Tables of Screening Designs

Second Edition

Donald J. Wheeler

SPC Press, Inc.

Knoxville, Tennessee

Contents

Contents

CONTENTS

"The fact that the criterion which we happen to use has a fine ancestry of highbrow statistical theorems does not justify its use. Such justification must come from empirical evidence that it works."

W. A. Shewhart

TABLES OF SCREENING DESIGNS

In 1946, R. L. Plackett and J. P. Burman published an article that defined a class of factorial designs based on maximal mutually orthogonal sets of contrasts. While they called these designs "Optimum Multifactorial Designs," they are now more commonly called "Screening Designs" since they provide an effective way to consider a large number of factors with a minimum number of observations. By using these designs, one can quickly separate inert factors from active factors, allowing most of the research effort to be concentrated on the active factors.

As a class, the Plackett-Burman designs have several characteristics. Among these are:

(1) The factors in a particular design will all have L levels, where L must be a prime number greater than 1, e.g. L = 2, 3, 5, 7, 11, etc.

(2) The number of runs (treatment combinations) for a particular design must be a multiple of L^2. Thus, if a design involves factors at two levels, it will have a number of runs that is equal to some multiple of 4, while a design that involves factors at three levels will have a number of runs that is equal to some multiple of 9.

(3) All main factor effects are estimated with the same precision. This means that one does not have to anticipate which factors are the most likely to be important when setting up the study.

(4) Because of the orthogonal contrasts, all main factor effects are estimated independently of each other. While interactions may contaminate the estimates of the main factor effects, at least the main effects do not contaminate one another.

It is these last two characteristics that make the Plackett-Burman designs especially well suited for exploratory studies.

In their article, Plackett and Burman provided an essentially complete set of screening designs. This set consists of 23 designs for factors at two levels each, 3 designs for factors at three levels each, 2 designs for factors at five levels each, and one design for factors with seven levels each. The 23 designs for two-level factors range from an 8-run design to a 100-run design, thus providing a way to study as many as 99 two-level factors.

Parts One and Two of these Tables give some designs for factors at two levels. Part Three gives some designs for factors at three levels. Part Four gives some hybrid designs that combine factors having two levels with factors having anywhere from three to sixteen levels.

The unique Data Collection Worksheets included in these tables help the user to organize the information needed to actually perform the experimental runs. In addition, many of the designs have Calculation Worksheets which facilitate the analysis of the experimental responses. These worksheets are constructed to minimize the chances of arithmetic errors, and should prove helpful for those designs that may not have been programmed.

The analysis of the experimental responses is simple enough that most of the users will be able to program the analysis on any simple spreadsheet program. Such programs may be checked for correctness using the numerical examples provided for many of the designs.

The orthogonal arrays in these tables are structured differently than the arrays presented by Plackett and Burman. This was done to provide the user with designs in which some factors change level only once or twice during the course of a set of experimental runs. Such designs facilitate the actual implementation of these designs since some factors will usually be harder to change than others.

Finally, one should note that the strategy for using these designs may change with changing needs. In basic experiments one will usually make bold choices for the different levels of a factor. By spacing the levels of a factor far apart, one makes the experiment sensitive to the effects of that factor. On the other hand, when experimenting with an operating process, one is faced with the restriction of avoiding nonconforming product. In this context one will typically choose factor levels that are closer together. If a factor is not found to have an effect with one spacing of factor levels, then one may confidently increase the distance between the factor levels in subsequent experiments. The factor levels used should always be reasonable in the context of the experiment, but subject to this constraint, they should be as far apart as possible.

While randomization is a proven and useful technique used in conjunction with many different types of experimental designs, it is not necessary when one is primarily concerned with using screening designs with one observation per run. For this reason, the following worksheets have been set up according to a standard order for the experimental runs. The confirmation provided by the replication of results between a basic design and a reflected design is much stronger than any assurance provided by the randomization of run order, and the use of a standard order makes the experiments much easier to conduct in practice. For a broader discussion of this point, see the book entitled **Understanding Industrial Experimentation** by this author.

GEOMETRIC TWO-LEVEL PLACKETT-BURMAN DESIGNS

The geometric two-level Plackett-Burman designs are the most useful of the Plackett-Burman screening designs. While they allow the experimenter to rapidly distinguish between active factors and inactive factors, they also provide information regarding which specific two-factor interaction effects are present, if any. It is this ability to identify specific two-factor interactions that sets the geometric two-level Placket-Burman designs apart from the remainder of the Plackett-Burman designs. Since this characteristic of the geometric two-level Plackett-Burman designs depends upon using a sequence of such designs, the experimenter will also be protected from interpreting counterfeit results by the replication of results from one study to another.

The Plackett-Burman designs are usually expressed in terms of an orthogonal array of plus signs and minus signs. These arrays are then read in two different ways. Each column in the array will define a contrast when the plus and minus signs have a coefficient of 1.0 attached. At the same time, each row of the array will define the treatment combination under which the response(s) for that row were obtained. In other words, the rows define the conditions under which each of the responses were obtained, while the columns define the contrasts to be used in the analysis for each factor effect. Rows are therefore associated with experimental runs, and columns are associated with specific factor labels.

When reading a particular row of an array the minus signs will indicate those factors that are set at their "low" levels, while the plus signs will indicate which factors are set at their "high" levels. The convention used by Plackett and Burman was to let the minus sign represent the "current" level of a factor, while the plus sign represented a change from the current factor level. Since they generally wanted one run to represent the current operating conditions, they always included one run with all the factors at their "minus" levels. In order to distinguish these designs from the many variations, the designs containing one run with all factors at their "minus" level will be called *basic* designs.

Another possible convention is to let the natural orderings of the factor levels be reflected in the minus and plus signs (minus for low level, plus for high level). When such a natural ordering exists, this convention facilitates the interpretation of the results.

In addition to the general features descfibed in the introduction, these geometric two-level Plackett-Burman designs have one additional feature that makes them especially useful. In every Plackett-Burman design each column uniquely corresponds to a particular main factor effect. In the geometric two-level designs there is a unique column for each and every interaction effect that can be estimated. It is this unique correspondence between interaction effects and contrasts (columns) that makes it feasible to specifically isolate any two-factor interaction effects that may be present.

Some users may find that they have encountered these geometric two-level Plackett-Burman designs under a different name. Some of the other names for these designs are Hadamard matrix designs, $2^{(k-p)}$ fractional factorial designs, or Taguchi orthogonal arrays.

BASIC 8-RUN PLACKETT-BURMAN DESIGNS

The Basic 8-Run Plackett-Burman Design shown below is useful for studying from three to seven factors having two-levels each. Specific Worksheets are provided for each number of factors on the following pages.

The Contrast Labels in the array below identify the columns of contrast coefficients associated with each of the seven factors in a fully saturated design. The same Contrast Labels are used with each of the five designs given on the following pages since each design utilizes the array below.

	Contrast Labels						
Run	A	B	C	D	E	F	G
1	-	-	-	-	-	-	-
2	-	-	-	+	+	+	+
3	-	+	+	+	+	-	-
4	-	+	+	-	-	+	+
5	+	+	-	-	+	+	-
6	+	+	-	+	-	-	+
7	+	-	+	+	-	+	-
8	+	-	+	-	+	-	+

Treatment combinations are defined by rows in this matrix.

Contrast coefficients are defined by columns in this matrix.

Number of changes in level:

A	B	C	D	E	F	G
1	2	3	4	5	6	7

EXAMPLE FOR THE BASIC 8-RUN DESIGN
OBTAINING THE DATA

The following data is provided for the user to review the calculations for a basic 8-Run design. The format is that given on the following worksheets.

A "run" consists of setting the seven (or fewer) factors at the levels indicated in the following array, and then observing the value for the response variable. As the eight different runs are performed the response values are written in the blanks as shown.

Changes in Factor Levels for Basic 8-Run Sequence with Seven Factors
Changes in factor levels are shown in boldface

Run								Response
1	Begin with all seven factors at their low level:							
	A-	**B-**	**C-**	**D-**	**E-**	**F-**	**G-**	77
2	Change the levels for Factors D, E, F, and G:							
	A-	B-	C-	**D+**	**E+**	**F+**	**G+**	187
3	Change the levels for Factors B, C, F, and G:							
	A-	**B+**	**C+**	D+	E+	**F-**	**G-**	172
4	Change the levels for Factors D, E, F, and G:							
	A-	B+	C+	**D-**	**E-**	**F+**	**G+**	58
5	Change the levels for Factors A, C, E, and G:							
	A+	B+	**C-**	D-	**E+**	F+	**G-**	102
6	Change the levels for Factors D, E, F, and G:							
	A+	B+	C-	**D+**	**E-**	**F-**	**G+**	77
7	Change the levels for Factors B, C, F, and G:							
	A+	**B-**	**C+**	D+	E-	**F+**	**G-**	58
8	Change the levels for Factors D, E, F, and G:							
	A+	B-	C+	**D-**	**E+**	**F-**	**G+**	73

EXAMPLE FOR THE BASIC 8-RUN DESIGN
CALCULATING THE ESTIMATED CONTRASTS

Next the eight response values are combined by means of contrasts. With the 8-Run Designs there will always be seven unique contrasts regardless of the number of Factors used in the study. These seven contrasts describe the contribution associated with each of seven unique components. The plus-signs and minus-signs in the following array define contrast coefficients of ±1. By multiplying the coefficients of a contrast by the corresponding responses and summing the products one will obtain the value for the Estimated Contrast.

CALCULATION WORKSHEET
FOR BASIC 8-RUN DESIGN WITH SEVEN FACTORS

Run No.	Response	Contrast Labels A	B	C	D	E	F	G
1	77	−	−	−	−	−	−	−
2	187	−	−	−	+	+	+	+
3	172	−	+	+	+	+	−	−
4	58	−	+	+	−	−	+	+
5	102	+	+	−	−	+	+	−
6	77	+	+	−	+	−	−	+
7	58	+	−	+	+	−	+	−
8	73	+	−	+	−	+	−	+

The plus-signs and minus-signs in the array indicate which responses to add and which responses to subtract in order to find the value for each of the Estimated Contrasts. The values for Contrasts A, B, C and D are found below. The user may practice finding the Estimated Contrasts for Contrasts E, F, and G. The correct values are shown on the following page.

For Contrast A: [(-1) 77 + (-1) 187 + (-1) 172 + (-1) 58 + (+1) 102 + (+1) 77 + (+1) 58 + (+1) 73] = -184

For Contrast B: [(-1) 77 + (-1) 187 + (+1) 172 + (+1) 58 + (+1) 102 + (+1) 77 + (-1) 58 + (-1) 73] =   14

For Contrast C: [(-1) 77 + (-1) 187 + (+1) 172 + (+1) 58 + (-1) 102 + (-1) 77 + (+1) 58 + (+1) 73] = -82

For Contrast D: [(-1) 77 + (+1) 187 + (+1) 172 + (-1) 58 + (-1) 102 + (+1) 77 + (+1) 58 + (-1) 73] = 184

EXAMPLE FOR THE BASIC 8-RUN DESIGN
CALCULATING THE SUMS OF SQUARES

The first column of the Single Degree of Freedom ANOVA Table consists of the Estimated Contrast values. The second column consists of the Sums of Squares for the contrasts. The Sum of Squares for a contrast is found by (1) squaring the Estimated Contrast value and (2) dividing this value by an adjustment term. The adjustment term is itself a ratio that depends upon the contrast coefficients and the number of responses per run.

$$\text{Adjustment Term} = \frac{\text{The sum of the squares of the contrast coefficients}}{\text{The number of responses per run}}$$

For 8-run designs with one response per run this adjustment term will be equal to:

$$\text{Adjustment Term} = \frac{1+1+1+1+1+1+1+1}{1} = 8.0.$$

So the Sums of Squares below are found by squaring the value in the first column and dividing by 8.

SINGLE DEGREE OF FREEDOM ANOVA TABLE

Contrast Labels	Estimated Contrasts	Sums of Squares		Estimated Effects
A	-184	4,232.0		
B	14	24.5		
C	-82	840.5		
D	184	4,232.0		
E	264			
F	6			
G	-14			
TOTAL Sum of Squares =		18,070.0		

The Total Sum of Squares is found by obtaining s^2 using all of the observations (8 in this case) and multiplying this s^2 value by [k-1]. (In this case, k-1 = 7.) The other sums of squares should sum to be equal to the Total Sum of Squares.

EXAMPLE FOR THE BASIC 8-RUN DESIGN
COMPARING THE SUMS OF SQUARES

There are several different methods available for comparing the Sums of Squares. The objective of each method is to identify those contrasts that can be said to represent "signals" rather than "noise." With multiple observations per run one may use the traditional F-ratios. With one observation per run one may either use *a priori* pooling or a *post hoc* analysis involving the Maximum F ratio and a Scree Plot. The post hoc analysis will be illustrated here. The other techniques are discussed in the companion text **Understanding Industrial Experimentation.**

SINGLE DEGREE OF FREEDOM ANOVA TABLE

Contrast Labels	Estimated Contrasts	Sums of Squares		Estimated Effects
A	-184	4,232.0		
B	14	24.5	pool	
C	-82	840.5		
D	184	4,232.0		
E	264	8,712.0	488.5	
F	6	4.5	pool	
G	-14	24.5	pool	
TOTAL	Sum of Squares =	18,070.0		

The Scree Plot suggests that three Sums of Squares might be pooled to form a Mean Square Error term:

$$MSE = (24.5 + 4.5 + 24.5)/3 = 17.833$$

So the Max F ratio will be

$$Max\ F = 8712.0 / 17.833 = 488.5$$

For $k = 7$ and $v = 3$ this value exceeds the 95th percentile of the Max F Distribution.

This suggests that the steep portion of the Scree Plot is due to signals rather than noise. Thus, Contrasts E, A and D are likely to represent signals, while Contrast C may represent a signal.

EXAMPLE FOR THE BASIC 8-RUN DESIGN
CALCULATING THE ESTIMATED EFFECTS

By comparing the Sums of Squares with each other in a Scree Plot it is possible to separate the the potentially active contrasts from those that appear to be inert.

For those contrasts which are thought to represent active factors or interactions one may calculate the Estimated Effects. The Estimated Effect for a contrast is found by dividing (the Estimated Contrast value) by (the sum of the positive contrast coefficients).

For the 8-Run Designs, the sum of the positive contrast coefficients is 4.0. Thus, for Contrast A, the Estimated Effect is -184 / 4 = -46. For Contrast C the Estimated Effect is -82/4 = -20.5.

Find the Estimated Effect for Contrast E.

SINGLE DEGREE OF FREEDOM ANOVA TABLE

Contrast Labels	Estimated Contrasts	Sums of Squares		Estimated Effects
A	-184	4,232.0		-46
B	14	24.5	pool	
C	-82	840.5		-20.5
D	184	4,232.0		46
E	264	8712.0	488.5	
F	6	4.5	pool	
G	-14	24.5	pool	
TOTAL	Sum of Squares =	18,070.0		

EXAMPLE FOR THE BASIC 8-RUN DESIGN
INTERPRETING THE ESTIMATED EFFECTS

The Calculation Worksheets on the following pages show the confounding pattern and some of the aliases for each contrast. These aliases help the user to interpret just which effects and interactions are represented by the active contrasts.

	Contrast Labels						
	A	B	C	D	E	F	G
Main Effects	A	B	C	D	E	F	G
Two-Factor Interactions	-BC	-AC	-AB	-AE	-AD	-AG	-AF
	-DE	-DF	-DG	-BF	-BG	-BD	-BE
	-FG	-EG	-EF	-CG	-CF	-CE	-CD
Three-Factor Interactions	BDG	ADG	ADF	ABG	ABF	ABE	ABD
	BEF	AEF	BDE	ACF	BCD	ACD	DEF
	CDF	CDE	BFG	BCE	DFG	DEG	BCF
	CEG	CFG	AEG	EFG	ACG	BCG	ACE

Contrast E has the greatest effect. Technically the Estimated Effect for Contrast E represents the sum of the effects of (1) the Main Effect for Factor E, (2) the negative of the AD Interaction, (3) the negative of the BG Interaction, (4) the negative of the CF Interaction, (5) the ABF Interaction, (6) the BCD Interaction, (7) the DFG Interaction, (8) the ACG Interaction and (9) other four-factor and higher order interactions. Since three-factor and higher-order interactions are rare, it is common practice to ignore all three-factor and higher-order interactions. In addition, it is usually safe to assume that an active contrast will represent only one real effect (main effect or interaction).

Thus, Contrast E is likely to be either the Main Effect for Factor E, or the negative of either the AD Interaction, the BG Interaction, or the CF Interaction. As the sign for Contrast E changes from - to + the average response increases 66 units.

Contrast A is most likely to be either the Main Effect for Factor A, or the negative of either the BC Interaction, the DE Interaction, or the FG Interaction. As Contrast A goes from - to + the average response decreases by 46 units.

Contrast D is most likely to be either the Main Effect for Factor D, or the negative of either the AE Interaction, the BF Interaction, or the CG Interaction. As Contrast D goes from - to + the average response increases by 46 units.

Contrast C, if it represents a signal at all, is most likely to be either the Main Effect for Factor C, or the negative of either the AB Interaction, the DG Interaction, or the EF Interaction. As Contrast C goes from - to + the average response decreases by 20.5 units.

DATA COLLECTION WORKSHEET
FOR THE BASIC 8-RUN DESIGN WITH SEVEN FACTORS

Factor Names	Low-Level	High-Level
A. _____	_____	_____
B. _____	_____	_____
C. _____	_____	_____
D. _____	_____	_____
E. _____	_____	_____
F. _____	_____	_____
G. _____	_____	_____

The Response Variable is _____

Changes in Factor Levels for Basic 8-Run Sequence with Seven Factors

Changes in factor levels are shown in boldface

Run	Begin with all seven factors at their low level:							Response
1	**A-**	**B-**	**C-**	**D-**	**E-**	**F-**	**G-**	_____
2	A-	B-	C-	**D+**	**E+**	**F+**	**G+**	_____
3	A-	**B+**	**C+**	D+	E+	**F-**	**G-**	_____
4	A-	B+	C+	**D-**	**E-**	**F+**	**G+**	_____
5	**A+**	B+	**C-**	D-	**E+**	F+	**G-**	_____
6	A+	B+	C-	**D+**	**E-**	**F-**	**G+**	_____
7	A+	**B-**	**C+**	D+	E-	**F+**	**G-**	_____
8	A+	B-	C+	**D-**	**E+**	**F-**	**G+**	_____

CALCULATION WORKSHEET
FOR BASIC 8-RUN DESIGN WITH SEVEN FACTORS

Run No.	Response	Contrast Labels A	B	C	D	E	F	G
1	_____	-	-	-	-	-	-	-
2	_____	-	-	-	+	+	+	+
3	_____	-	+	+	+	+	-	-
4	_____	-	+	+	-	-	+	+
5	_____	+	+	-	-	+	+	-
6	_____	+	+	-	+	-	-	+
7	_____	+	-	+	+	-	+	-
8	_____	+	-	+	-	+	-	+
	Main Effects	A	B	C	D	E	F	G

Two-Factor Interactions	-BC	-AC	-AB	-AE	-AD	-AG	-AF
	-DE	-DF	-DG	-BF	-BG	-BD	-BE
	-FG	-EG	-EF	-CG	-CF	-CE	-CD

Three-Factor Interactions	BDG	ADG	ADF	ABG	ABF	ABE	ABD
	BEF	AEF	BDE	ACF	BCD	ACD	DEF
	CDF	CDE	BFG	BCE	DFG	DEG	BCF
	CEG	CFG	AEG	EFG	ACG	BCG	ACE

(The ABC, ADE, AFG, BDF, BEG, CDG, and CEF Interactions are not estimated by any contrast in this design.)

SINGLE DEGREE OF FREEDOM ANOVA TABLE

Contrast Labels	Estimated Contrasts	Sums of Squares		Estimated Effects
A	_____	_____	_____	_____
B	_____	_____	_____	_____
C	_____	_____	_____	_____
D	_____	_____	_____	_____
E	_____	_____	_____	_____
F	_____	_____	_____	_____
G	_____	_____	_____	_____
TOTAL Sum of Squares		_____		

DATA COLLECTION WORKSHEET
FOR THE BASIC 8-RUN DESIGN WITH SIX FACTORS

Factor Names   Low-Level   High-Level

A. _____   _____   _____

B. _____   _____   _____

C. _____   _____   _____

D. _____   _____   _____

E. _____   _____   _____

F. _____   _____   _____

The Response Variable is _____

Changes in Factor Levels for Basic 8-Run Sequence with Six Factors

Changes in factor levels are shown in boldface

Run	Begin with all six factors at their low level:						Response
1	**A-**	**B-**	**C-**	**D-**	**E-**	**F -**	_____
2	A-	B-	C-	**D+**	**E+**	**F+**	_____
3	A-	**B+**	**C+**	D+	E+	**F -**	_____
4	A-	B+	C+	**D-**	**E-**	**F+**	_____
5	**A+**	B+	**C-**	D-	**E+**	F+	_____
6	A+	B+	C-	**D+**	**E-**	**F -**	_____
7	A+	**B-**	**C+**	D+	E-	**F+**	_____
8	A+	B-	C+	**D-**	**E+**	**F -**	_____

CALCULATION WORKSHEET
FOR BASIC 8-RUN DESIGN WITH SIX FACTORS

Run No.	Response	Contrast Labels A	B	C	D	E	F	G
1	_____	-	-	-	-	-	-	-
2	_____	-	-	-	+	+	+	+
3	_____	-	+	+	+	+	-	-
4	_____	-	+	+	-	-	+	+
5	_____	+	+	-	-	+	+	-
6	_____	+	+	-	+	-	-	+
7	_____	+	-	+	+	-	+	-
8	_____	+	-	+	-	+	-	+
	Main Effects	A	B	C	D	E	F	
Two-Factor Interactions		-BC -DE	-AC -DF	-AB -EF	-AE -BF	-AD -CF	-BD -CE	-AF -BE -CD
Three-Factor Interactions		BEF CDF	AEF CDE	ADF BDE	ACF BCE	ABF BCD	ABE ACD	ABD DEF BCF ACE

(The ABC, ADE, BDF, and CEF Interactions are not estimated by any contrast)

SINGLE DEGREE OF FREEDOM ANOVA TABLE

Contrast Labels	Estimated Contrasts	Sums of Squares		Estimated Effects
A	_____	_____	_____	_____
B	_____	_____	_____	_____
C	_____	_____	_____	_____
D	_____	_____	_____	_____
E	_____	_____	_____	_____
F	_____	_____	_____	_____
(G)	_____	_____	_____	_____
TOTAL Sum of Squares		_____		

DATA COLLECTION WORKSHEET
FOR THE BASIC 8-RUN DESIGN WITH FIVE FACTORS

Factor Names	Low-Level	High-Level
A. _____	_____	_____
B. _____	_____	_____
C. _____	_____	_____
D. _____	_____	_____
E. _____	_____	_____

The Response Variable is _____

Changes in Factor Levels for Basic 8-Run Sequence with Five Factors

Changes in factor levels are shown in boldface

Run	Begin with all five factors at their low level:					Response
1	**A-**	**B-**	**C-**	**D-**	**E-**	_____
2	A-	B-	C-	**D+**	**E+**	_____
3	A-	**B+**	**C+**	D+	E+	_____
4	A-	B+	C+	**D-**	**E-**	_____
5	**A+**	B+	**C-**	D-	**E+**	_____
6	A+	B+	C-	**D+**	E-	_____
7	A+	**B-**	**C+**	D+	E-	_____
8	A+	B-	C+	**D-**	**E+**	_____

CALCULATION WORKSHEET
FOR BASIC 8-RUN DESIGN WITH FIVE FACTORS

Run No.	Response	Contrast Labels A	B	C	D	E	F	G
1	_____	-	-	-	-	-	-	-
2	_____	-	-	-	+	+	+	+
3	_____	-	+	+	+	+	-	-
4	_____	-	+	+	-	-	+	+
5	_____	+	+	-	-	+	+	-
6	_____	+	+	-	+	-	-	+
7	_____	+	-	+	+	-	+	-
8	_____	+	-	+	-	+	-	+
	Main Effects	A	B	C	D	E		
	Two-Factor Interactions	-BC -DE	-AC	-AB	-AE	-AD	-BD -CE	-BE -CD
	Three-Factor Interactions		CDE	BDE	BCE	BCD	ACD ABE	ABD ACE

(The ABC and ADE Interactions are not estimated by any contrast in this design)

SINGLE DEGREE OF FREEDOM ANOVA TABLE

Contrast Labels	Estimated Contrasts	Sums of Squares	Estimated Effects
A	_____	_____	_____
B	_____	_____	_____
C	_____	_____	_____
D	_____	_____	_____
E	_____	_____	_____
(F)	_____	_____	_____
(G)	_____	_____	_____
TOTAL Sum of Squares	_____		

DATA COLLECTION WORKSHEET
FOR THE BASIC 8-RUN DESIGN WITH FOUR FACTORS

Only seven combinations of four Factor Labels will yield a Resolution IV Design. One of these sets of four Factor Labels is given below. Since this design is a one-half replicate of a fully crossed design, any follow-up study should be selected to provide the other one-half replicate. This is done by using a partially reflected design rather than a completely reflected design.

Factor Names	Low-Level	High-Level
A. _____	_____	_____
B. _____	_____	_____
D. _____	_____	_____
G. _____	_____	_____

The Response Variable is _____

Changes in Factor Levels for Basic 8-Run Sequence with Four Factors

Changes in factor levels are shown in boldface

Run	Begin with all four factors at their low level:				Response
1	**A-**	**B-**	**D-**	**G-**	_____
2	A-	B-	**D+**	**G+**	_____
3	A-	**B+**	D+	**G-**	_____
4	A-	B+	**D-**	**G+**	_____
5	**A+**	B+	D-	**G-**	_____
6	A+	B+	**D+**	**G+**	_____
7	A+	**B-**	D+	**G-**	_____
8	A+	B-	**D-**	**G+**	_____

CALCULATION WORKSHEET
FOR BASIC 8-RUN DESIGN WITH FOUR FACTORS

Run No.	Response	Contrast Labels A	B	C	D	E	F	G
1	_____	-	-	-	-	-	-	-
2	_____	-	-	-	+	+	+	+
3	_____	-	+	+	+	+	-	-
4	_____	-	+	+	-	-	+	+
5	_____	+	+	-	-	+	+	-
6	_____	+	+	-	+	-	-	+
7	_____	+	-	+	+	-	+	-
8	_____	+	-	+	-	+	-	+
	Main Effects	A	B		D			G

Two- and Three-Factor Interaction Effects	BDG	ADG	-AB -DG	ABG	-AD -BG	-AG -BD	ABD

(This design is of Resolution IV. All three-factor interactions are estimated by some contrast, and the two-factor interactions are no longer confounded with the main effects.)

SINGLE DEGREE OF FREEDOM ANOVA TABLE

Contrast Labels	Estimated Contrasts	Sums of Squares	Estimated Effects
A	_____	_____	_____
B	_____	_____	_____
(C)	_____	_____	_____
D	_____	_____	_____
(E)	_____	_____	_____
(F)	_____	_____	_____
G	_____	_____	_____
TOTAL Sum of Squares	_____		

DATA COLLECTION WORKSHEET
FOR THE BASIC 8-RUN DESIGN WITH THREE FACTORS

(Not all combinations of three Factor Labels will yield a fully-crossed design. The set of Factor Labels given below will result in a fully crossed design.)

Factor Names	Low-Level	High-Level
A. _____	_____	_____
B. _____	_____	_____
D. _____	_____	_____

The Response Variable is _____

Changes in Factor Levels for Basic 8-Run Sequence with Three Factors

Changes in factor levels are shown in boldface

Run	Begin with all three factors at their low level:			Response
1	**A-**	**B-**	**D-**	_____
2	A-	B-	**D+**	_____
3	A-	**B+**	D+	_____
4	A-	B+	**D-**	_____
5	**A+**	B+	D-	_____
6	A+	B+	**D+**	_____
7	A+	**B-**	D+	_____
8	A+	B-	**D-**	_____

CALCULATION WORKSHEET
FOR BASIC 8-RUN DESIGN WITH THREE FACTORS

Run No.	Response	Contrast Labels A	B	C	D	E	F	G
1	_____	-	-	-	-	-	-	-
2	_____	-	-	-	+	+	+	+
3	_____	-	+	+	+	+	-	-
4	_____	-	+	+	-	-	+	+
5	_____	+	+	-	-	+	+	-
6	_____	+	+	-	+	-	-	+
7	_____	+	-	+	+	-	+	-
8	_____	+	-	+	-	+	-	+
	Main Effects	A	B		D			
	Interactions			-AB		-AD	-BD	ABD

SINGLE DEGREE OF FREEDOM ANOVA TABLE

Contrast Labels	Estimated Contrasts	Sums of Squares		Estimated Effects
A	_____	_____	_____	_____
B	_____	_____	_____	_____
(C)	_____	_____	_____	_____
D	_____	_____	_____	_____
(E)	_____	_____	_____	_____
(F)	_____	_____	_____	_____
(G)	_____	_____	_____	_____
TOTAL Sum of Squares		_____		

REFLECTED 8-RUN PLACKETT-BURMAN DESIGNS

The Reflected 8-Run Plackett-Burman Design shown below has the same pattern as the Basic 8-Run Design, but with the signs reversed. This reversal makes this design complementary to the Basic 8-Run Design when used with at least five factors. Specific Worksheets are provided for each number of factors on the following pages.

The Contrast Labels in the array below identify the columns of contrast coefficients associated with each of the seven factors in a fully saturated design. The same Contrast Labels are used with each of the five designs given on the following pages since each design utilizes the array below.

Contrast Labels_____

Run	A	B	C	D	E	F	G
1	+	+	+	+	+	+	+
2	+	+	+	−	−	−	−
3	+	−	−	−	−	+	+
4	+	−	−	+	+	−	−
5	−	−	+	+	−	−	+
6	−	−	+	−	+	+	−
7	−	+	−	−	+	−	+
8	−	+	−	+	−	+	−

Treatment combinations are defined by rows in this matrix.

Contrast coefficients are defined by columns in this matrix.

Number of changes in level:

A	B	C	D	E	F	G
1	2	3	4	5	6	7

EXAMPLE OF REFLECTED 8-RUN DESIGN

Run No.	Response	Contrast Labels A	B	C	D	E	F	G
1	145	+	+	+	+	+	+	+
2	27	+	+	+	−	−	−	−
3	71	+	−	−	−	−	+	+
4	190	+	−	−	+	+	−	−
5	54	−	−	+	+	−	−	+
6	90	−	−	+	−	+	+	−
7	97	−	+	−	−	+	−	+
8	93	−	+	−	+	−	+	−
Main Effects		A	B	C	D	E	F	G

Two-Factor Interactions	BC	AC	AB	AE	AD	AG	AF
	DE	DF	DG	BF	BG	BD	BE
	FG	EG	EF	CG	CF	CE	CD

SINGLE DEGREE OF FREEDOM ANOVA TABLE

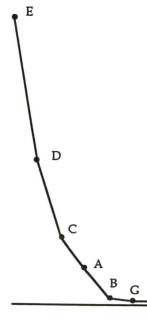

Contrast Labels	Estimated Contrasts	Sums of Squares		Estimated Effects
A	99	1,225.125		24.75
B	−43	231.125	pool	
C	−135	2,278.125		−33.75
D	197	4,851.125		49.25
E	277	9,591.125	59.04	69.25
F	31	120.125	pool	
G	−33	136.125	pool	
TOTAL Sum of Squares	18,432.875			

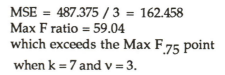

MSE = 487.375 / 3 = 162.458
Max F ratio = 59.04
which exceeds the Max $F_{.75}$ point
when $k = 7$ and $v = 3$.

COMBINING RESULTS OF BASIC AND REFLECTED 8-RUN STUDIES

If the factors and the response variable in the Basic 8-Run Study shown on pages 6 through 11 are the same as those used in the Reflected 8-Run Study shown on the preceding page, then one may combine the results of these two studies to obtain greater insight into the way the factors affect the response variable.

First one should look to see which contrasts show up as active in both studies. This persistence of a contrast from one study to another is the strongest indicator of the presence of a real effect. (If a contrast shows up in one study, but not in the other, then that contrast may well represent mere random variation. If it shows up in further experimentation it may be real, but with one vote for and one vote against the final outcome will be uncertain.)

Next one should check the estimated effects for the active contrasts. If the Estimated Effect changes signs from one study to the other, then that contrast can be said to represent a two-factor interaction effect. The table of aliases provided will identify the specific two-factor interactions that such a contrast may represent. If the sign of the Estimated Effect does not change sign from one study to the other, then the contrast may be safely interpreted as being a main effect. (It is either a main effect or a three-factor interaction. Since three-factor interaction effects are rare, one is usually safe in taking such contrasts to represent main effects.)

For the two 8-Run Studies (given on pages 6-11 and the preceding page) four contrasts stand out from the rubble at the bottom of the Scree Plot. Since these contrasts stand out in both studies they are likely to be real effects.

Contrast E showed the strongest effect in both studies.

Contrast D was tied for second place in the first study, and was in second place in the second.

Contrast C was in fourth and third place respectively.

Contrast A was tied for second and then was in fourth place.

Basic 8-Run Study		Reflected 8-Run Study	
Contrast	Est. Effect	Contrast	Est. Effect
A	-46	A	24.75
C	-20.5	C	-33.75
D	46	D	49.25
E	66	E	69.25

Contrasts E, D and C can be taken to represent main effects, while Contrast A must be taken to be an interaction effect. The interactions that are associated with Contrast A in the two studies are the BC Interaction Effect, the DE Interaction Effect, and the FG Interaction Effect. Of these three, one might be prone to suspect the DE Interaction Effect as most likely simply because Factors D and E are seen to be active main effects.

DATA COLLECTION WORKSHEET
FOR THE REFLECTED 8-RUN DESIGN WITH SEVEN FACTORS

Factor Names	Low-Level	High-Level
A. _____	_____	_____
B. _____	_____	_____
C. _____	_____	_____
D. _____	_____	_____
E. _____	_____	_____
F. _____	_____	_____
G. _____	_____	_____

The Response Variable is _____

Changes in Factor Levels for Reflected 8-Run Sequence with Seven Factors

Changes in factor levels are shown in boldface

Run	Begin with all seven factors at their high level:							Response
1	**A+**	**B+**	**C+**	**D+**	**E+**	**F+**	**G+**	_____
2	A+	B+	C+	**D-**	**E-**	**F-**	**G-**	_____
3	A+	**B-**	**C-**	D-	E-	**F+**	**G+**	_____
4	A+	B-	C-	**D+**	**E+**	**F-**	**G-**	_____
5	**A-**	B-	**C+**	D+	**E-**	F-	**G+**	_____
6	A-	B-	C+	**D-**	**E+**	**F+**	**G-**	_____
7	A-	**B+**	**C-**	D-	E+	**F-**	**G+**	_____
8	A-	B+	C-	**D+**	**E-**	**F+**	**G-**	_____

CALCULATION WORKSHEET
FOR REFLECTED 8-RUN DESIGN WITH SEVEN FACTORS

Run No.	Response	Contrast Labels A	B	C	D	E	F	G
1	_____	+	+	+	+	+	+	+
2	_____	+	+	+	-	-	-	-
3	_____	+	-	-	-	-	+	+
4	_____	+	-	-	+	+	-	-
5	_____	-	-	+	+	-	-	+
6	_____	-	-	+	-	+	+	-
7	_____	-	+	-	-	+	-	+
8	_____	-	+	-	+	-	+	-

	Main Effects	A	B	C	D	E	F	G
Two-Factor Interactions		BC	AC	AB	AE	AD	AG	AF
		DE	DF	DG	BF	BG	BD	BE
		FG	EG	EF	CG	CF	CE	CD
Three-Factor Interactions		BDG	ADG	ADF	ABG	ABF	ABE	ABD
		BEF	AEF	BDE	ACF	BCD	ACD	DEF
		CDF	CDE	BFG	BCE	DFG	DEG	BCF
		CEG	CFG	AEG	EFG	ACG	BCG	ACE

(The ABC, ADE, AFG, BDF, BEG, CDG, and CEF Interactions are not estimated by any contrast in this design.)

SINGLE DEGREE OF FREEDOM ANOVA TABLE

Contrast Labels	Estimated Contrasts	Sums of Squares	Estimated Effects
A	_____	_____	_____
B	_____	_____	_____
C	_____	_____	_____
D	_____	_____	_____
E	_____	_____	_____
F	_____	_____	_____
G	_____	_____	_____
TOTAL Sum of Squares	_____		

DATA COLLECTION WORKSHEET
FOR THE REFLECTED 8-RUN DESIGN WITH SIX FACTORS

Factor Names		Low-Level	High-Level
A.	_____	_____	_____
B.	_____	_____	_____
C.	_____	_____	_____
D.	_____	_____	_____
E.	_____	_____	_____
F.	_____	_____	_____

The Response Variable is _____

Changes in Factor Levels for Reflected 8-Run Sequence with Six Factors

Changes in factor levels are shown in boldface

Run	Begin with all six factors at their high level:						Response
1	**A+**	**B+**	**C+**	**D+**	**E+**	**F+**	_____
2	A+	B+	C+	**D-**	**E-**	**F-**	_____
3	A+	**B-**	**C-**	D-	E-	**F+**	_____
4	A+	B-	C-	**D+**	**E+**	**F-**	_____
5	**A-**	B-	**C+**	D+	**E-**	F-	_____
6	A-	B-	C+	**D-**	**E+**	**F+**	_____
7	A-	**B+**	**C-**	D-	**E+**	**F-**	_____
8	A-	B+	C-	**D+**	**E-**	**F+**	_____

CALCULATION WORKSHEET
FOR REFLECTED 8-RUN DESIGN WITH SIX FACTORS

Run No.	Response	Contrast Labels A	B	C	D	E	F	G
1	_____	+	+	+	+	+	+	+
2	_____	+	+	+	−	−	−	−
3	_____	+	−	−	−	−	+	+
4	_____	+	−	−	+	+	−	−
5	_____	−	−	+	+	−	−	+
6	_____	−	−	+	−	+	+	−
7	_____	−	+	−	−	+	−	+
8	_____	−	+	−	+	−	+	−
	Main Effects	A	B	C	D	E	F	
Two-Factor Interactions		BC	AC	AB	AE	AD	BD	AF
		DE	DF	EF	BF	CF	CE	BE
								CD
Three-Factor Interactions		BEF	AEF	ADF	ACF	ABF	ABE	ABD
		CDF	CDE	BDE	BCE	BCD	ACD	DEF
								BCF
								ACE

(The ABC, ADE, BDF, and CEF Interactions are not estimated by any contrast)

SINGLE DEGREE OF FREEDOM ANOVA TABLE

Contrast Labels	Estimated Contrasts	Sums of Squares		Estimated Effects
A	_____	_____	_____	_____
B	_____	_____	_____	_____
C	_____	_____	_____	_____
D	_____	_____	_____	_____
E	_____	_____	_____	_____
F	_____	_____	_____	_____
(G)	_____	_____	_____	_____
TOTAL Sum of Squares		_____		

DATA COLLECTION WORKSHEET
FOR THE REFLECTED 8-RUN DESIGN WITH FIVE FACTORS

Factor Names		Low-Level	High-Level
A. _____		_____	_____
B. _____		_____	_____
C. _____		_____	_____
D. _____		_____	_____
E. _____		_____	_____

The Response Variable is _____

Changes in Factor Levels for Reflected 8-Run Sequence with Five Factors

Changes in factor levels are shown in boldface

Run	Begin with all five factors at their high level:					Response
1	**A+**	**B+**	**C+**	**D+**	**E+**	_____
2	A+	B+	C+	**D-**	**E-**	_____
3	A+	**B-**	**C-**	D-	E-	_____
4	A+	B-	C-	**D+**	**E+**	_____
5	**A-**	B-	**C+**	D+	**E-**	_____
6	A-	B-	C+	**D-**	**E+**	_____
7	A-	**B+**	**C-**	D-	E+	_____
8	A-	B+	C-	**D+**	**E-**	_____

CALCULATION WORKSHEET
FOR REFLECTED 8-RUN DESIGN WITH FIVE FACTORS

Run No.	Response	Contrast Labels A	B	C	D	E	F	G
1	_____	+	+	+	+	+	+	+
2	_____	+	+	+	−	−	−	−
3	_____	+	−	−	−	−	+	+
4	_____	+	−	−	+	+	−	−
5	_____	−	−	+	+	−	−	+
6	_____	−	−	+	−	+	+	−
7	_____	−	+	−	−	+	−	+
8	_____	−	+	−	+	−	+	−
	Main Effects	A	B	C	D	E		
Two-Factor Interactions		BC DE	AC	AB	AE	AD	BD CE	BE CD
Three-Factor Interactions			CDE	BDE	BCE	BCD	ACD ABE	ABD ACE

(The ABC and ADE Interactions are not estimated by any contrast in this design)

SINGLE DEGREE OF FREEDOM ANOVA TABLE

Contrast Labels	Estimated Contrasts	Sums of Squares		Estimated Effects
A	_____	_____	_____	_____
B	_____	_____	_____	_____
C	_____	_____	_____	_____
D	_____	_____	_____	_____
E	_____	_____	_____	_____
(F)	_____	_____	_____	_____
(G)	_____	_____	_____	_____
TOTAL Sum of Squares	_____			

DATA COLLECTION WORKSHEET
FOR THE REFLECTED 8-RUN DESIGN WITH FOUR FACTORS

Only seven combinations of four Factor Labels will yield a Resolution IV Design. One of these sets of four Factor Labels is given below. Since this design is a one-half replicate of a fully crossed design, any follow-up study should be selected to provide the other one-half replicate. This is done by using a partially reflected design rather than a completely reflected design.

Factor Names   Low-Level   High-Level

A. _____   _____   _____

B. _____   _____   _____

D. _____   _____   _____

G. _____   _____   _____

The Response Variable is   _____

Changes in Factor Levels for Reflected 8-Run Sequence with Four Factors

Changes in factor levels are shown in boldface

Run	Begin with all four factors at their high level:				Response
1	**A+**	**B+**	**D+**	**G+**	_____
2	A+	B+	**D-**	**G-**	_____
3	A+	**B-**	D-	**G+**	_____
4	A+	B-	**D+**	**G-**	_____
5	**A-**	B-	D+	**G+**	_____
6	A-	B-	**D-**	**G-**	_____
7	A-	**B+**	D-	**G+**	_____
8	A-	B+	**D+**	**G-**	_____

CALCULATION WORKSHEET
FOR REFLECTED 8-RUN DESIGN WITH FOUR FACTORS

Run No.	Response	Contrast Labels A	B	C	D	E	F	G
1	_____	+	+	+	+	+	+	+
2	_____	+	+	+	−	−	−	−
3	_____	+	−	−	−	−	+	+
4	_____	+	−	−	+	+	−	−
5	_____	−	−	+	+	−	−	+
6	_____	−	−	+	−	+	+	−
7	_____	−	+	−	−	+	−	+
8	_____	−	+	−	+	−	+	−
Main Effects		A	B		D			G

Two- and Three-Factor Interaction Effects	BDG	ADG	A B DG	ABG	AD BG	AG BD	ABD

(This design is of Resolution IV. All three-factor interactions are estimated by some contrast, and the two-factor interactions are no longer confounded with the main effects.)

SINGLE DEGREE OF FREEDOM ANOVA TABLE

Contrast Labels	Estimated Contrasts	Sums of Squares		Estimated Effects
A	_____	_____	_____	_____
B	_____	_____	_____	_____
(C)	_____	_____	_____	_____
D	_____	_____	_____	_____
(E)	_____	_____	_____	_____
(F)	_____	_____	_____	_____
G	_____	_____	_____	_____
TOTAL Sum of Squares	_____			

DATA COLLECTION WORKSHEET
FOR THE REFLECTED 8-RUN DESIGN WITH THREE FACTORS

(Not all combinations of three Factor Labels will yield a fully-crossed design. The set of Factor Labels given below will result in a fully crossed design.)

Factor Names	Low-Level	High-Level
A. _____	_____	_____
B. _____	_____	_____
D. _____	_____	_____

The Response Variable is _____

Changes in Factor Levels for Reflected 8-Run Sequence with Three Factors

Changes in factor levels are shown in boldface

Run	Begin with all three factors at their high level:			Response
1	**A+**	**B+**	**D+**	_____
2	A+	B+	**D-**	_____
3	A+	**B-**	D-	_____
4	A+	B-	**D+**	_____
5	**A-**	B-	D+	_____
6	A-	B-	**D-**	_____
7	A-	**B+**	D-	_____
8	A-	B+	**D+**	_____

CALCULATION WORKSHEET
FOR REFLECTED 8-RUN DESIGN WITH THREE FACTORS

Run No.	Response	Contrast Labels A	B	C	D	E	F	G
1	_____	+	+	+	+	+	+	+
2	_____	+	+	+	-	-	-	-
3	_____	+	-	-	-	-	+	+
4	_____	+	-	-	+	+	-	-
5	_____	-	-	+	+	-	-	+
6	_____	-	-	+	-	+	+	-
7	_____	-	+	-	-	+	-	+
8	_____	-	+	-	+	-	+	-
	Main Effects	A	B		D			
	Interactions			AB		AD	BD	ABD

SINGLE DEGREE OF FREEDOM ANOVA TABLE

Contrast Labels	Estimated Contrasts	Sums of Squares		Estimated Effects
A	_____	_____	_____	_____
B	_____	_____	_____	_____
(C)	_____	_____	_____	_____
D	_____	_____	_____	_____
(E)	_____	_____	_____	_____
(F)	_____	_____	_____	_____
(G)	_____	_____	_____	_____
TOTAL Sum of Squares	_____			

BASIC 16-RUN PLACKETT-BURMAN DESIGNS

The Basic 16-Run Plackett-Burman Array shown below is useful for studying from four to fifteen factors having two-levels each. Specific tables of confounding patterns are given for designs using different numbers of factors. Data Collection Worksheets and Calculation Worksheets are included.

Contrast Labels

Run	A	B	C	D	E	F	G	H	I	J	K	L	M	N	O
1	−	−	−	−	−	−	−	−	−	−	−	−	−	−	−
2	−	−	−	−	−	−	−	+	+	+	+	+	+	+	+
3	−	−	−	+	+	+	+	+	+	+	+	−	−	−	−
4	−	−	−	+	+	+	+	−	−	−	−	+	+	+	+
5	−	+	+	+	+	−	−	−	−	+	+	+	+	−	−
6	−	+	+	+	+	−	−	+	+	−	−	−	−	+	+
7	−	+	+	−	−	+	+	+	+	−	−	+	+	−	−
8	−	+	+	−	−	+	+	−	−	+	+	−	−	+	+
9	+	+	−	−	+	+	−	−	+	+	−	−	+	+	−
10	+	+	−	−	+	+	−	+	−	−	+	+	−	−	+
11	+	+	−	+	−	−	+	+	−	−	+	−	+	+	−
12	+	+	−	+	−	−	+	−	+	+	−	+	−	−	+
13	+	−	+	+	−	+	−	−	+	−	+	+	−	+	−
14	+	−	+	+	−	+	−	+	−	+	−	−	+	−	+
15	+	−	+	−	+	−	+	+	−	+	−	+	−	+	−
16	+	−	+	−	+	−	+	−	+	−	+	−	+	−	+
	A	B	C	D	E	F	G	H	I	J	K	L	M	N	O

Treatment combinations are defined by rows in this matrix.

Contrast coefficients are defined by columns in this matrix.

Number of changes in level:

A	B	C	D	E	F	G	H	I	J	K	L	M	N	O
1	2	3	4	5	6	7	8	9	10	11	12	13	14	15

DATA COLLECTION WORKSHEET
FOR BASIC 16-RUN DESIGNS
PAGE ONE OF TWO PAGES
IDENTIFICATION OF FACTORS AND FACTOR LEVELS

When using less than fifteen factors some Contrast Labels will not represent a main effect. **These Contrast Labels should be crossed off the list below.** Suggested sets of Contrast Labels to use with different numbers of factors are shown in the tables of confounding patterns.

Contrast Labels	Factor Names	Low-Level	High-Level
A.			
B.			
C.			
D.			
E.			
F.			
G.			
H.			
I.			
J.			
K.			
L.			
M.			
N.			
O.			

The Response Variable is _____

DATA COLLECTION WORKSHEET
FOR BASIC 16-RUN DESIGNS
PAGE TWO OF TWO PAGES
CHANGES IN FACTOR LEVELS FOR BASIC 16-RUN DESIGNS

When using less than fifteen factors, **cross out all Factor Labels in the following array that do not represent a Main Effect in the study.** The resulting array will then show the factor levels to use in performing the experimental runs.

Changes in factor levels are shown in boldface.

Run	Begin with all factors set at their low levels															Response
1	**A-**	**B-**	**C-**	**D-**	**E-**	**F-**	**G-**	**H-**	**I-**	**J-**	**K-**	**L-**	**M-**	**N-**	**O-**	_____
2	A-	B-	C-	D-	E-	F-	G-	**H+**	**I+**	**J+**	**K+**	**L+**	**M+**	**N+**	**O+**	_____
3	A-	B-	C-	**D+**	**E+**	**F+**	**G+**	H+	I+	J+	K+	**L-**	**M-**	**N-**	**O-**	_____
4	A-	B-	C-	D+	E+	F+	G+	**H-**	**I-**	**J-**	**K-**	**L+**	**M+**	**N+**	**O+**	_____
5	A-	**B+**	**C+**	D+	E+	**F-**	**G-**	H-	I-	**J+**	**K+**	L+	M+	**N-**	**O-**	_____
6	A-	B+	C+	D+	E+	F-	G-	**H+**	**I+**	**J-**	**K-**	**L-**	**M-**	**N+**	**O+**	_____
7	A-	B+	C+	**D-**	**E-**	**F+**	**G+**	H+	I+	**J-**	**K-**	**L+**	**M+**	**N-**	**O-**	_____
8	A-	B+	C+	**D-**	**E-**	F+	G+	**H-**	**I-**	**J+**	**K+**	L-	M-	**N+**	**O+**	_____
9	**A+**	B+	**C-**	**D-**	**E+**	**F+**	**G-**	**H-**	**I+**	**J+**	**K-**	L-	**M+**	N+	**O-**	_____
10	A+	B+	C-	D-	E+	F+	G-	**H+**	**I-**	**J-**	**K+**	**L+**	**M-**	**N-**	**O+**	_____
11	A+	B+	C-	**D+**	**E-**	**F-**	**G+**	H+	I-	J-	K+	**L-**	**M+**	**N+**	**O-**	_____
12	A+	B+	C-	**D+**	E-	F-	**G+**	**H-**	**I+**	**J+**	**K-**	**L+**	**M-**	**N-**	**O+**	_____
13	A+	**B-**	**C+**	D+	E-	**F+**	**G-**	H-	I+	**J-**	**K+**	L+	M-	**N+**	**O-**	_____
14	A+	B-	C+	D+	E-	F+	G-	**H+**	**I-**	**J+**	**K-**	**L-**	**M+**	**N-**	**O+**	_____
15	A+	B-	C+	**D-**	**E+**	**F-**	**G+**	H+	I-	**J+**	**K-**	**L+**	**M-**	**N+**	**O-**	_____
16	A+	B-	C+	**D-**	**E+**	F-	**G+**	**H-**	**I+**	**J-**	**K+**	**L-**	**M+**	N-	**O+**	_____

CALCULATION WORKSHEET
FOR BASIC 16-RUN DESIGNS
PAGE ONE OF TWO PAGES

CONTRAST COEFFICIENTS

Run No.	Response	A	B	C	D	E	F	G	H	I	J	K	L	M	N	O
1	_____	-	-	-	-	-	-	-	-	-	-	-	-	-	-	-
2	_____	-	-	-	-	-	-	-	+	+	+	+	+	+	+	+
3	_____	-	-	-	+	+	+	+	+	+	+	+	-	-	-	-
4	_____	-	-	-	+	+	+	+	-	-	-	-	+	+	+	+
5	_____	-	+	+	+	+	-	-	-	-	+	+	+	+	-	-
6	_____	-	+	+	+	+	-	-	+	+	-	-	-	-	+	+
7	_____	-	+	+	-	-	+	+	+	+	-	-	+	+	-	-
8	_____	-	+	+	-	-	+	+	-	-	+	+	-	-	+	+
9	_____	+	+	-	-	+	+	-	-	+	+	-	-	+	+	-
10	_____	+	+	-	-	+	+	-	+	-	-	+	+	-	-	+
11	_____	+	+	-	+	-	-	+	+	-	-	+	-	+	+	-
12	_____	+	+	-	+	-	-	+	-	+	+	-	+	-	-	+
13	_____	+	-	+	+	-	+	-	-	+	-	+	+	-	+	-
14	_____	+	-	+	+	-	+	-	+	-	+	-	-	+	-	+
15	_____	+	-	+	-	+	-	+	+	-	+	-	+	-	+	-
16	_____	+	-	+	-	+	-	+	-	+	-	+	-	+	-	+

The main effects and interactions represented by each contrast are shown in the tables of confounding patterns for the 16-Run Designs. For Basic 16-Run Designs one should attach a negative sign to all two-factor interactions shown in the confounding pattern tables.

CALCULATION WORKSHEET
FOR BASIC 16-RUN DESIGNS
PAGE TWO OF TWO PAGES

SINGLE DEGREE OF FREEDOM ANOVA TABLE

Contrast Labels	Estimated Contrasts	Sums of Squares		Estimated Effects
A	_____	_____		_____
B	_____	_____		_____
C	_____	_____		_____
D	_____	_____		_____
E	_____	_____		_____
F	_____	_____		_____
G	_____	_____		_____
H	_____	_____		_____
I	_____	_____		_____
J	_____	_____		_____
K	_____	_____		_____
L	_____	_____		_____
M	_____	_____		_____
N	_____	_____		_____
O	_____	_____		_____
TOTAL Sum of Squares	_____			

EXAMPLE OF BASIC 16-RUN DESIGN

Run No.	Response	A	B	C	D	E	F	G	H	I	J	K	L	M	N	O
1	25	−	−	−	−	−	−	−	−	−	−	−	−	−	−	−
2	95	−	−	−	−	−	−	−	+	+	+	+	+	+	+	+
3	113	−	−	−	+	+	+	+	+	+	+	+	−	−	−	−
4	84	−	−	−	+	+	+	+	−	−	−	−	+	+	+	+
5	85	−	+	+	+	+	−	−	−	−	+	+	+	+	−	−
6	133	−	+	+	+	+	−	−	+	+	−	−	−	−	+	+
7	145	−	+	+	−	−	+	+	+	+	−	−	+	+	−	−
8	107	−	+	+	−	−	+	+	−	−	+	+	−	−	+	+
9	90	+	+	−	−	+	+	−	−	+	+	−	−	+	+	−
10	124	+	+	−	−	+	+	−	+	−	−	+	+	−	−	+
11	236	+	+	−	+	−	−	+	+	−	−	+	−	+	+	−
12	178	+	+	−	+	−	−	+	−	+	+	−	+	−	−	+
13	133	+	−	+	+	−	+	−	−	+	−	+	+	−	+	−
14	164	+	−	+	+	−	+	−	+	−	+	−	−	+	−	+
15	120	+	−	+	−	+	−	+	+	−	+	−	+	−	+	−
16	68	+	−	+	−	+	−	+	−	+	−	+	−	+	−	+

SINGLE DEGREE OF FREEDOM ANOVA TABLE

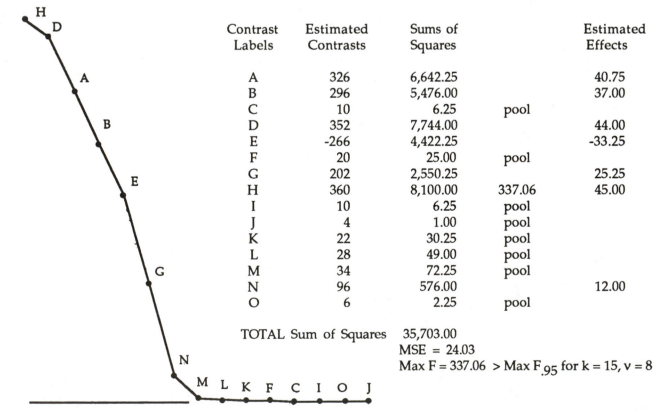

Contrast Labels	Estimated Contrasts	Sums of Squares		Estimated Effects
A	326	6,642.25		40.75
B	296	5,476.00		37.00
C	10	6.25	pool	
D	352	7,744.00		44.00
E	−266	4,422.25		−33.25
F	20	25.00	pool	
G	202	2,550.25		25.25
H	360	8,100.00	337.06	45.00
I	10	6.25	pool	
J	4	1.00	pool	
K	22	30.25	pool	
L	28	49.00	pool	
M	34	72.25	pool	
N	96	576.00		12.00
O	6	2.25	pool	

TOTAL Sum of Squares   35,703.00

MSE = 24.03

Max F = 337.06 > Max $F_{.95}$ for $k = 15$, $v = 8$

CONFOUNDING PATTERNS FOR 16-RUN PLACKETT-BURMAN DESIGNS

The 16-Run Plackett-Burman Arrays are useful for studying from four to fifteen factors having two-levels each. Specific tables of confounding patterns are given below for designs using different numbers of factors. When using the Basic 16-Run Array one should add a negative sign to all two-factor and four-factor interactions listed in the tables.

FIFTEEN FACTORS

Contrast Labels:	A	B	C	D	E	F	G	H	I	J	K	L	M	N	O
Main Effects:	A	B	C	D	E	F	G	H	I	J	K	L	M	N	O
Two-Factor Interactions:	BC	AC	AB	AE	AD	AG	AF	AI	AH	AK	AJ	AM	AL	AO	AN
	DE	DF	DG	BF	BG	BD	BE	BJ	BK	BH	BI	BN	BO	BL	BM
	FG	EG	EF	CG	CF	CE	CD	CK	CJ	CI	CH	CO	CN	CM	CL
	HI	HJ	HK	HL	HM	HN	HO	DL	DM	DN	DO	DH	DI	DJ	DK
	JK	IK	IJ	IM	IL	IO	IN	EM	EL	EO	EN	EI	EH	EK	EJ
	LM	LN	LO	JN	JO	JL	JM	FN	FO	FL	FM	FJ	FK	FH	FI
	NO	MO	MN	KO	KN	KM	KL	GO	GN	GM	GL	GK	GJ	GI	GH

(Change Signs of Two Factor Interactions when using Basic 16-Run Design.)

FOURTEEN FACTORS

Contrast Labels:	A	B	C	D	E	F	G	H	I	J	K	L	M	N	O
Main Effects:	A	B	C	D	E	F	G	H	I	J	K	L	M	N	
Two-Factor Interactions:	BC	AC	AB	AE	AD	AG	AF	AI	AH	AK	AJ	AM	AL	BL	AN
	DE	DF	DG	BF	BG	BD	BE	BJ	BK	BH	BI	BN	CN	CM	BM
	FG	EG	EF	CG	CF	CE	CD	CK	CJ	CI	CH	DH	DI	DJ	CL
	HI	HJ	HK	HL	HM	HN	IN	DL	DM	DN	EN	EI	EH	EK	DK
	JK	IK	IJ	IM	IL	JL	JM	EM	EL	FL	FM	FJ	FK	FH	EJ
	LM	LN	MN	JN	KN	KM	KL	FN	GN	GM	GL	GK	GJ	GI	FI
															GH

(Delete Factor Label O from Data Collection Worksheet.)
(Change Signs of Two Factor Interactions when using Basic 16-Run Design.)

CONFOUNDING PATTERNS FOR 16-RUN PLACKETT-BURMAN DESIGNS

The following designs for 11 to 13 factors are different from those in the first printing of these tables.

THIRTEEN FACTORS

Contrast Labels:	A	B	C	D	E	F	G	H	I	J	K	L	M	N	O
Main Effects:	A	B	C	D	E	F	G	H	I	J	K	L	M		

Two-Factor Interactions:															
BC	AC	AB	AE	AD	AG	AF	AI	AH	AK	AJ	AM	AL	BL	BM
DE	DF	DG	BF	BG	BD	BE	BJ	BK	BH	BI	DH	DI	CM	CL
FG	EG	EF	CG	CF	CE	CD	CK	CJ	CI	CH	EI	EH	DJ	DK
HI	HJ	HK	HL	HM	JL	JM	DL	DM	FL	FM	FJ	FK	EK	EJ
JK	IK	IJ	IM	IL	KM	KL	EM	EL	GM	GL	GK	GJ	FH	FI
LM				KN									GI	GH

(Delete Factor Labels N and O from Data Collection Worksheet.)
(Change Signs of Two Factor Interactions when using Basic 16-Run Design.)

TWELVE FACTORS

Contrast Labels:	A	B	C	D	E	F	G	H	I	J	K	L	M	N	O
Main Effects:	A	B	C	D	E	F	G	H	I	J	K	L			

Two-Factor Interactions:															
BC	AC	AB	AE	AD	AG	AF	AI	AH	AK	AJ	DH	AL	BL	CL
DE	DF	DG	BF	BG	BD	BE	BJ	BK	BH	BI	EI	DI	DJ	DK
FG	EG	EF	CG	CF	CE	CD	CK	CJ	CI	CH	FJ	EH	EK	EJ
HI	HJ	HK	HL	IL	JL	KL	DL	EL	FL	GL	GK	FK	FH	FI
JK	IK	IJ		KN								GJ	GI	GH

(Delete Factor Labels M, N and O from Data Collection Worksheet.)
(Change Signs of Two Factor Interactions when using Basic 16-Run Design.)

CONFOUNDING PATTERNS FOR 16-RUN PLACKETT-BURMAN DESIGNS

ELEVEN FACTORS

Contrast Labels:	A	B	C	D	E	F	G	H	I	J	K	L	M	N	O
Main Effects:	A	B	C	D	E	F	G	H	I	J	K				
Two-Factor Interactions:	BC	AC	AB	AE	AD	AG	AF	AI	AH	AK	AJ	DH	DI	DJ	DK
	DE	DF	DG	BF	BG	BD	BE	BJ	BK	BH	BI	EI	EH	EK	EJ
	FG	EG	EF	CG	CF	CE	CD	CK	CJ	CI	CH	FJ	FK	FH	FI
	HI	HJ	HK		KN							GK	GJ	GI	GH
	JK	IK	IJ												

(Delete Factor Labels L, M, N and O from Data Collection Worksheet.)

(Change Signs of Two Factor Interactions when using Basic 16-Run Design.)

TEN FACTORS

Contrast Labels:	A	B	C	D	E	F	G	H	I	J	K	L	M	N	O
Main Effects:	A	B	C	D	E		G	H			K		M	N	
Two-Factor Interactions:	BC	AC	AB	AE	AD	AG	BE	CK	AH	AK	CH	AM	CN	CM	AN
	DE	EG	DG	CG	BG	BD	CD	EM	BK	BH	EN	BN	EH	EK	BM
			HK		HM	CE			DM	DN		DH			DK
			MN		KN	HN			GN	GM		GK			GH
						KM									

(Delete Factor Labels F, I, J, L and O from Data Collection Worksheet.)

(Change Signs of Two Factor Interactions when using Basic 16-Run Design.)

CONFOUNDING PATTERNS FOR 16-RUN PLACKETT-BURMAN DESIGNS

NINE FACTORS

Contrast Labels:	A	B	C	D	E	F	G	H	I	J	K	L	M	N	O
Main Effects:	A	B	C	D			G	H			K		M	N	
Two-Factor Interactions:	BC	AC	AB	CG	AD	AG	CD	CK	AH	AK	CH	AM	CN	CM	AN
			DG		BG	BD			BK	BH		BN			BM
			HK		HM	HN			DM	DN		DH			DK
			MN		KN	KM			GN	GM		GK			GH

(Delete Factor Labels E, F, I, J, L and O from Data Collection Worksheet.)

(Change Signs of Two Factor Interactions when using Basic 16-Run Design.)

EIGHT FACTORS   (Resolution IV)

Contrast Labels:	A	B	C	D	E	F	G	H	I	J	K	L	M	N	O
Main Effects:	A	B		D			G	H			K		M	N	
Two-Factor Interactions:			AB		AD	AG			AH	AK		AM			AN
			DG		BG	BD			BK	BH		BN			BM
			HK		HM	HN			DM	DN		DH			DK
			MN		KN	KM			GN	GM		GK			GH
Three-Factor Interactions:	BDG	ADG		ABG			ABD	ABK			ABH		ABN	ABM	
	BHK	AHK		AHM			AHN	ADM			ADN		ADH	ADK	
	BMN	AMN		AKN			AKM	AGN			AGM		AGK	AGH	
	DHM	DHN		BHN			BHM	BDN			BDM		BDK	BDH	
	DKN	DKM		BKM			BKN	BGM			BGN		BGH	BGK	
	GHN	GHM		GHK			DHK	DGK			DGH		DGN	DGM	
	GKM	GKN		GMN			DMN	KMN			HMN		HKN	HKM	

(Delete Factor Labels C, E, F, I, J, L and O from Data Collection Worksheet.)

(Change Signs of Two Factor Interactions when using Basic 16-Run Design.)

CONFOUNDING PATTERNS FOR 16-RUN PLACKETT-BURMAN DESIGNS

SEVEN FACTORS _____ (Resolution IV)

Contrast Labels:	A	B	C	D	E	F	G	H	I	J	K	L	M	N	O
Main Effects:	A	B		D			G	H					M	N	
Two-Factor		AB		AD	AG			AH	BH		AM				AN
Interactions:		DG		BG	BD			DM	DN		BN				BM
		MN		HM	HN			GN	GM		DH				GH
Three-Factor	BDG	ADG		ABG			ABD	ADM			ABH		ABN	ABM	
Interactions:	BMN	AMN		AHM			AHN	AGN			ADN		ADH	AGH	
	DHM	DHN		BHN			BHM	BDN			AGM		BGH	BDH	
	GHN	GHM		GMN			DMN	BGM			BDM		DGN	DGM	
											BGN				
											DGH				
											HMN				

(Delete Factor Labels C, E, F, I, J, K, L and O from Data Collection Worksheet.)

(Change Signs of Two Factor Interactions when using Basic 16-Run Design.)

SIX FACTORS _____ (Resolution IV)

Contrast Labels:	A	B	C	D	E	F	G	H	I	J	K	L	M	N	O
Main Effects:	A	B		D			G	H						N	
Two-Factor		AB		AD	AG			AH	BH		BN				AN
Interactions:		DG		BG	BD			GN	DN		DH				GH
					HN										
Three-Factor	BDG	ADG		ABG			ABD	AGN			ABH		ABN	AGH	
Interactions:	GHN	DHN		BHN			AHN	BDN			ADN		ADH	BDH	
											BGN		BGH		
											DGH		DGN		

(Delete Factor Labels C, E, F, I, J, K, L, M and O from Data Collection Worksheet.)

(Change Signs of Two Factor Interactions when using Basic 16-Run Design.)

CONFOUNDING PATTERNS FOR 16-RUN PLACKETT-BURMAN DESIGNS

FIVE FACTORS _____ (Resolution V)

Contrast Labels: A   B   C   D   E   F   G   H   I   J   K   L   M   N   O

Main Effects: **A**   **B**   **D**   **H**   **O**

Interactions: AB   AD   BD   HO   AH   BH   DO   DH   BO   AO

BDHO   DHO   BHO   AHO   ABD   BDO   ADO   ABH   ABO   ADH   BDH

ADHO   ABHO   ABDO   ABDH

(Delete Factor Labels C, E, F, G, I, J, K, L, M and N from Data Collection Worksheet.)
(Change Signs of Two-Factor and Four-Factor Interactions when using Basic 16-Run Design.)
(Basic 16-Run Design plus Reflected 16-Run Design gives Fully Crossed Layout.)

FOUR FACTORS _____ (Fully Crossed)

Contrast Labels: A   B   C   D   E   F   G   H   I   J   K   L   M   N   O

Main Effects: **A**   **B**   **D**   **H**

Interactions: AB   AD   BD   AH   BH   DH   ABDH

ABD   ABH   ADH   BDH

(Delete Factor Labels C, E, F, G, I, J, K, L, M, N and O from Data Collection Worksheet.)
(Change Signs of Two-Factor and Four-Factor Interactions when using Basic 16-Run Design.)

REFLECTED 16-RUN PLACKETT-BURMAN DESIGNS

The Reflected 16-Run Plackett-Burman Array shown below is useful for studying from four to fifteen factors having two-levels each. Specific tables of confounding patterns are given for designs using different numbers of factors. Data Collection Worksheets and Calculation Worksheets are included.

Contrast Labels

Run	A	B	C	D	E	F	G	H	I	J	K	L	M	N	O
1	+	+	+	+	+	+	+	+	+	+	+	+	+	+	+
2	+	+	+	+	+	+	+	−	−	−	−	−	−	−	−
3	+	+	+	−	−	−	−	−	−	−	−	+	+	+	+
4	+	+	+	−	−	−	−	+	+	+	+	−	−	−	−
5	+	−	−	−	−	+	+	+	+	−	−	−	−	+	+
6	+	−	−	−	−	+	+	−	−	+	+	+	+	−	−
7	+	−	−	+	+	−	−	−	−	+	+	−	−	+	+
8	+	−	−	+	+	−	−	+	+	−	−	+	+	−	−
9	−	−	+	+	−	−	+	+	−	−	+	+	−	−	+
10	−	−	+	+	−	−	+	−	+	+	−	−	+	+	−
11	−	−	+	−	+	+	−	−	+	+	−	+	−	−	+
12	−	−	+	−	+	+	−	+	−	−	+	−	+	+	−
13	−	+	−	−	+	−	+	+	−	+	−	−	+	−	+
14	−	+	−	−	+	−	+	−	+	−	+	+	−	+	−
15	−	+	−	+	−	+	−	−	+	−	+	−	+	−	+
16	−	+	−	+	−	+	−	+	−	+	−	+	−	+	−
	A	B	C	D	E	F	G	H	I	J	K	L	M	N	O

Treatment combinations are defined by rows in this matrix.

Contrast coefficients are defined by columns in this matrix.

Number of changes in level:

A	B	C	D	E	F	G	H	I	J	K	L	M	N	O
1	2	3	4	5	6	7	8	9	10	11	12	13	14	15

DATA COLLECTION WORKSHEET
FOR REFLECTED 16-RUN DESIGNS
PAGE ONE OF TWO PAGES
IDENTIFICATION OF FACTORS AND FACTOR LEVELS

When using less than fifteen factors some Contrast Labels will not represent a main effect. **These Contrast Labels should be crossed off the list below.** Suggested sets of Contrast Labels to use with different numbers of factors are shown in the tables of confounding patterns.

Contrast Labels	Factor Names	Low-Level	High-Level
A.	_____	_____	_____
B.	_____	_____	_____
C.	_____	_____	_____
D.	_____	_____	_____
E.	_____	_____	_____
F.	_____	_____	_____
G.	_____	_____	_____
H.	_____	_____	_____
I.	_____	_____	_____
J.	_____	_____	_____
K.	_____	_____	_____
L.	_____	_____	_____
M.	_____	_____	_____
N.	_____	_____	_____
O.	_____	_____	_____

The Response Variable is   _____

Data Collection Worksheet
for Reflected 16-Run Designs
Page Two of Two Pages
Changes in Factor Levels for Reflected 16-Run Designs

When using less than fifteen factors, **cross out all Factor Labels in the following array that do not represent a Main Effect in the study.** The resulting array will then show the factor levels to use in performing the experimental runs.

Changes in level are shown in boldface.

Run	Begin with all factors set at their high levels															Response
1	A+	B+	C+	D+	E+	F+	G+	H+	I+	J+	K+	L+	M+	N+	O+	_____
2	A+	B+	C+	D+	E+	F+	G+	H-	I-	J-	K-	L-	M-	N-	O-	_____
3	A+	B+	C+	D-	E-	F-	G-	H-	I-	J-	K-	L+	M+	N+	O+	_____
4	A+	B+	C+	D-	E-	F-	G-	H+	I+	J+	K+	L-	M-	N-	O-	_____
5	A+	B-	C-	D-	E-	F+	G+	H+	I+	J-	K-	L-	M-	N+	O+	_____
6	A+	B-	C-	D-	E-	F+	G+	H-	I-	J+	K+	L+	M+	N-	O-	_____
7	A+	B-	C-	D+	E+	F-	G-	H-	I-	J+	K+	L-	M-	N+	O+	_____
8	A+	B-	C-	D+	E+	F-	G-	H+	I+	J-	K-	L+	M+	N-	O-	_____
9	A-	B-	C+	D+	E-	F-	G+	H+	I-	J-	K+	L+	M-	N-	O+	_____
10	A-	B-	C+	D+	E-	F-	G+	H-	I+	J+	K-	L-	M+	N+	O-	_____
11	A-	B-	C+	D-	E+	F+	G-	H-	I+	J+	K-	L+	M-	N-	O+	_____
12	A-	B-	C+	D-	E+	F+	G-	H+	I-	J-	K+	L-	M+	N+	O-	_____
13	A-	B+	C-	D-	E+	F-	G+	H+	I-	J+	K-	L-	M+	N-	O+	_____
14	A-	B+	C-	D-	E+	F-	G+	H-	I+	J-	K+	L+	M-	N+	O-	_____
15	A-	B+	C-	D+	E-	F+	G-	H-	I+	J-	K+	L-	M+	N-	O+	_____
16	A-	B+	C-	D+	E-	F+	G-	H+	I-	J+	K-	L+	M-	N+	O-	_____

CALCULATION WORKSHEET
FOR REFLECTED 16-RUN DESIGNS
PAGE ONE OF TWO PAGES

CONTRAST COEFFICIENTS

Run No.	Response	A	B	C	D	E	F	G	H	I	J	K	L	M	N	O
1	_____	+	+	+	+	+	+	+	+	+	+	+	+	+	+	+
2	_____	+	+	+	+	+	+	+	-	-	-	-	-	-	-	-
3	_____	+	+	+	-	-	-	-	-	-	-	-	+	+	+	+
4	_____	+	+	+	-	-	-	-	+	+	+	+	-	-	-	-
5	_____	+	-	-	-	-	+	+	+	+	-	-	-	-	+	+
6	_____	+	-	-	-	-	+	+	-	-	+	+	+	+	-	-
7	_____	+	-	-	+	+	-	-	-	-	+	+	-	-	+	+
8	_____	+	-	-	+	+	-	-	+	+	-	-	+	+	-	-
9	_____	-	-	+	+	-	-	+	+	-	-	+	+	-	-	+
10	_____	-	-	+	+	-	-	+	-	+	+	-	-	+	+	-
11	_____	-	-	+	-	+	+	-	-	+	+	-	+	-	-	+
12	_____	-	-	+	-	+	+	-	+	-	-	+	-	+	+	-
13	_____	-	+	-	-	+	-	+	+	-	+	-	-	+	-	+
14	_____	-	+	-	-	+	-	+	-	+	-	+	+	-	+	-
15	_____	-	+	-	+	-	+	-	-	+	-	+	-	+	-	+
16	_____	-	+	-	+	-	+	-	+	-	+	-	+	-	+	-

The main effects and interactions represented by each contrast are shown in the tables of confounding patterns for the 16-Run Designs.

CALCULATION WORKSHEET
FOR REFLECTED 16-RUN DESIGNS
PAGE TWO OF TWO PAGES

SINGLE DEGREE OF FREEDOM ANOVA TABLE

Contrast Labels	Estimated Contrasts	Sums of Squares		Estimated Effects
A	_____	_____	_____	_____
B	_____	_____	_____	_____
C	_____	_____	_____	_____
D	_____	_____	_____	_____
E	_____	_____	_____	_____
F	_____	_____	_____	_____
G	_____	_____	_____	_____
H	_____	_____	_____	_____
I	_____	_____	_____	_____
J	_____	_____	_____	_____
K	_____	_____	_____	_____
L	_____	_____	_____	_____
M	_____	_____	_____	_____
N	_____	_____	_____	_____
O	_____	_____	_____	_____
TOTAL Sum of Squares	_____			

EXAMPLE OF REFLECTED 16-RUN DESIGN

Run No.	Response	A	B	C	D	E	F	G	H	I	J	K	L	M	N	O
1	194	+	+	+	+	+	+	+	+	+	+	+	+	+	+	+
2	148	+	+	+	+	+	+	+	−	−	−	−	−	−	−	−
3	106	+	+	+	−	−	−	−	−	−	−	−	+	+	+	+
4	156	+	+	+	−	−	−	−	+	+	+	+	−	−	−	−
5	153	+	−	−	−	−	+	+	+	+	−	−	−	−	+	+
6	97	+	−	−	−	−	+	+	−	−	+	+	+	+	−	−
7	105	+	−	−	+	+	−	−	−	−	+	+	−	−	+	+
8	137	+	−	−	+	+	−	−	+	+	−	−	+	+	−	−
9	162	−	−	+	+	−	−	+	+	−	−	+	+	−	−	+
10	125	−	−	+	+	−	−	+	−	+	+	−	−	+	+	−
11	18	−	−	+	−	+	+	−	−	+	+	−	+	−	−	+
12	67	−	−	+	−	+	+	−	+	−	−	+	−	+	+	−
13	117	−	+	−	−	+	−	+	+	−	+	−	−	+	−	+
14	61	−	+	−	−	+	−	+	−	+	−	+	+	−	+	−
15	118	−	+	−	+	−	+	−	−	+	−	+	−	+	−	+
16	158	−	+	−	+	−	+	−	+	−	+	−	+	−	+	−

SINGLE DEGREE OF FREEDOM ANOVA TABLE

Contrast Labels	Estimated Contrasts	Sums of Squares		Estimated Effects
A	270	4,556.25		33.75
B	194	2,352.25		24.25
C	30	56.25	pool	
D	372	8,649.00	477.2	46.50
E	−228	3,249.00		−28.50
F	−16	16.00	pool	
G	192	2,304.00		24.00
H	366	8,372.25		45.75
I	2	0.25	pool	
J	18	20.25	pool	
K	−2	0.25	pool	
L	−56	196.00		
M	0	0.00	pool	
N	16	16.00	pool	
O	24	36.00	pool	

TOTAL Sum of Squares   29,823.75

MSE = 18.125

Max F = 477.2 > Max $F_{.95}$ for k = 15, v = 8

Combining both the Basic and Reflected 16-Run Examples, Contrasts D, H, A, E, B, and G are seen to represent main effects.

BASIC 32-RUN PLACKETT-BURMAN DESIGNS

The Basic 32-Run Array is useful for designs having from 16 to 31 factors with two-levels each. The rows in this array define treatment combinations and the columns define contrast coefficients. The number of changes in level for each factor is shown in the following table.

A	B	C	D	E	F	G	H	I	J	K	L	M	N	O	P	Q	R	S	T	U	V	W	X	Y	Z	*1*	*2*	*3*	*4*	*5*
1	2	3	4	5	6	7	8	9	10	11	12	13	14	15	16	17	18	19	20	21	22	23	24	25	26	27	28	29	30	31

The Contrast Labels above (A thru Z and 1 thru 5) will be used with each of the 32-Run designs even though there may not always be a main effect for each contrast.

For designs with less than 31 factors, the contrast labels to use for main effects may be found by referring to the tables of confounding patterns which follow. The designs given in these tables of confounding patterns will be Resolution III designs (except for the design for 16 factors). When used with the Basic 32-Run Array, the confounding tables need to have a negative sign attached to each two-factor interaction effect.

Due to the size of the 32-Run arrays, it is easy to make a error when computing the estimated contrast values. If the computations are to be carried out manually, it is best to break them into small segments. For this reason the Calculation Worksheets are set up to perform these computations in small steps. Each contrast is computed as the sum a set of partial sums, where each partial sum is computed using the responses and contrast coefficients for four runs. Since several different contrasts will have identical partial sums, this approach reduces the amount of computation while it makes errors less likely. In order to use this feature of the Calculation Worksheets begin by filling in each *row* of partial sums, and then sum the partial sums in each *column* to obtain the estimated contrast values.

THE BASIC 32-RUN PLACKETT-BURMAN ARRAY

Contrast Labels

Run	A	B	C	D	E	F	G	H	I	J	K	L	M	N	O	P	Q	R	S	T	U	V	W	X	Y	Z	1	2	3	4	5
1	−	−	−	−	−	−	−	−	−	−	−	−	−	−	−	−	−	−	−	−	−	−	−	−	−	−	−	−	−	−	−
2	−	−	−	−	−	−	−	−	−	−	−	−	−	−	−	+	+	+	+	+	+	+	+	+	+	+	+	+	+	+	+
3	−	−	−	−	−	−	−	+	+	+	+	+	+	+	+	+	+	+	+	+	+	+	+	−	−	−	−	−	−	−	−
4	−	−	−	−	−	−	−	+	+	+	+	+	+	+	+	−	−	−	−	−	−	−	−	+	+	+	+	+	+	+	+
5	−	−	−	+	+	+	+	+	+	+	+	−	−	−	−	−	−	−	−	+	+	+	+	+	+	+	+	−	−	−	−
6	−	−	−	+	+	+	+	+	+	+	+	−	−	−	−	+	+	+	+	−	−	−	−	−	−	−	−	+	+	+	+
7	−	−	−	+	+	+	+	−	−	−	−	+	+	+	+	+	+	+	+	−	−	−	−	−	+	+	+	−	−	−	−
8	−	−	−	+	+	+	+	−	−	−	−	+	+	+	+	−	−	−	−	−	+	+	+	−	−	−	−	+	+	+	+
9	−	+	+	+	+	−	−	−	−	+	+	+	+	−	−	−	−	+	+	+	+	−	−	−	−	+	+	+	+	−	−
10	−	+	+	+	+	−	−	−	−	+	+	+	+	−	−	+	+	−	−	−	−	+	+	+	+	−	−	−	−	+	+
11	−	+	+	+	+	−	−	+	+	−	−	−	−	+	+	+	+	−	−	−	−	+	+	−	−	+	+	+	+	−	−
12	−	+	+	+	+	−	−	+	+	−	−	−	−	+	+	−	−	+	+	+	+	−	−	+	+	−	−	−	−	+	+
13	−	+	+	−	−	+	+	+	+	−	−	+	+	−	−	−	−	+	+	−	−	+	+	+	+	−	−	+	+	−	−
14	−	+	+	−	−	+	+	+	+	−	−	+	+	−	−	−	+	−	−	+	+	−	−	−	−	+	+	−	−	+	+
15	−	+	+	−	−	+	+	−	−	+	+	−	−	+	+	+	−	+	+	+	+	−	−	+	+	−	−	+	+	−	−
16	−	+	+	−	−	+	+	−	−	+	+	−	−	+	+	−	−	+	+	−	−	+	+	−	−	+	+	−	−	+	+
17	+	+	−	−	+	+	−	−	+	+	−	−	+	+	−	−	+	+	−	−	+	+	−	−	+	+	−	−	+	+	−
18	+	+	−	−	+	+	−	−	+	+	−	−	+	+	−	+	−	−	+	+	−	−	+	+	−	−	+	+	−	−	+
19	+	+	−	−	+	+	−	+	−	−	+	+	−	−	+	+	−	−	+	+	−	−	+	+	+	+	−	−	+	+	−
20	+	+	−	−	+	+	−	+	−	−	+	−	−	+	+	−	−	+	+	−	+	+	−	−	+	+	−	+	−	−	+
21	+	+	−	+	−	−	+	+	−	−	+	−	+	+	−	−	+	+	−	+	−	−	+	+	−	−	+	−	+	+	−
22	+	+	−	+	−	−	+	+	−	−	+	−	+	+	−	+	−	−	+	−	+	+	−	−	+	+	−	+	−	−	+
23	+	+	−	+	−	−	+	−	+	+	−	+	−	−	+	−	+	+	−	+	−	−	+	+	−	−	+	−	+	+	−
24	+	+	−	+	−	−	+	−	+	+	−	+	−	−	+	−	+	+	−	+	−	−	+	−	+	+	−	+	−	−	+
25	+	−	+	+	−	−	−	−	+	−	+	+	−	+	−	−	+	−	+	+	−	+	−	−	+	−	+	+	−	+	+
26	+	−	+	+	−	+	−	−	+	−	+	+	−	+	−	+	−	+	−	−	+	−	+	+	−	+	−	−	+	−	+
27	+	−	+	+	−	+	−	+	−	+	−	−	+	−	+	+	−	+	−	−	+	−	+	−	+	−	+	+	−	+	−
28	+	−	+	+	−	+	−	+	−	+	−	−	+	−	+	−	+	−	+	+	−	+	−	+	−	+	−	+	−	+	+
29	+	−	+	−	+	−	+	+	−	+	−	+	−	+	−	+	−	+	−	+	−	+	−	+	−	+	−	+	−	+	+
30	+	−	+	−	+	−	+	+	−	+	−	+	−	+	−	+	−	+	−	+	−	+	−	+	−	+	+	−	+	−	+
31	+	−	+	−	+	−	+	−	+	−	+	−	+	−	+	−	+	−	+	−	+	−	+	−	+	−	+	−	−	+	−
32	+	−	+	−	+	−	+	−	+	−	+	−	+	−	+	−	+	−	+	−	+	−	+	−	+	−	+	−	+	−	+

A B C D E F G H I J K L M N O P Q R S T U V W X Y Z 1 2 3 4 5

EXAMPLE OF BASIC 32-RUN DESIGN

Twenty-eight factors were studied using the Basic 32-Run Array. As shown in the tables of confounding patterns for 28 factors, the unassigned factor labels are R, T and X.

DATA

Run	Response
1	46
2	46
3	94
4	46
5	90
6	291
7	116
8	66
9	59
10	123
11	284
12	107
13	64
14	89
15	33
16	55
17	57
18	46
19	90
20	79
21	106
22	295
23	116
24	76
25	69
26	98
27	290
28	100
29	73
30	85
31	57
32	37

SINGLE DEGREE OF FREEDOM ANOVA TABLE

Contrast Labels	Estimated Contrasts	Sums of Squares	Estimated Effects
A	65	132.03125	
B	75	175.78125	
C	-37	42.78125	
D	1289	51,922.53125	80.6
E	37	42.78125	
F	-17	9.03125	
G	15	7.03125	
H	1083	36,652.78125	67.7
I	-41	52.53125	
J	-15	7.03125	
K	-39	47.53125	
L	-597	11,137.78125	-37.3
M	7	1.53125	
N	-23	16.53125	
O	9	2.53125	
P	1023	32,704.03125	63.9
Q	63	124.03125	
(R)	77	185.28125	
S	33	34.03125	
(T)	-857	22,951.53125	-53.6
U	-25	19.53125	
V	77	185.28125	
W	-7	1.53125	
(X)	-683	14,577.78125	-42.7
Y	-35	38.28125	
Z	-21	13.78125	
1	-57	101.53125	
2	465	6,757.03125	29.1
3	-127	504.03125	
4	79	195.03125	
5	-5	0.78125	
Total		178,643.71800	

DATA COLLECTION WORKSHEET
FOR BASIC 32-RUN DESIGNS
PAGE ONE OF FIVE PAGES
IDENTIFICATION OF FACTORS AND FACTOR LEVELS

When using less than 31 factors some Contrast Labels will not represent a main effect. Customize this worksheet for a particular design by **crossing off the list below those Contrast Labels that do not represent a main effect.**

Factor Names	Low Level	High Level	Factor Names	Low Level	High Level
A. _____	___	___	P. _____	___	___
B. _____	___	___	Q. _____	___	___
C. _____	___	___	R. _____	___	___
D. _____	___	___	S. _____	___	___
E. _____	___	___	T. _____	___	___
F. _____	___	___	U. _____	___	___
G. _____	___	___	V. _____	___	___
H. _____	___	___	W. _____	___	___
I. _____	___	___	X. _____	___	___
J. _____	___	___	Y. _____	___	___
K. _____	___	___	Z. _____	___	___
L. _____	___	___	1. _____	___	___
M. _____	___	___	2. _____	___	___
N. _____	___	___	3. _____	___	___
O. _____	___	___	4. _____	___	___
			5. _____	___	___

The Response Variable is   _____

DATA COLLECTION WORKSHEET
PAGE TWO OF FIVE PAGES
CHANGES IN FACTOR LEVELS FOR BASIC 32-RUN DESIGNS

When using less than 31 factors, **cross out all Factor Labels in the following array that do not represent a Main Effect in the study.** The resulting array will then show the factor levels to use in performing the experimental runs.

Begin with all factors set at their low levels. Changes in factor levels shown in boldface.

Run   Response

1

A- B- C- D- E- F- G- H- I- J- K- L- M- N- O-

P- Q- R- S- T- U- V- W- X- Y- Z- 1- 2- 3- 4- 5-

2

A- B- C- D- E- F- G- H- I- J- K- L- M- N- O-

P+ Q+ R+ S+ T+ U+ V+ W+ X+ Y+ Z+ 1+ 2+ 3+ 4+ 5+

3

A- B- C- D- E- F- G- **H+ I+ J+ K+ L+ M+ N+ O+**

P+ Q+ R+ S+ T+ U+ V+ W+ **X- Y- Z- 1- 2- 3- 4- 5-**

4

A- B- C- D- E- F- G- **H+** I+ J+ K+ L+ M+ N+ O+

P- Q- R- S- T- U- V- W- X+ Y+ Z+ 1+ 2+ 3+ 4+ 5+

5

A- B- C- **D+ E+ F+ G+** H+ I+ J+ K+ **L- M- N- O-**

P- Q- R- S- **T+ U+ V+ W+** X+ Y+ Z+ 1+ **2- 3- 4- 5-**

6

A- B- C- D+ E+ F+ G+ H+ I+ J+ K+ L- M- N- O-

P+ Q+ R+ S+ T- U- V- W- X- Y- Z- 1- 2+ 3+ 4+ 5+

7

A- B- C- D+ E+ F+ G+ **H- I- J- K- L+ M+ N+ O+**

P+ Q+ R+ S+ T- U- V- W- **X+ Y+ Z+ 1+ 2- 3- 4- 5-**

8

A- B- C- D+ E+ F+ G+ H- I- J- K- L+ M+ N+ O+

P- Q- R- S- T+ U+ V+ W+ X- Y- Z- 1- 2+ 3+ 4+ 5+

DATA COLLECTION WORKSHEET
PAGE THREE OF FIVE PAGES
CHANGES IN FACTOR LEVELS FOR BASIC 32-RUN DESIGNS

Factors that change level from previous run are shown in boldface.

Run   Response

9

A- **B+ C+** D+ E+ **F- G- H-** I- **J+ K+ L+ M+ N- O-**

P- Q- **R+ S+** T+ U+ **V- W- X-** Y- **Z+ 1+** 2+ 3+ **4- 5-**

10

A- B+ C+ D+ E+ F- G- H- I- J+ K+ L+ M+ N- O-

P+ Q+ R- S- T- U- V+ W+ X+ Y+ Z- 1- 2- 3- 4+ 5+

11

A- B+ C+ D+ E+ F- G- **H+ I+ J- K- L- M- N+ O+**

P+ Q+ R- S- T- U- V+ W+ **X- Y- Z+ 1+** 2+ 3+ **4- 5-**

12

A- B+ C+ D+ E+ F- G- H+ I+ J- K- L- M- N+ O+

P- Q- R+ S+ T+ U+ V- W- X+ Y+ Z- 1- 2- 3- 4+ 5+

13

A- B+ C+ **D- E- F+ G+ H+** I+ J- K- **L+ M+ N- O-**

P- Q- R+ S+ **T- U- V+ W+** X+ Y+ Z- 1- **2+ 3+ 4- 5-**

14

A- B+ C+ D- E- F+ G+ H+ I+ J- K- L+ M+ N- O-

P+ Q+ R- S- T+ U+ V- W- X- Y- Z+ 1+ 2- 3- 4+ 5+

15

A- B+ C+ D- E- F+ G+ **H- I- J+ K+ L- M- N+ O+**

P+ Q+ R- S- T+ U+ V- W- **X+ Y+ Z- 1- 2+ 3+ 4- 5-**

16

A- B+ C+ D- E- F+ G+ H- I- J+ K+ L- M- N+ O+

P- Q- R+ S+ T- U- V+ W+ X- Y- Z+ 1+ 2- 3- 4+ 5+

DATA COLLECTION WORKSHEET
PAGE FOUR OF FIVE PAGES
CHANGES IN FACTOR LEVELS FOR BASIC 32-RUN DESIGNS

Factors that change level from previous run are shown in boldface.

Run   Response

17

A+ B+ **C-** D- E+ F+ **G-** H- I+ J+ **K-** L- **M+** N+ **O-**

P- **Q+** R+ **S-** T- **U+** V+ **W-** X- **Y+** Z+ **1-** 2- **3+** 4+ **5-**

18

A+ B+ C- D- E+ F+ G- H- I+ J+ K- L- M+ N+ O-

P+ **Q-** **R-** **S+** **T+** **U-** V- **W+** **X+** **Y-** **Z-** **1+** 2+ **3-** **4-** **5+**

19

A+ B+ C- D- E+ F+ G- **H+** **I-** **J-** **K+** **L+** **M-** **N-** **O+**

P+ Q- R- S+ T+ U- V- W+ **X-** **Y+** **Z+** **1-** 2- **3+** 4+ **5-**

20

A+ B+ C- D- E+ F+ G- H+ I- J- K+ L+ M- N- O+

P- **Q+** **R+** **S-** **T-** **U+** V+ **W-** **X+** **Y-** **Z-** **1+** 2+ **3-** **4-** 5+

21

A+ B+ C- **D+** **E-** **F-** **G+** H+ I- J- K+ **L-** **M+** **N+** **O-**

P- Q+ R+ S- **T+** **U-** **V-** **W+** X+ Y- Z- 1+ **2-** **3+** 4+ **5-**

22

A+ B+ C- D+ E- F- **G+** H+ I- J- K+ L- **M+** N+ O-

P+ **Q-** **R-** **S+** T- **U+** **V+** W+ **X-** **Y+** **Z+** **1-** 2+ **3-** **4-** **5+**

23

A+ B+ C- D+ E- F- G+ **H-** **I+** **J+** **K-** **L+** **M-** **N-** **O+**

P+ Q- R- S+ T- **U+** V+ W- **X+** **Y-** **Z-** 1+ 2- **3+** 4+ **5-**

24

A+ B+ C- D+ E- F- G+ **H-** **I+** J+ K- L+ M- N- O+

P- **Q+** **R+** **S-** **T+** **U-** **V-** **W+** **X-** **Y+** **Z+** **1-** 2+ **3-** **4-** 5+

DATA COLLECTION WORKSHEET
PAGE FIVE OF FIVE PAGES
CHANGES IN FACTOR LEVELS FOR BASIC 32-RUN DESIGNS

Factors that change level from previous run are shown in boldface.

Run   Response

25

A+ **B- C+** D+ E- **F+ G-** H- I+ **J- K+** L+ M- N+ **O-**

P- Q+ **R- S+** T+ U- **V+ W-** X- Y+ **Z- 1+** 2+ 3- **4+ 5-**

26

A+ B- C+ D+ E- F+ G- H- I+ J- K+ L+ M- N+ O-

P+ Q- R+ S- T- U+ V- W+ X+ Y- Z+ 1- 2- 3+ 4- 5+

27

A+ B- C+ D+ E- F+ G- **H+ I- J+ K- L- M+ N- O+**

P+ Q- R+ S- T- U+ V- W+ **X- Y+ Z- 1+** 2+ **3-** 4+ 5-

28

A+ B- C+ D+ E- F+ G- H+ I- J+ K- L- M+ N- O+

P- Q+ R- S+ T+ U- V+ W- X+ Y- Z+ 1- 2- 3+ 4- 5+

29

A+ B- C+ **D- E+ F- G+** H+ I- J+ K- **L+ M- N+ O-**

P- Q+ R- S+ **T- U+ V- W+** X+ Y- Z+ 1- **2+ 3- 4+ 5-**

30

A+ B- C+ D- E+ F- G+ H+ I- J+ K- L+ M- N+ O-

P+ Q- R+ S- T+ U- V+ W- X- Y+ Z- 1+ 2- **3+ 4- 5+**

31

A+ B- C+ D- E+ F- G+ **H- I+ J- K+ L- M+ N- O+**

P+ Q- R+ S- T+ U- V+ W- **X+ Y- Z+ 1- 2+** 3- **4+ 5-**

32

A+ B- C+ D- E+ F- G+ H- I+ J- K+ L- M+ N- O+

P- Q+ R- S+ T- U+ V- W+ X- Y+ Z- 1+ 2- 3+ 4- 5+

CALCULATION WORKSHEET FOR BASIC 32-RUN DESIGNS
PAGE ONE OF FIVE PAGES

Run No.	Response	A	B	C	D	E	F	G
1	_____	-	-	-	-	-	-	-
2	_____	-	-	-	-	-	-	-
3	_____	-	-	-	-	-	-	-
4	_____	-	-	-	-	-	-	-
sums for runs 1 to 4		____	____	____	____	____	____	____
5	_____	-	-	-	+	+	+	+
6	_____	-	-	-	+	+	+	+
7	_____	-	-	-	+	+	+	+
8	_____	-	-	-	+	+	+	+
sums for runs 5 to 8		____	____	____	____	____	____	____
9	_____	-	+	+	+	+	-	-
10	_____	-	+	+	+	+	-	-
11	_____	-	+	+	+	+	-	-
12	_____	-	+	+	+	+	-	-
sums for runs 9 to 12		____	____	____	____	____	____	____
13	_____	-	+	+	-	-	+	+
14	_____	-	+	+	-	-	+	+
15	_____	-	+	+	-	-	+	+
16	_____	-	+	+	-	-	+	+
sums for runs 13 to 16		____	____	____	____	____	____	____
17	_____	+	+	-	-	+	+	-
18	_____	+	+	-	-	+	+	-
19	_____	+	+	-	-	+	+	-
20	_____	+	+	-	-	+	+	-
sums for runs 17 to 20		____	____	____	____	____	____	____
21	_____	+	+	-	+	-	-	+
22	_____	+	+	-	+	-	-	+
23	_____	+	+	-	+	-	-	+
24	_____	+	+	-	+	-	-	+
sums for runs 21 to 24		____	____	____	____	____	____	____
25	_____	+	-	+	+	-	+	-
26	_____	+	-	+	+	-	+	-
27	_____	+	-	+	+	-	+	-
28	_____	+	-	+	+	-	+	-
sums for runs 25 to 28		____	____	____	____	____	____	____
29	_____	+	-	+	-	+	-	+
30	_____	+	-	+	-	+	-	+
31	_____	+	-	+	-	+	-	+
32	_____	+	-	+	-	+	-	+
sums for runs 29 to 32		____	____	____	____	____	____	____
Sum of Sums:		____	____	____	____	____	____	____
Est. Contrasts for		A	B	C	D	E	F	G

CALCULATION WORKSHEET FOR BASIC 32-RUN DESIGNS
PAGE TWO OF FIVE PAGES

Run No.	Response	H	I	J	K	L	M	N	O
1	_____	-	-	-	-	-	-	-	-
2	_____	-	-	-	-	-	-	-	-
3	_____	+	+	+	+	+	+	+	+
4	_____	+	+	+	+	+	+	+	+
sums for runs 1 to 4									
5	_____	+	+	+	+	-	-	-	-
6	_____	+	+	+	+	-	-	-	-
7	_____	-	-	-	-	+	+	+	+
8	_____	-	-	-	-	+	+	+	+
sums for runs 5 to 8									
9	_____	-	-	+	+	+	+	-	-
10	_____	-	-	+	+	+	+	-	-
11	_____	+	+	-	-	-	-	+	+
12	_____	+	+	-	-	-	-	+	+
sums for runs 9 to 12									
13	_____	+	+	-	-	+	+	-	-
14	_____	+	+	-	-	+	+	-	-
15	_____	-	-	+	+	-	-	+	+
16	_____	-	-	+	+	-	-	+	+
sums for runs 13 to 16									
17	_____	-	+	+	-	-	+	+	-
18	_____	-	+	+	-	-	+	+	-
19	_____	+	-	-	+	+	-	-	+
20	_____	+	-	-	+	+	-	-	+
sums for runs 17 to 20									
21	_____	+	-	-	+	-	+	+	-
22	_____	+	-	-	+	-	+	+	-
23	_____	-	+	+	-	+	-	-	+
24	_____	-	+	+	-	+	-	-	+
sums for runs 21 to 24									
25	_____	-	+	-	+	+	-	+	-
26	_____	-	+	-	+	+	-	+	-
27	_____	+	-	+	-	-	+	-	+
28	_____	+	-	+	-	-	+	-	+
sums for runs 25 to 28									
29	_____	+	-	+	-	+	-	+	-
30	_____	+	-	+	-	+	-	+	-
31	_____	-	+	-	+	-	+	-	+
32	_____	-	+	-	+	-	+	-	+
sums for runs 29 to 32									
Sum of Sums:									
Est. Contrasts for		H	I	J	K	L	M	N	O

64

CALCULATION WORKSHEET FOR BASIC 32-RUN DESIGNS
PAGE THREE OF FIVE PAGES

Run No.	Response	P	Q	R	S	T	U	V	W
1	_____	-	-	-	-	-	-	-	-
2	_____	+	+	+	+	+	+	+	+
3	_____	+	+	+	+	+	+	+	+
4	_____	-	-	-	-	-	-	-	-
sums for runs 1 to 4	_____	____	____	____	____	____	____	____	____
5	_____	-	-	-	-	+	+	+	+
6	_____	+	+	+	+	-	-	-	-
7	_____	+	+	+	+	-	-	-	-
8	_____	-	-	-	-	+	+	+	+
sums for runs 5 to 8	_____	____	____	____	____	____	____	____	____
9	_____	-	-	+	+	+	+	-	-
10	_____	+	+	-	-	-	-	+	+
11	_____	+	+	-	-	-	-	+	+
12	_____	-	-	+	+	+	+	-	-
sums for runs 9 to 12	_____	____	____	____	____	____	____	____	____
13	_____	-	-	+	+	-	-	+	+
14	_____	+	+	-	-	+	+	-	-
15	_____	+	+	-	-	+	+	-	-
16	_____	-	-	+	+	-	-	+	+
sums for runs 13 to 16	_____	____	____	____	____	____	____	____	____
17	_____	-	+	+	-	-	+	+	-
18	_____	+	-	-	+	+	-	-	+
19	_____	+	-	-	+	+	-	-	+
20	_____	-	+	+	-	-	+	+	-
sums for runs 17 to 20	_____	____	____	____	____	____	____	____	____
21	_____	-	+	+	-	+	-	-	+
22	_____	+	-	-	+	-	+	+	-
23	_____	+	-	-	+	-	+	+	-
24	_____	-	+	+	-	+	-	-	+
sums for runs 21 to 24	_____	____	____	____	____	____	____	____	____
25	_____	-	+	-	+	+	-	+	-
26	_____	+	-	+	-	-	+	-	+
27	_____	+	-	+	-	-	+	-	+
28	_____	-	+	-	+	+	-	+	-
sums for runs 25 to 28	_____	____	____	____	____	____	____	____	____
29	_____	-	+	-	+	-	+	-	+
30	_____	+	-	+	-	+	-	+	-
31	_____	+	-	+	-	+	-	+	-
32	_____	-	+	-	+	-	+	-	+
sums for runs 29 to 32	_____	____	____	____	____	____	____	____	____
Sum of Sums:		____	____	____	____	____	____	____	____
Est. Contrasts for		P	Q	R	S	T	U	V	W

Calculation Worksheet for Basic 32-Run Designs
Page Four of Five Pages

Run No.	Response	Contrast Labels X	Y	Z	1	2	3	4	5
1	_____	-	-	-	-	-	-	-	-
2	_____	+	+	+	+	+	+	+	+
3	_____	-	-	-	-	-	-	-	-
4	_____	+	+	+	+	+	+	+	+
sums for runs 1 to 4									
5	_____	+	+	+	+	-	-	-	-
6	_____	-	-	-	-	+	+	+	+
7	_____	+	+	+	+	-	-	-	-
8	_____	-	-	-	-	+	+	+	+
sums for runs 5 to 8									
9	_____	-	-	+	+	+	+	-	-
10	_____	+	+	-	-	-	-	+	+
11	_____	-	-	+	+	+	+	-	-
12	_____	+	+	-	-	-	-	+	+
sums for runs 9 to 12									
13	_____	+	+	-	-	+	+	-	-
14	_____	-	-	+	+	-	-	+	+
15	_____	+	+	-	-	+	+	-	-
16	_____	-	-	+	+	-	-	+	+
sums for runs 13 to 16									
17	_____	-	+	+	-	-	+	+	-
18	_____	+	-	-	+	+	-	-	+
19	_____	-	+	+	-	-	+	+	-
20	_____	+	-	-	+	+	-	-	+
sums for runs 17 to 20									
21	_____	+	-	-	+	-	+	+	-
22	_____	-	+	+	-	+	-	-	+
23	_____	+	-	-	+	-	+	+	-
24	_____	-	+	+	-	+	-	-	+
sums for runs 21 to 24									
25	_____	-	+	-	+	+	-	+	-
26	_____	+	-	+	-	-	+	-	+
27	_____	-	+	-	+	+	-	+	-
28	_____	+	-	+	-	-	+	-	+
sums for runs 25 to 28									
29	_____	+	-	+	-	+	-	+	-
30	_____	-	+	-	+	-	+	-	+
31	_____	+	-	+	-	+	-	+	-
32	_____	-	+	-	+	-	+	-	+
sums for runs 29 to 32									

Sum of Sums: _____ _____ _____ _____ _____ _____ _____ _____

Est. Contrasts for   X   Y   Z   1   2   3   4   5

CALCULATION WORKSHEET
FOR BASIC 32-RUN DESIGNS
PAGE FIVE OF FIVE PAGES

SINGLE DEGREE OF FREEDOM ANOVA TABLE

Contrast Labels	Estimated Contrasts	Sums of Squares		Estimated Effects
A	_____	_____	_____	_____
B	_____	_____	_____	_____
C	_____	_____	_____	_____
D	_____	_____	_____	_____
E	_____	_____	_____	_____
F	_____	_____	_____	_____
G	_____	_____	_____	_____
H	_____	_____	_____	_____
I	_____	_____	_____	_____
J	_____	_____	_____	_____
K	_____	_____	_____	_____
L	_____	_____	_____	_____
M	_____	_____	_____	_____
N	_____	_____	_____	_____
O	_____	_____	_____	_____
P	_____	_____	_____	_____
Q	_____	_____	_____	_____
R	_____	_____	_____	_____
S	_____	_____	_____	_____
T	_____	_____	_____	_____
U	_____	_____	_____	_____
V	_____	_____	_____	_____
W	_____	_____	_____	_____
X	_____	_____	_____	_____
Y	_____	_____	_____	_____
Z	_____	_____	_____	_____
1	_____	_____	_____	_____
2	_____	_____	_____	_____
3	_____	_____	_____	_____
4	_____	_____	_____	_____
5	_____	_____	_____	_____

TOTAL Sum of Squares _____

CONFOUNDING PATTERNS FOR 32-RUN PLACKETT-BURMAN DESIGNS

THIRTY-ONE FACTORS

Main Effects and Contrast Labels

A	B	C	D	E	F	G	H	I	J	K	L	M	N	O	P

Corresponding Two-Factor Interactions

A	B	C	D	E	F	G	H	I	J	K	L	M	N	O	P
BC	AC	AB	AE	AD	AG	AF	AI	AH	AK	AJ	AM	AL	AO	AN	AQ
DE	DF	DG	BF	BG	BD	BE	BJ	BK	BH	BI	BN	BO	BL	BM	BR
FG	EG	EF	CG	CF	CE	CD	CK	CJ	CI	CH	CO	CN	CM	CL	CS
HI	HJ	HK	HL	HM	HN	HO	DL	DM	DN	DO	DH	DI	DJ	DK	DT
JK	IK	IJ	IM	IL	IO	IN	EM	EL	EO	EN	EI	EH	EK	EJ	EU
LM	LN	LO	JN	JO	JL	JM	FN	FO	FL	FM	FJ	FK	FH	FI	FV
NO	MO	MN	KO	KN	KM	KL	GO	GN	GM	GL	GK	GJ	GI	GH	GW
PQ	PR	PS	PT	PU	PV	PW	PX	PY	PZ	P1	P2	P3	P4	P5	HX
RS	SQ	QR	QU	QT	QW	QV	QY	QX	Q1	QZ	Q3	Q2	Q5	Q4	IY
TU	TV	TW	RV	RW	RT	RU	RZ	R1	RX	RY	R4	R5	R2	R3	JZ
VW	UW	UV	SW	SV	SU	ST	S1	SZ	SY	SX	S5	S4	S3	S2	K1
XY	XZ	X1	X2	X3	X4	X5	T2	T3	T4	T5	TX	TY	TZ	T1	L2
Z1	Y1	YZ	Y3	Y2	Y5	Y4	U3	U2	U5	U4	UY	UX	U1	UZ	M3
23	24	25	Z4	Z5	Z2	Z3	V4	V5	V2	V3	VZ	V1	VX	VY	N4
45	35	34	15	14	13	12	W5	W4	W3	W2	W1	WZ	WY	WX	O5

Main Effects and Contrast Labels

Q	R	S	T	U	V	W	X	Y	Z	1	2	3	4	5

Corresponding Two-Factor Interactions

Q	R	S	T	U	V	W	X	Y	Z	1	2	3	4	5
AP	AS	AR	AU	AT	AW	AV	AY	AX	A1	AZ	A3	A2	A5	A4
BS	BP	BQ	BV	BW	BT	BU	BZ	B1	BX	BY	B4	B5	B2	B3
CR	CQ	CP	CW	CV	CU	CT	C1	CZ	CY	CX	C5	C4	C3	C2
DU	DV	DW	DP	DQ	DR	DS	D2	D3	D4	D5	DX	DY	DZ	D1
ET	EW	EV	EQ	EP	ES	ER	E3	E2	E5	E4	EY	EX	E1	EZ
FW	FT	FU	FR	FS	FP	FQ	F4	F5	F2	F3	FZ	F1	FX	FY
GV	GU	GT	GS	GR	GQ	GP	G5	G4	G3	G2	G1	GZ	GY	GX
HY	HZ	H1	H2	H3	H4	H5	HP	HQ	HR	HS	HT	HU	HV	HW
IX	I1	IZ	I3	I2	I5	I4	IQ	IP	IS	IR	IU	IT	IW	IV
J1	JX	JY	J4	J5	J2	J3	JR	JS	JP	JQ	JV	JW	JT	JU
KZ	KY	KX	K5	K4	K3	K2	KS	KR	KQ	KP	KW	KV	KU	KT
L3	L4	L5	LX	LY	LZ	L1	LT	LU	LV	LW	LP	LQ	LR	LS
M2	M5	M4	MY	MX	M1	MZ	MU	MT	MW	MV	MQ	MP	MS	MR
N5	N2	N3	NZ	N1	NX	NY	NV	NW	NT	NU	NR	NS	NP	NQ
O4	O3	O2	O1	OZ	OY	OX	OW	OV	OU	OT	OS	OR	OQ	OP

THIRTY-ONE FACTORS

Add minus sign to interactions when using Basic 32-Run Array.

CONFOUNDING PATTERNS FOR 32-RUN PLACKETT-BURMAN DESIGNS

THIRTY FACTORS

Contrast Labels

A	B	C	D	E	F	G	H	I	J	K	L	M	N	O	P

Corresponding Main Effects and Two-Factor Interactions

A	B	C	D	E	F	G	H	I	J	K	L	M	N	O	P
BC	AC	AB	AE	AD	AG	AF	AI	AH	AK	AJ	AM	AL	AO	AN	AQ
DE	DF	DG	BF	BG	BD	BE	BJ	BK	BH	BI	BN	BO	BL	BM	BR
FG	EG	EF	CG	CF	CE	CD	CK	CJ	CI	CH	CO	CN	CM	CL	CS
HI	HJ	HK	HL	HM	HN	HO	DL	DM	DN	DO	DH	DI	DJ	DK	DT
JK	IK	IJ	IM	IL	IO	IN	EM	EL	EO	EN	EI	EH	EK	EJ	EU
LM	LN	LO	JN	JO	JL	JM	FN	FO	FL	FM	FJ	FK	FH	FI	FV
NO	MO	MN	KO	KN	KM	KL	GO	GN	GM	GL	GK	GJ	GI	GH	GW
PQ	PR	PS	PT	PU	PV	PW	QY	PY	PZ	P1	P2	P3	P4	P5	IY
RS	SQ	QR	QU	QT	QW	QV	RZ	R1	Q1	QZ	Q3	Q2	Q5	Q4	JZ
TU	TV	TW	RV	RW	RT	RU	S1	SZ	SY	RY	R4	R5	R2	R3	K1
VW	UW	UV	SW	SV	SU	ST	T2	T3	T4	T5	S5	S4	S3	S2	L2
Z1	Y1	YZ	Y3	Y2	Y5	Y4	U3	U2	U5	U4	UY	TY	TZ	T1	M3
23	24	25	Z4	Z5	Z2	Z3	V4	V5	V2	V3	VZ	V1	U1	UZ	N4
45	35	34	15	14	13	12	W5	W4	W3	W2	W1	WZ	WY	VY	O5

Contrast Labels

Q	R	S	T	U	V	W	X	Y	Z	1	2	3	4	5

Corresponding Main Effects and Two-Factor Interactions

Q	R	S	T	U	V	W		Y	Z	1	2	3	4	5
AP	AS	AR	AU	AT	AW	AV	AY	B1	A1	AZ	A3	A2	A5	A4
BS	BP	BQ	BV	BW	BT	BU	BZ	CZ	CY	BY	B4	B5	B2	B3
CR	CQ	CP	CW	CV	CU	CT	C1	D3	D4	D5	C5	C4	C3	C2
DU	DV	DW	DP	DQ	DR	DS	D2	E2	E5	E4	EY	DY	DZ	D1
ET	EW	EV	EQ	EP	ES	ER	E3	F5	F2	F3	FZ	F1	E1	EZ
FW	FT	FU	FR	FS	FP	FQ	F4	G4	G3	G2	G1	GZ	GY	FY
GV	GU	GT	GS	GR	GQ	GP	G5	HQ	HR	HS	HT	HU	HV	HW
HY	HZ	H1	H2	H3	H4	H5	HP	IP	IS	IR	IU	IT	IW	IV
J1	I1	IZ	I3	I2	I5	I4	IQ	JS	JP	JQ	JV	JW	JT	JU
KZ	KY	JY	J4	J5	J2	J3	JR	KR	KQ	KP	KW	KV	KU	KT
L3	L4	L5	K5	K4	K3	K2	KS	LU	LV	LW	LP	LQ	LR	LS
M2	M5	M4	MY	LY	LZ	L1	LT	MT	MW	MV	MQ	MP	MS	MR
N5	N2	N3	NZ	N1	M1	MZ	MU	NW	NT	NU	NR	NS	NP	NQ
O4	O3	O2	O1	OZ	OY	NY	NV	OV	OU	OT	OS	OR	OQ	OP
						OW								

THIRTY FACTORS

Add minus sign to interactions when using Basic 32-Run Array.
On Data Collection Worksheet, delete Factor Label **X**.

CONFOUNDING PATTERNS FOR 32-RUN PLACKETT-BURMAN DESIGNS

TWENTY-NINE FACTORS

Contrast Labels

A	B	C	D	E	F	G	H	I	J	K	L	M	N	O	P

Corresponding Main Effects and Two-Factor Interactions

A	**B**	**C**	**D**	**E**	**F**	**G**	**H**	**I**	**J**	**K**	**L**	**M**	**N**	**O**	**P**
BC	AC	AB	AE	AD	AG	AF	AI	AH	AK	AJ	AM	AL	AO	AN	AQ
DE	DF	DG	BF	BG	BD	BE	BJ	BK	BH	BI	BN	BO	BL	BM	BR
FG	EG	EF	CG	CF	CE	CD	CK	CJ	CI	CH	CO	CN	CM	CL	CS
HI	HJ	HK	HL	HM	HN	HO	DL	DM	DN	DO	DH	DI	DJ	DK	EU
JK	IK	IJ	IM	IL	IO	IN	EM	EL	EO	EN	EI	EH	EK	EJ	FV
LM	LN	LO	JN	JO	JL	JM	FN	FO	FL	FM	FJ	FK	FH	FI	GW
NO	MO	MN	KO	KN	KM	KL	GO	GN	GM	GL	GK	GJ	GI	GH	IY
PQ	PR	PS	QU	PU	PV	PW	QY	PY	PZ	P1	P2	P3	P4	P5	JZ
RS	SQ	QR	RV	RW	QW	QV	RZ	R1	Q1	QZ	Q3	Q2	Q5	Q4	K1
VW	UW	UV	SW	SV	SU	RU	S1	SZ	SY	RY	R4	R5	R2	R3	L2
Z1	Y1	YZ	Y3	Y2	Y5	Y4	U3	U2	U5	U4	S5	S4	S3	S2	M3
23	24	25	Z4	Z5	Z2	Z3	V4	V5	V2	V3	UY	V1	U1	UZ	N4
45	35	34	15	14	13	12	W5	W4	W3	W2	VZ	WZ	WY	VY	O5
											W1				

Contrast Labels

Q	R	S	T	U	V	W	X	Y	Z	1	2	3	4	5

Corresponding Main Effects and Two-Factor Interactions

Q	**R**	**S**		**U**	**V**	**W**		**Y**	**Z**	**1**	**2**	**3**	**4**	**5**
AP	AS	AR	AU	BW	AW	AV	AY	B1	A1	AZ	A3	A2	A5	A4
BS	BP	BQ	BV	CV	CU	BU	BZ	CZ	CY	BY	B4	B5	B2	B3
CR	CQ	CP	CW	DQ	DR	DS	C1	D3	D4	D5	C5	C4	C3	C2
DU	DV	DW	DP	EP	ES	ER	D2	E2	E5	E4	EY	DY	DZ	D1
FW	EW	EV	EQ	FS	FP	FQ	E3	F5	F2	F3	FZ	F1	E1	EZ
GV	GU	FU	FR	GR	GQ	GP	F4	G4	G3	G2	G1	GZ	GY	FY
HY	HZ	H1	GS	H3	H4	H5	G5	HQ	HR	HS	IU	HU	HV	HW
J1	I1	IZ	H2	I2	I5	I4	HP	IP	IS	IR	JV	JW	IW	IV
KZ	KY	JY	I3	J5	J2	J3	IQ	JS	JP	JQ	KW	KV	KU	JU
L3	L4	L5	J4	K4	K3	K2	JR	KR	KQ	KP	LP	LQ	LR	LS
M2	M5	M4	K5	LY	LZ	L1	KS	LU	LV	LW	MQ	MP	MS	MR
N5	N2	N3	MY	N1	M1	MZ	MU	NW	MW	MV	NR	NS	NP	NQ
O4	O3	O2	NZ	OZ	OY	NY	NV	OV	OU	NU	OS	OR	OQ	OP
			O1				OW							

TWENTY-NINE FACTORS

Add minus sign to interactions when using Basic 32-Run Array.
On Data Collection Worksheet, delete Factor Labels **X** and **T**.

CONFOUNDING PATTERNS FOR 32-RUN PLACKETT-BURMAN DESIGNS

TWENTY-EIGHT FACTORS

Contrast Labels

A   B   C   D   E   F   G   H   I   J   K   L   M   N   O   P

Corresponding Main Effects and Two-Factor Interactions

A	B	C	D	E	F	G	H	I	J	K	L	M	N	O	P
BC	AC	AB	AE	AD	AG	AF	AI	AH	AK	AJ	AM	AL	AO	AN	AQ
DE	DF	DG	BF	BG	BD	BE	BJ	BK	BH	BI	BN	BO	BL	BM	CS
FG	EG	EF	CG	CF	CE	CD	CK	CJ	CI	CH	CO	CN	CM	CL	EU
HI	HJ	HK	HL	HM	HN	HO	DL	DM	DN	DO	DH	DI	DJ	DK	FV
JK	IK	IJ	IM	IL	IO	IN	EM	EL	EO	EN	EI	EH	EK	EJ	GW
LM	LN	LO	JN	JO	JL	JM	FN	FO	FL	FM	FJ	FK	FH	FI	IY
NO	MO	MN	KO	KN	KM	KL	GO	GN	GM	GL	GK	GJ	GI	GH	JZ
PQ	SQ	PS	QU	PU	PV	PW	QY	PY	PZ	P1	P2	P3	P4	P5	K1
VW	UW	UV	SW	SV	QW	QV	S1	SZ	Q1	QZ	Q3	Q2	Q5	Q4	L2
Z1	Y1	YZ	Y3	Y2	SU	Y4	U3	U2	SY	U4	S5	S4	S3	S2	M3
23	24	25	Z4	Z5	Y5	Z3	V4	V5	U5	V3	UY	V1	U1	UZ	N4
45	35	34	15	14	Z2	12	W5	W4	V2	W2	VZ	WZ	WY	VY	O5
					13				W3		W1				

Contrast Labels

Q   R   S   T   U   V   W   X   Y   Z   *1*   *2*   *3*   *4*   *5*

Corresponding Main Effects and Two-Factor Interactions

Q	R	S	T	U	V	W	X	Y	Z	1	2	3	4	5
AP	AS	BQ	AU	BW	AW	AV	AY	B1	A1	AZ	A3	A2	A5	A4
BS	BP	CP	BV	CV	CU	BU	BZ	CZ	CY	BY	B4	B5	B2	B3
DU	CQ	DW	CW	DQ	ES	DS	C1	D3	D4	D5	C5	C4	C3	C2
FW	DV	EV	DP	EP	FP	FQ	D2	E2	E5	E4	EY	DY	DZ	D1
GV	EW	FU	EQ	FS	GQ	GP	E3	F5	F2	F3	FZ	F1	E1	EZ
HY	GU	H1	GS	H3	H4	H5	F4	G4	G3	G2	G1	GZ	GY	FY
J1	HZ	IZ	H2	I2	I5	I4	G5	HQ	IS	HS	IU	HU	HV	HW
KZ	I1	JY	I3	J5	J2	J3	HP	IP	JP	JQ	JV	JW	IW	IV
L3	KY	L5	J4	K4	K3	K2	IQ	JS	KQ	KP	KW	KV	KU	JU
M2	L4	M4	K5	LY	LZ	L1	KS	LU	LV	LW	LP	LQ	MS	LS
N5	M5	N3	MY	N1	M1	MZ	MU	NW	MW	MV	MQ	MP	NP	NQ
O4	N2	O2	NZ	OZ	OY	NY	NV	OV	OU	NU	OS	NS	OQ	OP
	O3		O1				OW							

Add minus sign to interactions when using Basic 32-Run Array.
On Data Collection Worksheet, delete Factor Labels **X, T** and **R**.

CONFOUNDING PATTERNS FOR 32-RUN PLACKETT-BURMAN DESIGNS

TWENTY-SEVEN FACTORS

Contrast Labels

A	B	C	D	E	F	G	H	I	J	K	L	M	N	O	P

Corresponding Main Effects and Two-Factor Interactions

A	B	C	D	E	F	G	H	I	J	K	L	M	N	O	P
BC	AC	AB	AE	AD	AG	AF	AI	AH	AK	AJ	AM	AL	AO	AN	CS
DE	DF	DG	BF	BG	BD	BE	BJ	BK	BH	BI	BN	BO	BL	BM	EU
FG	EG	EF	CG	CF	CE	CD	CK	CJ	CI	CH	CO	CN	CM	CL	FV
HI	HJ	HK	HL	HM	HN	HO	DL	DM	DN	DO	DH	DI	DJ	DK	GW
JK	IK	IJ	IM	IL	IO	IN	EM	EL	EO	EN	EI	EH	EK	EJ	IY
LM	LN	LO	JN	JO	JL	JM	FN	FO	FL	FM	FJ	FK	FH	FI	JZ
NO	MO	MN	KO	KN	KM	KL	GO	GN	GM	GL	GK	GJ	GI	GH	K1
VW	UW	PS	SW	PU	PV	PW	S1	PY	PZ	P1	P2	P3	P4	P5	L2
Z1	Y1	UV	Y3	SV	SU	Y4	U3	SZ	SY	U4	S5	S4	S3	S2	M3
23	24	YZ	Z4	Y2	Y5	Z3	V4	U2	U5	V3	UY	V1	U1	UZ	N4
45	35	25	15	Z5	Z2	12	W5	V5	V2	W2	VZ	WZ	WY	VY	O5
		34		14	13		W4	W3			W1				

Contrast Labels

Q	R	S	T	U	V	W	X	Y	Z	1	2	3	4	5

Corresponding Main Effects and Two-Factor Interactions

Q	R	S	T	U	V	W	X	Y	Z	1	2	3	4	5
		S		U	V	W		Y	Z	1	2	3	4	5
AP	AS	CP	AU	BW	AW	AV	AY	B1	A1	AZ	A3	A2	A5	A4
BS	BP	DW	BV	CV	CU	BU	BZ	CZ	CY	BY	B4	B5	B2	B3
DU	DV	EV	CW	EP	ES	DS	C1	D3	D4	D5	C5	C4	C3	C2
FW	EW	FU	DP	FS	FP	GP	D2	E2	E5	E4	EY	DY	DZ	D1
GV	GU	H1	GS	H3	H4	H5	E3	F5	F2	F3	FZ	F1	E1	EZ
HY	HZ	IZ	H2	I2	I5	I4	F4	G4	G3	G2	G1	GZ	GY	FY
J1	I1	JY	I3	J5	J2	J3	G5	IP	IS	HS	IU	HU	HV	HW
KZ	KY	L5	J4	K4	K3	K2	HP	JS	JP	KP	JV	JW	IW	IV
L3	L4	M4	K5	LY	LZ	L1	KS	LU	LV	LW	KW	KV	KU	JU
M2	M5	N3	MY	N1	M1	MZ	MU	NW	MW	MV	LP	MP	MS	LS
N5	N2	O2	NZ	OZ	OY	NY	NV	OV	OU	NU	OS	NS	NP	OP
O4	O3	O1				OW								

Add minus sign to interactions when using Basic 32-Run Array.
On Data Collection Worksheet, delete Factor Labels **X, T, R** and **Q.**

CONFOUNDING PATTERNS FOR 32-RUN PLACKETT-BURMAN DESIGNS

TWENTY-SIX FACTORS

Contrast Labels

A	B	C	D	E	F	G	H	I	J	K	L	M	N	O	P

Corresponding Main Effects and Two-Factor Interactions

A	B	C	D	E	F	G	H	I	J	K		M	N	O	P
BC	AC	AB	AE	AD	AG	AF	AI	AH	AK	AJ	AM	BO	AO	AN	CS
DE	DF	DG	BF	BG	BD	BE	BJ	BK	BH	BI	BN	CN	CM	BM	EU
FG	EG	EF	CG	CF	CE	CD	CK	CJ	CI	CH	CO	DI	DJ	DK	FV
HI	HJ	HK	IM	HM	HN	HO	EM	DM	DN	DO	DH	EH	EK	EJ	GW
JK	IK	IJ	JN	JO	IO	IN	FN	FO	EO	EN	EI	FK	FH	FI	IY
NO	MO	MN	KO	KN	KM	JM	GO	GN	GM	FM	FJ	GJ	GI	GH	JZ
VW	UW	PS	SW	PU	PV	PW	S1	PY	PZ	P1	GK	P3	P4	P5	K1
Z1	Y1	UV	Y3	SV	SU	Y4	U3	SZ	SY	U4	P2	S4	S3	S2	M3
23	24	YZ	Z4	Y2	Y5	Z3	V4	U2	U5	V3	S5	V1	U1	UZ	N4
45	35	25	15	Z5	Z2	12	W5	V5	V2	W2	UY	WZ	WY	VY	O5
		34		14	13		W4	W3			VZ				
											W1				

Contrast Labels

Q	R	S	T	U	V	W	X	Y	Z	1	2	3	4	5

Corresponding Main Effects and Two-Factor Interactions

		S		U	V	W		Y	Z	1	2	3	4	5
AP	AS	CP	AU	BW	AW	AV	AY	B1	A1	AZ	A3	A2	A5	A4
BS	BP	DW	BV	CV	CU	BU	BZ	CZ	CY	BY	B4	B5	B2	B3
DU	DV	EV	CW	EP	ES	DS	C1	D3	D4	D5	C5	C4	C3	C2
FW	EW	FU	DP	FS	FP	GP	D2	E2	E5	E4	EY	DY	DZ	D1
GV	GU	H1	GS	H3	H4	H5	E3	F5	F2	F3	FZ	F1	E1	EZ
HY	HZ	IZ	H2	I2	I5	I4	F4	G4	G3	G2	G1	GZ	GY	FY
J1	I1	JY	I3	J5	J2	J3	G5	IP	IS	HS	IU	HU	HV	HW
KZ	KY	M4	J4	K4	K3	K2	HP	JS	JP	KP	JV	JW	IW	IV
M2	M5	N3	K5	N1	M1	MZ	KS	NW	MW	MV	KW	KV	KU	JU
N5	N2	O2	MY	OZ	OY	NY	MU	OV	OU	NU	OS	MP	MS	OP
O4	O3	NZ					NV					NS	NP	
		O1					OW							

Add minus sign to interactions when using Basic 32-Run Array.
On Data Collection Worksheet, delete Factor Labels **X, T, R, Q** and **L.**

CONFOUNDING PATTERNS FOR 32-RUN PLACKETT-BURMAN DESIGNS

TWENTY-FIVE FACTORS

Contrast Labels

A	B	C	D	E	F	G	H	I	J	K	L	M	N	O	P

Corresponding Main Effects and Two-Factor Interactions

A	B	C	D	E	F	G	H	I		K		M	N	O	P
BC	AC	AB	AE	AD	AG	AF	AI	AH	AK	BI	AM	BO	AO	AN	CS
DE	DF	DG	BF	BG	BD	BE	CK	BK	BH	CH	BN	CN	CM	BM	EU
FG	EG	EF	CG	CF	CE	CD	EM	DM	CI	DO	CO	DI	EK	DK	FV
HI	IK	HK	IM	HM	HN	HO	FN	FO	DN	EN	DH	EH	FH	FI	GW
NO	MO	MN	KO	KN	IO	IN	GO	GN	EO	FM	EI	FK	GI	GH	IY
VW	UW	PS	SW	PU	KM	PW	S1	PY	GM	P1	GK	P3	P4	P5	K1
Z1	Y1	UV	Y3	SV	PV	Y4	U3	SZ	PZ	U4	P2	S4	S3	S2	M3
23	24	YZ	Z4	Y2	SU	Z3	V4	U2	SY	V3	S5	V1	U1	UZ	N4
45	35	25	15	Z5	Y5	12	W5	V5	U5	W2	UY	WZ	WY	VY	O5
		34		14	Z2			W4	V2		VZ				
					13				W3		W1				

Contrast Labels

Q	R	S	T	U	V	W	X	Y	Z	1	2	3	4	5

Corresponding Main Effects and Two-Factor Interactions

		S		U	V	W		Y	Z	1	2	3	4	5
AP	AS	CP	AU	BW	AW	AV	AY	B1	A1	AZ	A3	A2	A5	A4
BS	BP	DW	BV	CV	CU	BU	BZ	CZ	CY	BY	B4	B5	B2	B3
DU	DV	EV	CW	EP	ES	DS	C1	D3	D4	D5	C5	C4	C3	C2
FW	EW	FU	DP	FS	FP	GP	D2	E2	E5	E4	EY	DY	DZ	D1
GV	GU	H1	GS	H3	H4	H5	E3	F5	F2	F3	FZ	F1	E1	EZ
HY	HZ	IZ	H2	I2	I5	I4	F4	G4	G3	G2	G1	GZ	GY	FY
KZ	I1	M4	I3	K4	K3	K2	G5	IP	IS	HS	IU	HU	HV	HW
M2	KY	N3	K5	N1	M1	MZ	HP	NW	MW	KP	KW	KV	IW	IV
O4	M5	O2	MY	OZ	OY	NY	KS	OV	OU	MV	OS	MP	KU	OP
	N2		NZ				MU			NU		NS	MS	
	O3		O1				NV					NP		
							OW							

TWENTY-FIVE FACTORS

Add minus sign to interactions when using Basic 32-Run Array.
On Data Collection Worksheet, delete Factor Labels **X, T, R, Q, L** and **J.**

CONFOUNDING PATTERNS FOR 32-RUN PLACKETT-BURMAN DESIGNS

TWENTY-FOUR FACTORS

Contrast Labels

A	B	C	D	E	F	G	H	I	J	K	L	M	N	O	P

Corresponding Main Effects and Two-Factor Interactions

A	B	C	D	E	F	G	H			K		M	N	O	P
BC	AC	AB	AE	AD	AG	AF	CK	AH	AK	CH	AM	BO	AO	AN	CS
DE	DF	DG	BF	BG	BD	BE	EM	BK	BH	DO	BN	CN	CM	BM	EU
FG	EG	EF	CG	CF	CE	CD	FN	DM	DN	EN	CO	EH	EK	DK	FV
NO	MO	HK	KO	HM	HN	HO	GO	FO	EO	FM	DH	FK	FH	GH	GW
VW	UW	MN	SW	KN	KM	PW	S1	GN	GM	P1	GK	P3	P4	P5	K1
Z1	Y1	PS	Y3	PU	PV	Y4	U3	PY	PZ	U4	P2	S4	S3	S2	M3
23	24	UV	Z4	SV	SU	Z3	V4	SZ	SY	V3	S5	V1	U1	UZ	N4
45	35	YZ	15	Y2	Y5	12	W5	U2	U5	W2	UY	WZ	WY	VY	O5
		25		Z5	Z2			V5	V2		VZ				
		34		14	13			W4	W3		W1				

Contrast Labels

Q	R	S	T	U	V	W	X	Y	Z	1	2	3	4	5

Corresponding Main Effects and Two-Factor Interactions

		S		U	V	W		Y	Z	1	2	3	4	5
AP	AS	CP	AU	BW	AW	AV	AY	B1	A1	AZ	A3	A2	A5	A4
BS	BP	DW	BV	CV	CU	BU	BZ	CZ	CY	BY	B4	B5	B2	B3
DU	DV	EV	CW	EP	ES	DS	C1	D3	D4	D5	C5	C4	C3	C2
FW	EW	FU	DP	FS	FP	GP	D2	E2	E5	E4	EY	DY	DZ	D1
GV	GU	H1	GS	H3	H4	H5	E3	F5	F2	F3	FZ	F1	E1	EZ
HY	HZ	M4	H2	K4	K3	K2	F4	G4	G3	G2	G1	GZ	GY	FY
KZ	KY	N3	K5	N1	M1	MZ	G5	NW	MW	HS	KW	HU	HV	HW
M2	M5	O2	MY	OZ	OY	NY	HP	OV	OU	KP	OS	KV	KU	OP
N5	N2	NZ					KS			MV		MP	MS	
O4	O3	O1					MU			NU		NS	NP	
							NV							
							OW							

Add minus sign to interactions when using Basic 32-Run Array.
On Data Collection Worksheet, delete Factor Labels X, T, R, Q, L, J and I.

CONFOUNDING PATTERNS FOR 32-RUN PLACKETT-BURMAN DESIGNS

TWENTY-THREE FACTORS

Contrast Labels

A	B	C	D	E	F	G	H	I	J	K	L	M	N	O	P

Corresponding Main Effects and Two-Factor Interactions

A	B	C	D	E		G	H			K		M	N	O	P
BC	AC	AB	AE	AD	AG	BE	CK	AH	AK	CH	AM	BO	AO	AN	CS
DE	EG	DG	CG	BG	BD	CD	EM	BK	BH	DO	BN	CN	CM	BM	EU
NO	MO	HK	KO	HM	CE	HO	GO	DM	DN	EN	CO	EH	EK	DK	GW
VW	UW	MN	SW	KN	HN	PW	S1	GN	EO	P1	DH	P3	P4	GH	K1
Z1	Y1	PS	Y3	PU	KM	Y4	U3	PY	GM	U4	GK	S4	S3	P5	M3
23	24	UV	Z4	SV	PV	Z3	V4	SZ	PZ	V3	P2	V1	U1	S2	N4
45	35	YZ	15	Y2	SU	12	W5	U2	SY	W2	S5	WZ	WY	UZ	O5
		25		Z5	Y5			V5	U5		UY			VY	
		34		14	Z2			W4	V2		VZ				
					13				W3		W1				

Contrast Labels

Q	R	S	T	U	V	W	X	Y	Z	1	2	3	4	5

Corresponding Main Effects and Two-Factor Interactions

		S		U	V	W		Y	Z	1	2	3	4	5
AP	AS	CP	AU	BW	AW	AV	AY	B1	A1	AZ	A3	A2	A5	A4
BS	BP	DW	BV	CV	CU	BU	BZ	CZ	CY	BY	B4	B5	B2	B3
DU	DV	EV	CW	EP	ES	DS	C1	D3	D4	D5	C5	C4	C3	C2
GV	EW	H1	DP	H3	H4	GP	D2	E2	E5	E4	EY	DY	DZ	D1
HY	GU	M4	GS	K4	K3	H5	E3	G4	G3	G2	G1	GZ	E1	EZ
KZ	HZ	N3	H2	N1	M1	K2	G5	NW	MW	HS	KW	HU	GY	HW
M2	KY	O2	K5	OZ	OY	MZ	HP	OV	OU	KP	OS	KV	HV	OP
N5	M5		MY			NY	KS			MV		MP	KU	
O4	N2		NZ				MU			NU		NS	MS	
	O3		O1				NV						NP	
							OW							

TWENTY-THREE FACTORS

Add minus sign to interactions when using Basic 32-Run Array.
On Data Collection Worksheet, delete Factor Labels X, T, R, Q, L, J, I and F.

CONFOUNDING PATTERNS FOR 32-RUN PLACKETT-BURMAN DESIGNS

TWENTY-TWO FACTORS

Contrast Labels

A	B	C	D	E	F	G	H	I	J	K	L	M	N	O	P

Corresponding Main Effects and Two-Factor Interactions

A	B	C	D	E	F	G	H	I	J	K	L	M	N	O	P
A	B	C	D			G	H			K		M	N	O	P
BC	AC	AB	CG	AD	AG	CD	CK	AH	AK	CH	AM	BO	AO	AN	CS
NO	MO	DG	KO	BG	BD	HO	GO	BK	BH	DO	BN	CN	CM	BM	GW
VW	UW	HK	SW	HM	HN	PW	S1	DM	DN	P1	CO	P3	P4	DK	K1
Z1	Y1	MN	Y3	KN	KM	Y4	U3	GN	GM	U4	DH	S4	S3	GH	M3
23	24	PS	Z4	PU	PV	Z3	V4	PY	PZ	V3	GK	V1	U1	P5	N4
45	35	UV	15	SV	SU	12	W5	SZ	SY	W2	P2	WZ	WY	S2	O5
		YZ		Y2	Y5			U2	U5		S5			UZ	
		25		Z5	Z2			V5	V2		UY			VY	
		34		14	13			W4	W3		VZ				
											W1				

Contrast Labels

Q	R	S	T	U	V	W	X	Y	Z	1	2	3	4	5

Corresponding Main Effects and Two-Factor Interactions

Q	R	S	T	U	V	W	X	Y	Z	1	2	3	4	5
		S		U	V	W		Y	Z	1	2	3	4	5
AP	AS	CP	AU	BW	AW	AV	AY	B1	A1	AZ	A3	A2	A5	A4
BS	BP	DW	BV	CV	CU	BU	BZ	CZ	CY	BY	B4	B5	B2	B3
DU	DV	H1	CW	H3	H4	DS	C1	D3	D4	D5	C5	C4	C3	C2
GV	GU	M4	DP	K4	K3	GP	D2	G4	G3	G2	G1	DY	DZ	D1
HY	HZ	N3	GS	N1	M1	H5	G5	NW	MW	HS	KW	GZ	GY	HW
KZ	KY	O2	H2	OZ	OY	K2	HP	OV	OU	KP	OS	HU	HV	OP
M2	M5	K5				MZ	KS			MV		KV	KU	
N5	N2	MY				NY	MU			NU		MP	MS	
O4	O3	NZ				NV						NS	NP	
		O1				OW								

Add minus sign to interactions when using Basic 32-Run Array.
On Data Collection Worksheet, delete Factor Labels **X, T, R, Q, L, J, I, F and E.**

CONFOUNDING PATTERNS FOR 32-RUN PLACKETT-BURMAN DESIGNS

TWENTY-ONE FACTORS

Contrast Labels

A	B	C	D	E	F	G	H	I	J	K	L	M	N	O	P

Corresponding Main Effects and Two-Factor Interactions

A	B		D			G	H			K		M	N	O	P
NO	MO	AB	KO	AD	AG	HO	GO	AH	AK	DO	AM	BO	AO	AN	GW
VW	UW	DG	SW	BG	BD	PW	S1	BK	BH	P1	BN	P3	P4	BM	K1
Z1	Y1	HK	Y3	HM	HN	Y4	U3	DM	DN	U4	DH	S4	S3	DK	M3
23	24	MN	Z4	KN	KM	Z3	V4	GN	GM	V3	GK	V1	U1	GH	N4
45	35	PS	15	PU	PV	12	W5	PY	PZ	W2	P2	WZ	WY	P5	O5
		UV		SV	SU			SZ	SY		S5			S2	
		YZ		Y2	Y5			U2	U5		UY			UZ	
		25		Z5	Z2			V5	V2		VZ			VY	
		34		14	13			W4	W3		W1				

Contrast Labels

Q	R	S	T	U	V	W	X	Y	Z	1	2	3	4	5

Corresponding Main Effects and Two-Factor Interactions

		S		U	V	W		Y	Z	1	2	3	4	5
AP	AS	DW	AU	BW	AW	AV	AY	B1	A1	AZ	A3	A2	A5	A4
BS	BP	H1	BV	H3	H4	BU	BZ	D3	D4	BY	B4	B5	B2	B3
DU	DV	M4	DP	K4	K3	DS	D2	G4	G3	D5	G1	DY	DZ	D1
GV	GU	N3	GS	N1	M1	GP	G5	NW	MW	G2	KW	GZ	GY	HW
HY	HZ	O2	H2	OZ	OY	H5	HP	OV	OU	HS	OS	HU	HV	OP
KZ	KY	K5				K2	KS			KP		KV	KU	
M2	M5	MY				MZ	MU			MV		MP	MS	
N5	N2	NZ				NY	NV			NU		NS	NP	
O4	O3	O1				OW								

Add minus sign to interactions when using Basic 32-Run Array.
On Data Collection Worksheet, delete Factor Labels X, T, R, Q, L, J, I, F, E and C.

CONFOUNDING PATTERNS FOR 32-RUN PLACKETT-BURMAN DESIGNS

TWENTY FACTORS

Contrast Labels

A	B	C	D	E	F	G	H	I	J	K	L	M	N	O	P

Corresponding Main Effects and Two-Factor Interactions

A	B		D			G	H			K		M	N	O	P
NO	MO	AB	KO	AD	AG	HO	GO	AH	AK	DO	AM	BO	AO	AN	GW
VW	UW	DG	SW	BG	BD	PW	S1	BK	BH	P1	BN	P3	S3	BM	K1
Z1	Y1	HK	Y3	HM	HN	Z3	U3	DM	DN	V3	DH	V1	U1	DK	M3
23	35	MN	15	KN	KM	12	W5	GN	GM	W2	GK	WZ	WY	GH	O5
		PS		PU	PV			PY	PZ		P2			P5	
		UV		SV	SU			SZ	SY		S5			S2	
		YZ		Y2	Y5			U2	U5		UY			UZ	
		25		Z5	Z2			V5	V2		VZ			VY	
					13				W3		W1				

Contrast Labels

Q	R	S	T	U	V	W	X	Y	Z	1	2	3	4	5

Corresponding Main Effects and Two-Factor Interactions

		S		U	V	W		Y	Z	1	2	3		5
AP	AS	DW	AU	BW	AW	AV	AY	B1	A1	AZ	A3	A2	A5	B3
BS	BP	H1	BV	H3	K3	BU	BZ	D3	G3	BY	G1	B5	B2	D1
DU	DV	N3	DP	N1	M1	DS	D2	NW	MW	D5	KW	DY	DZ	HW
GV	GU	O2	GS	OZ	OY	GP	G5	OV	OU	G2	OS	GZ	GY	OP
HY	HZ		H2			H5	HP			HS		HU	HV	
KZ	KY		K5			K2	KS			KP		KV	KU	
M2	M5		MY			MZ	MU			MV		MP	MS	
N5	N2		NZ			NY	NV			NU		NS	NP	
	O3		O1			OW								

TWENTY FACTORS

Add minus sign to interactions when using Basic 32-Run Array.
On Data Collection Worksheet, delete Factor Labels **X, T, R, Q, L, J, I, F, E, C** and **4.**

CONFOUNDING PATTERNS FOR 32-RUN PLACKETT-BURMAN DESIGNS

NINETEEN FACTORS

Contrast Labels

A	B	C	D	E	F	G	H	I	J	K	L	M	N	O	P

Corresponding Main Effects and Two-Factor Interactions

A	B	C	D	E	F	G	H	I	J	K	L	M	N	O	P
A	**B**		**D**			**G**	**H**			**K**		**M**	**N**	**O**	**P**
NO	MO	AB	KO	AD	AG	HO	GO	AH	AK	DO	AM	BO	AO	AN	GW
VW	UW	DG	SW	BG	BD	PW	S1	BK	BH	P1	BN	V1	U1	BM	K1
Z1	Y1	HK	15	HM	HN	12	W5	DM	DN	W2	DH	WZ	WY	DK	O5
		MN		KN	KM			GN	GM		GK			GH	
		PS		PU	PV			PY	PZ		P2			P5	
		UV		SV	SU			SZ	SY		S5			S2	
		YZ		Y2	Y5			U2	U5		UY			UZ	
		25		Z5	Z2			V5	V2		VZ			VY	
											W1				

Contrast Labels

Q	R	S	T	U	V	W	X	Y	Z	1	2	3	4	5

Corresponding Main Effects and Two-Factor Interactions

Q	R	S	T	U	V	W	X	Y	Z	1	2	3	4	5
		S		**U**	**V**	**W**		**Y**	**Z**	**1**	**2**			**5**
AP	AS	DW	AU	BW	AW	AV	AY	B1	A1	AZ	G1	A2	A5	D1
BS	BP	H1	BV	N1	M1	BU	BZ	NW	MW	BY	KW	B5	B2	HW
DU	DV	O2	DP	OZ	OY	DS	D2	OV	OU	D5	OS	DY	DZ	OP
GV	GU		GS			GP	G5			G2		GZ	GY	
HY	HZ		H2			H5	HP			HS		HU	HV	
KZ	KY		K5			K2	KS			KP		KV	KU	
M2	M5		MY			MZ	MU			MV		MP	MS	
N5	N2		NZ			NY	NV			NU		NS	NP	
			O1				OW							

NINETEEN FACTORS

Add minus sign to interactions when using Basic 32-Run Array.
On Data Collection Worksheet, delete Factor Labels **X, T, R, Q, L, J, I, F, E, C, 4** and **3.**

CONFOUNDING PATTERNS FOR 32-RUN PLACKETT-BURMAN DESIGNS

EIGHTEEN FACTORS

Contrast Labels

A	B	C	D	E	F	G	H	I	J	K	L	M	N	O	P

Corresponding Main Effects and Two-Factor Interactions

A	B		D			G	H			K		M	N	O	P
NO	MO	AB	KO	AD	AG	HO	GO	AH	AK	DO	AM	BO	AO	AN	GW
VW	UW	DG	SW	BG	BD	PW	W5	BK	BH	W2	BN	WZ	WY	BM	O5
		HK		HM	HN			DM	DN		DH			DK	
		MN		KN	KM			GN	GM		GK			GH	
		PS		PU	PV			PY	PZ		P2			P5	
		UV		SV	SU			SZ	SY		S5			S2	
		YZ		Y2	Y5			U2	U5		UY			UZ	
		25		Z5	Z2			V5	V2		VZ			VY	

Contrast Labels

Q	R	S	T	U	V	W	X	Y	Z	1	2	3	4	5

Corresponding Main Effects and Two-Factor Interactions

		S		U	V	W		Y	Z		2			5
AP	AS	DW	AU	BW	AW	AV	AY	NW	MW	AZ	KW	A2	A5	HW
BS	BP	O2	BV	OZ	OY	BU	BZ	OV	OU	BY	OS	B5	B2	OP
DU	DV	DP				DS	D2					D5	DY	DZ
GV	GU	GS				GP	G5					G2	GZ	GY
HY	HZ	H2				H5	HP					HS	HU	HV
KZ	KY	K5				K2	KS					KP	KV	KU
M2	M5	MY				MZ	MU					MV	MP	MS
N5	N2	NZ				NY	NV					NU	NS	NP
						OW								

EIGHTEEN FACTORS

Add minus sign to interactions when using Basic 32-Run Array.
On Data Collection Worksheet, delete Factor Labels **X, T, R, Q, L, J, I, F, E, C, 4, 3** and **1.**

CONFOUNDING PATTERNS FOR 32-RUN PLACKETT-BURMAN DESIGNS

SEVENTEEN FACTORS

Contrast Labels

A	B	C	D	E	F	G	H	I	J	K	L	M	N	O	P

Corresponding Main Effects and Two-Factor Interactions

A	B	C	D	E	F	G	H	I	J	K	L	M	N	O	P
A	B		D			G	H			K		M	N	O	P
NO	MO	AB	KO	AD	AG	HO	GO	AH	AK	DO	AM	BO	AO	AN	O5
		DG		BG	BD			BK	BH		BN			BM	
		HK		HM	HN			DM	DN		DH			DK	
		MN		KN	KM			GN	GM		GK			GH	
		PS		PU	PV			PY	PZ		P2			P5	
		UV		SV	SU			SZ	SY		S5			S2	
		YZ		Y2	Y5			U2	U5		UY			UZ	
		25		Z5	Z2			V5	V2		VZ			VY	

Contrast Labels

Q	R	S	T	U	V	W	X	Y	Z	1	2	3	4	5

Corresponding Main Effects and Two-Factor Interactions

Q	R	S	T	U	V	W	X	Y	Z	1	2	3	4	5
		S		U	V			Y	Z		2			5
AP	AS	O2	AU	OZ	OY	AV	AY	OV	OU	AZ	OS	A2	A5	OP
BS	BP	BV				BU	BZ			BY		B5	B2	
DU	DV	DP				DS	D2			D5		DY	DZ	
GV	GU	GS				GP	G5			G2		GZ	GY	
HY	HZ	H2				H5	HP			HS		HU	HV	
KZ	KY	K5				K2	KS			KP		KV	KU	
M2	M5	MY				MZ	MU			MV		MP	MS	
N5	N2	NZ				NY	NV			NU		NS	NP	

SEVENTEEN FACTORS

Add minus sign to interactions when using Basic 32-Run Array.
On Data Collection Worksheet, delete Factor Labels **X, T, R, Q, L, J, I, F, E, C, 4, 3, 1** and **W.**

CONFOUNDING PATTERNS FOR 32-RUN PLACKETT-BURMAN DESIGNS

SIXTEEN FACTORS

Contrast Labels

A	B	C	D	E	F	G	H	I	J	K	L	M	N	O	P

Corresponding Main Effects and Two-Factor Interactions

A	B		D			G	H			K		M	N		P
		AB	AD	AG			AH	AK		AM			AN		
		DG	BG	BD			BK	BH		BN			BM		
		HK	HM	HN			DM	DN		DH			DK		
		MN	KN	KM			GN	GM		GK			GH		
		PS	PU	PV			PY	PZ		P2			P5		
		UV	SV	SU			SZ	SY		S5			S2		
		YZ	Y2	Y5			U2	U5		UY			UZ		
		25	Z5	Z2			V5	V2		VZ			VY		

Contrast Labels

Q	R	S	T	U	V	W	X	Y	Z	1	2	3	4	5

Corresponding Main Effects and Two-Factor Interactions

		S		U	V			Y	Z		2			5
AP	AS		AU			AV	AY			AZ		A2	A5	
BS	BP		BV			BU	BZ			BY		B5	B2	
DU	DV		DP			DS	D2			D5		DY	DZ	
GV	GU		GS			GP	G5			G2		GZ	GY	
HY	HZ		H2			H5	HP			HS		HU	HV	
KZ	KY		K5			K2	KS			KP		KV	KU	
M2	M5		MY			MZ	MU			MV		MP	MS	
N5	N2		NZ			NY	NV			NU		NS	NP	

SIXTEEN FACTORS

Add minus sign to interactions when using Basic 32-Run Array.
On Data Collection Worksheet, delete Factor Labels **X, T, R, Q, L, J, I, F, E, C, 4, 3, 1, W** and **O.**

This design is a Resolution IV design.

REFLECTED 32-RUN PLACKETT-BURMAN DESIGNS

The Reflected 32-Run Array is useful for designs having from 16 to 31 factors with two-levels each. The rows in this array define treatment combinations and the columns define contrast coefficients. The number of changes in level for each factor is shown in the following table.

A	B	C	D	E	F	G	H	I	J	K	L	M	N	O	P	Q	R	S	T	U	V	W	X	Y	Z	1	2	3	4	5
1	2	3	4	5	6	7	8	9	10	11	12	13	14	15	16	17	18	19	20	21	22	23	24	25	26	27	28	29	30	31

The Contrast Labels above (A thru Z and 1 thru 5) will be used with each of the 32-Run designs even though there may not always be a main effect for each contrast.

For designs with less than 31 factors, the contrast labels to use for main effects may be found by referring to the tables of confounding patterns. The designs given in the tables of confounding patterns will be Resolution III designs (except for the design for 16 factors).

Due to the size of the 32-Run arrays, it is easy to make a error when computing the estimated contrast values. If the computations are to be carried out manually, it is best to break them into small segments. For this reason the Calculation Worksheets are set up to perform these computations in small steps. Each contrast is computed as the sum a set of partial sums, where each partial sum is computed using the responses and contrast coefficients for four runs. Since several different contrasts will have identical partial sums, this approach reduces the amount of computation while it makes errors less likely. In order to use this feature of the Calculation Worksheets begin by filling in each *row* of partial sums, and then sum the partial sums in each *column* to obtain the estimated contrast values.

THE REFLECTED 32-RUN PLACKETT-BURMAN ARRAY

Contrast Labels

Run	A	B	C	D	E	F	G	H	I	J	K	L	M	N	O	P	Q	R	S	T	U	V	W	X	Y	Z	1	2	3	4	5
1	+	+	+	+	+	+	+	+	+	+	+	+	+	+	+	+	+	+	+	+	+	+	+	+	+	+	+	+	+	+	+
2	+	+	+	+	+	+	+	+	+	+	+	+	+	+	+	−	−	−	−	−	−	−	−	−	−	−	−	−	−	−	−
3	+	+	+	+	+	+	+	−	−	−	−	−	−	−	−	−	−	−	−	+	+	+	+	+	+	+	+	+	+	+	+
4	+	+	+	+	+	+	+	−	−	−	−	−	−	−	+	+	+	+	+	+	+	−	−	−	−	−	−	−	−	−	−
5	+	+	+	−	−	−	−	−	−	−	−	+	+	+	+	+	+	+	−	−	−	−	−	−	−	+	+	+	+	+	+
6	+	+	+	−	−	−	−	−	−	−	−	+	+	+	−	−	−	−	+	+	+	+	+	+	+	−	−	−	−	−	−
7	+	+	+	−	−	−	−	+	+	+	+	−	−	−	−	−	−	−	+	+	+	−	−	−	−	+	+	+	+	+	+
8	+	+	+	−	−	−	−	+	+	+	+	−	−	−	+	+	+	+	−	−	−	+	+	+	+	−	−	−	−	−	−
9	+	−	−	−	−	+	+	+	+	−	−	−	−	+	+	+	+	−	−	−	−	+	+	+	+	−	−	−	−	+	+
10	+	−	−	−	−	+	+	+	+	−	−	−	−	+	+	−	−	+	+	+	+	−	−	−	−	+	+	+	+	−	−
11	+	−	−	−	−	+	+	+	−	+	+	+	+	−	−	−	−	+	+	+	+	−	−	+	+	−	−	−	−	+	+
12	+	−	−	−	−	+	+	+	−	+	+	+	+	−	−	+	+	−	−	−	−	+	+	+	+	−	−	+	+	−	−
13	+	−	−	+	+	−	−	−	−	+	+	−	−	+	+	+	+	−	−	+	+	−	−	−	−	+	+	−	−	+	+
14	+	−	−	+	+	−	−	−	−	+	+	−	−	+	+	−	−	+	+	−	−	+	+	+	+	−	−	+	+	−	−
15	+	−	−	+	+	−	−	+	+	−	−	+	+	−	−	−	−	+	+	−	−	+	+	−	−	+	+	−	−	+	+
16	+	−	−	+	+	−	−	+	+	−	−	+	+	−	−	−	−	+	+	−	+	−	−	+	+	−	−	+	+	−	−
17	−	−	+	+	−	−	+	+	−	−	+	+	−	−	+	+	−	−	+	+	−	−	+	+	−	−	+	+	−	−	+
18	−	−	+	+	−	−	+	+	−	−	+	+	−	−	+	−	+	+	−	−	+	+	−	−	+	+	−	−	+	+	−
19	−	−	+	+	−	−	−	+	+	+	−	−	+	+	−	−	+	+	−	−	+	+	−	+	−	−	+	+	−	−	+
20	−	−	+	+	−	−	+	−	+	+	−	−	+	+	−	+	−	−	+	+	−	−	+	−	+	+	−	−	+	+	−
21	−	−	+	−	+	+	−	−	+	+	−	+	−	−	+	+	−	−	+	−	+	+	−	−	+	+	−	+	−	−	+
22	−	−	+	−	+	+	−	−	+	+	−	+	−	−	+	−	+	+	−	+	−	−	+	+	−	−	+	−	+	+	−
23	−	−	+	−	+	+	−	+	−	−	+	−	+	+	−	+	+	+	−	−	+	+	−	−	+	+	−	+	−	−	+
24	−	−	+	−	+	+	−	+	−	−	+	−	+	+	−	+	−	−	+	−	+	+	−	+	−	−	+	−	+	+	−
25	−	+	−	−	+	−	+	+	−	+	−	−	+	−	+	+	−	+	−	−	+	−	+	+	−	+	−	−	+	−	+
26	−	+	−	−	+	−	+	+	−	+	−	−	+	−	+	−	+	−	+	+	−	+	−	−	+	−	+	+	−	+	−
27	−	+	−	−	+	−	+	−	+	−	+	+	−	+	−	−	+	−	+	+	−	+	−	+	−	−	+	+	−	+	−
28	−	+	−	−	+	−	+	−	+	−	+	+	−	+	−	+	−	+	−	+	+	−	+	−	+	−	+	+	−	+	−
29	−	+	−	+	−	+	−	−	−	+	−	+	−	+	−	+	+	−	+	−	+	−	−	+	−	+	−	+	−	+	−
30	−	+	−	+	−	+	−	−	+	−	+	−	+	−	+	−	+	−	+	+	−	+	−	+	+	−	+	−	+	−	−
31	−	+	−	+	−	+	−	+	−	+	−	+	−	+	−	+	−	+	−	+	−	+	−	+	−	+	−	+	−	+	−
32	−	+	−	+	−	+	−	+	−	+	−	+	−	+	−	+	−	+	−	+	−	+	−	+	−	+	−	+	−	+	−

    A B C D   E F G H   I J K L   M N O P   Q R S T   U V W X   Y Z 1 2   3 4 5

EXAMPLE OF REFLECTED 32-RUN DESIGN

Twenty-eight factors were studied using the Reflected 32-Run Array. As shown in the tables of confounding patterns for 28 factors, the unassigned factor labels are R, T and X.

DATA

Run	Response
1	290
2	88
3	77
4	111
5	41
6	42
7	60
8	73
9	99
10	66
11	50
12	40
13	105
14	81
15	85
16	282
17	294
18	77
19	60
20	104
21	50
22	32
23	49
24	78
25	96
26	58
27	51
28	63
29	95
30	57
31	103
32	283

SINGLE DEGREE OF FREEDOM ANOVA TABLE

Contrast Labels	Estimated Contrasts	Sums of Squares	Estimated Effects
A	40	50.0	
B	36	40.5	
C	-88	242.0	
D	1244	48,360.5	77.8
E	52	84.5	
F	-4	0.5	
G	108	364.5	
H	1022	32,640.125	63.9
I	-30	28.125	
J	6	1.125	
K	-38	45.125	
L	602	11,325.125	37.6
M	-110	378.125	
N	66	136.125	
O	2	0.125	
P	1068	35,644.5	66.8
Q	-84	220.5	
(R)	-36	40.5	
S	44	60.5	
(T)	804	20,200.5	50.3
U	40	50.0	
V	-20	12.5	
W	72	162.0	
(X)	750	17,578.125	46.9
Y	46	66.125	
Z	-50	78.125	
1	-18	10.125	
2	562	9,870.125	35.1
3	6	1.125	
4	-22	15.125	
5	70	153.125	
Total		177,859.5	

DATA COLLECTION WORKSHEET
FOR REFLECTED 32-RUN DESIGNS
PAGE ONE OF FIVE PAGES
IDENTIFICATION OF FACTORS AND FACTOR LEVELS

When using less than 31 factors some Contrast Labels will not represent a main effect. Customize this worksheet for a particular design by **crossing off the list below those Contrast Labels that do not represent a main effect.**

	Factor Names	Low Level	High Level		Factor Names	Low Level	High Level
A.				P.			
B.				Q.			
C.				R.			
D.				S.			
E.				T.			
F.				U.			
G.				V.			
H.				W.			
I.				X.			
J.				Y.			
K.				Z.			
L.				1.			
M.				2.			
N.				3.			
O.				4.			
				5.			

The Response Variable is _____

DATA COLLECTION WORKSHEET
PAGE TWO OF FIVE PAGES
CHANGES IN FACTOR LEVELS FOR REFLECTED 32-RUN DESIGNS

When using less than 31 factors, **cross out all Factor Labels in the following array that do not represent a Main Effect in the study.** The resulting array will then show the factor levels to use in performing the experimental runs.

Begin with all factors set at their high levels. Changes in factor level shown in boldface.

Run   Response

1

A+ B+ C+ D+ E+ F+ G+ H+ I+ J+ K+ L+ M+ N+ O+

P+ Q+ R+ S+ T+ U+ V+ W+ X+ Y+ Z+ 1+ 2+ 3+ 4+ 5+

2

A+ B+ C+ D+ E+ F+ G+ H+ I+ J+ K+ L+ M+ N+ O+

P- Q- R- S- T- U- V- W- X- Y- Z- 1- 2- 3- 4- 5-

3

A+ B+ C+ D+ E+ F+ G+ **H- I- J- K- L- M- N- O-**

P- Q- R- S- T- U- V- W- **X+ Y+ Z+ 1+ 2+ 3+ 4+ 5+**

4

A+ B+ C+ D+ E+ F+ G+ H- I- J- K- L- M- N- O-

P+ Q+ R+ S+ T+ U+ V+ W+ X- Y- Z- 1- 2- 3- 4- 5-

5

A+ B+ C+ **D- E- F- G-** H- I- J- K- **L+ M+ N+ O+**

P+ Q+ R+ S+ **T- U- V- W-** X- Y- Z- 1- **2+ 3+ 4+ 5+**

6

A+ B+ C+ D- E- F- G- H- I- J- K- L+ M+ N+ O+

P- Q- R- S- T+ U+ V+ W+ X+ Y+ Z+ 1+ 2- 3- 4- 5-

7

A+ B+ C+ D- E- F- G- **H+ I+ J+ K+ L- M- N- O-**

P- Q- R- S- **T+ U+ V+ W+ X- Y- Z- 1- 2+ 3+ 4+ 5+**

8

A+ B+ C+ D- E- F- G- H+ I+ J+ K+ L- M- N- O-

P+ Q+ R+ S+ T- U- V- W- X+ Y+ Z+ 1+ 2- 3- 4- 5-

DATA COLLECTION WORKSHEET
PAGE THREE OF FIVE PAGES
CHANGES IN FACTOR LEVELS FOR REFLECTED 32-RUN DESIGNS

Factors that change level from previous run are shown in boldface.

Run   Response

9

A+ **B-** **C-** D- E- **F+** **G+** H+ I+ **J-** **K-** L- M- **N+** **O+**

P+ Q+ **R-** **S-** T- U- **V+** **W+** X+ Y+ **Z-** *1-* 2- 3- **4+** 5+

10

A+ B- C- D- E- F+ G+ H+ I+ J- K- L- M- N+ O+

P- **Q-** **R+** **S+** **T+** **U+** **V-** **W-** **X-** **Y-** **Z+** *1+* 2+ 3+ *4-* *5-*

11

A+ B- C- D- E- F+ G+ **H-** **I-** **J+** **K+** **L+** **M+** **N-** **O-**

P- Q- **R+** **S+** T+ U+ V- W- **X+** **Y+** **Z-** *1-* 2- 3- **4+** 5+

12

A+ B- C- D- E- F+ G+ H- I- J+ K+ L+ M+ N- O-

P+ **Q+** **R-** **S-** T- U- **V+** **W+** X- Y- **Z+** *1+* 2+ 3+ *4-* *5-*

13

A+ B- C- **D+** **E+** **F-** **G-** H- I- **J+** **K+** **L-** **M-** **N+** **O+**

P+ Q+ R- S- **T+** **U+** **V-** **W-** X- Y- Z+ 1+ **2-** *3-* **4+** 5+

14

A+ B- C- D+ E+ F- G- H- I- J+ K+ L- M- N+ O+

P- **Q-** **R+** **S+** T- **U-** **V+** **W+** X+ Y+ **Z-** *1-* 2+ 3+ *4-* *5-*

15

A+ B- C- D+ E+ F- G- **H+** **I+** **J-** **K-** **L+** **M+** **N-** **O-**

P- Q- **R+** **S+** T- U- **V+** **W+** **X-** **Y-** **Z+** *1+* 2- 3- **4+** 5+

16

A+ B- C- D+ E+ F- G- H+ I+ J- K- L+ M+ N- O-

P+ **Q+** **R-** **S-** **T+** **U+** V- **W-** **X+** **Y+** **Z-** *1-* 2+ 3+ *4-* *5-*

DATA COLLECTION WORKSHEET
PAGE FOUR OF FIVE PAGES
CHANGES IN FACTOR LEVELS FOR REFLECTED 32-RUN DESIGNS

Factors that change level from previous run are shown in boldface.

Run

Response

17

A- B- **C+** D+ E- F- **G+** H+ I- J- **K+** L+ **M-** N- **O+**

P+ **Q-** R- **S+** T+ **U-** V- **W+** X+ **Y-** **Z-** **1+** 2+ 3- 4- 5+

18

A- B- C+ D+ E- F- G+ H+ I- J- K+ L+ M- N- O+

P- **Q+** **R+** **S-** **T-** **U+** **V+** **W-** **X-** **Y+** **Z+** **1-** 2- 3+ 4+ 5-

19

A- B- C+ D+ E- F- G+ **H-** **I+** **J+** **K-** **L-** **M+** **N+** **O-**

P- Q+ R+ S- **T-** U+ V+ W- **X+** **Y-** **Z-** 1+ 2+ 3- 4- 5+

20

A- B- C+ D+ E- F- G+ H- I+ J+ K- L- M+ N+ O-

P+ **Q-** **R-** **S+** **T+** **U-** **V-** **W+** **X-** **Y+** **Z+** **1-** 2- 3+ 4+ 5-

21

A- B- C+ **D-** **E+** **F+** **G-** H- I+ J+ K- **L+** **M-** N- **O+**

P+ Q- R- S+ **T-** **U+** **V+** **W-** X- Y+ Z+ 1- **2+** 3- 4- 5+

22

A- B- C+ D- E+ F+ G- H- I+ J+ K- L+ M- N- O+

P- **Q+** **R+** **S-** **T+** **U-** V- **W+** **X+** **Y-** **Z-** **1+** 2- 3+ 4+ 5-

23

A- B- C+ D- E+ F+ G- **H+** **I-** **J-** **K+** **L-** **M+** **N+** **O-**

P- Q+ R+ S- T+ U- V- W+ **X-** **Y+** **Z+** 1- 2+ 3- 4- 5+

24

A- B- C+ D- E+ F+ G- H+ I- J- K+ L- M+ N+ O-

P+ **Q-** **R-** **S+** **T-** **U+** **V+** **W-** **X+** **Y-** **Z-** 1+ 2- 3+ 4+ 5-

Data Collection Worksheet
Page Five of Five Pages
Changes in Factor Levels for Reflected 32-Run Designs

Factors that change level from previous run are shown in boldface.

Run   Response

25

A- **B+** **C-** D- **E+** **F-** **G+** H+ I- **J+** **K-** L- **M+** **N-** **O+**

P+ **Q-** **R+** **S-** T- **U+** **V-** **W+** X+ Y- **Z+** **1-** 2- 3+ **4-** **5+**

26

A- B+ C- D- E+ F- G+ H+ I- J+ K- L- M+ N- O+

P- **Q+** **R-** **S+** **T+** **U-** **V+** **W-** **X-** **Y+** **Z-** **1+** 2+ **3-** **4+** **5-**

27

A- B+ C- D- E+ F- G+ **H-** **I+** **J-** **K+** **L+** **M-** **N+** **O-**

P- Q+ R- S+ T+ U- V+ W- **X+** **Y-** **Z+** **1-** 2- 3+ **4-** **5+**

28

A- B+ C- D- E+ F- G+ H- I+ J- K+ L+ M- N+ O-

P+ **Q-** **R+** **S-** **T-** **U+** **V-** **W+** **X-** **Y+** **Z-** **1+** 2+ **3-** **4+** **5-**

29

A- B+ C- **D+** **E-** **F+** **G-** H- I+ J- K+ **L-** **M+** **N-** **O+**

P+ Q- R+ S- **T+** **U-** **V+** **W-** X- Y+ Z- 1+ **2-** 3+ **4-** **5+**

30

A- B+ C- D+ E- F+ G- H- I+ J- K+ L- **M+** N- O+

P- **Q+** **R-** **S+** **T-** **U+** **V-** **W+** **X+** **Y-** **Z+** **1-** 2+ **3-** **4+** **5-**

31

A- B+ C- D+ E- F+ G- **H+** **I-** **J+** **K-** **L+** **M-** **N+** **O-**

P- Q+ R- S+ T- U+ V- W+ **X-** **Y+** **Z-** **1+** 2- 3+ **4-** **5+**

32

A- B+ C- D+ E- F+ G- H+ I- J+ K- L+ M- N+ O-

P+ **Q-** **R+** **S-** **T+** **U-** **V+** **W-** **X+** **Y-** **Z+** **1-** 2+ **3-** **4+** **5-**

CALCULATION WORKSHEET FOR REFLECTED 32-RUN DESIGNS
PAGE ONE OF FIVE PAGES

Run No.	Response	Contrast Labels A	B	C	D	E	F	G
1	_____	+	+	+	+	+	+	+
2	_____	+	+	+	+	+	+	+
3	_____	+	+	+	+	+	+	+
4	_____	+	+	+	+	+	+	+
sums for runs 1 to 4		_____	_____	_____	_____	_____	_____	_____
5	_____	+	+	+	-	-	-	-
6	_____	+	+	+	-	-	-	-
7	_____	+	+	+	-	-	-	-
8	_____	+	+	+	-	-	-	-
sums for runs 5 to 8		_____	_____	_____	_____	_____	_____	_____
9	_____	+	-	-	-	-	+	+
10	_____	+	-	-	-	-	+	+
11	_____	+	-	-	-	-	+	+
12	_____	+	-	-	-	-	+	+
sums for runs 9 to 12		_____	_____	_____	_____	_____	_____	_____
13	_____	+	-	-	+	+	-	-
14	_____	+	-	-	+	+	-	-
15	_____	+	-	-	+	+	-	-
16	_____	+	-	-	+	+	-	-
sums for runs 13 to 16		_____	_____	_____	_____	_____	_____	_____
17	_____	-	-	+	+	-	-	+
18	_____	-	-	+	+	-	-	+
19	_____	-	-	+	+	-	-	+
20	_____	-	-	+	+	-	-	+
sums for runs 17 to 20		_____	_____	_____	_____	_____	_____	_____
21	_____	-	-	+	-	+	+	-
22	_____	-	-	+	-	+	+	-
23	_____	-	-	+	-	+	+	-
24	_____	-	-	+	-	+	+	-
sums for runs 21 to 24		_____	_____	_____	_____	_____	_____	_____
25	_____	-	+	-	-	+	-	+
26	_____	-	+	-	-	+	-	+
27	_____	-	+	-	-	+	-	+
28	_____	-	+	-	-	+	-	+
sums for runs 25 to 28		_____	_____	_____	_____	_____	_____	_____
29	_____	-	+	-	+	-	+	-
30	_____	-	+	-	+	-	+	-
31	_____	-	+	-	+	-	+	-
32	_____	-	+	-	+	-	+	-
sums for runs 29 to 32		_____	_____	_____	_____	_____	_____	_____
Sum of Sums:		_____	_____	_____	_____	_____	_____	_____
Est. Contrasts for		A	B	C	D	E	F	G

CALCULATION WORKSHEET FOR REFLECTED 32-RUN DESIGNS
PAGE TWO OF FIVE PAGES

Run No.	Response	H	I	J	K	L	M	N	O
1	_____	+	+	+	+	+	+	+	+
2	_____	+	+	+	+	+	+	+	+
3	_____	-	-	-	-	-	-	-	-
4	_____	-	-	-	-	-	-	-	-
sums for runs 1 to 4									
5	_____	-	-	-	-	+	+	+	+
6	_____	-	-	-	-	+	+	+	+
7	_____	+	+	+	+	-	-	-	-
8	_____	+	+	+	+	-	-	-	-
sums for runs 5 to 8									
9	_____	+	+	-	-	-	-	+	+
10	_____	+	+	-	-	-	-	+	+
11	_____	-	-	+	+	+	+	-	-
12	_____	-	-	+	+	+	+	-	-
sums for runs 9 to 12									
13	_____	-	-	+	+	-	-	+	+
14	_____	-	-	+	+	-	-	+	+
15	_____	+	+	-	-	+	+	-	-
16	_____	+	+	-	-	+	+	-	-
sums for runs 13 to 16									
17	_____	+	-	-	+	+	-	-	+
18	_____	+	-	-	+	+	-	-	+
19	_____	-	+	+	-	-	+	+	-
20	_____	-	+	+	-	-	+	+	-
sums for runs 17 to 20									
21	_____	-	+	+	-	+	-	-	+
22	_____	-	+	+	-	+	-	-	+
23	_____	+	-	-	+	-	+	+	-
24	_____	+	-	-	+	-	+	+	-
sums for runs 21 to 24									
25	_____	+	-	+	-	-	+	-	+
26	_____	+	-	+	-	-	+	-	+
27	_____	-	+	-	+	+	-	+	-
28	_____	-	+	-	+	+	-	+	-
sums for runs 25 to 28									
29	_____	-	+	-	+	-	+	-	+
30	_____	-	+	-	+	-	+	-	+
31	_____	+	-	+	-	+	-	+	-
32	_____	+	-	+	-	+	-	+	-
sums for runs 29 to 32									
Sum of Sums:		___	___	___	___	___	___	___	___
Est. Contrasts for		H	I	J	K	L	M	N	O

CALCULATION WORKSHEET FOR REFLECTED 32-RUN DESIGNS
PAGE THREE OF FIVE PAGES

Run No.	Response	P	Q	R	S	T	U	V	W
1	_____	+	+	+	+	+	+	+	+
2	_____	-	-	-	-	-	-	-	-
3	_____	-	-	-	-	-	-	-	-
4	_____	+	+	+	+	+	+	+	+
sums for runs 1 to 4		___	___	___	___	___	___	___	___
5	_____	+	+	+	+	-	-	-	-
6	_____	-	-	-	-	+	+	+	+
7	_____	-	-	-	-	+	+	+	+
8	_____	+	+	+	+	-	-	-	-
sums for runs 5 to 8		___	___	___	___	___	___	___	___
9	_____	+	+	-	-	-	-	+	+
10	_____	-	-	+	+	+	+	-	-
11	_____	-	-	+	+	+	+	-	-
12	_____	+	+	-	-	-	-	+	+
sums for runs 9 to 12		___	___	___	___	___	___	___	___
13	_____	+	+	-	-	+	+	-	-
14	_____	-	-	+	+	-	-	+	+
15	_____	-	-	+	+	-	-	+	+
16	_____	+	+	-	-	+	+	-	-
sums for runs 13 to 16		___	___	___	___	___	___	___	___
17	_____	+	-	-	+	+	-	-	+
18	_____	-	+	+	-	-	+	+	-
19	_____	-	+	+	-	-	+	+	-
20	_____	+	-	-	+	+	-	-	+
sums for runs 17 to 20		___	___	___	___	___	___	___	___
21	_____	+	-	-	+	-	+	+	-
22	_____	-	+	+	-	+	-	-	+
23	_____	-	+	+	-	+	-	-	+
24	_____	+	-	-	+	-	+	+	-
sums for runs 21 to 24		___	___	___	___	___	___	___	___
25	_____	+	-	+	-	-	+	-	+
26	_____	-	+	-	+	+	-	+	-
27	_____	-	+	-	+	+	-	+	-
28	_____	+	-	+	-	-	+	-	+
sums for runs 25 to 28		___	___	___	___	___	___	___	___
29	_____	+	-	+	-	+	-	+	-
30	_____	-	+	-	+	-	+	-	+
31	_____	-	+	-	+	-	+	-	+
32	_____	+	-	+	-	+	-	+	-
sums for runs 29 to 32		___	___	___	___	___	___	___	___
Sum of Sums:		___	___	___	___	___	___	___	___
Est. Contrasts for		P	Q	R	S	T	U	V	W

CALCULATION WORKSHEET FOR REFLECTED 32-RUN DESIGNS
PAGE FOUR OF FIVE PAGES

Run No.	Response	Contrast Labels							
		X	Y	Z	1	2	3	4	5
1	_____	+	+	+	+	+	+	+	+
2	_____	-	-	-	-	-	-	-	-
3	_____	+	+	+	+	+	+	+	+
4	_____	-	-	-	-	-	-	-	-
sums for runs 1 to 4		___	___	___	___	___	___	___	___
5	_____	-	-	-	-	+	+	+	+
6	_____	+	+	+	+	-	-	-	-
7	_____	-	-	-	-	+	+	+	+
8	_____	+	+	+	+	-	-	-	-
sums for runs 5 to 8		___	___	___	___	___	___	___	___
9	_____	+	+	-	-	-	-	+	+
10	_____	-	-	+	+	+	+	-	-
11	_____	+	+	-	-	-	-	+	+
12	_____	-	-	+	+	+	+	-	-
sums for runs 9 to 12		___	___	___	___	___	___	___	___
13	_____	-	-	+	+	-	-	+	+
14	_____	+	+	-	-	+	+	-	-
15	_____	-	-	+	+	-	-	+	+
16	_____	+	+	-	-	+	+	-	-
sums for runs 13 to 16		___	___	___	___	___	___	___	___
17	_____	+	-	-	+	+	-	-	+
18	_____	-	+	+	-	-	+	+	-
19	_____	+	-	-	+	+	-	-	+
20	_____	-	+	+	-	-	+	+	-
sums for runs 17 to 20		___	___	___	___	___	___	___	___
21	_____	-	+	+	-	+	-	-	+
22	_____	+	-	-	+	-	+	+	-
23	_____	-	+	+	-	+	-	-	+
24	_____	+	-	-	+	-	+	+	-
sums for runs 21 to 24		___	___	___	___	___	___	___	___
25	_____	+	-	+	-	-	+	-	+
26	_____	-	+	-	+	+	-	+	-
27	_____	+	-	+	-	-	+	-	+
28	_____	-	+	-	+	+	-	+	-
sums for runs 25 to 28		___	___	___	___	___	___	___	___
29	_____	-	+	-	+	-	+	-	+
30	_____	+	-	+	-	+	-	+	-
31	_____	-	+	-	+	-	+	-	+
32	_____	+	-	+	-	+	-	+	-
sums for runs 29 to 32		___	___	___	___	___	___	___	___
Sum of Sums:		___	___	___	___	___	___	___	___
Est. Contrasts for		X	Y	Z	1	2	3	4	5

CALCULATION WORKSHEET
FOR REFLECTED 32-RUN DESIGNS
PAGE FIVE OF FIVE PAGES

SINGLE DEGREE OF FREEDOM ANOVA TABLE

Contrast Labels	Estimated Contrasts	Sums of Squares		Estimated Effects
A	_____	_____	_____	_____
B	_____	_____	_____	_____
C	_____	_____	_____	_____
D	_____	_____	_____	_____
E	_____	_____	_____	_____
F	_____	_____	_____	_____
G	_____	_____	_____	_____
H	_____	_____	_____	_____
I	_____	_____	_____	_____
J	_____	_____	_____	_____
K	_____	_____	_____	_____
L	_____	_____	_____	_____
M	_____	_____	_____	_____
N	_____	_____	_____	_____
O	_____	_____	_____	_____
P	_____	_____	_____	_____
Q	_____	_____	_____	_____
R	_____	_____	_____	_____
S	_____	_____	_____	_____
T	_____	_____	_____	_____
U	_____	_____	_____	_____
V	_____	_____	_____	_____
W	_____	_____	_____	_____
X	_____	_____	_____	_____
Y	_____	_____	_____	_____
Z	_____	_____	_____	_____
1	_____	_____	_____	_____
2	_____	_____	_____	_____
3	_____	_____	_____	_____
4	_____	_____	_____	_____
5	_____	_____	_____	_____

TOTAL Sum of Squares   _____

PART TWO

NON-GEOMETRIC TWO-LEVEL PLACKETT-BURMAN DESIGNS

The two-level Plackett-Burman designs with 4, 8, 16, 32, 64 and 128 runs are called *geometric* designs. All other two-level Plackett-Burman designs are said to be *non-geometric* designs. The major difference between the geometric designs and the non-geometric designs is the way that the interaction effects are confounded with the main effects.

With the geometric designs each interaction effect was confounded with exactly one main effect (i.e., the AB interaction effect might be confounded with the main effect for Factor C). This unique correspondence between an interaction and a particular contrast can be exploited to identify two-factor interaction effects as well as main effects.

With the non-geometric designs this unique correspondence is missing. In these designs a two-factor interaction will be partially confounded with each of the other main effects in the study (i.e., the AB interaction effect will be partially confounded with Factors C, D, E, F, G, H, I, J ,K, etc.). Any particular interaction will be positively confounded with some main effects, and negatively confounded with others. At the same time, the degree of confounding for any particular interaction will vary from main effect to main effects. Thus, for non-geometric designs, the confounding pattern is so complex that it is of little use in isolating individual interaction effects. Moreover, since one significant interaction effect will impact every other main effect, interactions can appreciably cloud the interpretation of results.

For these reasons, the non-geometric designs are essentially "main-effect designs." That is, they are most useful where there is strong prior reason to believe that any interactions are of little practical importance. Any contrast that shows up in both a basic study and also in the reflection of this study is quite likely to represent a real effect. If the contrast changes sign from one study to the other, then it is most surely not a main effect, but rather the effect of one or more interactions. One cannot identify just which particular interaction effects are represented by such a contrast, but the difference between main effects and two-factor interaction effects will still be clear.

These characteristics do somewhat limit the usefulness of the following designs. If the user is indeed interested in discovering as much as possible about a large number of factors, he will generally do best with one of the geometric two-level Plackett-Burman designs from Part One.

BASIC 12-RUN PLACKETT-BURMAN DESIGNS

The Basic 12-Run Plackett-Burman Design may be used with as many as 11 two-level factors.

The Contrast Labels in the array below identify the columns of contrast coefficients associated with each of the eleven factors in a fully saturated design.

Contrast Labels

Run	A	B	C	D	E	F	G	H	I	J	K
1	−	−	−	−	−	−	−	−	−	−	−
2	−	−	−	+	+	+	−	−	+	+	+
3	−	−	+	−	+	+	+	+	−	−	+
4	−	+	+	−	+	−	−	+	+	+	−
5	−	+	+	+	−	−	+	−	+	−	+
6	−	+	−	+	−	+	+	+	−	+	−
7	+	+	−	+	+	−	−	+	−	−	+
8	+	+	−	−	+	+	+	−	+	−	−
9	+	+	+	−	−	+	−	−	−	+	+
10	+	−	+	+	−	+	−	+	+	−	−
11	+	−	+	+	+	−	+	−	−	+	−
12	+	−	−	−	−	−	+	+	+	+	+

Treatment combinations are defined by rows in this matrix.

Contrast coefficients are defined by columns in this matrix.

Number of changes in level:

A	B	C	D	E	F	G	H	I	J	K
1	2	4	6	6	6	7	7	9	9	9

DATA COLLECTION WORKSHEET
FOR THE BASIC 12-RUN DESIGN

Delete labels on this page that do not correspond to a main effect.

Factor Names	Low-Level	High-Level
A. _____	_____	_____
B. _____	_____	_____
C. _____	_____	_____
D. _____	_____	_____
E. _____	_____	_____
F. _____	_____	_____
G. _____	_____	_____
H. _____	_____	_____
I. _____	_____	_____
J. _____	_____	_____
K. _____	_____	_____

The Response Variable is _____

Changes in Factor Levels for Basic 12-Run Sequence

Changes in factor levels are shown in boldface

Run	Begin with all factors at their low level:											Response
1	**A-**	**B-**	**C-**	**D-**	**E-**	**F-**	**G-**	**H-**	**I-**	**J-**	**K-**	_____
2	A-	B-	C-	**D+**	**E+**	**F+**	G-	H-	**I+**	**J+**	**K+**	_____
3	A-	B-	**C+**	**D-**	E+	F+	**G+**	**H+**	I-	J-	K+	_____
4	A-	**B+**	C+	D-	E+	**F-**	**G-**	H+	**I+**	**J+**	**K-**	_____
5	A-	B+	C+	**D+**	**E-**	F-	**G+**	**H-**	I+	J-	**K+**	_____
6	A-	B+	**C-**	**D+**	E-	**F+**	G+	**H+**	**I-**	**J+**	**K-**	_____
7	**A+**	B+	C-	D+	**E+**	**F-**	**G-**	H+	I-	J-	**K+**	_____
8	A+	B+	C-	**D-**	E+	**F+**	**G+**	**H-**	**I+**	J-	**K-**	_____
9	A+	B+	**C+**	D-	**E-**	F+	**G-**	H-	I-	**J+**	**K+**	_____
10	A+	**B-**	C+	**D+**	E-	F+	G-	**H+**	**I+**	J-	**K-**	_____
11	A+	B-	C+	D+	**E+**	**F-**	**G+**	**H-**	I-	**J+**	K-	_____
12	A+	B-	**C-**	**D-**	E-	F-	G+	**H+**	**I+**	J+	**K+**	_____

CALCULATION WORKSHEET
FOR BASIC 12-RUN DESIGN

Run No.	Response	A	B	C	D	E	F	G	H	I	J	K
1	_____	−	−	−	−	−	−	−	−	−	−	−
2	_____	−	−	−	+	+	+	−	−	+	+	+
3	_____	−	−	+	−	+	+	+	+	−	−	+
4	_____	−	+	+	−	+	−	−	+	+	+	−
5	_____	−	+	+	+	−	−	+	−	+	−	+
6	_____	−	+	−	+	−	+	+	+	−	+	−
7	_____	+	+	−	+	+	−	−	+	−	−	+
8	_____	+	+	−	−	+	+	+	−	+	−	−
9	_____	+	+	+	−	−	+	−	−	−	+	+
10	_____	+	−	+	+	−	+	−	+	+	−	−
11	_____	+	−	+	+	+	−	+	−	−	+	−
12	_____	+	−	−	−	−	−	+	+	+	+	+

SINGLE DEGREE OF FREEDOM ANOVA TABLE

Contrast Labels	Estimated Contrasts	Sums of Squares	Estimated Effects
A	_____	_____	_____
B	_____	_____	_____
C	_____	_____	_____
D	_____	_____	_____
E	_____	_____	_____
F	_____	_____	_____
G	_____	_____	_____
H	_____	_____	_____
I	_____	_____	_____
J	_____	_____	_____
K	_____	_____	_____

TOTAL Sum of Squares _____

EXAMPLE OF BASIC 12-RUN DESIGN

The basic 12-run design was used to study seven factors. Contrast Labels H, I, J and K were unassigned, and so represent the effects of interactions and noise. It was decided, *a priori*, to pool these four contrasts to form a Mean Square Error term for use in testing the other seven contrasts.

Run No.	Response	A	B	C	D	E	F	G	H	I	J	K
1	46.31	-	-	-	-	-	-	-	-	-	-	-
2	47.33	-	-	-	+	+	+	-	-	+	+	+
3	53.51	-	-	+	-	+	+	+	+	-	-	+
4	47.08	-	+	+	-	+	-	-	+	+	+	-
5	54.77	-	+	+	+	-	-	+	-	+	-	+
6	44.99	-	+	-	+	-	+	+	+	-	+	-
7	47.41	+	+	-	+	+	-	-	+	-	-	+
8	47.01	+	+	-	-	+	+	+	-	+	-	-
9	50.27	+	+	+	-	-	+	-	-	-	+	+
10	57.91	+	-	+	+	-	+	-	+	+	-	-
11	55.56	+	-	+	+	+	-	+	-	-	+	-
12	44.71	+	-	-	-	-	-	+	+	+	+	+

The contrast labels heading row: Contrast Labels

SINGLE DEGREE OF FREEDOM ANOVA TABLE

Contrast Labels	Estimated Contrasts	Sums of Squares	F-ratios	Estimated Effects	
A	8.88	6.571	0.98		
B	-13.80	15.870	2.37		
C	41.34	142.416	21.26*	6.89	Contrast C is significant.
D	19.08	30.337	4.53		Contrast D may be significant.
E	-1.06	0.094	0.01		
F	5.18	2.236	0.33		
G	4.24	1.498	0.22		
(H)	-5.64	2.651	pool		
(I)	0.76	0.048	pool		
(J)	-16.98	24.027	pool		$MSE = 6.697$ with 4 d.f.
(K)	-0.86	0.062	pool		
TOTAL Sum of Squares		225.810			$F_{.90}(1,4) = 4.54$

REFLECTED 12-RUN PLACKETT-BURMAN DESIGNS

The Reflected 12-Run Plackett-Burman Design may be used with as many as 11 two-level factors.

The Contrast Labels in the array below identify the columns of contrast coefficients associated with each of the eleven factors in a fully saturated design.

Contrast Labels

Run	A	B	C	D	E	F	G	H	I	J	K
1	+	+	+	+	+	+	+	+	+	+	+
2	+	+	+	-	-	-	+	+	-	-	-
3	+	+	-	+	-	-	-	-	+	+	-
4	+	-	-	+	-	+	+	-	-	-	+
5	+	-	-	-	+	+	-	+	-	+	-
6	+	-	+	-	+	-	-	-	+	-	+
7	-	-	+	-	-	+	+	-	+	+	-
8	-	-	+	+	-	-	-	+	-	+	+
9	-	-	-	+	+	-	+	+	+	-	-
10	-	+	-	-	+	-	+	-	-	+	+
11	-	+	-	-	-	+	-	+	+	-	+
12	-	+	+	+	+	+	-	-	-	-	-

Treatment combinations are defined by rows in this matrix.

Contrast coefficients are defined by columns in this matrix.

Number of changes in level:

A	B	C	D	E	F	G	H	I	J	K
1	2	4	6	6	6	7	7	9	9	9

DATA COLLECTION WORKSHEET
FOR THE REFLECTED 12-RUN DESIGN

Delete labels on this page that do not correspond to a main effect.

Factor Names	Low-Level	High-Level
A. _____	_____	_____
B. _____	_____	_____
C. _____	_____	_____
D. _____	_____	_____
E. _____	_____	_____
F. _____	_____	_____
G. _____	_____	_____
H. _____	_____	_____
I. _____	_____	_____
J. _____	_____	_____
K. _____	_____	_____

The Response Variable is _____

Changes in Factor Levels for Reflected 12-Run Sequence

Changes in factor levels are shown in boldface

Run	Begin with all factors at their high level:											Response
1	**A+**	**B+**	**C+**	**D+**	**E+**	**F+**	**G+**	**H+**	**I+**	**J+**	**K+**	_____
2	A+	B+	C+	**D-**	**E-**	**F-**	G+	H+	**I-**	**J-**	**K-**	_____
3	A+	B+	**C-**	**D+**	E-	F-	**G-**	**H-**	**I+**	**J+**	K-	_____
4	A+	**B-**	C-	D+	E-	**F+**	**G+**	H-	**I-**	**J-**	**K+**	_____
5	A+	B-	C-	**D-**	**E+**	F+	**G-**	**H+**	I-	**J+**	**K-**	_____
6	A+	B-	**C+**	D-	E+	**F-**	G-	**H-**	**I+**	J-	**K+**	_____
7	**A-**	B-	C+	D-	**E-**	**F+**	**G+**	H-	I+	**J+**	K-	_____
8	A-	B-	C+	**D+**	E-	**F-**	**G-**	**H+**	**I-**	J+	**K+**	_____
9	A-	B-	**C-**	D+	**E+**	F-	**G+**	H+	**I+**	**J-**	**K-**	_____
10	A-	**B+**	C-	**D-**	E+	F-	G+	**H-**	I-	**J+**	**K+**	_____
11	A-	B+	C-	D-	**E-**	**F+**	**G-**	**H+**	**I+**	J-	K+	_____
12	A-	B+	**C+**	**D+**	E+	F+	G-	**H-**	**I-**	J-	**K-**	_____

106

CALCULATION WORKSHEET
FOR REFLECTED 12-RUN DESIGN

Run No.	Response	A	B	C	D	E	F	G	H	I	J	K
						Contrast Labels						
1	_____	+	+	+	+	+	+	+	+	+	+	+
2	_____	+	+	+	-	-	-	+	+	-	-	-
3	_____	+	+	-	+	-	-	-	-	+	+	-
4	_____	+	-	-	+	-	+	+	-	-	-	+
5	_____	+	-	-	-	+	+	-	+	-	+	-
6	_____	+	-	+	-	+	-	-	-	+	-	+
7	_____	-	-	+	-	-	+	+	-	+	+	-
8	_____	-	-	+	+	-	-	-	+	-	+	+
9	_____	-	-	-	+	+	-	+	+	+	-	-
10	_____	-	+	-	-	+	-	+	-	-	+	+
11	_____	-	+	-	-	-	+	-	+	+	-	+
12	_____	-	+	+	+	+	+	-	-	-	-	-

SINGLE DEGREE OF FREEDOM ANOVA TABLE

Contrast Labels	Estimated Contrasts	Sums of Squares		Estimated Effects
A	_____	_____	_____	_____
B	_____	_____	_____	_____
C	_____	_____	_____	_____
D	_____	_____	_____	_____
E	_____	_____	_____	_____
F	_____	_____	_____	_____
G	_____	_____	_____	_____
H	_____	_____	_____	_____
I	_____	_____	_____	_____
J	_____	_____	_____	_____
K	_____	_____	_____	_____
TOTAL Sum of Squares	_____			

EXAMPLE OF REFLECTED 12-RUN DESIGN

The reflected 12-run design was used to study seven factors. Contrast Labels H, I, J and K were unassigned, and so represent the effects of interactions and noise. It was decided, *a priori*, to pool these four contrasts to form a Mean Square Error term for use in testing the other seven contrasts.

Run No.	Response	Contrast Labels A	B	C	D	E	F	G	H	I	J	K
1	56.94	+	+	+	+	+	+	+	+	+	+	+
2	50.20	+	+	+	-	-	-	+	+	-	-	-
3	45.96	+	+	-	+	-	-	-	-	+	+	-
4	49.01	+	-	-	+	-	+	+	-	-	-	+
5	45.79	+	-	-	-	+	+	-	+	-	+	-
6	47.08	+	-	+	-	+	-	-	-	+	-	+
7	54.10	-	-	+	-	-	+	+	-	+	+	-
8	54.17	-	-	+	+	-	-	-	+	-	+	+
9	48.83	-	-	-	+	+	-	+	+	+	-	-
10	45.10	-	+	-	-	+	-	+	-	-	+	+
11	46.40	-	+	-	-	-	+	-	+	+	-	+
12	57.00	-	+	+	+	+	+	-	-	-	-	-

SINGLE DEGREE OF FREEDOM ANOVA TABLE

Contrast Labels	Estimated Contrasts	Sums of Squares		Estimated Effects
A	-10.62	9.399	10.5*	-1.77
B	2.62	0.572	0.6	
C	38.40	122.880	136.8*	6.40
D	23.24	45.008	50.1*	3.87
E	0.90	0.068	0.1	
F	17.90	26.701	29.7*	2.98
G	7.78	5.044	5.6*	1.30
(H)	4.08	1.387	pool	
(I)	-1.96	0.320	pool	
(J)	3.54	1.044	pool	
(K)	-3.18	0.843	pool	
TOTAL Sum of Squares		213.266		

Contrasts C, D, F, A, and G are found to be significant at the $\alpha = 0.10$ level based on the *a priori* pooling.

MSE = 0.8985 with 4 d.f.

$F_{.90}(1,4) = 4.54$

BASIC 20-RUN PLACKETT-BURMAN DESIGNS

The Basic 20-Run Plackett-Burman Design may be used with as many as 19 two-level factors.

The Contrast Labels in the array below identify the columns of contrast coefficients associated with each of the nineteen factors in a fully saturated design.

Contrast Labels

Run	A	B	C	D	E	F	G	H	I	J	K	L	M	N	O	P	Q	R	S
1	-	-	-	-	-	-	-	-	-	-	-	-	-	-	-	-	-	-	-
2	-	-	-	-	+	-	+	+	-	+	+	+	-	-	+	-	+	+	+
3	-	-	-	+	+	+	+	+	+	-	+	+	-	+	-	+	-	-	-
4	-	-	+	+	-	+	+	-	+	-	-	+	+	-	+	-	-	+	+
5	-	-	+	+	+	-	-	+	-	-	-	-	+	+	+	+	+	+	-
6	-	+	+	+	+	-	-	-	+	+	+	-	-	+	-	-	-	+	+
7	-	+	+	-	+	+	+	-	-	+	+	-	+	-	+	+	-	-	-
8	-	+	+	-	-	+	+	+	+	+	-	+	-	+	+	-	+	-	-
9	-	+	-	-	-	+	-	+	+	-	+	-	+	-	-	+	+	+	+
10	-	+	-	+	-	-	+	-	-	+	-	+	+	+	-	+	+	-	+
11	+	+	-	+	-	+	+	-	-	-	+	-	-	+	+	-	+	+	-
12	+	+	-	+	+	+	-	+	-	+	-	+	+	-	-	-	-	+	-
13	+	+	-	-	+	-	+	+	+	-	-	-	+	+	+	-	-	-	+
14	+	+	+	-	+	-	+	-	+	-	-	+	-	-	-	+	+	+	-
15	+	+	+	+	-	-	-	+	-	-	+	+	-	-	+	+	-	-	+
16	+	-	+	+	-	-	+	+	+	+	+	-	+	-	-	-	+	-	-
17	+	-	+	-	-	+	+	+	-	+	-	-	-	+	-	+	-	+	+
18	+	-	+	-	+	+	-	-	-	-	+	+	+	+	-	-	+	-	+
19	+	-	-	-	-	-	-	-	+	+	+	+	+	+	+	+	-	+	-
20	+	-	-	+	+	+	-	-	+	+	-	-	-	-	+	+	+	-	+
	A	B	C	D	E	F	G	H	I	J	K	L	M	N	O	P	Q	R	S

Treatment combinations are defined by rows in this matrix.

Contrast coefficients are defined by columns in this matrix.

Number of changes in level:

A	B	C	D	E	F	G	H	I	J	K	L	M	N	O	P	Q	R	S
1	2	4	7	9	9	10	10	11	11	12	12	12	12	13	13	13	14	15

DATA COLLECTION WORKSHEET
FOR THE BASIC 20-RUN DESIGN
PAGE ONE OF TWO PAGES

Delete labels on this worksheet that do not correspond to a main effect.

Factor Names	Low-Level	High-Level
A. _____	_____	_____
B. _____	_____	_____
C. _____	_____	_____
D. _____	_____	_____
E. _____	_____	_____
F. _____	_____	_____
G. _____	_____	_____
H. _____	_____	_____
I. _____	_____	_____
J. _____	_____	_____
K. _____	_____	_____
L. _____	_____	_____
M. _____	_____	_____
N. _____	_____	_____
O. _____	_____	_____
P. _____	_____	_____
Q. _____	_____	_____
R. _____	_____	_____
S. _____	_____	_____

The Response Variable is _____

DATA COLLECTION WORKSHEET
FOR THE BASIC 20-RUN DESIGN
PAGE TWO OF TWO PAGES

Changes in Factor Levels for Basic 20-Run Sequence

Changes in factor levels are shown in boldface

Run   Begin with all factors at their low level: Response

Run	A	B	C	D	E	F	G	H	I	J	K	L	M	N	O	P	Q	R	S	Response
1	**A-**	**B-**	**C-**	**D-**	**E-**	**F-**	**G-**	**H-**	**I-**	**J-**	**K-**	**L-**	**M-**	N-	**O-**	P-	**Q-**	R-	S-	_____
2	A-	B-	C-	D-	**E+**	F-	**G+**	**H+**	I-	**J+**	**K+**	**L+**	M-	N-	O+	P-	**Q+**	R+	S+	_____
3	A-	B-	C-	**D+**	E+	**F+**	G+	H+	**I+**	**J-**	K+	L+	M-	**N+**	**O-**	**P+**	**Q-**	R-	S-	_____
4	A-	B-	**C+**	D+	**E-**	F+	G+	**H-**	I+	J-	**K-**	L+	**M+**	N-	**O+**	**P-**	Q-	**R+**	**S+**	_____
5	A-	B-	C+	D+	**E+**	F-	**G-**	**H+**	**I-**	J-	K-	**L-**	**M+**	**N+**	O+	**P+**	**Q+**	R+	**S-**	_____
6	A-	**B+**	C+	D+	E+	F-	G-	**H-**	**I+**	**J+**	**K+**	**L-**	**M-**	N+	**O-**	P-	**Q-**	R+	S+	_____
7	A-	B+	C+	**D-**	E+	**F+**	**G+**	H-	**I-**	J+	K+	L-	**M+**	**N-**	**O+**	**P+**	Q-	R-	S-	_____
8	A-	B+	C+	D-	**E-**	F+	**G-**	**H+**	**I+**	J+	**K-**	**L+**	**M-**	**N+**	O+	**P-**	**Q+**	R-	S-	_____
9	A-	B+	**C-**	D-	E-	F+	G-	**H+**	I+	**J-**	**K+**	**L+**	**M+**	N-	**O-**	**P+**	Q+	R+	S+	_____
10	A-	B+	C-	**D+**	E-	**F-**	**G+**	**H-**	**I-**	**J+**	**K-**	L+	**M+**	**N+**	O-	P+	Q+	R-	S+	_____
11	**A+**	B+	C-	D+	E-	**F+**	G+	H-	I-	**J-**	K+	L+	**M-**	N+	**O+**	**P-**	Q+	R+	S-	_____
12	A+	B+	C-	D+	**E+**	F+	**G-**	**H+**	I-	**J+**	**K-**	L+	**M+**	N+	**O-**	P-	**Q-**	R+	S-	_____
13	A+	B+	C-	**D-**	E+	**F-**	**G+**	**H+**	**I+**	J-	K-	**L-**	**M+**	**N+**	**O+**	P-	Q-	R-	**S+**	_____
14	A+	B+	**C+**	D-	E+	F-	G+	**H-**	I+	J-	K-	**L+**	**M-**	N-	**O-**	**P+**	**Q+**	R+	S-	_____
15	A+	B+	C+	**D+**	**E-**	F-	**G-**	**H+**	**I-**	J-	**K+**	L+	M-	N-	**O+**	P+	**Q-**	R-	S+	_____
16	A+	**B-**	C+	D+	E-	F-	**G+**	**H+**	**I+**	**J+**	K+	**L-**	**M+**	N-	**O-**	P-	**Q+**	R-	S-	_____
17	A+	B-	C+	**D-**	E-	**F+**	**G+**	H+	**I-**	**J+**	**K-**	L-	M-	**N+**	O-	**P+**	**Q-**	**R+**	S+	_____
18	A+	B-	C+	D-	**E+**	F+	**G-**	**H-**	I-	**J-**	**K+**	**L+**	**M+**	N+	O-	P-	**Q+**	R-	S+	_____
19	A+	B-	**C-**	D-	**E-**	F-	G-	H-	**I+**	**J+**	K+	L+	M+	N-	**O+**	**P+**	Q-	R+	S-	_____
20	A+	B-	C-	**D+**	**E+**	**F+**	G-	H-	**I+**	J+	**K-**	L-	**M-**	N-	O+	P+	**Q+**	R+	**S+**	_____

CALCULATION WORKSHEET
FOR BASIC 20-RUN DESIGN
PAGE ONE OF THREE PAGES

Run No.	Response	Contrast Labels									
		A	B	C	D	E	F	G	H	I	J
1	_____	-	-	-	-	-	-	-	-	-	-
2	_____	-	-	-	-	+	-	+	+	-	+
3	_____	-	-	-	+	+	+	+	+	+	-
4	_____	-	-	+	+	-	+	+	-	+	-
sums/runs 1 to 4		____	____	____	____	____	____	____	____	____	____
5	_____	-	-	+	+	+	-	-	+	-	-
6	_____	-	+	+	+	+	-	-	-	+	+
7	_____	-	+	+	-	+	+	+	-	-	+
8	_____	-	+	+	-	-	+	-	+	+	+
sums/runs 5 to 8		____	____	____	____	____	____	____	____	____	____
9	_____	-	+	-	-	-	+	-	+	+	-
10	_____	-	+	-	+	-	-	+	-	-	+
11	_____	+	+	-	+	-	+	+	-	-	-
12	_____	+	+	-	+	+	+	-	+	-	+
sums/runs 9 to 12		____	____	____	____	____	____	____	____	____	____
13	_____	+	+	-	-	+	-	+	+	+	-
14	_____	+	+	+	-	+	-	+	-	+	-
15	_____	+	+	+	+	-	-	-	+	-	-
16	_____	+	-	+	+	-	-	+	+	+	+
sums/runs 13 to 16		____	____	____	____	____	____	____	____	____	____
17	_____	+	-	+	-	-	+	+	+	-	+
18	_____	+	-	+	-	+	+	-	-	-	-
19	_____	+	-	-	-	-	-	-	-	+	+
20	_____	+	-	-	+	+	+	-	-	+	+
sums/runs 17 to 20		____	____	____	____	____	____	____	____	____	____
Sums of Partial Sums		____	____	____	____	____	____	____	____	____	____
Est. Contrasts for		A	B	C	D	E	F	G	H	I	J

CALCULATION WORKSHEET
FOR BASIC 20-RUN DESIGN
PAGE TWO OF THREE PAGES

Run No.	Response	K	L	M	N	O	P	Q	R	S
1	_____	−	−	−	−	−	−	−	−	−
2	_____	+	+	−	−	+	−	+	+	+
3	_____	+	+	−	+	−	+	−	−	−
4	_____	−	+	+	−	+	−	−	+	+
sums/runs 1 to 4		____	____	____	____	____	____	____	____	____
5	_____	−	−	+	+	+	+	+	+	−
6	_____	+	−	−	+	−	−	−	+	+
7	_____	+	−	+	−	+	+	−	−	−
8	_____	−	+	−	+	+	−	+	−	−
sums/runs 5 to 8		____	____	____	____	____	____	____	____	____
9	_____	+	−	+	−	−	+	+	+	+
10	_____	−	+	+	+	−	+	+	−	+
11	_____	+	−	−	+	+	−	+	+	−
12	_____	−	+	+	−	−	−	−	+	−
sums/runs 9 to 12		____	____	____	____	____	____	____	____	____
13	_____	−	−	+	+	+	−	−	−	+
14	_____	−	+	−	−	−	+	+	+	−
15	_____	+	+	−	−	+	+	−	−	+
16	_____	+	−	+	−	−	−	+	−	−
sums/runs 13 to 16		____	____	____	____	____	____	____	____	____
17	_____	−	−	−	+	−	+	−	+	+
18	_____	+	+	+	+	−	−	+	−	+
19	_____	+	+	+	+	+	+	−	+	−
20	_____	−	−	−	−	+	+	+	−	+
sums/runs 17 to 20		____	____	____	____	____	____	____	____	____
Sums of Partial Sums		____	____	____	____	____	____	____	____	____
Est. Contrasts for		K	L	M	N	O	P	Q	R	S

CALCULATION WORKSHEET
FOR BASIC 20-RUN DESIGNS
PAGE THREE OF THREE PAGES

SINGLE DEGREE OF FREEDOM ANOVA TABLE

Contrast Labels	Estimated Contrasts	Sums of Squares	Estimated Effects
A	_____	_____	_____
B	_____	_____	_____
C	_____	_____	_____
D	_____	_____	_____
E	_____	_____	_____
F	_____	_____	_____
G	_____	_____	_____
H	_____	_____	_____
I	_____	_____	_____
J	_____	_____	_____
K	_____	_____	_____
L	_____	_____	_____
M	_____	_____	_____
N	_____	_____	_____
O	_____	_____	_____
P	_____	_____	_____
Q	_____	_____	_____
R	_____	_____	_____
S	_____	_____	_____
TOTAL Sum of Squares	_____		

EXAMPLE OF BASIC 20-RUN DESIGN

Run	Response	A	B	C	D	E	F	G	H	I	J	K	L	M	N	O	P	Q	R	S
1	64	-	-	-	-	-	-	-	-	-	-	-	-	-	-	-	-	-	-	-
2	46	-	-	-	-	+	-	+	+	-	+	+	+	-	-	+	-	+	+	+
3	96	-	-	-	+	+	+	+	+	+	-	+	+	-	+	-	+	-	-	-
4	94	-	-	+	+	-	+	+	-	+	-	-	+	+	-	+	-	-	+	+
5	91	-	-	+	+	+	-	-	+	-	-	-	-	+	+	+	+	+	+	-
6	77	-	+	+	+	+	-	-	-	+	+	+	-	-	+	-	-	-	+	+
7	31	-	+	+	-	+	+	+	-	-	+	+	-	+	-	+	+	-	-	-
8	58	-	+	+	-	-	+	-	+	+	+	-	-	-	+	+	-	+	-	-
9	32	-	+	-	-	-	+	-	+	+	-	+	-	+	-	-	+	+	+	+
10	100	-	+	-	+	-	-	+	-	-	+	-	+	+	+	-	+	+	-	+
11	133	+	+	-	+	-	+	+	-	-	-	+	-	-	+	+	-	+	+	-
12	140	+	+	-	+	+	+	-	+	-	+	-	+	+	-	-	-	-	+	-
13	106	+	+	-	-	+	-	+	+	+	-	-	-	+	+	+	-	-	-	+
14	96	+	+	+	-	+	-	+	-	+	-	-	-	-	-	-	+	+	+	-
15	138	+	+	+	+	-	-	-	+	-	-	+	+	-	-	+	+	-	-	+
16	154	+	-	+	+	-	-	+	+	+	+	+	-	+	-	-	-	+	-	-
17	100	+	-	+	-	-	+	+	+	-	+	-	-	-	+	-	+	-	+	+
18	113	+	-	+	-	+	+	-	-	-	-	+	+	+	+	-	-	+	-	+
19	106	+	-	-	-	-	-	-	-	+	+	+	+	+	+	+	+	-	+	-
20	149	+	-	-	+	+	+	-	-	+	+	-	-	-	-	+	+	+	-	+

SINGLE DEGREE OF FREEDOM ANOVA TABLE

Contrast Labels	Estimated Contrasts	Sums of Squares	Estimated Effects	Contrast Labels	Estimated Contrasts	Sums of Squares	Estimated Effects
A	546	14,905.8	54.6	K	-72	259.2	
B	-102	520.2		L	50	125.0	
C	-20	20.0		M	10	5.0	
D	420	8,820.0	42.0	N	36	64.8	
E	-34	57.8		O	-20	20.0	
F	-32	51.2		P	-46	105.8	
G	-12	7.2		Q	20	20.0	
H	-2	0.2		R	-94	441.8	
I	12	7.2		S	-14	9.8	
J	-2	0.2					

TOTAL Sum of Squares   25,441.2

REFLECTED 20-RUN PLACKETT-BURMAN DESIGNS

The Reflected 20-Run Plackett-Burman Design may be used with as many as 19 two-level factors.

The Contrast Labels in the array below identify the columns of contrast coefficients associated with each of the nineteen factors in a fully saturated design.

Contrast Labels

Run	A	B	C	D	E	F	G	H	I	J	K	L	M	N	O	P	Q	R	S
1	+	+	+	+	+	+	+	+	+	+	+	+	+	+	+	+	+	+	+
2	+	+	+	+	-	+	-	-	+	-	-	-	+	+	-	+	-	-	-
3	+	+	+	-	-	-	-	-	-	+	-	-	+	-	+	-	+	+	+
4	+	+	-	-	+	-	-	+	-	+	+	-	-	+	-	+	+	-	-
5	+	+	-	-	-	+	+	-	+	+	+	+	-	-	-	-	-	-	+
6	+	-	-	-	-	+	+	+	-	-	-	+	+	-	+	+	+	-	-
7	+	-	-	+	-	-	-	+	+	-	-	+	-	+	-	-	+	+	+
8	+	-	-	+	+	-	+	-	-	-	+	-	+	-	-	+	-	+	+
9	+	-	+	+	+	-	+	-	-	+	-	+	-	+	+	-	-	-	-
10	+	-	+	-	+	+	-	+	+	-	+	-	-	-	+	-	-	+	-
11	-	-	+	-	+	-	-	+	+	+	-	+	+	-	-	+	-	-	+
12	-	-	+	-	-	-	+	-	+	-	+	-	-	+	+	+	+	-	+
13	-	-	+	+	-	+	-	-	-	+	+	+	-	-	-	+	+	+	-
14	-	-	-	+	-	+	-	+	-	+	+	-	+	+	+	-	-	-	+
15	-	-	-	-	+	+	+	-	+	+	-	-	+	+	-	-	+	+	-
16	-	+	-	-	+	+	-	-	-	-	-	+	-	+	+	+	-	+	+
17	-	+	-	+	+	-	-	-	+	-	+	+	+	-	+	-	+	-	-
18	-	+	-	+	-	-	+	+	+	+	-	-	-	-	+	+	-	+	-
19	-	+	+	+	+	+	+	+	-	-	-	-	-	-	-	-	+	-	+
20	-	+	+	-	-	-	+	+	-	-	+	+	+	+	-	-	-	+	-
	A	B	C	D	E	F	G	H	I	J	K	L	M	N	O	P	Q	R	S

Treatment combinations are defined by rows in this matrix.

Contrast coefficients are defined by columns in this matrix.

Number of changes in level:

A	B	C	D	E	F	G	H	I	J	K	L	M	N	O	P	Q	R	S
1	2	4	7	9	9	10	10	11	11	12	12	12	12	13	13	13	14	15

DATA COLLECTION WORKSHEET
FOR THE REFLECTED 20-RUN DESIGN
PAGE ONE OF TWO PAGES

Delete labels on this worksheet that do not correspond to a main effect.

Factor Names	Low-Level	High-Level
A. _____	_____	_____
B. _____	_____	_____
C. _____	_____	_____
D. _____	_____	_____
E. _____	_____	_____
F. _____	_____	_____
G. _____	_____	_____
H. _____	_____	_____
I. _____	_____	_____
J. _____	_____	_____
K. _____	_____	_____
L. _____	_____	_____
M. _____	_____	_____
N. _____	_____	_____
O. _____	_____	_____
P. _____	_____	_____
Q. _____	_____	_____
R. _____	_____	_____
S. _____	_____	_____

The Response Variable is   _____

DATA COLLECTION WORKSHEET
FOR THE REFLECTED 20-RUN DESIGN
PAGE TWO OF TWO PAGES

Changes in Factor Levels for Reflected 20-Run Sequence

Changes in factor levels are shown in boldface

Run	Begin with all factors at their high level:				Response
1	**A+B+C+D+**	**E+ F+ G+ H+**	**I+ J+ K+ L+**	**M+N+O+P+**	**Q+R+S+** _____
2	A+ B+ C+ D+	**E-** F+ **G- H-**	I+ **J- K- L-**	M+ N+ **O-** P+	**Q- R- S-** _____
3	A+ B+ C+ **D-**	E- **F- G-** H-	**I-** J+ K- L-	M+ **N-O+P-**	**Q+R+S+** _____
4	A+ B+ **C-** D-	**E+** F- G- **H+**	I- J+ **K+** L-	**M-N+O- P+**	Q+ **R-** S- _____
5	A+ B+ C- D-	**E- F+G+ H-**	**I+** J+ K+ **L+**	**M-** N- O- **P-**	**Q-** R- **S+** _____
6	A+ **B-** C- D-	E- F+ G+ **H+**	**I- J-** K- L+	**M+N- O+P+**	**Q+** R- S- _____
7	A+ B- C- **D+**	E- **F- G-** H+	**I+** J- K- L+	**M-N+O- P-**	Q+ **R+S+** _____
8	A+ B- C- D+	**E+** F- **G+ H-**	**I-** J- **K+** L+	**M+N-** O- P+	**Q-** R+ S+ _____
9	A+ B- **C+D+**	E+ F- **G+** H-	**I-** **J+** K- **L+**	**M-N+O+** P-	**Q-** R- S- _____
10	A+ B- C+ **D-**	E+ **F+ G-H+**	**I+** J- **K+** L+	M- N- O+ P-	**Q-** R+ S- _____
11	**A-** B- C+ D-	E+ **F-** G- H+	I+ **J+** K- **L+**	**M+N-** O- **P+**	Q- **R-** S+ _____
12	A- B- C+ D-	**E-** F- **G+ H-**	I+ **J-** K+ L+	**M-N+O+** P+	**Q+** R- S+ _____
13	A- B- C+ **D+**	E- **F+ G-** H-	**I-** J+ K+ L+	M- N- **O-** P+	**Q+R+** S- _____
14	A- B- **C-** D+	E- F+ G- **H+**	I- J+ K+ **L-**	**M+N+O+P-**	**Q-** R- S+ _____
15	A- B- C- **D-**	**E+** F+ **G+ H-**	**I+** J+ **K-** L-	M+ N+ **O-** P-	**Q+R+** S- _____
16	A- **B+** C- D-	E+ F+ **G-** H-	**I- J-** K- L+	**M-N+O+P+**	**Q-** R+ S+ _____
17	A- B+ C- **D+**	E+ **F-** G- H-	**I+** J- **K+** L+	**M+N-** O+ **P-**	**Q+** R- S- _____
18	A- B+ C- D+	**E-** F- **G+H+**	I+ **J+** K- **L-**	**M-** N- O+ P+	**Q-** R+ S- _____
19	A- B+ **C+D+**	**E+ F+** G+ H+	**I- J-** K- L-	M- N- **O-** P-	**Q+** R- S+ _____
20	A- B+ C+ **D-**	**E-** F- G+ H+	I- J- **K+L+**	**M+N+** O- P-	**Q-** R+ S- _____

CALCULATION WORKSHEET
FOR REFLECTED 20-RUN DESIGN
PAGE ONE OF THREE PAGES

Run No.	Response	A	B	C	D	E	F	G	H	I	J
		Contrast Labels									
1	_____	+	+	+	+	+	+	+	+	+	+
2	_____	+	+	+	+	-	+	-	-	+	-
3	_____	+	+	+	-	-	-	-	-	-	+
4	_____	+	+	-	-	+	-	-	+	-	+
sums/runs 1 to 4		____	____	____	____	____	____	____	____	____	____
5	_____	+	+	-	-	-	+	+	-	+	+
6	_____	+	-	-	-	-	+	+	+	-	-
7	_____	+	-	-	+	-	-	-	+	+	-
8	_____	+	-	-	+	+	-	+	-	-	-
sums/runs 5 to 8		____	____	____	____	____	____	____	____	____	____
9	_____	+	-	+	+	+	-	+	-	-	+
10	_____	+	-	+	-	+	+	-	+	+	-
11	_____	-	-	+	-	+	-	-	+	+	+
12	_____	-	-	+	-	-	-	+	-	+	-
sums/runs 9 to 12		____	____	____	____	____	____	____	____	____	____
13	_____	-	-	+	+	-	+	-	-	-	+
14	_____	-	-	-	+	-	+	-	+	-	+
15	_____	-	-	-	-	+	+	+	-	+	+
16	_____	-	+	-	-	+	+	-	-	-	-
sums/runs 13 to 16		____	____	____	____	____	____	____	____	____	____
17	_____	-	+	-	+	+	-	-	-	+	-
18	_____	-	+	-	+	-	-	+	+	+	+
19	_____	-	+	+	+	+	+	+	+	-	-
20	_____	-	+	+	-	-	-	+	+	-	-
sums/runs 17 to 20		____	____	____	____	____	____	____	____	____	____
Sums of Partial Sums		____	____	____	____	____	____	____	____	____	____
Est. Contrasts for		A	B	C	D	E	F	G	H	I	J

CALCULATION WORKSHEET
FOR REFLECTED 20-RUN DESIGN
PAGE TWO OF THREE PAGES

Run No.	Response	K	L	M	N	O	P	Q	R	S
1	_____	+	+	+	+	+	+	+	+	+
2	_____	−	−	+	+	−	+	−	−	−
3	_____	−	−	+	−	+	−	+	+	+
4	_____	+	−	−	+	−	+	+	−	−
sums/runs 1 to 4		___	___	___	___	___	___	___	___	___
5	_____	+	+	−	−	−	−	−	−	+
6	_____	−	+	+	−	+	+	+	−	−
7	_____	−	+	−	+	−	−	+	+	+
8	_____	+	−	+	−	−	+	−	+	+
sums/runs 5 to 8		___	___	___	___	___	___	___	___	___
9	_____	−	+	−	+	+	−	−	−	−
10	_____	+	−	−	−	+	−	−	+	−
11	_____	−	+	+	−	−	+	−	−	+
12	_____	+	−	−	+	+	+	+	−	+
sums/runs 9 to 12		___	___	___	___	___	___	___	___	___
13	_____	+	+	−	−	−	+	+	+	−
14	_____	+	−	+	+	+	−	−	−	+
15	_____	−	−	+	+	−	−	+	+	−
16	_____	−	+	−	+	+	+	−	+	+
sums/runs 13 to 16		___	___	___	___	___	___	___	___	___
17	_____	+	+	+	−	+	−	+	−	−
18	_____	−	−	−	−	+	+	−	+	−
19	_____	−	−	−	−	−	−	+	−	+
20	_____	+	+	+	+	−	−	−	+	−
sums/runs 17 to 20		___	___	___	___	___	___	___	___	___
Sums of Partial Sums		___	___	___	___	___	___	___	___	___
Est. Contrasts for		K	L	M	N	O	P	Q	R	S

CALCULATION WORKSHEET
FOR REFLECTED 20-RUN DESIGNS
PAGE THREE OF THREE PAGES

SINGLE DEGREE OF FREEDOM ANOVA TABLE

Contrast Labels	Estimated Contrasts	Sums of Squares		Estimated Effects
A	_____	_____	_____	_____
B	_____	_____	_____	_____
C	_____	_____	_____	_____
D	_____	_____	_____	_____
E	_____	_____	_____	_____
F	_____	_____	_____	_____
G	_____	_____	_____	_____
H	_____	_____	_____	_____
I	_____	_____	_____	_____
J	_____	_____	_____	_____
K	_____	_____	_____	_____
L	_____	_____	_____	_____
M	_____	_____	_____	_____
N	_____	_____	_____	_____
O	_____	_____	_____	_____
P	_____	_____	_____	_____
Q	_____	_____	_____	_____
R	_____	_____	_____	_____
S	_____	_____	_____	_____
TOTAL Sum of Squares	_____			

EXAMPLE OF REFLECTED 20-RUN DESIGN

Run	Response	A	B	C	D	E	F	G	H	I	J	K	L	M	N	O	P	Q	R	S
1	165	+	+	+	+	+	+	+	+	+	+	+	+	+	+	+	+	+	+	+
2	149	+	+	+	+	−	+	−	−	+	−	−	−	+	+	−	+	−	−	−
3	107	+	+	+	−	−	−	−	−	−	+	−	−	+	−	+	−	+	+	+
4	115	+	+	−	−	+	−	−	+	−	+	+	−	−	+	−	+	+	−	−
5	103	+	+	−	−	−	+	+	−	+	+	+	+	−	−	−	−	−	−	+
6	104	+	−	−	−	−	+	+	+	−	−	−	+	+	−	+	+	+	−	−
7	153	+	−	−	+	−	−	−	+	+	−	−	+	−	+	−	−	+	+	+
8	152	+	−	−	+	+	−	+	−	−	−	+	−	+	−	−	+	−	+	+
9	160	+	−	+	+	+	−	+	−	−	+	−	+	−	+	+	−	−	−	−
10	108	+	−	+	−	+	+	−	+	+	−	+	−	−	−	+	+	−	+	−
11	61	−	−	+	−	+	−	−	+	+	+	−	+	+	−	−	+	−	−	+
12	51	−	−	+	−	−	−	+	−	+	−	+	−	−	+	+	+	+	−	+
13	103	−	−	+	+	−	+	−	−	−	+	+	+	−	−	−	+	+	+	−
14	81	−	−	−	+	−	+	−	+	−	+	+	−	+	+	+	−	−	−	+
15	44	−	−	−	−	+	+	+	−	+	+	−	−	+	+	−	−	+	+	−
16	46	−	+	−	−	+	+	−	−	−	−	−	+	−	+	+	+	−	+	+
17	92	−	+	−	+	+	−	−	−	+	−	+	+	+	−	+	−	+	−	−
18	90	−	+	−	+	−	−	+	+	+	+	−	−	−	−	+	+	−	+	−
19	99	−	+	+	+	+	+	+	+	−	−	−	−	−	−	−	−	+	−	+
20	40	−	+	+	−	−	−	+	+	−	−	+	+	+	+	−	−	−	+	−

SINGLE DEGREE OF FREEDOM ANOVA TABLE

Contrast Labels	Estimated Contrasts	Sums of Squares	Estimated Effects	Contrast Labels	Estimated Contrasts	Sums of Squares	Estimated Effects
A	609	18,544.05	60.9	K	−3	0.45	
B	−11	6.05		L	31	48.05	
C	63	198.45		M	−33	54.45	
D	465	10,811.25	46.5	N	−15	11.25	
E	61	186.05		O	−15	11.25	
F	−19	18.05		P	49	120.05	
G	−7	2.45		Q	43	92.45	
H	9	4.05		R	−7	2.45	
I	9	4.05		S	13	8.45	
J	35	61.25					

TOTAL Sum of Squares   30,184.55

EXAMPLE OF BASIC 24-RUN DESIGN

SINGLE DEGREE OF FREEDOM ANOVA TABLE

DATA			Contrast	Estimated	Sum of	Estimated
Run	Response		Label	Contrast	Squares	Effect
1	53		A	775	25,026.042	64.6
2	15		B	1125	52,734.375	93.8
3	32		C	1099	50,325.042	91.6
4	27		D	-51	108.375	
5	47		E	-239	2,380.042	
6	56		F	-97	392.042	
7	183		G	-335	4,676.042	
8	166		H	-395	6,501.042	-32.9
9	179		I	-445	8,251.042	-37.1
10	19		J	-213	1,890.375	
11	10		K	195	1,584.375	
12	7		L	29	35.042	
13	119		M	115	551.042	
14	129		N	9	3.375	
15	109		O	1	0.042	
16	275		P	-97	392.042	
17	282		Q	-149	925.042	
18	266		R	-31	40.042	
19	79		S	-277	3,197.042	
20	91		T	113	532.042	
21	80		U	-337	4,732.042	
22	51		V	41	70.042	
23	45		W	255	2,709.375	
24	43					
			TOTAL		167,055.958	

BASIC 24-RUN PLACKETT-BURMAN DESIGNS

Contrast Labels

Run	A	B	C	D	E	F	G	H	I	J	K	L	M	N	O	P	Q	R	S	T	U	V	W
1	-	-	-	-	-	-	-	-	-	-	-	-	-	-	-	-	-	-	-	-	-	-	-
2	-	-	-	-	-	-	+	-	+	-	+	+	+	+	+	+	-	-	-	+	+	+	+
3	-	-	-	+	-	+	-	+	-	-	+	+	+	-	-	-	+	+	+	+	-	+	+
4	-	-	+	+	+	+	+	-	+	+	+	+	-	-	-	-	-	+	-	+	+	-	-
5	-	-	+	+	-	+	+	+	-	+	-	+	-	+	+	+	-	-	+	-	-	-	+
6	-	-	+	-	+	+	-	-	-	-	-	-	-	+	+	+	+	+	+	+	+	+	-
7	-	+	+	-	+	+	-	-	+	+	+	-	+	-	+	-	-	-	+	-	-	+	+
8	-	+	+	-	+	-	-	+	+	-	+	+	-	+	-	+	+	+	-	-	-	-	+
9	-	+	+	+	-	-	-	+	-	+	+	-	+	+	+	-	+	-	-	+	+	-	-
10	-	+	-	+	-	-	+	-	+	+	-	-	-	+	-	-	+	+	+	-	+	+	+
11	-	+	-	+	+	-	+	+	+	-	-	-	+	-	+	+	-	+	+	+	-	-	-
12	-	+	-	-	+	+	+	+	-	+	-	+	+	-	-	+	+	-	-	-	+	+	-
13	+	+	-	-	+	+	+	+	-	-	+	-	-	+	-	-	-	-	+	+	+	-	+
14	+	+	-	-	-	+	-	+	+	+	-	+	-	+	+	-	-	+	-	+	-	+	-
15	+	+	-	+	-	+	-	-	+	-	+	+	-	-	+	+	+	-	+	-	+	-	-
16	+	+	+	+	+	-	+	-	-	-	-	+	-	-	+	-	+	-	-	+	-	+	+
17	+	+	+	+	-	+	+	-	-	-	+	-	+	+	-	+	-	+	-	-	-	+	-
18	+	+	+	-	-	-	-	-	-	+	-	+	+	-	-	+	-	+	+	+	+	-	+
19	+	-	+	-	-	-	+	+	+	+	+	-	-	-	-	+	+	-	+	+	-	+	-
20	+	-	+	-	-	+	+	+	+	-	-	-	+	-	+	-	+	+	-	-	+	-	+
21	+	-	+	+	+	-	-	+	+	-	-	+	+	+	-	-	-	-	+	-	+	+	-
22	+	-	-	+	+	+	-	-	+	+	-	-	+	+	-	+	+	-	-	+	-	-	+
23	+	-	-	+	+	-	-	+	-	+	+	-	-	-	+	+	-	+	-	-	+	+	+
24	+	-	-	-	+	-	+	-	-	+	+	+	+	+	+	-	+	+	+	-	-	-	-
	A	B	C	D	E	F	G	H	I	J	K	L	M	N	O	P	Q	R	S	T	U	V	W
	1	2	4	8	9	10	11	12	12	13	13	13	13	13	13	14	15	15	15	16	18	18	18

Number of changes in level for each factor shown above:
Treatment combinations are defined by rows in this matrix.
Contrast coefficients are defined by columns in this matrix.

DATA COLLECTION WORKSHEET
FOR THE BASIC 24-RUN DESIGN
PAGE ONE OF TWO PAGES

Delete labels on this worksheet that do not correspond to a main effect.

Factor Names	Low-Level	High-Level
A.		
B.		
C.		
D.		
E.		
F.		
G.		
H.		
I.		
J.		
K.		
L.		
M.		
N.		
O.		
P.		
Q.		
R.		
S.		
T.		
U.		
V.		
W.		

The Response Variable is _____

DATA COLLECTION WORKSHEET
FOR THE BASIC 24-RUN DESIGN
PAGE TWO OF TWO PAGES

Changes in Factor Levels for Basic 24-Run Sequence

Changes in factor levels are shown in boldface

Run   Begin with all factors at their low level:
       Response

1   A- B- C- D-   E- F- G- H-   I- J- K- L-   M- N- O- P-   Q- R- S- T-   U- V- W- _____

2   A- B- C- D-   E- F- G+ H-   I+ J- K+ L+   M+ N+ O+ P+   Q- R- S- T+   U+ V+ W+ _____

3   A- B- C- D+   E- F+ G- H+   I- J- K+ L+   M+ N- O- P-   Q+ R+ S+ T+   U- V+ W+ _____

4   A- B- C+ D+   E+ F+ G+ H-   I+ J+ K+ L+   M- N- O- P-   Q- R+ S- T+   U+ V- W- _____

5   A- B- C+ D+   E- F+ G+ H+   I- J+ K- L+   M- N+ O+ P+   Q- R- S+ T-   U- V- W+ _____

6   A- B- C+ D-   E+ F+ G- H-   I- J- K- L-   M- N+ O+ P+   Q+ R+ S+ T+   U+ V+ W- _____

7   A- B+ C+ D-   E+ F+ G- H-   I+ J+ K+ L-   M+ N- O+ P-   Q- R- S+ T-   U- V+ W+ _____

8   A- B+ C+ D-   E+ F- G- H+   I+ J- K+ L+   M- N- O+ P+   Q+ R+ S- T-   U- V- W+ _____

9   A- B+ C+ D+   E- F- G- H+   I- J+ K+ L-   M+ N+ O+ P-   Q+ R- S- T+   U+ V- W- _____

10   A- B+ C- D+   E- F- G+ H-   I+ J+ K- L-   M- N+ O- P-   Q+ R+ S+ T-   U+ V+ W+ _____

11   A- B+ C- D+   E+ F- G+ H+   I+ J- K- L-   M+ N- O+ P+   Q- R+ S+ T+   U- V- W- _____

12   A- B+ C- D-   E+ F+ G+ H+   I- J+ K- L+   M+ N- O- P+   Q+ R- S- T-   U+ V+ W- _____

13   A+ B+ C- D-   E+ F+ G+ H+   I- J- K+ L+   M- N+ O- P-   Q- R- S+ T+   U+ V- W+ _____

14   A+ B+ C- D-   E- F+ G- H+   I+ J+ K- L+   M- N+ O+ P-   Q- R+ S- T+   U- V+ W- _____

15   A+ B+ C- D+   E- F+ G- H-   I+ J- K+ L+   M- N- O+ P+   Q+ R+ S+ T-   U+ V- W- _____

16   A+ B+ C+ D+   E+ F- G+ H-   I- J- K- L+   M- N- O+ P-   Q+ R- S- T+   U- V+ W+ _____

17   A+ B+ C+ D+   E- F+ G- H-   I- J- K+ L+   M+ N+ O- P+   Q- R+ S- T-   U- V+ W- _____

18   A+ B+ C+ D-   E- F- G- H-   I- J+ K- L+   M+ N- O- P+   Q- R+ S+ T+   U+ V- W+ _____

19   A+ B- C+ D-   E- F- G+ H+   I+ J+ K+ L+   M- N- O- P+   Q+ R+ S- T+   U- V+ W- _____

20   A+ B- C+ D-   E- F+ G- H+   I+ J- K- L-   M+ N- O+ P+   Q- R+ S- T-   U+ V- W+ _____

21   A+ B- C+ D+   E+ F- G- H+   I+ J- K- L+   M+ N+ O- P-   Q- R- S+ T-   U+ V+ W- _____

22   A+ B- C- D+   E+ F+ G- H-   I+ J+ K- L-   M+ N+ O- P+   Q+ R+ S- T+   U- V+ W+ _____

23   A+ B- C- D+   E+ F- G- H+   I- J+ K+ L-   M- N- O+ P+   Q- R+ S- T-   U+ V+ W+ _____

24   A+ B- C- D-   E+ F- G+ H-   I- J+ K+ L+   M+ N+ O+ P-   Q+ R+ S+ T-   U- V- W- _____

CALCULATION WORKSHEET FOR BASIC 24-RUN DESIGN
PAGE ONE OF FOUR PAGES

Run No.	Response	A	B	C	D	E	F	G	H
1	_____	-	-	-	-	-	-	-	-
2	_____	-	-	-	-	-	-	+	-
3	_____	-	-	-	+	-	+	-	+
sums/runs 1 to 3		_____	_____	_____	_____	_____	_____	_____	_____
4	_____	-	-	+	+	+	+	+	-
5	_____	-	-	+	+	-	+	+	+
6	_____	-	-	+	-	+	+	-	-
sums/runs 4 to 6		_____	_____	_____	_____	_____	_____	_____	_____
7	_____	-	+	+	-	+	+	-	-
8	_____	-	+	+	-	+	-	-	+
9	_____	-	+	+	+	-	-	-	+
sums/runs 7 to 9		_____	_____	_____	_____	_____	_____	_____	_____
10	_____	-	+	-	+	-	-	+	-
11	_____	-	+	-	+	+	-	+	+
12	_____	-	+	-	-	+	+	+	+
sums/runs 10 to 12		_____	_____	_____	_____	_____	_____	_____	_____
13	_____	+	+	-	-	+	+	+	+
14	_____	+	+	-	-	-	+	-	+
15	_____	+	+	-	+	-	+	-	-
sums/runs 13 to 15		_____	_____	_____	_____	_____	_____	_____	_____
16	_____	+	+	+	+	+	-	+	-
17	_____	+	+	+	+	-	+	+	-
18	_____	+	+	+	-	-	-	-	-
sums/runs 16 to 18		_____	_____	_____	_____	_____	_____	_____	_____
19	_____	+	-	+	-	-	-	+	+
20	_____	+	-	+	-	-	+	+	+
21	_____	+	-	+	+	+	-	-	+
sums/runs 19 to 21		_____	_____	_____	_____	_____	_____	_____	_____
22	_____	+	-	-	+	+	+	-	-
23	_____	+	-	-	+	+	-	-	+
24	_____	+	-	-	-	+	-	+	-
sums/runs 22 to 24		_____	_____	_____	_____	_____	_____	_____	_____
Sums of Partial Sums		_____	_____	_____	_____	_____	_____	_____	_____
Est. Contrasts for		A	B	C	D	E	F	G	H

CALCULATION WORKSHEET FOR BASIC 24-RUN DESIGN
PAGE TWO OF FOUR PAGES

Run No.	Response	I	J	K	L	M	N	O	P
		Contrast Labels							
1	_____	-	-	-	-	-	-	-	-
2	_____	+	-	+	+	+	+	+	+
3	_____	-	-	+	+	+	-	-	-
sums/runs 1 to 3									
4	_____	+	+	+	+	-	-	-	-
5	_____	-	+	-	+	-	+	+	+
6	_____	-	-	-	-	-	+	+	+
sums/runs 4 to 6									
7	_____	+	+	+	-	+	-	+	-
8	_____	+	-	+	+	-	+	-	+
9	_____	-	+	+	-	+	+	+	-
sums/runs 7 to 9									
10	_____	+	+	-	-	-	+	-	-
11	_____	+	-	-	-	+	-	+	+
12	_____	-	+	-	+	+	-	-	+
sums/runs 10 to 12									
13	_____	-	-	+	-	-	+	-	-
14	_____	+	+	-	+	-	+	+	-
15	_____	+	-	+	+	-	-	+	+
sums/runs 13 to 15									
16	_____	-	-	-	+	-	-	+	-
17	_____	-	-	+	-	+	+	-	+
18	_____	-	+	-	+	+	-	-	+
sums/runs 16 to 18									
19	_____	+	+	+	-	-	-	-	+
20	_____	+	-	-	-	+	-	+	-
21	_____	+	-	-	+	+	+	-	-
sums/runs 19 to 21									
22	_____	+	+	-	-	+	+	-	+
23	_____	-	+	+	-	-	-	+	+
24	_____	-	+	+	+	+	+	+	-
sums/runs 22 to 24									
Sums of Partial Sums									
Est. Contrasts for		I	J	K	L	M	N	O	P

CALCULATION WORKSHEET FOR BASIC 24-RUN DESIGN
PAGE THREE OF FOUR PAGES

Run No.	Response	Q	R	S	T	U	V	W
1	_____	-	-	-	-	-	+	-
2	_____	-	-	-	+	+	+	+
3	_____	+	+	+	+	-	+	+
sums/runs 1 to 3		_____	_____	_____	_____	_____	_____	_____
4	_____	-	+	-	+	+	-	-
5	_____	-	-	+	-	-	-	+
6	_____	+	+	+	+	+	+	-
sums/runs 4 to 6		_____	_____	_____	_____	_____	_____	_____
7	_____	-	-	+	-	-	+	+
8	_____	+	+	-	-	-	-	+
9	_____	+	-	-	+	+	-	-
sums/runs 7 to 9		_____	_____	_____	_____	_____	_____	_____
10	_____	+	+	+	-	+	+	+
11	_____	-	+	+	+	-	-	-
12	_____	+	-	-	-	+	+	-
sums/runs 10 to 12		_____	_____	_____	_____	_____	_____	_____
13	_____	-	-	+	+	+	-	+
14	_____	-	+	-	+	-	+	-
15	_____	+	-	+	-	+	-	-
sums/runs 13 to 15		_____	_____	_____	_____	_____	_____	_____
16	_____	+	-	-	+	-	+	+
17	_____	-	+	-	-	-	+	-
18	_____	-	+	+	+	+	-	+
sums/runs 16 to 18		_____	_____	_____	_____	_____	_____	_____
19	_____	+	-	+	+	-	+	-
20	_____	+	+	-	-	+	-	+
21	_____	-	-	+	-	+	+	-
sums/runs 19 to 21		_____	_____	_____	_____	_____	_____	_____
22	_____	+	-	-	+	-	-	+
23	_____	-	+	-	-	+	+	+
24	_____	+	+	+	-	-	-	-
sums/runs 22 to 24		_____	_____	_____	_____	_____	_____	_____
Sums of Partial Sums		_____	_____	_____	_____	_____	_____	_____
Est. Contrasts for		Q	R	S	T	U	V	W

CALCULATION WORKSHEET
FOR BASIC 24-RUN DESIGNS
PAGE FOUR OF FOUR PAGES

SINGLE DEGREE OF FREEDOM ANOVA TABLE

Contrast Labels	Estimated Contrasts	Sums of Squares		Estimated Effects
A	_____	_____	_____	_____
B	_____	_____	_____	_____
C	_____	_____	_____	_____
D	_____	_____	_____	_____
E	_____	_____	_____	_____
F	_____	_____	_____	_____
G	_____	_____	_____	_____
H	_____	_____	_____	_____
I	_____	_____	_____	_____
J	_____	_____	_____	_____
K	_____	_____	_____	_____
L	_____	_____	_____	_____
M	_____	_____	_____	_____
N	_____	_____	_____	_____
O	_____	_____	_____	_____
P	_____	_____	_____	_____
Q	_____	_____	_____	_____
R	_____	_____	_____	_____
S	_____	_____	_____	_____
T	_____	_____	_____	_____
U	_____	_____	_____	_____
V	_____	_____	_____	_____
W	_____	_____	_____	_____

TOTAL Sum of Squares   _____

EXAMPLE OF REFLECTED 24-RUN DESIGN

SINGLE DEGREE OF FREEDOM ANOVA TABLE

DATA			Contrast	Estimated	Sum of	Estimated
Run	Response		Label	Contrast	Squares	Effect
1	270		A	802	26,800.167	66.8
2	261		B	1176	57,624.0	98.0
3	247		C	944	37,130.667	78.7
4	121		D	-36	54.0	
5	141		E	158	1,040.167	
6	130		F	120	600.0	
7	51		G	262	2,860.167	
8	54		H	432	7,776.0	36.0
9	60		I	398	6,600.167	33.2
10	71		J	72	216.0	
11	70		K	-236	2,320.667	
12	61		L	-114	541.5	
13	27		M	-24	24.0	
14	47		N	-62	160.167	
15	45		O	-78	253.5	
16	24		P	-60	150.0	
17	25		Q	136	770.667	
18	13		R	24	24.0	
19	26		S	272	3,082.667	
20	9		T	-124	640.667	
21	10		U	320	4,266.667	26.7
22	172		V	30	37.5	
23	168		W	-204	1,734.0	
24	169					
			TOTAL		154,707.333	

REFLECTED 24-RUN PLACKETT-BURMAN DESIGNS

This design may be used with as many as 23 two-level factors.

Contrast Labels_____

Run	A	B	C	D	E	F	G	H	I	J	K	L	M	N	O	P	Q	R	S	T	U	V	W
1	+	+	+	+	+	+	+	+	+	+	+	+	+	+	+	+	+	+	+	+	+	+	+
2	+	+	+	+	+	+	−	+	−	+	−	−	−	−	−	−	+	+	+	−	−	−	−
3	+	+	+	−	+	−	+	−	+	+	−	−	−	+	+	+	−	−	−	−	+	−	−
4	+	+	−	−	−	−	−	+	−	−	−	−	+	+	+	+	+	−	+	−	−	+	+
5	+	+	−	−	+	−	−	−	+	−	+	−	+	−	−	−	+	+	−	+	+	+	−
6	+	+	−	+	−	−	+	+	+	+	+	+	+	−	−	−	−	−	−	−	−	−	+
7	+	−	−	+	−	−	+	+	−	−	−	+	−	+	−	+	+	+	−	+	+	−	−
8	+	−	−	+	−	+	+	−	−	+	−	−	+	−	+	−	−	−	+	+	+	+	−
9	+	−	−	−	+	+	+	−	+	−	−	+	−	−	−	+	−	+	+	−	−	+	+
10	+	−	+	−	+	+	−	+	−	−	+	+	+	−	+	+	−	−	−	+	−	−	−
11	+	−	+	−	−	+	−	−	−	+	+	+	−	+	−	−	+	−	−	−	+	+	+
12	+	−	+	+	−	−	−	−	+	−	+	−	−	+	+	−	−	+	+	+	−	−	+
13	−	−	+	+	−	−	−	−	+	+	−	+	+	−	+	+	+	+	−	−	−	+	−
14	−	−	+	+	+	−	+	−	−	−	+	−	+	−	−	+	+	−	+	−	+	−	+
15	−	−	+	−	+	−	+	+	−	+	−	−	+	+	−	−	−	+	−	+	−	+	+
16	−	−	−	−	−	+	−	+	+	+	+	−	+	+	−	+	−	+	+	−	+	−	−
17	−	−	−	−	+	−	−	+	+	+	−	+	−	−	+	−	+	−	+	+	+	−	+
18	−	−	−	+	+	+	+	+	+	−	+	−	−	+	+	−	+	−	−	−	−	+	−
19	−	+	−	+	+	+	−	−	−	−	−	+	+	+	+	−	−	+	−	−	+	−	+
20	−	+	−	+	+	−	−	−	−	+	+	+	−	+	−	+	−	−	+	+	−	+	−
21	−	+	−	−	−	+	+	−	−	+	+	−	−	−	+	+	+	+	−	+	−	−	+
22	−	+	+	−	−	−	+	+	−	−	+	+	−	−	+	−	−	+	+	−	+	+	−
23	−	+	+	−	−	+	+	−	+	−	−	+	+	+	−	−	+	−	+	+	−	−	−
24	−	+	+	+	−	+	−	+	+	−	−	−	−	−	−	+	−	−	−	+	+	+	+

A	B	C	D	E	F	G	H	I	J	K	L	M	N	O	P	Q	R	S	T	U	V	W
1	2	4	8	9	10	11	12	12	13	13	13	13	13	13	14	15	15	15	16	18	18	18

The number of changes in level for each factor is shown above:
Treatment combinations are defined by rows in this matrix.
Contrast coefficients are defined by columns in this matrix.

Data Collection Worksheet
for the Reflected 24-Run Design
PAGE ONE OF TWO PAGES

Delete labels on this worksheet that do not correspond to a main effect.

Factor Names	Low-Level	High-Level
A. _____	_____	_____
B. _____	_____	_____
C. _____	_____	_____
D. _____	_____	_____
E. _____	_____	_____
F. _____	_____	_____
G. _____	_____	_____
H. _____	_____	_____
I. _____	_____	_____
J. _____	_____	_____
K. _____	_____	_____
L. _____	_____	_____
M. _____	_____	_____
N. _____	_____	_____
O. _____	_____	_____
P. _____	_____	_____
Q. _____	_____	_____
R. _____	_____	_____
S. _____	_____	_____
T. _____	_____	_____
U. _____	_____	_____
V. _____	_____	_____
W. _____	_____	_____

The Response Variable is _____

DATA COLLECTION WORKSHEET
FOR THE REFLECTED 24-RUN DESIGN
PAGE TWO OF TWO PAGES

Changes in Factor Levels for Reflected 24-Run Sequence

Changes in factor levels are shown in boldface

Run　　Begin with all factors at their high level:
　　　　Response

1 A+ B+ C+ D+ E+ F+ G+ H+ I+ J+ K+ L+ M+ N+ O+ P+ Q+ R+ S+ T+ U+ V+ W+ _____

2 A+ B+ C+ D+ E+ F+ G- H+ I- J+ K- L- M- N- O- P- Q+ R+ S+ T- U- V- W- _____

3 A+ B+ C+ D- E+ F- G+ H- I+ J+ K- L- M- N+ O+ P+ Q- R- S- T- U+ V- W- _____

4 A+ B+ C- D- E- F- G- H+ I- J- K- L- M+ N+ O+ P+ Q+ R- S+ T- U- V+ W+ _____

5 A+ B+ C- D- E+ F- G- H- I+ J- K+ L- M+ N- O- P- Q+ R+ S- T+ U+ V+ W- _____

6 A+ B+ C- D+ E- F- G+ H+ I+ J+ K+ L+ M+ N- O- P- Q- R- S- T- U- V- W+ _____

7 A+ B- C- D+ E- F- G+ H+ I- J- K- L+ M- N+ O- P+ Q+ R+ S- T+ U+ V- W- _____

8 A+ B- C- D+ E- F+ G+ H- I- J+ K- L- M+ N+ O- P- Q- R- S+ T+ U+ V+ W- _____

9 A+ B- C- D- E+ F+ G+ H- I+ J- K- L+ M- N- O- P+ Q- R+ S+ T- U- V+ W+ _____

10 A+ B- C+ D- E+ F+ G- H+ I- J- K+ L+ M+ N+ O- P+ Q- R- S- T+ U- V- W- _____

11 A+ B- C+ D- E- F+ G- H- I- J+ K+ L+ M- N+ O- P- Q+ R- S- T- U+ V+ W+ _____

12 A+ B- C+ D+ E- F- G- H- I+ J- K+ L- M- N+ O+ P- Q- R+ S+ T+ U- V- W+ _____

13 A- B- C+ D+ E- F- G- H- I+ J+ K- L+ M+ N+ O- P+ Q+ R+ S- T- U- V+ W- _____

14 A- B- C+ D+ E+ F- G+ H- I- J- K+ L+ M+ N- O- P+ Q+ R- S+ T- U+ V- W+ _____

15 A- B- C+ D- E+ F- G+ H+ I- J+ K- L- M+ N+ O+ P- Q- R+ S+ T+ U- V+ W+ _____

16 A- B- C- D- E- F+ G- H+ I+ J+ K+ L+ M+ N+ O+ P+ Q- R+ S+ T- U+ V- W- _____

17 A- B- C- D- E+ F- G- H+ I+ J+ K- L+ M- N- O+ P- Q+ R- S+ T+ U+ V- W+ _____

18 A- B- C- D+ E+ F+ G+ H+ I+ J- K+ L+ M- N+ O+ P- Q+ R- S- T- U- V+ W- _____

19 A- B+ C- D+ E+ F+ G- H- I- J- K- L+ M+ N+ O+ P- Q- R+ S- T- U+ V+ W+ _____

20 A- B+ C- D+ E+ F- G- H- I- J+ K+ L+ M- N+ O+ P+ Q- R- S+ T+ U+ V+ W+ _____

21 A- B+ C- D- E- F+ G+ H+ I- J+ K+ L+ M- N- O+ P+ Q+ R+ S- T+ U- V+ W+ _____

22 A- B+ C+ D- E- F- G+ H+ I- J- K+ L+ M- N- O+ P- Q- R+ S+ T- U+ V+ W- _____

23 A- B+ C+ D- E- F+ G+ H- I+ J- K- L+ M+ N+ O- P- Q+ R- S+ T+ U- V- W- _____

24 A- B+ C+ D+ E- F+ G- H+ I+ J- K- L- M- N- O- P+ Q- R- S- T+ U+ V+ W+ _____

CALCULATION WORKSHEET FOR REFLECTED 24-RUN DESIGN
PAGE ONE OF FOUR PAGES

Run No.	Response	Contrast Labels A	B	C	D	E	F	G	H
1	_____	+	+	+	+	+	+	+	+
2	_____	+	+	+	+	+	+	−	+
3	_____	+	+	+	−	+	−	+	−
sums/runs 1 to 3		_____	_____	_____	_____	_____	_____	_____	_____
4	_____	+	+	−	−	−	−	−	+
5	_____	+	+	−	−	+	−	−	−
6	_____	+	+	−	+	−	−	+	+
sums/runs 4 to 6		_____	_____	_____	_____	_____	_____	_____	_____
7	_____	+	−	−	+	−	−	+	+
8	_____	+	−	−	+	−	+	+	−
9	_____	+	−	−	−	+	+	+	−
sums/runs 7 to 9		_____	_____	_____	_____	_____	_____	_____	_____
10	_____	+	−	+	−	+	+	−	+
11	_____	+	−	+	−	−	+	−	−
12	_____	+	−	+	+	−	−	−	−
sums/runs 10 to 12		_____	_____	_____	_____	_____	_____	_____	_____
13	_____	−	−	+	+	−	−	−	−
14	_____	−	−	+	+	+	−	+	−
15	_____	−	−	+	−	+	−	+	+
sums/runs 13 to 15		_____	_____	_____	_____	_____	_____	_____	_____
16	_____	−	−	−	−	−	+	−	+
17	_____	−	−	−	−	+	−	−	+
18	_____	−	−	−	+	+	+	+	+
sums/runs 16 to 18		_____	_____	_____	_____	_____	_____	_____	_____
19	_____	−	+	−	+	+	+	−	−
20	_____	−	+	−	+	+	−	−	−
21	_____	−	+	−	−	−	+	+	−
sums/runs 19 to 21		_____	_____	_____	_____	_____	_____	_____	_____
22	_____	−	+	+	−	−	−	+	+
23	_____	−	+	+	−	−	+	+	−
24	_____	−	+	+	+	−	+	−	+
sums/runs 22 to 24		_____	_____	_____	_____	_____	_____	_____	_____
Sums of Partial Sums		_____	_____	_____	_____	_____	_____	_____	_____
Est. Contrasts for		A	B	C	D	E	F	G	H

CALCULATION WORKSHEET FOR REFLECTED 24-RUN DESIGN
PAGE TWO OF FOUR PAGES

Run No.	Response	Contrast Labels I	J	K	L	M	N	O	P
1	_____	+	+	+	+	+	+	+	+
2	_____	-	+	-	-	-	-	-	-
3	_____	+	+	-	-	-	+	+	+
sums/runs 1 to 3		_____	_____	_____	_____	_____	_____	_____	_____
4	_____	-	-	-	-	+	+	+	+
5	_____	+	-	+	-	+	-	-	-
6	_____	+	+	+	+	+	-	-	-
sums/runs 4 to 6		_____	_____	_____	_____	_____	_____	_____	_____
7	_____	-	-	-	+	-	+	-	+
8	_____	-	+	-	-	+	-	+	-
9	_____	+	-	-	+	-	-	-	+
sums/runs 7 to 9		_____	_____	_____	_____	_____	_____	_____	_____
10	_____	-	-	+	+	+	-	+	+
11	_____	-	+	+	+	-	+	-	-
12	_____	+	-	+	-	-	+	+	-
sums/runs 10 to 12		_____	_____	_____	_____	_____	_____	_____	_____
13	_____	+	+	-	+	+	-	+	+
14	_____	-	-	+	-	+	-	-	+
15	_____	-	+	-	-	+	+	-	-
sums/runs 13 to 15		_____	_____	_____	_____	_____	_____	_____	_____
16	_____	+	+	+	-	+	+	-	+
17	_____	+	+	-	+	-	-	+	-
18	_____	+	-	+	-	-	+	+	-
sums/runs 16 to 18		_____	_____	_____	_____	_____	_____	_____	_____
19	_____	-	-	-	+	+	+	+	-
20	_____	-	+	+	+	-	+	-	+
21	_____	-	+	+	-	-	-	+	+
sums/runs 19 to 21		_____	_____	_____	_____	_____	_____	_____	_____
22	_____	-	-	+	+	-	-	+	-
23	_____	+	-	-	+	+	+	-	-
24	_____	+	-	-	-	-	-	-	+
sums/runs 22 to 24		_____	_____	_____	_____	_____	_____	_____	_____
Sums of Partial Sums		_____	_____	_____	_____	_____	_____	_____	_____
Est. Contrasts for		I	J	K	L	M	N	O	P

CALCULATION WORKSHEET FOR REFLECTED 24-RUN DESIGN
PAGE THREE OF FOUR PAGES

Run No.	Response	Contrast Labels Q	R	S	T	U	V	W
1	_____	+	+	+	+	+	+	+
2	_____	+	+	+	-	-	-	-
3	_____	-	-	-	-	+	-	-
sums/runs 1 to 3		_____	_____	_____	_____	_____	_____	_____
4	_____	+	-	+	-	-	+	+
5	_____	+	+	-	+	+	+	-
6	_____	-	-	-	-	-	-	+
sums/runs 4 to 6		_____	_____	_____	_____	_____	_____	_____
7	_____	+	+	-	+	+	-	-
8	_____	-	-	+	+	+	+	-
9	_____	-	+	+	-	-	+	+
sums/runs 7 to 9		_____	_____	_____	_____	_____	_____	_____
10	_____	-	-	-	+	-	-	-
11	_____	+	-	-	-	+	+	+
12	_____	-	+	+	+	-	-	+
sums/runs 10 to 12		_____	_____	_____	_____	_____	_____	_____
13	_____	+	+	-	-	-	+	-
14	_____	+	-	+	-	+	-	+
15	_____	-	+	-	+	-	+	+
sums/runs 13 to 15		_____	_____	_____	_____	_____	_____	_____
16	_____	-	+	+	-	+	-	-
17	_____	+	-	+	+	+	-	+
18	_____	+	-	-	-	-	+	-
sums/runs 16 to 18		_____	_____	_____	_____	_____	_____	_____
19	_____	-	+	-	-	+	-	+
20	_____	-	-	+	+	-	+	-
21	_____	+	+	-	+	-	-	+
sums/runs 19 to 21		_____	_____	_____	_____	_____	_____	_____
22	_____	-	+	+	-	+	+	-
23	_____	+	-	+	+	-	-	-
24	_____	-	-	-	+	+	+	+
sums/runs 22 to 24		_____	_____	_____	_____	_____	_____	_____
Sums of Partial Sums		_____	_____	_____	_____	_____	_____	_____
Est. Contrasts for		Q	R	S	T	U	V	W

CALCULATION WORKSHEET
FOR REFLECTED 24-RUN DESIGNS
PAGE FOUR OF FOUR PAGES

SINGLE DEGREE OF FREEDOM ANOVA TABLE

Contrast Labels	Estimated Contrasts	Sums of Squares		Estimated Effects
A	_____	_____	_____	_____
B	_____	_____	_____	_____
C	_____	_____	_____	_____
D	_____	_____	_____	_____
E	_____	_____	_____	_____
F	_____	_____	_____	_____
G	_____	_____	_____	_____
H	_____	_____	_____	_____
I	_____	_____	_____	_____
J	_____	_____	_____	_____
K	_____	_____	_____	_____
L	_____	_____	_____	_____
M	_____	_____	_____	_____
N	_____	_____	_____	_____
O	_____	_____	_____	_____
P	_____	_____	_____	_____
Q	_____	_____	_____	_____
R	_____	_____	_____	_____
S	_____	_____	_____	_____
T	_____	_____	_____	_____
U	_____	_____	_____	_____
V	_____	_____	_____	_____
W	_____	_____	_____	_____

TOTAL Sum of Squares   _____

BASIC 28-RUN PLACKETT-BURMAN DESIGNS

Contrast Labels

Run	A B C D	E F G H	I J K L	M N O P	Q R S T	U V W X	Y Z 1
1	- - - -	- - - -	- - - -	- - - -	- - - -	- - - -	- - -
2	- - - -	+ - - -	- + - -	- - + +	+ + + +	+ + + -	+ + +
3	- - - +	+ + - +	+ + + -	- + + -	- - + +	- + - +	+ - -
4	- - - +	- - + +	- + + +	+ - + -	- + - +	+ - - +	- + +
5	- - + +	- - - +	- - + +	+ + + +	+ + - -	- + + -	+ - -
6	- - + -	- + - +	+ + - +	- + - +	- - - -	+ + + +	- + +
7	- - + -	+ - + -	+ - - +	+ + - -	- + + +	- - + +	+ + +
8	- + + -	+ - + -	+ - + +	- - + +	+ - - +	- + - +	- - +
9	- + + +	+ - - +	+ - + -	+ - - +	- - + -	+ - - -	+ + +
10	- + + +	+ + - -	+ + - -	+ - + -	+ + - -	+ - + +	- - -
11	- + + +	- + + -	- + - -	+ + - +	- + + +	- + - -	- - +
12	- + - +	- + + +	- + + +	- - - +	+ - + -	- - + +	+ + -
13	- + - -	- + + +	+ - + -	- + - -	+ + - +	+ - + -	+ - +
14	- + - -	+ + + +	- - - +	+ + + -	+ - + -	+ + - -	- + -
15	+ + - -	+ - + +	- + - -	+ + + +	- - - -	- - + +	+ - +
16	+ + - +	+ - - +	+ + - +	- + - +	+ + - +	- - - -	- + -
17	+ + - +	+ - - -	- - + +	- + - -	- + + -	+ + + +	- - +
18	+ + - +	- + - -	+ - - +	+ - + -	- - - +	- + + -	+ + +
19	+ + + -	- + - +	- - - +	- - + +	- + + +	+ - - +	+ - -
20	+ + + -	- - + +	+ + + -	- - + -	- + + -	- + + -	- + -
21	+ + + -	- - - -	- + + -	+ + - -	+ - - +	+ + - +	+ + -
22	+ - + -	+ + - +	- + + +	+ - - -	+ - + +	- - + -	- - +
23	+ - + +	+ + + +	- - - -	- - - -	+ + - -	- + - +	+ + +
24	+ - + +	+ + + -	- - + -	- + + +	- - - +	+ - + -	- + -
25	+ - + +	- - + -	+ + - +	- + + -	+ - + -	+ - - -	+ - +
26	+ - - +	- - + +	+ - - -	+ - - +	+ - + +	+ + + +	- - -
27	+ - - -	- + - -	+ - + -	+ + + +	+ + + -	- - - +	- + +
28	+ - - -	+ + + -	+ + + +	+ - - +	- + - +	+ + - -	+ - -
	A B C D	E F G H	I J K L	M N O P	Q R S T	U V W X	Y Z 1
	1 2 4 8	9 11 11 12	13 13 13 13	13 14 14 15	16 17 18 18	19 19 20 20	21 22 22

EXAMPLE OF BASIC 28-RUN DESIGN

DATA

Run	Response
1	33
2	54
3	6
4	40
5	96
6	38
7	44
8	81
9	3
10	51
11	61
12	46
13	92
14	90
15	32
16	58
17	31
18	77
19	10
20	64
21	46
22	96
23	94
24	91
25	49
26	6
27	13
28	10

SINGLE DEGREE OF FREEDOM ANOVA TABLE

Contrast Labels	Estimated Contrasts	Sums of Squares	Estimated Effects
A	-58	120.143	
B	72	185.143	
C	236	1,989.143	16.9
D	6	1.286	
E	70	175.000	
F	138	680.143	
G	188	1,262.286	13.4
H	38	51.571	
I	-228	1,856.571	-16.3
J	-110	432.143	
K	18	11.571	
L	120	514.286	
M	-82	240.143	
N	82	240.143	
O	96	329.143	
P	-214	1,635.571	-15.3
Q	332	3,936.571	23.7
R	24	20.571	
S	-266	2,527.000	-19.0
T	112	448.000	
U	-190	1,289.286	-13.6
V	96	329.143	
W	224	1,729.000	16.0
X	-336	4,032.000	-24.0
Y	-94	315.571	
Z	104	386.286	
1	110	432.143	
Total		25,232.857	

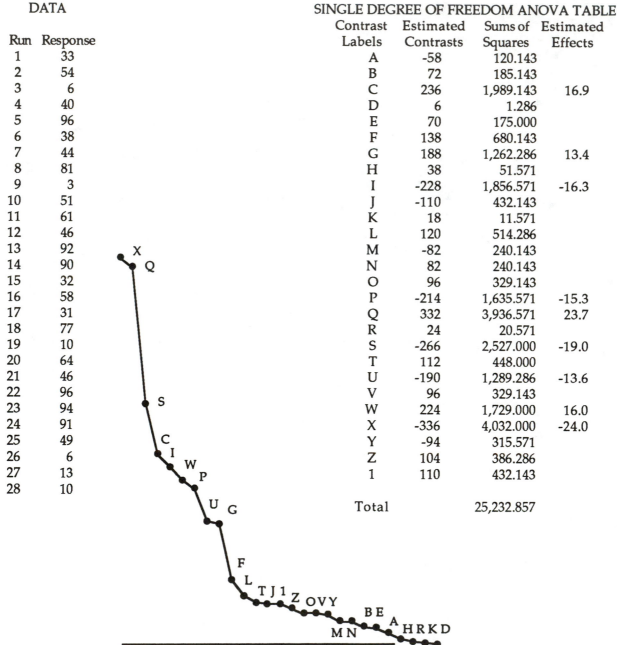

Data Collection Worksheet
for Basic 28-Run Designs
Page One of Four Pages
Identification of Factors and Factor Levels

Delete Contrast Labels on this worksheet that do not represent a main effect.

Factor Names	Low Level	High Level	Factor Names	Low Level	High Level
A.			N.		
B.			O.		
C.			P.		
D.			Q.		
E.			R.		
F.			S.		
G.			T.		
H.			U.		
I.			V.		
J.			W.		
K.			X.		
L.			Y.		
M.			Z.		
			1.		

The Response Variable is _____

DATA COLLECTION WORKSHEET
PAGE TWO OF FOUR PAGES
CHANGES IN FACTOR LEVELS FOR BASIC 28-RUN DESIGNS

Begin with all factors set at their low levels. Changes in factor levels shown in boldface.

Run   Response

1

A- B- C- D- E- F- G- H- I- J- K- L- M-
N- **O-** P- Q- R- S- T- U- V- W- X- Y- Z- *1-*

2

A- B- C- D- **E+** F- G- H- I- **J+** K- L- M-
N- **O+ P+ Q+ R+ S+ T+ U+ V+ W+** X- **Y+ Z+ 1+**

3

A- B- C- **D+ E+ F+** G- **H+ I+** J+ **K+** L- M-
N+ O+ **P- Q- R-** S+ T+ **U-** V+ **W- X+** Y+ **Z- 1-**

4

A- B- C- **D+** E- F- **G+ H+** I- **J+ K+ L+ M+**
N- O+ **P- Q-** R+ **S-** T+ U+ **V- W-** X+ **Y- Z+ 1+**

5

A- B- **C+ D+** E- F- **G-** H+ I- **J-** K+ L+ M+
N+ O+ **P+ Q+** R+ **S- T- U- V+ W+** X- **Y+ Z- 1-**

6

A- B- **C+ D-** E- **F+** G- H+ **I+ J+** K- L+ **M-**
N+ O- P+ Q- R- S- T- **U+** V+ W+ **X+ Y- Z+ 1+**

7

A- B- **C+ D- E+** F- **G+ H-** I+ **J-** K- L+ **M+**
N+ O- P- Q- R+ S+ T+ **U- V-** W+ X+ **Y+ Z+** *1-*

8

A- **B+ C+ D-** E+ F- **G+** H- I+ **J-** K+ **L+ M-**
N- O+ P+ Q+ R- **S-** T+ **U-** V+ **W-** X+ **Y- Z- 1+**

9

A- **B+ C+ D+ E+** F- **G-** H+ I+ **J-** K+ **L- M+**
N- O- P+ Q- R- **S+ T- U+ V- W-** X- **Y+ Z+** *1+*

10

A- **B+ C+ D+ E+ F+** G- **H-** I+ **J+** K- **L-** M+
N- O+ P- **Q+ R+ S- T-** U+ **V- W+ X+** Y- **Z- 1-**

DATA COLLECTION WORKSHEET
PAGE THREE OF FOUR PAGES
CHANGES IN FACTOR LEVELS FOR BASIC 28-RUN DESIGNS

Factors that change level from previous run are shown in boldface.

Run   Response

11

A- B+ C+ D+ E- F+ **G+** H- I- J+ K- L- M+
N+ O- P+ Q- R+ **S+ T+ U- V+ W- X-** Y- Z- *1+*

12

A- B+ **C-** D+ E- F+ G+ H- I- J+ **K+ L+ M-**
N- O- P+ **Q+ R-** S+ **T-** U- **V- W+ X+ Y+ Z+** *1-*

13

A- B+ C- **D-** E- F+ G+ **H+ I+ J-** K+ **L-** M-
N+ O- **P-** Q+ R+ **S- T+ U+** V- **W+ X-** Y+ **Z-** *1+*

14

A- B+ C- D- **E+** F+ G+ H+ **I-** J- **K- L+ M+**
N+ O+ P- Q+ **R- S+ T-** U+ **V+ W-** X- Y- **Z+** *1-*

15

A+ B+ C- D- E+ **F-** G+ H+ I- **J+** K- L- M+
N+ O+ **P+ Q-** R- **S-** T- U- V- **W+** X+ **Y+ Z-** 1+

16

A+ B+ C- **D+** E+ F- **G-** H+ **I+** J+ K- **L+ M-**
N+ **O-** P+ **Q+** R+ **S-** T+ U- V- **W-** X- Y- **Z+** *1-*

17

A+ B+ C- D+ E+ F- G- **H- I-** J- **K+** L+ M-
N+ **O- P- Q-** R+ **S+** T- **U+ V+** W+ X+ Y- **Z-** *1+*

18

A+ B+ C- D+ **E-** **F+** G- H- **I+** J- **K-** L+ **M+**
N- **O+** P- Q- R- **S-** T+ U- **V+** W+ **X-** Y+ **Z+** 1+

19

A+ B+ **C+** **D-** E- F+ G- **H+** I- J- K- L+ **M-**
N- O+ **P+** Q- **R+** S+ **T+** U+ **V- W-** X+ Y+ **Z-** *1-*

DATA COLLECTION WORKSHEET
PAGE FOUR OF FOUR PAGES
CHANGES IN FACTOR LEVELS FOR BASIC 28-RUN DESIGNS

Factors that change level from previous run are shown in boldface.

Run | Response

20

A+ B+ C+ D- E- **F-** G+ H+ I+ J+ K+ L- M-
N- O+ **P-** Q- R+ S+ **T-** U- **V+ W+ X-** Y- Z+ 1-

21

A+ B+ C+ D- E- F- **G-** H- I- J+ K+ L- **M+**
N+ O- P- **Q+ R- S-** T+ U+ V+ **W-** X+ Y+ Z+ 1-

22

A+ **B-** C+ D- **E+ F+** G- **H+** I- J+ K+ **L+** M+
N- O- P- **Q+** R- **S+** T+ **U- V-** W+ X- Y- **Z- 1+**

23

A+ B- C+ **D+** E+ F+ **G+** H+ I- **J- K- L-** M-
N- O- P- **Q+ R+ S-** T- U- **V+ W- X+** Y+ **Z+** 1+

24

A+ B- C+ D+ E+ F+ G+ **H-** I- **J-** K+ L- M-
N+ O+ P+ Q- R- S- **T+** U+ **V- W+ X-** Y- **Z+ 1-**

25

A+ B- C+ D+ **E-** F- G+ H- **I+** J+ **K-** L+ M-
N+ O+ **P- Q+** R- **S+** T- U+ V- **W-** X- **Y+ Z- 1+**

26

A+ B- **C-** D+ E- F- G+ **H+** I+ **J-** K- L- **M+**
N- O- **P+** Q+ R- **S+** T+ U+ **V+ W+ X+** Y- Z- 1-

27

A+ B- C- **D-** E- **F+** G- H- **I+** J- K+ L- M+
N+ O+ P+ Q+ **R+** S+ **T-** U- **V- W-** X+ Y- **Z+ 1+**

28

A+ B- C- D- **E+** F+ **G+** H- I+ **J+** K+ **L+** M+
N- O- **P+ Q-** R+ **S-** T- **U+** V+ **W-** X- **Y+ Z- 1-**

CALCULATION WORKSHEET FOR BASIC 28-RUN DESIGNS
PAGE ONE OF FOUR PAGES

Run No.	Response	A	B	C	D	E	F	G	H	I
		Contrast Labels								
1	_____	-	-	-	-	-	-	-	-	-
2	_____	-	-	-	-	+	-	-	-	-
3	_____	-	-	-	+	+	+	-	+	+
4	_____	-	-	-	+	-	-	+	+	-
sums/runs 1 to 4	_____	_____	_____	_____	_____	_____	_____	_____	_____	_____
5	_____	-	-	+	+	-	-	-	+	-
6	_____	-	-	+	-	-	+	-	+	+
7	_____	-	-	+	-	+	-	+	-	+
sums/runs 5 to 7	_____	_____	_____	_____	_____	_____	_____	_____	_____	_____
8	_____	-	+	+	-	+	-	+	-	+
9	_____	-	+	+	+	+	-	-	+	+
10	_____	-	+	+	+	+	+	-	-	+
sums/runs 8 to 10	_____	_____	_____	_____	_____	_____	_____	_____	_____	_____
11	_____	-	+	+	+	-	+	+	-	-
12	_____	-	+	-	+	-	+	+	-	-
13	_____	-	+	-	-	-	+	+	+	+
sums/runs 11 to 13	_____	_____	_____	_____	_____	_____	_____	_____	_____	_____
14	_____	-	+	-	-	+	+	+	+	
15	_____	+	+	-	-	+	-	+	+	-
16	_____	+	+	-	+	+	-	-	+	+
sums/runs 14 to 16	_____	_____	_____	_____	_____	_____	_____	_____	_____	_____
17	_____	+	+	-	+	+	-	-	-	-
18	_____	+	+	-	+	-	+	-	-	+
19	_____	+	+	+	-	-	+	-	+	-
sums/runs 17 to 19	_____	_____	_____	_____	_____	_____	_____	_____	_____	_____
20	_____	+	+	+	-	-	-	+	+	+
21	_____	+	+	+	-	-	-	-	-	-
22	_____	+	-	+	-	+	+	-	+	-
sums/runs 20 to 22	_____	_____	_____	_____	_____	_____	_____	_____	_____	_____
23	_____	+	-	+	+	+	+	+	+	-
24	_____	+	-	+	+	+	+	+	-	-
25	_____	+	-	+	+	-	-	+	-	+
sums/runs 23 to 25	_____	_____	_____	_____	_____	_____	_____	_____	_____	_____
26	_____	+	-	-	+	-	-	+	+	+
27	_____	+	-	-	-	-	+	-	-	+
28	_____	+	-	-	-	+	+	+	-	+
sums/runs 26 to 28		_____	_____	_____	_____	_____	_____	_____	_____	_____
Sums of Partial Sums		_____	_____	_____	_____	_____	_____	_____	_____	_____
Est. Contrasts for		A	B	C	D	E	F	G	H	I

CALCULATION WORKSHEET FOR BASIC 28-RUN DESIGNS
PAGE TWO OF FOUR PAGES

Run No.	Response	J	K	L	M	N	O	P	Q	R
1	_____	-	-	-	-	-	-	-	-	-
2	_____	+	-	-	-	-	+	+	+	+
3	_____	+	+	-	-	+	+	-	-	-
4	_____	+	+	+	+	-	+	-	-	+
sums/runs 1 to 4										
5	_____	-	+	+	+	+	+	+	+	+
6	_____	+	-	+	-	+	-	+	-	-
7	_____	-	-	+	+	+	-	-	-	+
sums/runs 5 to 7										
8	_____	-	+	+	-	-	+	+	+	-
9	_____	-	+	-	+	-	-	+	-	-
10	_____	+	-	-	+	-	+	-	+	+
sums/runs 8 to 10										
11	_____	+	-	-	+	+	-	+	-	+
12	_____	+	+	+	-	-	-	+	+	-
13	_____	-	+	-	-	+	-	-	+	+
sums/runs 11 to 13										
14	_____	-	-	+	+	+	+	-	+	-
15	_____	+	-	-	+	+	+	+	-	-
16	_____	+	-	+	-	+	-	+	+	+
sums/runs 14 to 16										
17	_____	-	+	+	-	+	-	-	-	+
18	_____	-	-	+	+	-	+	-	-	-
19	_____	-	-	+	-	-	+	+	-	+
sums/runs 17 to 19										
20	_____	+	+	-	-	-	+	-	-	+
21	_____	+	+	-	+	+	-	-	+	-
22	_____	+	+	+	+	-	-	-	+	-
sums/runs 20 to 22										
23	_____	-	-	-	-	-	-	-	+	+
24	_____	-	+	-	-	+	+	+	-	-
25	_____	+	-	+	-	+	+	-	+	-
sums/runs 23 to 25										
26	_____	-	-	-	+	-	-	+	+	-
27	_____	-	+	-	+	+	+	+	+	+
28	_____	+	+	+	+	-	-	+	-	+
sums/runs 26 to 28										
Sums of Partial Sums										
Est. Contrasts for		J	K	L	M	N	O	P	Q	R

CALCULATION WORKSHEET FOR BASIC 28-RUN DESIGNS
PAGE THREE OF FOUR PAGES

Run No.	Response	Contrast Labels S	T	U	V	W	X	Y	Z	1
1	_____	-	-	-	-	-	-	-	-	-
2	_____	+	+	+	+	+	-	+	+	+
3	_____	+	+	-	+	-	+	+	-	-
4	_____	-	+	+	-	-	+	-	+	+
sums/runs 1 to 4										
5	_____	-	-	-	+	+	-	+	-	-
6	_____	-	-	+	+	+	+	-	+	+
7	_____	+	+	-	-	+	+	+	+	-
sums/runs 5 to 7										
8	_____	-	+	-	+	-	+	-	-	+
9	_____	+	-	+	-	-	-	+	+	+
10	_____	-	-	+	-	+	+	-	-	-
sums/runs 8 to 10										
11	_____	+	+	-	+	-	-	-	-	+
12	_____	+	-	-	-	+	+	+	+	-
13	_____	-	+	+	-	+	-	+	-	+
sums/runs 11 to 13										
14	_____	+	-	+	+	-	-	-	+	-
15	_____	-	-	-	-	+	+	+	-	+
16	_____	-	+	-	-	-	-	-	+	-
sums/runs 14 to 16										
17	_____	+	-	+	+	+	+	-	-	+
18	_____	-	+	-	+	+	-	+	+	+
19	_____	+	+	+	-	-	+	+	-	-
sums/runs 17 to 19										
20	_____	+	-	-	+	+	-	-	+	-
21	_____	-	+	+	+	-	+	+	+	-
22	_____	+	+	-	-	+	-	-	-	+
sums/runs 20 to 22										
23	_____	-	-	-	+	-	+	+	+	+
24	_____	-	+	+	-	+	-	-	+	-
25	_____	+	-	+	-	-	-	+	-	+
sums/runs 23 to 25										
26	_____	+	+	+	+	+	+	-	-	-
27	_____	+	-	-	-	-	+	-	+	+
28	_____	-	-	+	+	-	-	+	-	-
sums/runs 26 to 28										
Sums of Partial Sums										
Est. Contrasts for		S	T	U	V	W	X	Y	Z	1

CALCULATION WORKSHEET
FOR BASIC 28-RUN DESIGNS
PAGE FOUR OF FOUR PAGES

SINGLE DEGREE OF FREEDOM ANOVA TABLE

Contrast Labels	Estimated Contrasts	Sums of Squares		Estimated Effects
A	_____	_____	_____	_____
B	_____	_____	_____	_____
C	_____	_____	_____	_____
D	_____	_____	_____	_____
E	_____	_____	_____	_____
F	_____	_____	_____	_____
G	_____	_____	_____	_____
H	_____	_____	_____	_____
I	_____	_____	_____	_____
J	_____	_____	_____	_____
K	_____	_____	_____	_____
L	_____	_____	_____	_____
M	_____	_____	_____	_____
N	_____	_____	_____	_____
O	_____	_____	_____	_____
P	_____	_____	_____	_____
Q	_____	_____	_____	_____
R	_____	_____	_____	_____
S	_____	_____	_____	_____
T	_____	_____	_____	_____
U	_____	_____	_____	_____
V	_____	_____	_____	_____
W	_____	_____	_____	_____
X	_____	_____	_____	_____
Y	_____	_____	_____	_____
Z	_____	_____	_____	_____
1	_____	_____	_____	_____

TOTAL Sum of Squares = _____

REFLECTED 28-RUN PLACKETT-BURMAN DESIGNS

Contrast Labels

Run	A	B	C	D	E	F	G	H	I	J	K	L	M	N	O	P	Q	R	S	T	U	V	W	X	Y	Z	1
1	+	+	+	+	+	+	+	+	+	+	+	+	+	+	+	+	+	+	+	+	+	+	+	+	+	+	+
2	+	+	+	+	-	+	+	+	+	-	+	+	+	+	-	-	-	-	-	-	-	-	-	+	-	-	-
3	+	+	+	-	-	-	+	-	-	-	-	+	+	-	-	+	+	+	-	-	+	-	+	-	-	+	+
4	+	+	+	-	+	+	-	-	+	-	-	-	-	+	-	+	+	-	+	-	-	+	+	-	+	-	-
5	+	+	-	-	+	+	+	-	+	+	-	-	-	-	-	-	-	-	+	+	+	-	-	+	-	+	+
6	+	+	-	+	+	-	+	-	-	-	+	-	+	-	+	-	+	+	+	+	-	-	-	-	+	-	-
7	+	+	-	+	-	+	-	+	-	+	+	-	-	-	+	+	+	-	-	-	+	+	-	-	-	-	+
8	+	-	-	+	-	+	-	+	-	+	-	-	+	+	-	-	-	+	+	-	+	-	+	-	+	+	-
9	+	-	-	-	-	+	+	-	-	+	-	+	-	+	+	-	+	+	-	+	-	+	+	+	-	-	-
10	+	-	-	-	-	-	+	+	-	-	+	+	-	+	-	+	-	-	+	+	-	+	-	-	+	+	+
11	+	-	-	-	+	-	-	+	+	-	+	+	-	-	+	-	+	-	-	-	+	-	+	+	+	+	-
12	+	-	+	-	+	-	-	+	+	-	-	-	+	+	+	-	-	+	-	+	+	+	-	-	-	-	+
13	+	-	+	+	+	-	-	-	-	+	-	+	+	-	+	+	-	-	+	-	-	+	-	+	-	+	-
14	+	-	+	+	-	-	-	-	+	+	+	-	-	-	-	+	-	+	-	+	-	-	+	+	+	-	+
15	-	-	+	+	-	+	-	-	+	-	+	+	-	-	-	-	+	+	+	+	+	+	-	-	-	+	-
16	-	-	+	-	-	+	+	-	-	-	+	-	+	-	+	-	-	-	+	-	+	+	+	+	+	-	+
17	-	-	+	-	-	+	+	+	+	+	-	-	+	-	+	+	+	+	-	+	-	-	-	-	+	+	-
18	-	-	+	-	+	-	+	+	-	+	+	-	-	+	-	+	+	+	+	-	+	-	-	+	-	-	-
19	-	-	-	+	+	-	+	-	+	+	+	-	+	+	-	-	+	-	-	-	-	+	+	-	-	+	+
20	-	-	-	+	+	+	-	-	-	-	-	+	+	+	-	+	+	-	-	+	+	-	-	+	+	-	+
21	-	-	-	+	+	+	+	+	+	-	-	+	-	-	+	+	-	+	+	-	-	-	+	-	-	-	+
22	-	+	-	+	-	-	+	-	+	-	-	-	-	+	+	+	-	+	-	-	+	+	-	+	+	+	-
23	-	+	-	-	-	-	-	-	+	+	+	+	+	+	+	+	-	-	+	+	+	-	+	-	-	-	-
24	-	+	-	-	-	-	-	+	+	+	-	+	+	-	-	-	+	+	+	-	-	+	-	+	+	-	+
25	-	+	-	-	+	+	-	+	-	-	+	-	+	-	-	+	-	+	-	+	-	+	+	+	-	+	-
26	-	+	+	-	+	+	-	-	-	+	+	+	-	+	+	-	-	+	-	-	-	-	-	-	+	+	+
27	-	+	+	+	+	-	+	+	-	+	-	+	-	-	-	-	-	-	-	+	+	+	+	-	+	-	-
28	-	+	+	+	-	-	-	+	-	-	-	-	-	+	+	-	+	-	+	+	-	-	+	+	-	+	+
	A	B	C	D	E	F	G	H	I	J	K	L	M	N	O	P	Q	R	S	T	U	V	W	X	Y	Z	1
	1	2	4	8	9	11	11	12	13	13	13	13	13	14	14	15	16	17	18	18	19	19	20	20	21	22	22

EXAMPLE OF REFLECTED 28-RUN DESIGN

The following data involve a completely different set of factors than those used in the example for the basic 28-run design.

DATA

Run	Response
1	117
2	110
3	111
4	93
5	92
6	103
7	99
8	89
9	110
10	89
11	123
12	111
13	96
14	93
15	97
16	77
17	91
18	100
19	101
20	110
21	104
22	101
23	100
24	89
25	91
26	77
27	91
28	100

SINGLE DEGREE OF FREEDOM ANOVA TABLE

Contrast Labels	Estimated Contrasts	Sums of Squares	Estimated Effects
A	107	408.893	
B	-17	10.321	
C	-37	48.893	
D	57	116.036	
E	53	100.321	
F	-51	92.893	
G	29	30.036	
H	43	66.036	
I	79	222.893	
J	-75	200.893	
K	-11	4.321	
L	83	246.036	
M	27	26.036	
N	51	92.893	
O	53	100.321	
P	25	22.321	
Q	123	540.321	
R	21	15.750	
S	-73	190.321	
T	25	22.321	
U	71	180.036	
V	-41	60.036	
W	35	43.750	
X	53	100.321	
Y	-79	222.893	
Z	-15	8.036	
1	-25	22.321	
Total		3195.250	

DATA COLLECTION WORKSHEET
FOR REFLECTED 28-RUN DESIGNS
PAGE ONE OF FOUR PAGES
IDENTIFICATION OF FACTORS AND FACTOR LEVELS

Delete Contrast Labels on this worksheet that do not represent a main effect.

Factor Names	Low Level	High Level	Factor Names	Low Level	High Level
A. _____	____	____	N. _____	____	____
B. _____	____	____	O. _____	____	____
C. _____	____	____	P. _____	____	____
D. _____	____	____	Q. _____	____	____
E. _____	____	____	R. _____	____	____
F. _____	____	____	S. _____	____	____
G. _____	____	____	T. _____	____	____
H. _____	____	____	U. _____	____	____
I. _____	____	____	V. _____	____	____
J. _____	____	____	W. _____	____	____
K. _____	____	____	X. _____	____	____
L. _____	____	____	Y. _____	____	____
M. _____	____	____	Z. _____	____	____
			1. _____	____	____

The Response Variable is _____

DATA COLLECTION WORKSHEET
PAGE TWO OF FOUR PAGES
CHANGES IN FACTOR LEVELS FOR REFLECTED 28-RUN DESIGNS

Begin with all factors set at their high levels. Changes in factor levels shown in boldface.

Run   Response

1

A+ B+ C+ D+ E+ F+ G+ H+ I+ J+ K+ L+ M+
N+ O+ P+ Q+ R+ S+ T+ U+ V+ W+ X+ Y+ Z+ 1+

2

A+ B+ C+ D+ **E-** F+ G+ H+ I+ **J-** K+ L+ M+
N+ **O-** **P-** **Q-** **R-** **S-** **T-** **U-** **V-** **W-** X+ **Y-** **Z-** **1-**

3

A+ B+ C+ **D-** **E-** **F-** G+ **H-** **I-** **J-** **K-** L+ M+
N- **O-** **P+** Q+ R+ **S-** **T-** U+ **V-** **W+** **X-** **Y-** Z+ 1+

4

A+ B+ C+ **D-** **E+** F+ **G-** **H-** I+ **J-** **K-** **L-** **M-**
N+ **O-** **P+** Q+ **R-** **S+** **T-** **U-** **V+** W+ **X-** **Y+** **Z-** **1-**

5

A+ B+ **C-** **D-** **E+** F+ **G+** **H-** I+ **J+** **K-** **L-** **M-**
N- **O-** **P-** **Q-** **R-** **S+** **T+** U+ **V-** **W-** **X+** **Y-** **Z+** **1+**

6

A+ B+ **C-** **D+** E+ **F-** G+ **H-** **I-** **J-** K+ **L-** **M+**
N- **O+** P- **Q+** R+ S+ T+ **U-** **V-** **W-** **X-** **Y+** **Z-** **1-**

7

A+ B+ **C-** D+ **E-** F+ **G-** H+ **I-** J+ K+ **L-** **M-**
N- **O+** **P+** Q+ **R-** **S-** **T-** U+ V+ **W-** **X-** **Y-** Z- **1+**

8

A+ **B-** **C-** D+ E- F+ **G-** H+ **I-** J+ **K-** **L-** **M+**
N+ **O-** **P-** **Q-** R+ **S+** **T-** U+ **V-** **W+** **X-** **Y+** Z+ **1-**

9

A+ **B-** **C-** **D-** E- F+ **G+** **H-** **I-** J+ **K-** **L+** **M-**
N+ **O+** P- **Q+** R+ **S-** **T+** **U-** **V+** W+ **X+** **Y-** **Z-** 1-

10

A+ **B-** **C-** **D-** E- **F-** G+ H+ **I-** **J-** K+ L+ **M-**
N+ **O-** **P+** **Q-** **R-** **S+** T+ **U-** **V+** **W-** **X-** **Y+** **Z+** **1+**

DATA COLLECTION WORKSHEET
PAGE THREE OF FOUR PAGES
CHANGES IN FACTOR LEVELS FOR REFLECTED 28-RUN DESIGNS

Factors that change level from previous run are shown in boldface.

Run   Response

11

A+ B- C- D- **E+** F- **G** **H+** **I+** J- **K+** **L+** **M-**
N- **O+** **P-** **Q+** R- **S-** T- **U+** V- **W+** **X+** Y+ Z+ *1-*

12

A+ B- **C+** D- **E+** F- **G-** **H+** I+ J- **K-** **L-** **M+**
N+ O+ P- **Q-** **R+** S- **T+** U+ **V+** **W-** **X-** Y- Z- 1+

13

A+ B- **C+** **D+** **E+** F- G- **H-** **I-** **J+** **K-** **L+** **M+**
N- O+ **P+** **Q-** R- **S+** T- **U-** **V+** W- **X+** Y- **Z+** *1-*

14

A+ B- **C+** D+ **E-** F- G- H- **I+** J+ **K+** **L-** **M-**
N- **O-** **P+** Q- **R+** **S-** **T+** U- **V-** **W+** X+ Y+ **Z-** 1+

15

A- B- C+ D+ **E-** **F+** G- **H-** **I+** **J-** **K+** **L+** M-
N- O- **P-** **Q+** **R+** **S+** **T+** **U+** **V+** **W-** X- Y- **Z+** 1-

16

A- B- C+ **D-** E- F+ **G+** **H-** **I-** J- **K+** **L-** **M+**
N- **O+** P- **Q-** **R-** **S+** **T-** **U+** V+ **W+** X+ Y+ **Z-** 1+

17

A- B- C+ **D-** E- F+ **G+** **H+** **I+** **J+** **K-** **L-** **M+**
N- **O+** **P+** **Q+** R- **S-** **T+** **U-** V- W- X- **Y+** **Z+** *1-*

18

A- B- C+ D- **E+** F- **G+** **H+** **I-** **J+** **K+** **L-** **M-**
N+ **O-** **P+** Q+ **R+** **S+** T- **U+** V- W- **X+** **Y-** **Z-** 1-

19

A- B- **C-** **D+** **E+** F- G+ **H-** **I+** J+ **K+** L- **M+**
N+ O- **P-** **Q+** **R-** **S-** **T-** U- **V+** **W+** **X-** Y- **Z+** 1+

DATA COLLECTION WORKSHEET
PAGE FOUR OF FOUR PAGES
CHANGES IN FACTOR LEVELS FOR REFLECTED 28-RUN DESIGNS

Factors that change level from previous run are shown in boldface.

Run   Response

20

A- B- C- D+ E+ **F+** **G-** H- I- J- K- L+ M+
N+ O- **P+** Q+ R- S- **T+** U+ **V-** **W-** X+ Y+ Z- *1+*

21

A- B- C- D+ E+ F+ **G+** **H+** **I+** J- K- L+ **M-**
N- O+ P+ **Q-** **R+** **S+** T- U- V- **W+** X- Y- Z- *1+*

22

A- **B+** C- D+ **E-** **F-** **G+** **H-** **I+** J- K- **L-** M-
N+ O+ P+ **Q-** **R+** **S-** T- **U+** **V+** **W-** **X+** Y+ **Z+** *1-*

23

A- B+ C- **D-** E- F- **G-** H- I+ **J+** K+ L+ M+
N+ O+ P+ Q- **R-** **S+** **T+** U+ **V-** **W+** X- Y- Z- *1-*

24

A- B+ C- D- E- F- G- **H+** I+ J+ **K-** L+ M+
N- **O-** P- **Q+** **R+** S+ **T-** **U-** **V+** **W-** **X+** Y+ Z- *1+*

25

A- B+ C- D- **E+** **F+** G- **H+** **I-** J- **K+** L- M+
N- O- **P+** **Q-** **R+** **S-** **T+** U- **V+** **W+** X+ **Y-** **Z+** *1-*

26

A- B+ **C+** D- **E+** F+ G- **H-** I- **J+** K+ **L+** **M-**
N+ **O+** **P-** Q- **R+** S- **T-** U- **V-** W- X- **Y+** **Z+** *1+*

27

A- B+ C+ **D+** E+ **F-** **G+** **H+** I- J+ **K-** L+ M-
N- **O-** P- Q- **R-** S- **T+** **U+** **V+** **W+** X- **Y+** **Z-** *1-*

28

A- B+ C+ D+ **E-** F- **G-** **H+** I- **J-** K- **L-** M-
N+ **O+** P- **Q+** **R-** **S+** T+ **U-** V- **W+** **X+** **Y-** **Z+** *1+*

CALCULATION WORKSHEET FOR REFLECTED 28-RUN DESIGNS
PAGE ONE OF FOUR PAGES

Run No.	Response	Contrast Labels A	B	C	D	E	F	G	H	I
1	_____	+	+	+	+	+	+	+	+	+
2	_____	+	+	+	+	-	+	+	+	+
3	_____	+	+	+	-	-	-	+	-	-
4	_____	+	+	+	-	+	+	-	-	+
sums/runs 1 to 4		___	___	___	___	___	___	___	___	___
5	_____	+	+	-	-	+	+	+	-	+
6	_____	+	+	-	+	+	-	+	-	-
7	_____	+	+	-	+	-	+	-	+	-
sums/runs 5 to 7		___	___	___	___	___	___	___	___	___
8	_____	+	-	-	+	-	+	-	+	-
9	_____	+	-	-	-	-	+	+	-	-
10	_____	+	-	-	-	-	-	+	+	-
sums/runs 8 to 10		___	___	___	___	___	___	___	___	___
11	_____	+	-	-	-	+	-	-	+	+
12	_____	+	-	+	-	+	-	-	+	+
13	_____	+	-	+	+	+	-	-	-	-
sums/runs 11 to 13		___	___	___	___	___	___	___	___	___
14	_____	+	-	+	+	-	-	-	-	+
15	_____	-	-	+	+	-	+	-	-	+
16	_____	-	-	+	-	-	+	+	-	-
sums/runs 14 to 16		___	___	___	___	___	___	___	___	___
17	_____	-	-	+	-	-	+	+	+	+
18	_____	-	-	+	-	+	-	+	+	-
19	_____	-	-	-	+	+	-	+	-	+
sums/runs 17 to 19		___	___	___	___	___	___	___	___	___
20	_____	-	-	-	+	+	+	-	-	-
21	_____	-	-	-	+	+	+	+	+	+
22	_____	-	+	-	+	-	-	+	-	+
sums/runs 20 to 22		___	___	___	___	___	___	___	___	___
23	_____	-	+	-	-	-	-	-	-	+
24	_____	-	+	-	-	-	-	-	+	+
25	_____	-	+	-	-	+	+	-	+	-
sums/runs 23 to 25		___	___	___	___	___	___	___	___	___
26	_____	-	+	+	-	+	+	-	-	-
27	_____	-	+	+	+	+	-	+	+	-
28	_____	-	+	+	+	-	-	-	+	-
sums/runs 26 to 28		___	___	___	___	___	___	___	___	___
Sums of Partial Sums		___	___	___	___	___	___	___	___	___
Est. Contrasts for		A	B	C	D	E	F	G	H	I

CALCULATION WORKSHEET FOR REFLECTED 28-RUN DESIGNS
PAGE TWO OF FOUR PAGES

Run No.	Response	Contrast Labels J	K	L	M	N	O	P	Q	R
1	_____	+	+	+	+	+	+	+	+	+
2	_____	−	+	+	+	+	−	−	−	−
3	_____	−	−	+	+	−	−	+	+	+
4	_____	−	−	−	−	+	−	+	+	−
sums/runs 1 to 4										
5	_____	+	−	−	−	−	−	−	−	−
6	_____	−	+	−	+	−	+	−	+	+
7	_____	+	+	−	−	−	+	+	+	−
sums/runs 5 to 7										
8	_____	+	−	−	+	+	−	−	−	+
9	_____	+	−	+	−	+	+	−	+	+
10	_____	−	+	+	−	+	−	+	−	−
sums/runs 8 to 10										
11	_____	−	+	+	−	−	+	−	+	−
12	_____	−	−	−	+	+	+	−	−	+
13	_____	+	−	+	+	−	+	+	−	−
sums/runs 11 to 13										
14	_____	+	+	−	−	−	−	+	−	+
15	_____	−	+	+	−	−	−	−	+	+
16	_____	−	+	−	+	−	+	−	−	−
sums/runs 14 to 16										
17	_____	+	−	−	+	−	+	+	+	−
18	_____	+	+	−	−	+	−	+	+	+
19	_____	+	+	−	+	+	−	−	+	−
sums/runs 17 to 19										
20	_____	−	−	+	+	+	−	+	+	−
21	_____	−	−	+	−	−	+	+	−	+
22	_____	−	−	−	−	+	+	+	−	+
sums/runs 20 to 22										
23	_____	+	+	+	+	+	+	+	−	−
24	_____	+	−	+	+	−	−	−	+	+
25	_____	−	+	−	+	−	−	+	−	+
sums/runs 23 to 25										
26	_____	+	+	+	−	+	+	−	−	+
27	_____	+	−	+	−	−	−	−	−	−
28	_____	−	−	−	−	+	+	−	+	−
sums/runs 26 to 28										
Sums of Partial Sums										
Est. Contrasts for		J	K	L	M	N	O	P	Q	R

CALCULATION WORKSHEET FOR REFLECTED 28-RUN DESIGNS
PAGE THREE OF FOUR PAGES

Run No.	Response	S	T	U	V	W	X	Y	Z	1
		Contrast Labels								
1	_____	+	+	+	+	+	+	+	+	+
2	_____	-	-	-	-	-	+	-	-	-
3	_____	-	-	+	-	+	-	-	+	+
4	_____	+	-	-	+	+	-	+	-	-
sums/runs 1 to 4		_____	_____	_____	_____	_____	_____	_____	_____	_____
5	_____	+	+	+	-	-	+	-	+	+
6	_____	+	+	-	-	-	-	+	-	-
7	_____	-	-	+	+	-	-	-	-	+
sums/runs 5 to 7		_____	_____	_____	_____	_____	_____	_____	_____	_____
8	_____	+	-	+	-	+	-	+	+	-
9	_____	-	+	-	+	+	+	-	-	-
10	_____	+	+	-	+	-	-	+	+	+
sums/runs 8 to 10		_____	_____	_____	_____	_____	_____	_____	_____	_____
11	_____	-	-	+	-	+	+	+	+	-
12	_____	-	+	+	+	-	-	-	-	+
13	_____	+	-	-	+	-	+	-	+	-
sums/runs 11 to 13		_____	_____	_____	_____	_____	_____	_____	_____	_____
14	_____	-	+	-	-	+	+	+	-	+
15	_____	+	+	+	+	-	-	-	+	-
16	_____	+	-	+	+	+	+	+	-	+
sums/runs 14 to 16		_____	_____	_____	_____	_____	_____	_____	_____	_____
17	_____	-	+	-	-	-	-	+	+	-
18	_____	+	-	+	-	-	+	-	-	-
19	_____	-	-	-	+	+	-	-	+	+
sums/runs 17 to 19		_____	_____	_____	_____	_____	_____	_____	_____	_____
20	_____	-	+	+	-	-	+	+	-	+
21	_____	+	-	-	-	+	-	-	-	+
22	_____	-	-	+	+	-	+	+	+	-
sums/runs 20 to 22		_____	_____	_____	_____	_____	_____	_____	_____	_____
23	_____	+	+	+	-	+	-	-	-	-
24	_____	+	-	-	+	-	+	+	-	+
25	_____	-	+	-	+	+	+	-	+	-
sums/runs 23 to 25		_____	_____	_____	_____	_____	_____	_____	_____	_____
26	_____	-	-	-	-	-	-	+	+	+
27	_____	-	+	+	+	+	-	+	-	-
28	_____	+	+	-	-	+	+	-	+	+
sums/runs 26 to 28		_____	_____	_____	_____	_____	_____	_____	_____	_____
Sums of Partial Sums		_____	_____	_____	_____	_____	_____	_____	_____	_____
Est. Contrasts for		S	T	U	V	W	X	Y	Z	1

Calculation Worksheet
for Reflected 28-Run Designs
Page Four of Four Pages

Single Degree of Freedom ANOVA Table

Contrast Labels	Estimated Contrasts	Sums of Squares		Estimated Effects
A	_____	_____	_____	_____
B	_____	_____	_____	_____
C	_____	_____	_____	_____
D	_____	_____	_____	_____
E	_____	_____	_____	_____
F	_____	_____	_____	_____
G	_____	_____	_____	_____
H	_____	_____	_____	_____
I	_____	_____	_____	_____
J	_____	_____	_____	_____
K	_____	_____	_____	_____
L	_____	_____	_____	_____
M	_____	_____	_____	_____
N	_____	_____	_____	_____
O	_____	_____	_____	_____
P	_____	_____	_____	_____
Q	_____	_____	_____	_____
R	_____	_____	_____	_____
S	_____	_____	_____	_____
T	_____	_____	_____	_____
U	_____	_____	_____	_____
V	_____	_____	_____	_____
W	_____	_____	_____	_____
X	_____	_____	_____	_____
Y	_____	_____	_____	_____
Z	_____	_____	_____	_____
1	_____	_____	_____	_____

TOTAL Sum of Squares _____

THREE-LEVEL PLACKETT-BURMAN DESIGNS

Plackett-Burman designs for factors at three levels each will require that the number of runs be a multiple of nine. The most commonly used three-level Plackett-Burman designs are the 9-run, the 18-run and the 27-run designs. The 9-run and 27-run designs can be said to be geometric three-level designs. These designs use all of the available degrees of freedom for factors at three levels. The existence of the 18-run design was only mentioned in a footnote to the original article. J.P. Burman had discovered this design after the article had gone to press, and he simply observed that it could only be used for a maximum of seven factors at three levels each. Since 7 three-level factors will only require 14 degrees of freedom for main effects, there are three extra degrees of freedom with the 18-run design. One of these three degrees of freedom is customarily used to include an eighth factor having two levels.

The need for two degrees of freedom to estimate the main effect for each three-level factor will reduce the number of factors that can be considered by each design. For example, while an 8-run design can be used to study as many as 7 two-level factors, a 9-run design will accommodate 4 factors at three levels each. While a 28-run design will accommodate up to 27 two-level factors, the 27-run design can only handle up to 13 factors at three levels each. This reduction in the number of factors makes these designs less efficient than the two-level designs for screening large numbers of factors.

The three-level designs give up the ability to study a larger number of factors in order to investigate the possibility of non-linear effects upon the response. Unfortunately this trade-off has a side effect. While one gains the ability to check for non-linear effects, one looses the ability to easily discriminate between main effects and even the simplest of interactions. Unlike the geometric two-level designs, the geometric three-level designs do not have a simple and clean confounding pattern. One simple two-factor interaction may be confounded with four or more different contrasts. In order to disentangle the simple two-factor interaction effects from the various main effects one will generally have to run three different rotations of a given three-level design. Thus, in the presence of interaction effects, the 9-run design turns into a 27-run design, while the 27-run design becomes an 81-run design. Moreover, at least for the 27-run design, some interactions will still be confounded with some main effects even after the 81 runs of the three rotations! Thus, in the presence of interaction effects, the three-level Plackett-Burman designs can be very expensive to use.

For these reasons, the three-level Plackett-Burman designs must be considered to be exactly what they were intended to be: designs for discovering main effects only. They are of greatest use in those situations where theory or experience has shown that there are few interaction effects. If one is in doubt concerning interaction effects, one will do much better to screen out the inert factors using geometric two-level designs, and then to study the active factors in greater depth with designs that are less highly fractionated than the three-level Plackett-Burman designs.

An alternative to the use of these three-level designs consists of adding a centroid point to one of the geometric two-level designs. The response at the centroid would not be used in computing the contrasts for the different effects, but it would be included on the response plot as a visual check on the possibility of non-linear effects. If the response values for the centroid are inconsistent with the average of the responses in diagonally opposite corners of the design, then non-linear effects are likely. This approach preserves the screening nature of the two-level designs and the concise confounding patterns that allow one to check for two-factor interactions, while providing at least a simple check for non-linearity of effects.

In the following tables the "low" level for a factor will be denoted by a minus symbol (-). The "medium" level for each factor will be denoted by a lower case letter "o." The "high" level of each factor will be denoted by a plus symbol (+). As with the two-level designs, one must carefully define the levels of each of the factors in order to avoid confusion in performing the experiment.

The "linear contrast" for each factor will compare the low level (-) with the high level (+). For a quantitative factor this is equivalent to testing for a significant linear effect. The coefficients for this linear contrast are found from the columns of the design matrix. The plus sign (+) will denote a coefficient of +1, the minus sign (-) will denote a coefficient of -1, and the letter "o" will denote a contrast coefficient of 0.

The "quadratic contrast" for a factor will compare the average of the responses at the high and low levels with the average response at the middle level. For a quantitative factor with equally spaced levels this is equivalent to testing for a significant quadratic effect. The contrast coefficients for the quadratic contrast will be given in a separate array from the design matrix. The contrast labels for such quadratic contrasts will have an exponent of 2.

THE LOW-LEVEL 9-RUN PLACKETT-BURMAN DESIGN

	Treatment Combinations Linear Contrasts					Quadratic Contrasts			
Run	A	B	C	D		A^2	B^2	C^2	D^2
1	-	-	-	-		-1	-1	-1	-1
2	-	o	o	o		-1	2	2	2
3	-	+	+	+		-1	-1	-1	-1
4	o	+	-	o		2	-1	-1	2
5	o	-	o	+		2	-1	2	-1
6	o	o	+	-		2	2	-1	-1
7	+	o	-	+		-1	2	-1	-1
8	+	+	o	-		-1	-1	2	-1
9	+	-	+	o		-1	-1	-1	2

DATA COLLECTION WORKSHEET FOR LOW-LEVEL 9-RUN DESIGN

Factor Names	Low-Level	Mid-Level	High-Level
A. _____	_____	_____	_____
B. _____	_____	_____	_____
C. _____	_____	_____	_____
D. _____	_____	_____	_____

Changes in Factor Levels for Low-Level 9-Run Design
Changes in factor levels are shown in boldface

Run	Begin with all four factors at their low level:				Response
1	**A-**	**B-**	**C-**	**D-**	_____
2	A-	**Bo**	**Co**	**Do**	_____
3	A-	**B+**	**C+**	**D+**	_____
4	**Ao**	B+	**C-**	**Do**	_____
5	Ao	**B-**	**Co**	**D+**	_____
6	Ao	**Bo**	**C+**	**D-**	_____
7	**A+**	Bo	**C-**	**D+**	_____
8	A+	**B+**	**Co**	**D-**	_____
9	A+	**B-**	**C+**	**Do**	_____

THE MID-LEVEL 9-RUN PLACKETT-BURMAN DESIGN

	Treatment Combinations Linear Contrasts					Quadratic Contrasts			
Run	A	B	C	D		A^2	B^2	C^2	D^2
1	0	0	0	0		2	2	2	2
2	0	+	+	+		2	-1	-1	-1
3	0	-	-	-		2	-1	-1	-1
4	+	-	0	+		-1	-1	2	-1
5	+	0	+	-		-1	2	-1	-1
6	+	+	-	0		-1	-1	-1	2
7	-	+	0	-		-1	-1	2	-1
8	-	-	+	0		-1	-1	-1	2
9	-	0	-	+		-1	2	-1	-1

DATA COLLECTION WORKSHEET FOR MID-LEVEL 9-RUN DESIGN

Factor Names	Low-Level	Mid-Level	High-Level
A. _____	_____	_____	_____
B. _____	_____	_____	_____
C. _____	_____	_____	_____
D. _____	_____	_____	_____

Changes in Factor Levels for Mid-Level 9-Run Design
Changes in factor levels are shown in boldface

Run	Begin with all four factors at their middle level:				Response
1	**Ao**	**Bo**	**Co**	**Do**	_____
2	Ao	**B+**	**C+**	**D+**	_____
3	Ao	**B-**	**C-**	**D-**	_____
4	**A+**	B-	**Co**	**D+**	_____
5	A+	**Bo**	**C+**	**D-**	_____
6	A+	**B+**	**C-**	**Do**	_____
7	**A-**	B+	**Co**	**D-**	_____
8	A-	**B-**	**C+**	**Do**	_____
9	A-	**Bo**	**C-**	**D+**	_____

THE HIGH-LEVEL 9-RUN PLACKETT-BURMAN DESIGN

	Treatment Combinations Linear Contrasts				Quadratic Contrasts			
Run	A	B	C	D	A^2	B^2	C^2	D^2
1	+	+	+	+	-1	-1	-1	-1
2	+	-	-	-	-1	-1	-1	-1
3	+	0	0	0	-1	2	2	2
4	-	0	+	-	-1	2	-1	-1
5	-	+	-	0	-1	-1	-1	2
6	-	-	0	+	-1	-1	2	-1
7	0	-	+	0	2	-1	-1	-1
8	0	0	-	+	2	2	-1	2
9	0	+	0	-	2	-1	2	-1

DATA COLLECTION WORKSHEET FOR HIGH-LEVEL 9-RUN DESIGN

Factor Names		Low-Level	Mid-Level	High-Level
A.	_____	_____	_____	_____
B.	_____	_____	_____	_____
C.	_____	_____	_____	_____
D.	_____	_____	_____	_____

Changes in Factor Levels for High-Level 9-Run Design
Changes in factor levels are shown in boldface

Run	Begin with all four factors at their high level:				Response
1	**A+**	**B+**	**C+**	**D+**	_____
-1	A+	**B-**	**C-**	**D-**	_____
3	A+	**Bo**	**Co**	**Do**	_____
4	**A-**	Bo	**C+**	**D-**	_____
5	A-	**B+**	**C-**	**Do**	_____
6	A-	**B-**	**Co**	**D+**	_____
7	**Ao**	B-	**C+**	**Do**	_____
8	Ao	**Bo**	**C-**	**D+**	_____
9	Ao	**B+**	**Co**	**D-**	_____

THE LOW-LEVEL 18-RUN PLACKETT-BURMAN DESIGN

Contrast Label A represents a two-level factor. Only 15 degrees of freedom are used for contrasts. Since there will be a total of 17 degrees of fredom the two extra degrees of freedom may be used to obtain a two degree-of-freedom Mean Square Error term for testing the sums of squares for the contrasts. The Error Sum of Squares would be found by subtracting the 15 SS(C) values from the Total Sum of Squares. Since this would be *a priori* pooling, one would use the regular F-ratio critical values.

Treatment Combinations and
Linear Contrast Coefficients   Quadratic Contrast Coefficients

Run	A	B	C	D	E	F	G	H	B^2	C^2	D^2	E^2	F^2	G^2	H^2
1	-	-	-	-	-	-	-	-	-1	-1	-1	-1	-1	-1	-1
2	-	-	o	o	o	o	o	o	-1	2	2	2	2	2	2
3	-	-	+	+	+	+	+	+	-1	-1	-1	-1	-1	-1	-1
4	-	o	+	o	+	o	-	-	2	-1	2	-1	2	-1	-1
5	-	o	o	-	o	-	+	+	2	2	-1	2	-1	-1	-1
6	-	o	-	+	-	+	o	o	2	-1	-1	-1	-1	2	2
7	-	+	-	+	o	o	+	-	-1	-1	-1	2	2	-1	-1
8	-	+	o	-	+	+	-	o	-1	2	-1	-1	-1	-1	2
9	-	+	+	o	-	-	o	+	-1	-1	2	-1	-1	2	-1
10	+	+	+	+	o	-	-	o	-1	-1	-1	2	-1	-1	2
11	+	+	o	o	-	+	+	-	-1	2	2	-1	-1	-1	-1
12	+	+	-	-	+	o	o	+	-1	-1	-1	-1	2	2	-1
13	+	o	-	o	+	-	+	o	2	-1	2	-1	-1	-1	2
14	+	o	o	+	-	o	-	+	2	2	-1	-1	2	-1	-1
15	+	o	+	-	o	+	o	-	2	-1	-1	2	-1	2	-1
16	+	-	+	-	-	o	+	o	-1	-1	-1	-1	2	-1	2
17	+	-	o	+	+	-	o	-	-1	2	-1	-1	-1	2	-1
18	+	-	-	o	o	+	-	+	-1	-1	2	2	-1	-1	-1

DATA COLLECTION WORKSHEET
FOR THE LOW-LEVEL 18-RUN DESIGN

Delete labels on this page that do not correspond to a main effect.

Factor Names	Low-Level	Mid-Level	High-Level
A. _____	_____		_____
B. _____	_____	_____	_____
C. _____	_____	_____	_____
D. _____	_____	_____	_____
E. _____	_____	_____	_____
F. _____	_____	_____	_____
G. _____	_____	_____	_____
H. _____	_____	_____	_____

The Response Variable is _____

DATA COLLECTION WORKSHEET
FOR THE LOW-LEVEL 18-RUN DESIGN

Changes in Factor Levels for Low-Level 18-Run Sequence

Changes in factor levels are shown in boldface

Run	Begin with all factors at their low level:								Response
1	**A-**	**B-**	**C-**	**D-**	**E-**	**F-**	**G-**	**H-**	_____
2	A-	B-	**Co**	**Do**	**Eo**	**Fo**	**Go**	**Ho**	_____
3	A-	B-	**C+**	**D+**	**E+**	**F+**	**G+**	**H+**	_____
4	A-	**Bo**	C+	**Do**	E+	**Fo**	**G-**	**H-**	_____
5	A-	Bo	**Co**	**D-**	**Eo**	**F-**	**G+**	**H+**	_____
6	A-	Bo	**C-**	**D+**	**E-**	**F+**	**Go**	**Ho**	_____
7	A-	**B+**	C-	D+	**Eo**	**Fo**	**G+**	**H-**	_____
8	A-	B+	**Co**	**D-**	**E+**	**F+**	**G-**	**Ho**	_____
9	A-	B+	**C+**	**Do**	**E-**	**F-**	**Go**	**H+**	_____
10	**A+**	B+	C+	**D+**	**Eo**	F-	**G-**	**Ho**	_____
11	A+	B+	**Co**	**Do**	**E-**	**F+**	**G+**	**H-**	_____
12	A+	B+	**C+**	**D-**	**E+**	**Fo**	**Go**	**H+**	_____
13	A+	**Bo**	C+	**Do**	E+	**F-**	**G+**	**Ho**	_____
14	A+	Bo	**Co**	**D+**	**E-**	**Fo**	**G-**	**H+**	_____
15	A+	Bo	**C+**	**D-**	**Eo**	**F+**	**Go**	**H-**	_____
16	A+	**B-**	C+	D-	**E-**	**Fo**	**G+**	**Ho**	_____
17	A+	B-	**Co**	**D+**	**E+**	**F-**	**Go**	**H-**	_____
18	A+	B-	**C-**	**Do**	**Eo**	**F+**	**G-**	**H+**	_____

THE MID-LEVEL 18-RUN PLACKETT-BURMAN DESIGN

Contrast Label A represents a two-level factor. Only 15 degrees of freedom are used for contrasts. Since there will be a total of 17 degrees of fredom the two extra degrees of freedom may be used to obtain a two degree-of-freedom Mean Square Error term for testing the sums of squares for the contrasts. The Error Sum of Squares would be found by subtracting the 15 SS(C) values from the Total Sum of Squares. Since this would be *a priori* pooling, one would use the regular F-ratio critical values.

Treatment Combinations and
Linear Contrast Coefficients   Quadratic Contrast Coefficients

Run	A	B	C	D	E	F	G	H	B^2	C^2	D^2	E^2	F^2	G^2	H^2
1	-	o	o	o	o	o	o	o	2	2	2	2	2	2	2
2	-	o	+	+	+	+	+	+	2	-1	-1	-1	-1	-1	-1
3	-	o	-	-	-	-	-	-	2	-1	-1	-1	-1	-1	-1
4	-	+	-	+	-	+	o	o	-1	-1	-1	-1	-1	2	2
5	-	+	+	o	+	o	-	-	-1	-1	2	-1	2	-1	-1
6	-	+	o	-	o	-	+	+	-1	2	-1	2	-1	-1	-1
7	-	-	o	-	+	+	-	o	-1	2	-1	-1	-1	-1	2
8	-	-	+	o	-	-	o	+	-1	-1	2	-1	-1	2	-1
9	-	-	-	+	o	o	+	-	-1	-1	-1	2	2	-1	-1
10	+	-	-	-	+	o	o	+	-1	-1	-1	-1	2	2	-1
11	+	-	+	+	o	-	-	o	-1	-1	-1	2	-1	-1	2
12	+	-	o	o	-	+	+	-	-1	2	2	-1	-1	-1	-1
13	+	+	o	+	-	o	-	+	-1	2	-1	-1	2	-1	-1
14	+	+	+	-	o	+	o	-	-1	-1	-1	2	-1	2	-1
15	+	+	-	o	+	-	+	o	-1	-1	2	-1	-1	-1	2
16	+	o	-	o	o	+	-	+	2	-1	2	2	-1	-1	-1
17	+	o	+	-	-	o	+	o	2	-1	-1	-1	2	-1	2
18	+	o	o	+	+	-	o	-	2	2	-1	-1	-1	2	-1

Data Collection Worksheet
for the Mid-Level 18-Run Design

Delete labels on this page that do not correspond to a main effect.

Factor Names	Low-Level	Mid-Level	High-Level
A. _____	_____		_____
B. _____	_____	_____	_____
C. _____	_____	_____	_____
D. _____	_____	_____	_____
E. _____	_____	_____	_____
F. _____	_____	_____	_____
G. _____	_____	_____	_____
H. _____	_____	_____	_____

The Response Variable is   _____

DATA COLLECTION WORKSHEET
FOR THE MID-LEVEL 18-RUN DESIGN

Changes in Factor Levels for Mid-Level 18-Run Sequence

Changes in factor levels are shown in boldface

Begin with Factor A at its low level and Factors B through H at their middle level:

Run:									Response
1	**A-**	**Bo**	Co	Do	Eo	Fo	Go	Ho	_____
2	A-	Bo	**C+**	**D+**	**E+**	**F+**	**G+**	**H+**	_____
3	A-	Bo	**C-**	**D-**	**E-**	**F-**	**G-**	**H-**	_____
4	A-	**B+**	C-	**D+**	E-	**F+**	Go	Ho	_____
5	A-	B+	**C+**	**Do**	**E+**	**Fo**	**G-**	**H-**	_____
6	A-	B+	**Co**	**D-**	**Eo**	F-	**G+**	**H+**	_____
7	A-	**B-**	Co	**D-**	**E+**	**F+**	**G-**	**Ho**	_____
8	A-	B-	**C+**	**Do**	**E-**	F-	**Go**	**H+**	_____
9	A-	B-	**C-**	**D+**	**Eo**	Fo	**G+**	**H-**	_____
10	**A+**	B-	C-	**D-**	**E+**	Fo	**Go**	**H+**	_____
11	A+	B-	**C+**	**D+**	**Eo**	**F-**	**G-**	**Ho**	_____
12	A+	B-	**C-**	**Do**	**E-**	**F+**	**G+**	**H-**	_____
13	A+	**B+**	C-	**D+**	E-	**Fo**	**G-**	**H+**	_____
14	A+	B+	**C+**	**D-**	**Eo**	**F+**	**Go**	**H-**	_____
15	A+	B+	**C-**	**Do**	**E+**	**F-**	**G+**	**Ho**	_____
16	A+	**Bo**	C-	Do	**Eo**	**F+**	**G-**	**H+**	_____
17	A+	Bo	**C+**	**D-**	**E-**	**Fo**	**G+**	**Ho**	_____
18	A+	Bo	**Co**	**D+**	**E+**	**F-**	**Go**	**H-**	_____

THE HIGH-LEVEL 18-RUN PLACKETT-BURMAN DESIGN

Contrast Label A represents a two-level factor. Only 15 degrees of freedom are used for contrasts. Since there will be a total of 17 degrees of fredom the two extra degrees of freedom may be used to obtain a two degree-of-freedom Mean Square Error term for testing the sums of squares for the contrasts. The Error Sum of Squares would be found by subtracting the 15 SS(C) values from the Total Sum of Squares. Since this would be *a priori* pooling, one would use the regular F-ratio critical values.

Treatment Combinations and Linear Contrast Coefficients | Quadratic Contrast Coefficients

Run	A	B	C	D	E	F	G	H	B^2	C^2	D^2	E^2	F^2	G^2	H^2
1	+	+	+	+	+	+	+	+	-1	-1	-1	-1	-1	-1	-1
2	+	+	-	-	-	-	-	-	-1	-1	-1	-1	-1	-1	-1
3	+	+	o	o	o	o	o	o	-1	2	2	2	2	2	2
4	+	-	o	-	o	-	+	+	-1	2	-1	2	-1	-1	-1
5	+	-	-	+	-	+	o	o	-1	-1	-1	-1	-1	2	2
6	+	-	+	o	+	o	-	-	-1	-1	2	-1	2	-1	-1
7	+	o	+	o	-	-	o	+	2	-1	2	-1	-1	2	-1
8	+	o	-	+	o	o	+	-	2	-1	-1	2	2	-1	-1
9	+	o	o	-	+	+	-	o	2	2	-1	-1	-1	-1	2
10	-	o	o	o	-	+	+	-	2	2	2	-1	-1	-1	-1
11	-	o	-	-	+	o	o	+	2	-1	-1	-1	2	2	-1
12	-	o	+	+	o	-	-	o	2	-1	-1	2	-1	-1	2
13	-	-	+	-	o	+	o	-	-1	-1	-1	2	-1	2	-1
14	-	-	-	o	+	-	+	o	-1	-1	2	-1	-1	-1	2
15	-	-	o	+	-	o	-	+	-1	2	-1	-1	2	-1	-1
16	-	+	o	+	+	-	o	-	-1	2	-1	-1	-1	2	-1
17	-	+	-	o	o	+	-	+	-1	-1	2	2	-1	-1	-1
18	-	+	+	-	-	o	+	o	-1	-1	-1	-1	2	-1	2

DATA COLLECTION WORKSHEET
FOR THE HIGH-LEVEL 18-RUN DESIGN

Delete labels on this page that do not correspond to a main effect.

Factor Names	Low-Level	Mid-Level	High-Level
A. _____	_____		_____
B. _____	_____	_____	_____
C. _____	_____	_____	_____
D. _____	_____	_____	_____
E. _____	_____	_____	_____
F. _____	_____	_____	_____
G. _____	_____	_____	_____
H. _____	_____	_____	_____

The Response Variable is _____

Data Collection Worksheet
for the High-Level 18-Run Design

Changes in Factor Levels for High-Level 18-Run Sequence

Changes in factor levels are shown in boldface

Run	Begin with all factors at their high level:								Response
1	**A+**	**B+**	**C+**	**D+**	**E+**	**F+**	**G+**	**H+**	_____
2	A+	B+	**C-**	**D-**	**E-**	**F-**	**G-**	**H-**	_____
3	A+	B+	**Co**	**Do**	**Eo**	**Fo**	**Go**	**Ho**	_____
4	A+	**B-**	Co	**D-**	Eo	**F-**	**G+**	**H+**	_____
5	A+	B-	**C-**	**D+**	**E-**	**F+**	**Go**	**Ho**	_____
6	A+	B-	**C+**	**Do**	**E+**	**Fo**	**G-**	**H-**	_____
7	A+	**Bo**	C+	Do	**E-**	**F-**	**Go**	**H+**	_____
8	A+	Bo	**C-**	**D+**	**Eo**	**Fo**	**G+**	**H-**	_____
9	A+	Bo	**Co**	**D-**	**E+**	**F+**	**G-**	**Ho**	_____
10	**A-**	Bo	Co	**Do**	**E-**	F+	**G+**	**H-**	_____
11	A-	Bo	**C-**	**D-**	**E+**	**Fo**	**Go**	**H+**	_____
12	A-	Bo	**Co**	**D+**	**Eo**	**F-**	**G-**	**Ho**	_____
13	A-	**B-**	Co	**D-**	Eo	**F+**	**Go**	**H-**	_____
14	A-	B-	**C-**	**Do**	**E+**	**F-**	**G+**	**Ho**	_____
15	A-	B-	**Co**	**D+**	**E-**	**Fo**	**G-**	**H+**	_____
16	A-	**B+**	Co	D+	**E+**	**F-**	**Go**	**H-**	_____
17	A-	B+	**C-**	**Do**	**Eo**	**F+**	**G-**	**H+**	_____
18	A-	B+	**C+**	**D-**	**E-**	**Fo**	**G+**	**Ho**	_____

THE LOW-LEVEL 27-RUN PLACKETT-BURMAN DESIGN

Treatment Combinations and Linear Contrast Coefficients

Run	A	B	C	D	E	F	G	H	I	J	K	L	M
1	-	-	-	-	-	-	-	-	-	-	-	-	-
2	-	-	-	-	o	o	o	o	+	o	o	+	o
3	-	-	-	-	+	+	+	+	o	+	+	o	+
4	-	o	o	+	+	+	+	-	+	-	-	+	o
5	-	o	o	+	-	-	-	o	o	o	o	o	+
6	-	o	o	+	o	o	o	+	-	+	+	-	-
7	-	+	+	o	o	o	o	-	o	-	-	o	+
8	-	+	+	o	+	+	+	o	-	o	o	-	-
9	-	+	+	o	-	-	-	+	+	+	+	+	o
10	o	+	-	+	-	o	+	+	+	-	o	-	+
11	o	+	-	+	o	+	-	-	o	o	+	+	-
12	o	+	-	+	+	-	o	o	-	+	-	o	o
13	o	-	o	o	+	-	o	+	o	-	o	+	-
14	o	-	o	o	-	o	+	-	-	o	+	o	o
15	o	-	o	o	o	+	-	o	+	+	-	-	+
16	o	o	+	-	o	+	-	+	-	-	o	o	o
17	o	o	+	-	+	-	o	-	+	o	+	-	+
18	o	o	+	-	-	o	+	o	o	+	-	+	-
19	+	o	-	o	-	+	o	o	o	-	+	-	o
20	+	o	-	o	o	-	+	+	-	o	-	+	+
21	+	o	-	o	+	o	-	-	+	+	o	o	-
22	+	+	o	-	+	o	-	o	-	-	+	+	+
23	+	+	o	-	-	+	o	+	+	o	-	o	-
24	+	+	o	-	o	-	+	-	o	+	o	-	o
25	+	-	+	+	o	-	+	o	+	-	+	o	-
26	+	-	+	+	+	o	-	+	o	o	-	-	o
27	+	-	+	+	-	+	o	-	-	+	o	+	+

THE LOW-LEVEL 27-RUN PLACKETT-BURMAN DESIGN

Quadratic Contrast Coefficients

Run	A^2	B^2	C^2	D^2	E^2	F^2	G^2	H^2	I^2	J^2	K^2	L^2	M^2
1	-1	-1	-1	-1	-1	-1	-1	-1	-1	-1	-1	-1	-1
2	-1	-1	-1	-1	2	2	2	2	-1	2	2	-1	2
3	-1	-1	-1	-1	-1	-1	-1	-1	2	-1	-1	2	-1
4	-1	2	2	-1	-1	-1	-1	-1	-1	-1	-1	-1	2
5	-1	2	2	-1	-1	-1	-1	2	2	2	2	2	-1
6	-1	2	2	-1	2	2	2	-1	-1	-1	-1	-1	-1
7	-1	-1	-1	2	2	2	2	-1	2	-1	-1	2	-1
8	-1	-1	-1	2	-1	-1	-1	2	-1	2	2	-1	-1
9	-1	-1	-1	2	-1	-1	-1	-1	-1	-1	-1	-1	2
10	2	-1	-1	-1	-1	2	-1	-1	-1	-1	2	-1	-1
11	2	-1	-1	-1	2	-1	-1	-1	2	2	-1	-1	-1
12	2	-1	-1	-1	-1	-1	2	2	-1	-1	-1	2	2
13	2	-1	2	2	-1	-1	2	-1	2	-1	2	-1	-1
14	2	-1	2	2	-1	2	-1	-1	-1	2	-1	2	2
15	2	-1	2	2	2	-1	-1	2	-1	-1	-1	-1	-1
16	2	2	-1	-1	2	-1	-1	-1	-1	-1	2	2	2
17	2	2	-1	-1	-1	-1	2	-1	-1	2	-1	-1	-1
18	2	2	-1	-1	-1	2	-1	2	2	-1	-1	-1	-1
19	-1	2	-1	2	-1	-1	2	2	2	-1	-1	-1	2
20	-1	2	-1	2	2	-1	-1	-1	-1	2	-1	-1	-1
21	-1	2	-1	2	-1	2	-1	-1	-1	-1	2	2	-1
22	-1	-1	2	-1	-1	2	-1	2	-1	-1	-1	-1	-1
23	-1	-1	2	-1	-1	-1	2	-1	-1	2	-1	2	-1
24	-1	-1	2	-1	2	-1	-1	-1	2	-1	2	-1	2
25	-1	-1	-1	-1	2	-1	-1	2	-1	-1	-1	2	-1
26	-1	-1	-1	-1	-1	2	-1	-1	2	2	-1	-1	2
27	-1	-1	-1	-1	-1	-1	2	-1	-1	-1	2	-1	-1

Data Collection Worksheet
for the Low-Level 27-Run Design

Delete labels on this page that do not correspond to a main effect.

Factor Names	Low-Level	Mid-Level	High-Level
A. _____	_____	_____	_____
B. _____	_____	_____	_____
C. _____	_____	_____	_____
D. _____	_____	_____	_____
E. _____	_____	_____	_____
F. _____	_____	_____	_____
G. _____	_____	_____	_____
H. _____	_____	_____	_____
I. _____	_____	_____	_____
J. _____	_____	_____	_____
K. _____	_____	_____	_____
L. _____	_____	_____	_____
M. _____	_____	_____	_____

The Response Variable is   _____

DATA COLLECTION WORKSHEET
FOR THE LOW-LEVEL 27-RUN DESIGN

Changes in Factor Levels for Low-Level 27-Run Sequence
Changes in factor levels are shown in boldface

Run	Begin with all factors at their low level:													Response
1	A-	B-	C-	D-	E-	F-	G-	H-	I-	J-	K-	L-	M-	_____
2	A-	B-	C-	D-	Eo	Fo	Go	Ho	I+	Jo	Ko	L+	Mo	_____
3	A-	B-	C-	D-	E+	F+	G+	H+	Io	J+	K+	Lo	M+	_____
4	A-	Bo	Co	D+	E+	F+	G+	H-	I+	J-	K-	L+	Mo	_____
5	A-	Bo	Co	D+	E-	F-	G-	Ho	Io	Jo	Ko	Lo	M+	_____
6	A-	Bo	Co	D+	Eo	Fo	Go	H+	I-	J+	K+	L-	M-	_____
7	A-	B+	C+	Do	Eo	Fo	Go	H-	Io	J-	K-	Lo	M+	_____
8	A-	B+	C+	Do	E+	F+	G+	Ho	I-	Jo	Ko	L-	M-	_____
9	A-	B+	C+	Do	E-	F-	G-	H+	I+	J+	K+	L+	Mo	_____
10	Ao	B+	C-	D+	E-	Fo	G+	H+	I+	J-	Ko	L-	M+	_____
11	Ao	B+	C-	D+	Eo	F+	G-	H-	Io	Jo	K+	L+	M-	_____
12	Ao	B+	C-	D+	E+	F-	Go	Ho	I-	J+	K-	Lo	Mo	_____
13	Ao	B-	Co	Do	E+	F-	Go	H+	Io	J-	Ko	L+	M-	_____
14	Ao	B-	Co	Do	E-	Fo	G+	H-	I-	Jo	K+	Lo	Mo	_____
15	Ao	B-	Co	Do	Eo	F+	G-	Ho	I+	J+	K-	L-	M+	_____
16	Ao	Bo	C+	D-	Eo	F+	G-	H+	I-	J-	Ko	Lo	Mo	_____
17	Ao	Bo	C+	D-	E+	F-	Go	H-	I+	Jo	K+	L-	M+	_____
18	Ao	Bo	C+	D-	E-	Fo	G+	Ho	Io	J+	K-	L+	M-	_____
19	A+	Bo	C-	Do	E-	F+	Go	Ho	Io	J-	K+	L-	Mo	_____
20	A+	Bo	C-	Do	Eo	F-	G+	H+	I-	Jo	K-	L+	M+	_____
21	A+	Bo	C-	Do	E+	Fo	G-	H-	I+	J+	Ko	Lo	M-	_____
22	A+	B+	Co	D-	E+	Fo	G-	Ho	I-	J-	K+	L+	M+	_____
23	A+	B+	Co	D-	E-	F+	Go	H+	I+	Jo	K-	Lo	M-	_____
24	A+	B+	Co	D-	Eo	F-	G+	H-	Io	J+	Ko	L-	Mo	_____
25	A+	B-	C+	D+	Eo	F-	G+	Ho	I+	J-	K+	Lo	M-	_____
26	A+	B-	C+	D+	E+	Fo	G-	H+	Io	Jo	K-	L-	Mo	_____
27	A+	B-	C+	D+	E-	F+	Go	H-	I-	J+	Ko	L+	M+	_____

181

THE MID-LEVEL 27-RUN PLACKETT-BURMAN DESIGN

Treatment Combinations and Linear Contrast Coefficients

Run	A	B	C	D	E	F	G	H	I	J	K	L	M
1	o	o	o	o	o	o	o	o	o	o	o	o	o
2	o	o	o	o	+	+	+	+	−	+	+	−	+
3	o	o	o	o	−	−	−	−	+	−	−	+	−
4	o	+	+	−	−	−	−	o	−	o	o	−	+
5	o	+	+	−	o	o	o	+	+	+	+	+	−
6	o	+	+	−	+	+	+	−	o	−	−	o	o
7	o	−	−	+	+	+	+	o	+	o	o	+	−
8	o	−	−	+	−	−	−	+	o	+	+	o	o
9	o	−	−	+	o	o	o	−	−	−	−	−	+
10	+	−	o	−	o	+	−	−	−	o	+	o	−
11	+	−	o	−	+	−	o	o	+	+	−	−	o
12	+	−	o	−	−	o	+	+	o	−	o	+	+
13	+	o	+	+	−	o	+	−	+	o	+	−	o
14	+	o	+	+	o	+	−	o	o	+	−	+	+
15	+	o	+	+	+	−	o	+	−	−	o	o	−
16	+	+	−	o	+	−	o	−	o	o	+	+	+
17	+	+	−	o	−	o	+	o	−	+	−	o	−
18	+	+	−	o	o	+	−	+	+	−	o	−	o
19	−	+	o	+	o	−	+	+	+	o	−	o	+
20	−	+	o	+	+	o	−	−	o	+	o	−	−
21	−	+	o	+	−	+	o	o	−	−	+	+	o
22	−	−	+	o	−	+	o	+	o	o	−	−	−
23	−	−	+	o	o	−	+	−	−	+	o	+	o
24	−	−	+	o	+	o	−	o	+	−	+	o	+
25	−	o	−	−	+	o	−	+	−	o	−	+	o
26	−	o	−	−	−	+	o	−	+	+	o	o	+
27	−	o	−	−	o	−	+	o	o	−	+	−	−

THE MID-LEVEL 27-RUN PLACKETT-BURMAN DESIGN

Quadratic Contrast Coefficients

Run	A^2	B^2	C^2	D^2	E^2	F^2	G^2	H^2	I^2	J^2	K^2	L^2	M^2
1	2	2	2	2	2	2	2	2	2	2	2	2	2
2	2	2	2	2	-1	-1	-1	-1	-1	-1	-1	-1	-1
3	2	2	2	2	-1	-1	-1	-1	-1	-1	-1	-1	-1
4	2	-1	-1	-1	-1	-1	-1	2	-1	2	2	-1	-1
5	2	-1	-1	-1	2	2	2	-1	-1	-1	-1	-1	-1
6	2	-1	-1	-1	-1	-1	-1	-1	2	-1	-1	2	2
7	2	-1	-1	-1	-1	-1	-1	2	-1	2	2	-1	-1
8	2	-1	-1	-1	-1	-1	-1	-1	2	-1	-1	2	2
9	2	-1	-1	-1	2	2	2	-1	-1	-1	-1	-1	-1
10	-1	-1	2	-1	2	-1	-1	-1	-1	2	-1	2	-1
11	-1	-1	2	-1	-1	-1	2	2	-1	-1	-1	-1	2
12	-1	-1	2	-1	-1	2	-1	-1	2	-1	2	-1	-1
13	-1	2	-1	-1	-1	2	-1	-1	-1	2	-1	-1	2
14	-1	2	-1	-1	2	-1	-1	2	2	-1	-1	-1	-1
15	-1	2	-1	-1	-1	-1	2	-1	-1	-1	2	2	-1
16	-1	-1	-1	2	-1	-1	2	-1	2	2	-1	-1	-1
17	-1	-1	-1	2	-1	2	-1	2	-1	-1	-1	2	-1
18	-1	-1	-1	2	2	-1	-1	-1	-1	-1	2	-1	2
19	-1	-1	2	-1	2	-1	-1	-1	-1	2	-1	2	-1
20	-1	-1	2	-1	-1	2	-1	-1	2	-1	2	-1	-1
21	-1	-1	2	-1	-1	-1	2	2	-1	-1	-1	-1	2
22	-1	-1	-1	2	-1	-1	2	-1	2	2	-1	-1	-1
23	-1	-1	-1	2	2	-1	-1	-1	-1	-1	2	-1	2
24	-1	-1	-1	2	-1	2	-1	2	-1	-1	-1	2	-1
25	-1	2	-1	-1	-1	2	-1	-1	-1	2	-1	-1	2
26	-1	2	-1	-1	-1	-1	2	-1	-1	-1	2	2	-1
27	-1	2	-1	-1	2	-1	-1	2	2	-1	-1	-1	-1

DATA COLLECTION WORKSHEET
FOR THE MID-LEVEL 27-RUN DESIGN

Delete labels on this page that do not correspond to a main effect.

Factor Names		Low-Level	Mid-Level	High-Level
A.	_____	_____	_____	_____
B.	_____	_____	_____	_____
C.	_____	_____	_____	_____
D.	_____	_____	_____	_____
E.	_____	_____	_____	_____
F.	_____	_____	_____	_____
G.	_____	_____	_____	_____
H.	_____	_____	_____	_____
I.	_____	_____	_____	_____
J.	_____	_____	_____	_____
K.	_____	_____	_____	_____
L.	_____	_____	_____	_____
M.	_____	_____	_____	_____

The Response Variable is   _____

Data Collection Worksheet
for the Mid-Level 27-Run Design

Changes in Factor Levels for Mid-Level 27-Run Sequence
Changes in factor levels are shown in boldface

Run	Begin with all factors at their middle level:													Response
1	Ao	Bo	Co	Do	Eo	Fo	Go	Ho	Io	Jo	Ko	Lo	Mo	_____
2	Ao	Bo	Co	Do	E+	F+	G+	H+	I-	J+	K+	L-	M+	_____
3	Ao	Bo	Co	Do	E-	F-	G-	H-	I+	J-	K-	L+	M-	_____
4	Ao	B+	C+	D-	E-	F-	G-	Ho	I-	Jo	Ko	L-	M+	_____
5	Ao	B+	C+	D-	Eo	Fo	Go	H+	I+	J+	K+	L+	M-	_____
6	Ao	B+	C+	D-	E+	F+	G+	H-	Io	J-	K-	Lo	Mo	_____
7	Ao	B-	C-	D+	E+	F+	G+	Ho	I+	Jo	Ko	L+	M-	_____
8	Ao	B-	C-	D+	E-	F-	G-	H+	Io	J+	K+	Lo	Mo	_____
9	Ao	B-	C-	D+	Eo	Fo	Go	H-	I-	J-	K-	L-	M+	_____
10	A+	B-	Co	D-	Eo	F+	G-	H-	I-	Jo	K+	Lo	M-	_____
11	A+	B-	Co	D-	E+	F-	Go	Ho	I+	J+	K-	L-	Mo	_____
12	A+	B-	Co	D-	E-	Fo	G+	H+	Io	J-	Ko	L+	M+	_____
13	A+	Bo	C+	D+	E-	Fo	G+	H-	I+	Jo	K+	L-	Mo	_____
14	A+	Bo	C+	D+	Eo	F+	G-	Ho	Io	J+	K-	L+	M+	_____
15	A+	Bo	C+	D+	E+	F-	Go	H+	I-	J-	Ko	Lo	M-	_____
16	A+	B+	C-	Do	E+	F-	Go	H-	Io	Jo	K+	L+	M+	_____
17	A+	B+	C-	Do	E-	Fo	G+	Ho	I-	J+	K-	Lo	M-	_____
18	A+	B+	C-	Do	Eo	F+	G-	H+	I+	J-	Ko	L-	Mo	_____
19	A-	B+	Co	D+	Eo	F-	G+	H+	I+	Jo	K-	Lo	M+	_____
20	A-	B+	Co	D+	E+	Fo	G-	H-	Io	J+	Ko	L-	M-	_____
21	A-	B+	Co	D+	E-	F+	Go	Ho	I-	J-	K+	L+	Mo	_____
22	A-	B-	C+	Do	E-	F+	Go	H+	Io	Jo	K-	L-	M-	_____
23	A-	B-	C+	Do	Eo	F-	G+	H-	I-	J+	Ko	L+	Mo	_____
24	A-	B-	C+	Do	E+	Fo	G-	Ho	I+	J-	K+	Lo	M+	_____
25	A-	Bo	C-	D-	E+	Fo	G-	H+	I-	Jo	K-	L+	Mo	_____
26	A-	Bo	C-	D-	E-	F+	Go	H-	I+	J+	Ko	Lo	M+	_____
27	A-	Bo	C-	D-	Eo	F-	G+	Ho	Io	J-	K+	L-	M-	_____

THE HIGH-LEVEL 27-RUN PLACKETT-BURMAN DESIGN

Treatment Combinations and Linear Contrast Coefficients

Run	A	B	C	D	E	F	G	H	I	J	K	L	M
1	+	+	+	+	+	+	+	+	+	+	+	+	+
2	+	+	+	+	-	-	-	-	o	-	-	o	-
3	+	+	+	+	o	o	o	o	-	o	o	-	o
4	+	-	-	o	o	o	o	+	o	+	+	o	-
5	+	-	-	o	+	+	+	-	-	-	-	-	o
6	+	-	-	o	-	-	-	o	+	o	o	+	+
7	+	o	o	-	-	-	-	+	-	+	+	-	o
8	+	o	o	-	o	o	o	-	+	-	-	+	+
9	+	o	o	-	+	+	+	o	o	o	o	o	-
10	-	o	+	o	+	-	o	o	o	+	-	+	o
11	-	o	+	o	-	o	+	+	-	-	o	o	+
12	-	o	+	o	o	+	-	-	+	o	+	-	-
13	-	+	-	-	o	+	-	o	-	+	-	o	+
14	-	+	-	-	+	-	o	+	+	-	o	-	-
15	-	+	-	-	-	o	+	-	o	o	+	+	o
16	-	-	o	+	-	o	+	o	+	+	-	-	-
17	-	-	o	+	o	+	-	+	o	-	o	+	o
18	-	-	o	+	+	-	o	-	-	o	+	o	+
19	o	-	+	-	+	o	-	-	-	+	o	+	-
20	o	-	+	-	-	+	o	o	+	-	+	o	o
21	o	-	+	-	o	-	+	+	o	o	-	-	+
22	o	o	-	+	o	-	+	-	+	+	o	o	o
23	o	o	-	+	+	o	-	o	o	-	+	-	+
24	o	o	-	+	-	+	o	+	-	o	-	+	-
25	o	+	o	o	-	+	o	-	o	+	o	-	+
26	o	+	o	o	o	-	+	o	-	-	+	+	-
27	o	+	o	o	+	o	-	+	+	o	-	o	o

THE HIGH-LEVEL 27-RUN PLACKETT-BURMAN DESIGN

Quadratic Contrast Coefficients

Run	A^2	B^2	C^2	D^2	E^2	F^2	G^2	H^2	I^2	J^2	K^2	L^2	M^2
1	-1	-1	-1	-1	-1	-1	-1	-1	-1	-1	-1	-1	-1
2	-1	-1	-1	-1	-1	-1	-1	-1	2	-1	-1	2	-1
3	-1	-1	-1	-1	2	2	2	2	-1	2	2	-1	2
4	-1	-1	-1	2	2	2	2	-1	2	-1	-1	2	-1
5	-1	-1	-1	2	-1	-1	-1	-1	-1	-1	-1	-1	2
6	-1	-1	-1	2	-1	-1	-1	2	-1	2	2	-1	-1
7	-1	2	2	-1	-1	-1	-1	-1	-1	-1	-1	-1	2
8	-1	2	2	-1	2	2	2	-1	-1	-1	-1	-1	-1
9	-1	2	2	-1	-1	-1	-1	2	2	2	2	2	-1
10	-1	2	-1	2	-1	-1	2	2	2	-1	-1	-1	2
11	-1	2	-1	2	-1	2	-1	-1	-1	-1	2	2	-1
12	-1	2	-1	2	2	-1	-1	-1	-1	2	-1	-1	-1
13	-1	-1	-1	-1	2	-1	-1	2	-1	-1	-1	2	-1
14	-1	-1	-1	-1	-1	-1	2	-1	-1	-1	2	-1	-1
15	-1	-1	-1	-1	-1	2	-1	-1	2	2	-1	-1	2
16	-1	-1	2	-1	-1	2	-1	2	-1	-1	-1	-1	-1
17	-1	-1	2	-1	2	-1	-1	-1	2	-1	2	-1	2
18	-1	-1	2	-1	-1	-1	2	-1	-1	2	-1	2	-1
19	2	-1	-1	-1	-1	2	-1	-1	-1	-1	2	-1	-1
20	2	-1	-1	-1	-1	-1	2	2	-1	-1	-1	2	2
21	2	-1	-1	-1	2	-1	-1	-1	2	2	-1	-1	-1
22	2	2	-1	-1	2	-1	-1	-1	-1	-1	2	2	2
23	2	2	-1	-1	-1	2	-1	2	2	-1	-1	-1	-1
24	2	2	-1	-1	-1	-1	2	-1	-1	2	-1	-1	-1
25	2	-1	2	2	-1	-1	2	-1	2	-1	2	-1	-1
26	2	-1	2	2	2	-1	-1	2	-1	-1	-1	-1	-1
27	2	-1	2	2	-1	2	-1	-1	-1	2	-1	2	2

DATA COLLECTION WORKSHEET
FOR THE HIGH-LEVEL 27-RUN DESIGN

Delete labels on this page that do not correspond to a main effect.

Factor Names	Low-Level	Mid-Level	High-Level
A. _____	_____	_____	_____
B. _____	_____	_____	_____
C. _____	_____	_____	_____
D. _____	_____	_____	_____
E. _____	_____	_____	_____
F. _____	_____	_____	_____
G. _____	_____	_____	_____
H. _____	_____	_____	_____
I. _____	_____	_____	_____
J. _____	_____	_____	_____
K. _____	_____	_____	_____
L. _____	_____	_____	_____
M. _____	_____	_____	_____

The Response Variable is   _____

DATA COLLECTION WORKSHEET
FOR THE HIGH-LEVEL 27-RUN DESIGN

Changes in Factor Levels for High-Level 27-Run Sequence
Changes in factor levels are shown in boldface

Run	Begin with all factors at their high level:													Response
1	A+	B+	C+	D+	E+	F+	G+	H+	I+	J+	K+	L+	M+	_____
2	A+	B+	C+	D+	E-	F-	G-	H-	Io	J-	K-	Lo	M-	_____
3	A+	B+	C+	D+	Eo	Fo	Go	Ho	I-	Jo	Ko	L-	Mo	_____
4	A+	B-	C-	Do	Eo	Fo	Go	H+	Io	J+	K+	Lo	M-	_____
5	A+	B-	C-	Do	E+	F+	G+	H-	I-	J-	K-	L-	Mo	_____
6	A+	B-	C-	Do	E-	F-	G-	Ho	I+	Jo	Ko	L+	M+	_____
7	A+	Bo	Co	D-	E-	F-	G-	H+	I-	J+	K+	L-	Mo	_____
8	A+	Bo	Co	D-	Eo	Fo	Go	H-	I+	J-	K-	L+	M+	_____
9	A+	Bo	Co	D-	E+	F+	G+	Ho	Io	Jo	Ko	Lo	M-	_____
10	A-	Bo	C+	Do	E+	F-	Go	Ho	Io	J+	K-	L+	Mo	_____
11	A-	Bo	C+	Do	E-	Fo	G+	H+	I-	J-	Ko	Lo	M+	_____
12	A-	Bo	C+	Do	Eo	F+	G-	H-	I+	Jo	K+	L-	M-	_____
13	A-	B+	C-	D-	Eo	F+	G-	Ho	I-	J+	K-	Lo	M+	_____
14	A-	B+	C-	D-	E+	F-	Go	H+	I+	J-	Ko	L-	M-	_____
15	A-	B+	C-	D-	E-	Fo	G+	H-	Io	Jo	K+	L+	Mo	_____
16	A-	B-	Co	D+	E-	Fo	G+	Ho	I+	J+	K-	L-	M-	_____
17	A-	B-	Co	D+	Eo	F+	G-	H+	Io	J-	Ko	L+	Mo	_____
18	A-	B-	Co	D+	E+	F-	Go	H-	I-	Jo	K+	Lo	M+	_____
19	Ao	B-	C+	D-	E+	Fo	G-	H-	I-	J+	Ko	L+	M-	_____
20	Ao	B-	C+	D-	E-	F+	Go	Ho	I+	J-	K+	Lo	Mo	_____
21	Ao	B-	C+	D-	Eo	F-	G+	H+	Io	Jo	K-	L-	M+	_____
22	Ao	Bo	C-	D+	Eo	F-	G+	H-	I+	J+	Ko	Lo	Mo	_____
23	Ao	Bo	C-	D+	E+	Fo	G-	Ho	Io	J-	K+	L-	M+	_____
24	Ao	Bo	C-	D+	E-	F+	Go	H+	I-	Jo	K-	L+	M-	_____
25	Ao	B+	Co	Do	E-	F+	Go	H-	Io	J+	Ko	L-	M+	_____
26	Ao	B+	Co	Do	Eo	F-	G+	Ho	I-	J-	K+	L+	M-	_____
27	Ao	B+	Co	Do	E+	Fo	G-	H+	I+	Jo	K-	Lo	Mo	_____

PART FOUR

HYBRID DESIGNS:

SOME DESIGNS THAT COMBINE

FACTORS HAVING TWO LEVELS

WITH FACTORS HAVING MORE THAN TWO LEVELS

When studying quantitative factors the levels of each factor will consist of different values of some measurable quantity such as time, pressure, temperature, feed rate, concentration, etc. With such factors the underlying continuum will allow one to initiate an investigation of the effect of the factor upon the response variable by using only two points out of the continuum. It is this aspect of quantitative factors that justifies the recommendation of the two-level designs for the initial screening studies. In particular, with such factors, the geometric two-level designs of Part One of these tables will yield the greatest clarity of results with the minimum number of experimental runs.

However, one may occasionally wish to use more than two levels when studying some quantitative factors. The designs in this section provide a means of doing this.

With qualitative factors one cannot manipulate the choice of factor levels as easily as with quantitative factors. With qualitative factors there may be no underlying natural order or continuum to use in defining "extreme levels" of the factor. Quite often the levels of a qualitative factor are simply categories that may be listed in any order. When this happens, one will have to respect the number of discrete levels that are inherent in any qualitative factor, and this number may be greater than two.

When faced with either of the situations described in the previous paragraphs one will need effective designs that combine factors with two levels with factors having more than two levels. Several such designs are given in this portion of these tables. While such designs are, in theory, easy to obtain from the designs given earlier, in practice there are some pitfalls that complicate this task. This is the reason that the following designs are listed.

While the 12-Run design is a special design, having its own set of contrasts coefficients and its own confounding pattern, the remainder of the designs included in this section are based upon one of the geometric two-level designs from Part One. Because of this, the contrast coefficients will remain the same and one may use the same computational programs for the analysis of these combined designs as for the corresponding geometric Plackett-Burman designs. In addition, by building these combined designs upon the geometric two-level Plackett-Burman Designs one may take advantage of the known confounding patterns in interpreting the various contrasts.

Since the standard notation for factorial designs expresses the number of factors (k) and the number of levels (L) as L^k, this notation has been adopted for these tables as a convenience. In some instances the degree of fractionation is indicated with the design.

As before, the emphasis has been upon the main effects and two-factor interactions. By convention, the three-level factors will have a "linear" main effect contrast and a "quadratic" main effect contrast even though these terms have no clear meaning when applied to qualitative factors. They are simply names to use in identifying certain contrasts between the levels of the qualitative factors.

If it is especially difficult to change the levels of a particular factor, then one may rearrange the order of the runs to minimize the number of changes in level for that factor. When this is done, one should undo this rearrangement of the responses prior to the computations. The responses will need to be arranged in the order shown in the design arrays in order to utilize the geometric Plackett-Burman contrast coefficients and the confounding patterns given. Otherwise the contrasts will not make the stated comparisons. In other words, one may perform the runs in any order, but prior to analysis one should list the responses by their corresponding run in the order shown in the design arrays.

The use of the computations for the geometric two-level Plackett-Burman designs makes most of the designs in this section very easy to use. The use of the confounding patterns given will facilitate the interpretation of the results. Because of the presence of factors at more than two levels, one may not always be able to completely separate the main effects and the two-factor interactions, but one can still narrow the list of possibilities and can be aware of possible alternative explanations for the behavior of the response variable.

A BASIC EIGHT-RUN DESIGN WITH A FOUR-LEVEL FACTOR

The following design is based upon the Basic 8-Run Plackett-Burman Design. It can accommodate one factor at 4 levels and up to four factors at 2 levels each.

A BASIC 4×2^4 DESIGN_____

	Treatment Combinations									
Run	A	D	E	F	G					
1	1	-	-	-	-		-	-	-
2	1	+	+	+	+		-	-	-
3	2	+	+	-	-		-	+	+
4	2	-	-	+	+		-	+	+
5	3	-	+	+	-		+	+	-
6	3	+	-	-	+		+	+	-
7	4	+	-	+	-		+	-	+
8	4	-	+	-	+		+	-	+
		D	E	F	G		A	B	C

Contrast Labels

Treatment combinations are defined by the first five elements in each row.

Contrast coefficients are defined by the seven columns on the right of this array. These coefficients are the same as those of the Basic 8-Run Plackett-Burman Design.

The Confounding Pattern for this design is shown in the following table. Contrasts A, B and C represent the three degrees of freedom for the four-level Factor A. Contrast A will compare levels 1 and 2 with levels 3 and 4. Denote this as Main Effect A. Contrast B will compare levels 1 and 4 with levels 2 and 3. Denote this as Main Effect A'. Contrast C will compare levels 1 and 3 with levels 2 and 4. Denote this as Main Effect A".

Contrast Label	A	B	C	D	E	F	G
Main Effect	A	A'	A"	D	E	F	G
Interaction	-DE	-DF	-DG	-AE	-AD	-A'D	-A"D
	-FG	-EG	-EF	-A'F	-A"F	-A"E	-A'E
			-A"G	-A'G	-AG	-AF

A Reflected Eight-Run Design With A Four-Level Factor

The following design is based upon the Reflected 8-Run Plackett-Burman Design. It can accommodate one factor at 4 levels and up to four factors at 2 levels each.

A REFLECTED 4×2^4 DESIGN_____

	Treatment Combinations							
Run	A	D	E	F	G			
1	4	+	+	+	+	+	+	+
2	4	-	-	-	-	+	+	+
3	3	-	-	+	+	+	-	-
4	3	+	+	-	-	+	-	-
5	2	+	-	-	+	-	-	+
6	2	-	+	+	-	-	-	+
7	1	-	+	-	+	-	+	-
8	1	+	-	+	-	-	+	-
	D	E	F	G	A	B	C
		Contrast Labels						

Treatment combinations for each run are defined by the first five elements in each row.

Contrast coefficients are defined by the seven columns on the right of this array. These coefficients are the same as those of the Reflected 8-Run Plackett-Burman Design.

The Confounding Pattern for this design is shown in the following table. Main Effects A, A' and A" represent the same comparisons defined with the Basic Design given earlier. Note that Contrast B represents the negative of Main Effect A', and the two-factor interactions involving A' do not change sign between the basic design and this reflected design. These departures from the behavior of the confounding pattern for the two-level Plackett Burman designs are unavoidable when using four level factors with these designs.

Contrast Label	A	B	C	D	E	F	G
Main Effect	**A**	**-A'**	**A"**	D	E	F	G
Interaction	DE	DF	DG	AE	AD	-A'D	A"D
	FG	EG	EF	-A'F	A"F	A"E	-A'E
				A"G	-A'G	AG	AF

194

EIGHT-RUN DESIGNS WITH A THREE-LEVEL FACTOR

The four-level factor may be converted into a three-level factor by substituting any one specific level for Level 4:

Four-Level Factor		Three-Level Factor
Level 1	stays	Level 1
Level 2	stays	Level 2
Level 3	stays	Level 3
Level 4	**becomes**	**Level 1 or Level 2 or Level 3**

Once such a substitution has been made it must be used in both the basic and reflected designs in order to enable one to combine the results from the two studies. Since any one of the three levels may be used in this way, the experimenter is free to choose just which of the three levels will have twice as much data as the other levels.

A natural consequence of making a three-level factor appear to have four levels is that there will be one more degree of freedom than one would expect. Instead of two degrees of freedom, there will be three degrees of freedom for the three level factor. Since the contrasts are still orthogonal, there will have to be a redundancy in the main effects represented by these contrasts. If, for example, Level 4 is replaced by Level 2, then Main Effect A (Contrast A) will compare Levels 1 and 2 with levels 2 and 3, and Main Effect A' (Contrast B) will also compare Levels 1 and 2 with Levels 2 and 3! Since Contrast A will still be orthogonal to Contrast B, these two comparisons will be independent of each other. Thus, the Main Effects A and A' will separately and independently represent the same Main Effect. Main Effect A" (Contrast C) will compare Levels 1 and 3 with Level 2. Similar results will be found when Level 4 is replaced by Level 1 or Level 3.

These redundancies are sometimes quite useful in undoing the confounding when combining a basic design with a reflected design. For example, even though the two-factor interactions involving A' do not change signs, those involving A do change signs. Since, in this case, A and A' represent the same Main Effect, both A'F and AF represent the same interaction effect. This is a useful tool in undoing the algebraic jigsaw puzzle represented by the alias equations.

The confounding pattern for these 8-run designs will remain the same as shown above even though Factor A is taken to represent a three-level factor.

Any significant effect involving a four-level factor or a three-level factor should be examined by means of a response plot. Interpretations based upon such plots will usually be better than those based solely upon a consideration of the contrast coefficients.

A ONE HALF REPLICATE OF A $2^3 \times 3$ DESIGN USING 12 RUNS

While the previous designs can accommodate one factor at three levels and up to four factors at two levels each, the combination of both versions of the design will require 16 runs. If one is only using three factors at two levels and one factor at three levels a one-half replicate will only require 12 runs. This design can be thought of as a Plackett-Burman 4-Run design crossed with a factor at three levels. The contrasts will be somewhat different from those for the other designs, but the low degree of confounding will allow most effects to be teased out with a little simple arithmetic.

TREATMENT COMBINATIONS

Run	A	B	C	D
1	+	+	+	+
2	+	-	-	+
3	-	-	+	+
4	-	+	-	+
5	-	+	-	o
6	-	-	+	o
7	+	-	-	o
8	+	+	+	o
9	+	+	-	-
10	+	-	+	-
11	-	-	-	-
12	-	+	+	-

Treatment combinations are defined by rows in this matrix.

Contrasts for
A One Half Replicate of a $2^3 \times 3$ Design Using 12 Runs

Run	A	B	C	D	D^2	AB C	AC B	AD BC	BC A	BD AC	CD AB
1	+	+	+	+	-1	0	0	+	0	+	+
2	+	-	-	+	-1	0	0	+	0	-	-
3	-	-	+	+	-1	0	0	-	0	-	+
4	-	+	-	+	-1	0	0	-	0	+	-
5	0	0	0	0	2	-	+	0	-	0	0
6	0	0	0	0	2	+	-	0	-	0	0
7	0	0	0	0	2	-	-	0	+	0	0
8	0	0	0	0	2	+	+	0	+	0	0
9	+	+	-	-	-1	0	0	-	0	-	+
10	+	-	+	-	-1	0	0	-	0	+	-
11	-	-	-	-	-1	0	0	+	0	+	+
12	-	+	+	-	-1	0	0	+	0	-	-

To find estimates of those interaction effects which are confounded with a main effect (such as AB) subtract the $\hat{l}$ value for the confounded main effect (the effect for C) from the $\hat{l}$ value for the contrast involving that interaction (the contrast for AB + C).

To find estimates of other interaction effects (such as CD) subtract the estimated effect for the other interaction (such as AB) from the estimated effect for the contrast (the contrast for CD + AB).

An interaction effect will be judged to be significant when its estimated effect is as large as that of a significant main effect.

EXAMPLE FOR THE
ONE HALF REPLICATE OF A $2^3 \times 3$ DESIGN USING 12 RUNS

The following data are artificial. They are simply provided to illustrate how to tease out the effects.

Contrasts and Data _____   ANOVA Table _____

Run	A	B	C	D	D^2	AB C	AC B	AD BC	BC A	BD AC	CD AB	Response
1	+	+	+	+	-1	0	0	+	0	+	+	75
2	+	-	-	+	-1	0	0	+	0	-	-	9
3	-	-	+	+	-1	0	0	-	0	-	+	5
4	-	+	-	+	-1	0	0	-	0	+	-	7
5	0	0	0	0	2	-	+	0	-	0	0	0
6	0	0	0	0	2	+	-	0	-	0	0	0
7	0	0	0	0	2	-	-	0	+	0	0	0
8	0	0	0	0	2	+	+	0	+	0	0	60
9	+	+	-	-	-1	0	0	-	0	-	+	19
10	+	-	+	-	-1	0	0	-	0	+	-	17
11	-	-	-	-	-1	0	0	+	0	+	+	13
12	-	+	+	-	-1	0	0	+	0	-	-	15

Factor	Estimated Contrast	Sum of Squares	Estimated Contrast Effect
A	80	800.0	20
B	72	648.0	18
C	64	512.0	16
D	32	128.0	8
D^2	40	66.67	5
AB+C	60	900.0	30
AC+B	60	900.0	30
AD+BC	64	512.0	16
BC+A	60	900.0	30
BD+AC	64	512.0	16
CD+AB	64	512.0	16
Total		6390.67	

198

EXAMPLE FOR THE
ONE HALF REPLICATE OF A $2^3 \times 3$ DESIGN USING 12 RUNS

The first five contrasts provide estimates of the main effects that are not confounded with any two-factor interactions. These estimates may be used to isolate the estimated effects of AB, AC and BC. The logic and the arithmetic are shown below.

The estimated contrast effect for (AB+C) is 30. The estimated effect for C alone is 16. Thus, the estimated effect of AB is 30 - 16 = 14. If this interaction effect is as large as that of a significant main effect, this interaction will be judged to also be significant.

The estimated contrast effect for (AC+B) is 30. The estimated effect for B alone is 18. Thus, the estimated effect of AC is 30 - 18 = 12.

The estimated contrast effect for (BC+A) is 30. The estimated effect for A alone is 20. Thus, the estimated effect of BC is 30 - 20 = 10.

Given these estimates, one may also isolate the estimated effects of AD, BD, and CD in a manner similar to that shown above.

The estimated contrast effect for (AD+BC) is 16. The estimated effect for BC alone is 10. Thus, the estimated effect of AD is 16 - 10 = 6.

The estimated contrast effect for (BD+AC) is 16. The estimated effect for AC alone is 12. Thus, the estimated effect of BD is 16 - 12 = 4.

The estimated contrast effect for (CD+AB) is 16. The estimated effect for AB alone is 14. Thus, the estimated effect of CD is 16 - 14 = 2.

A Basic 16-Run Design With An Eight-Level Factor

The following design is based upon the Basic 16-Run Plackett-Burman Design. It can accommodate one factor at eight levels and up to eight factors at 2 levels each. When used with nine factors it is a (1/128)th replicate of the fully crossed design.

A BASIC 8×2^8 DESIGN

TREATMENT COMBINATIONS

Run	A	H	I	J	K	L	M	N	O	A	B	C	D	E	F	G
1	1	−	−	−	−	−	−	−	−	−	−	−	−	−	−	−
2	1	+	+	+	+	+	+	+	+	−	−	−	−	−	−	−
3	2	+	+	+	+	−	−	−	−	−	−	−	+	+	+	+
4	2	−	−	−	−	+	+	+	+	−	−	−	+	+	+	+
5	3	−	−	+	+	+	+	−	−	−	+	+	+	+	−	−
6	3	+	+	−	−	−	−	+	+	−	+	+	+	+	−	−
7	4	+	+	−	−	+	+	−	−	−	+	+	−	−	+	+
8	4	−	−	+	+	−	−	+	+	−	+	+	−	−	+	+
9	5	−	+	+	−	−	+	+	−	+	+	−	−	+	+	−
10	5	+	−	−	+	+	−	−	+	+	+	−	−	+	+	−
11	6	+	−	−	+	−	+	+	−	+	+	−	+	−	−	+
12	6	−	+	+	−	+	−	−	+	+	+	−	+	−	−	+
13	7	−	+	−	+	+	−	+	−	+	−	+	+	−	+	−
14	7	+	−	+	−	−	+	−	+	+	−	+	+	−	+	−
15	8	+	−	+	−	+	−	+	−	+	−	+	−	+	−	+
16	8	−	+	−	+	−	+	−	+	+	−	+	−	+	−	+

| | H | I | J | K | L | M | N | O | A | B | C | D | E | F | G |

CONTRAST LABELS

Treatment combinations are defined by the first nine elements in each row.

Contrast coefficients are defined by the last 15 columns of the array above.

CONFOUNDING PATTERN FOR THE
BASIC 16-RUN DESIGN WITH AN EIGHT-LEVEL FACTOR

The 15 degrees of freedom for these sixteen runs are represented by the 15 contrasts for the Basic 16-Run Plackett-Burman Design. Use the contrast coefficients for the Basic 16-Run Plackett-Burman design to analyze the data from this experiment.

Contrasts A, B, C, D, E, F, and G will compare levels of the eight-level factor, Factor A. The exact comparisons being made may be found by an examination of the contrast coefficients. These seven comparisons are denoted by the symbols A_1, A_2, A_3, A_4, A_5, A_6, and A_7 in the following table.

Due to the complex nature of the comparisons made by the seven contrasts for Factor A, the interpretation of estimated effects for significant interaction contrasts is quite difficult. If any interaction involving Factor A is judged to be significant, one should use a response plot or ANOM plot to interpret the interaction effect.

Contrast Labels:	A	B	C	D	E	F	G	H	I	J	K	L	M	N	O
Main Effects:	A_1	A_2	A_3	A_4	A_5	A_6	A_7	H	I	J	K	L	M	N	O

Two-Factor	-HI	-HJ	-HK	-HL	-HM	-HN	-HO	$-A_1I$	$-A_1H$	$-A_1K$	$-A_1J$	$-A_1M$	$-A_1L$	$-A_1O$	$-A_1N$
Interactions:	-JK	-IK	-IJ	-IM	-IL	-IO	-IN	$-A_2J$	$-A_2K$	$-A_2H$	$-A_2I$	$-A_2N$	$-A_2O$	$-A_2L$	$-A_2M$
	-LM	-LN	-LO	-JN	-JO	-JL	-JM	$-A_3K$	$-A_3J$	$-A_3I$	$-A_3H$	$-A_3O$	$-A_3N$	$-A_3M$	$-A_3L$
	-NO	-MO	-MN	-KO	-KN	-KM	-KL	$-A_4L$	$-A_4M$	$-A_4N$	$-A_4O$	$-A_4H$	$-A_4I$	$-A_4J$	$-A_4K$
								$-A_5M$	$-A_5L$	$-A_5O$	$-A_5N$	$-A_5I$	$-A_5H$	$-A_5K$	$-A_5J$
								$-A_6N$	$-A_6O$	$-A_6L$	$-A_6M$	$-A_6J$	$-A_6K$	$-A_6H$	$-A_6I$
								$-A_7O$	$-A_7N$	$-A_7M$	$-A_7L$	$-A_7K$	$-A_7J$	$-A_7I$	$-A_7H$

A Reflected 16-Run Design With An Eight-Level Factor

The following design is based upon the Reflected 16-Run Plackett-Burman Design. It can accommodate one factor at eight levels and up to eight factors at 2 levels each. When used with nine factors it is a (1/128)th replicate of the fully crossed design.

A REFLECTED 8×2^8 DESIGN

TREATMENT COMBINATIONS

Run	A	H	I	J	K	L	M	N	O							
1	8	+	+	+	+	+	+	+	+	+	+	+	+	+	+	+
2	8	-	-	-	-	-	-	-	-	+	+	+	+	+	+	+
3	7	-	-	-	-	+	+	+	+	+	+	+	-	-	-	-
4	7	+	+	+	+	-	-	-	-	+	+	+	-	-	-	-
5	6	+	+	-	-	-	-	+	+	+	-	-	-	-	+	+
6	6	-	-	+	+	+	+	-	-	+	-	-	-	-	+	+
7	5	-	-	+	+	-	-	+	+	+	-	-	+	+	-	-
8	5	+	+	-	-	+	+	-	-	+	-	-	+	+	-	-
9	4	+	-	-	+	+	-	-	+	-	-	+	+	-	-	+
10	4	-	+	+	-	-	+	+	-	-	-	+	+	-	-	+
11	3	-	+	+	-	+	-	-	+	-	-	+	-	+	+	-
12	3	+	-	-	+	-	+	+	-	-	-	+	-	+	+	-
13	2	+	-	+	-	-	+	-	+	-	+	-	-	+	-	+
14	2	-	+	-	+	+	-	+	-	-	+	-	-	+	-	+
15	1	-	+	-	+	-	+	-	+	-	+	-	+	-	+	-
16	1	+	-	+	-	+	-	+	-	-	+	-	+	-	+	-
		H	I	J	K	L	M	N	O	A	B	C	D	E	F	G

CONTRAST LABELS

Treatment combinations are defined by the first nine elements in each row.

Contrast coefficients are defined by the last 15 columns of the array above.

CONFOUNDING PATTERN FOR THE
REFLECTED 16-RUN DESIGN WITH AN EIGHT-LEVEL FACTOR

The 15 degrees of freedom for these sixteen runs are represented by the 15 contrasts for the Reflected 16-Run Plackett-Burman Design. Use the contrast coefficients for the Reflected 16-Run Plackett-Burman design to analyze the data from this experiment.

Contrasts A, B, C, D, E, F, and G will compare levels of the eight-level factor, Factor A. The exact comparisons being made may be found by an examination of the contrast coefficients. These seven comparisons are denoted by the symbols A_1, A_2, A_3, A_4, A_5, A_6, and A_7 in the following table.

Due to the complex nature of the comparisons made by the seven contrasts for Factor A, the interpretation of estimated effects for significant interaction contrasts is quite difficult. If any interaction involving Factor A is judged to be significant, one should use a response plot or ANOM plot to interpret the interaction effect.

Contrast Labels:	A	B	C	D	E	F	G	H	I	J	K	L	M	N	O
Main Effects:	A_1	$-A_2$	A_3	$-A_4$	A_5	$-A_6$	A_7	H	I	J	K	L	M	N	O

Two-Factor Interactions:	HI	HJ	HK	HL	HM	HN	HO	A_1I	A_1H	A_1K	A_1J	A_1M	A_1L	A_1O	A_1N
	JK	IK	IJ	IM	IL	IO	IN	$-A_2J$	$-A_2K$	$-A_2H$	$-A_2I$	$-A_2N$	$-A_2O$	$-A_2L$	$-A_2M$
	LM	LN	LO	JN	JO	JL	JM	A_3K	A_3J	A_3I	A_3H	A_3O	A_3N	A_3M	A_3L
	NO	MO	MN	KO	KN	KM	KL	$-A_4L$	$-A_4M$	$-A_4N$	$-A_4O$	$-A_4H$	$-A_4I$	$-A_4J$	$-A_4K$
								A_5M	A_5L	A_5O	A_5N	A_5I	A_5H	A_5K	A_5J
								$-A_6N$	$-A_6O$	$-A_6L$	$-A_6M$	$-A_6J$	$-A_6K$	$-A_6H$	$-A_6I$
								A_7O	A_7N	A_7M	A_7L	A_7K	A_7J	A_7I	A_7H

16-Run Designs With One Factor At 5, 6, or 7 Levels

The following modifications refer to the designs given on pages 200–203.

The 16-Run Designs having one factor at 8 levels can be modified to allow for one factor having either 5, 6 or 7 levels. The modified designs will involve some redundancy for the multi-level factor, but they still use the same set of contrast coefficients for the analysis.

A (1/112)th REPLICATE OF A 7×2^8 DESIGN:

For a (1/112)th replicate of a 7×2^8 Design change the treatment combinations for either of the 8×2^8 Designs as follows. For Factor A: let levels 1 through 7 remain as shown in the array and change level 8 into any specific one of the seven levels. You will collect twice as much data at this level of Factor A than you will at the other 6 levels of Factor A. For Factor H through Factor O there will be no changes. The Confounding Patterns given with the Combined 16-Run Designs will remain the unchanged, although the comparisons made by the contrasts for Factor A will be slightly different.

A (1/96)th REPLICATE OF A 6×2^8 DESIGN:

For a (1/96)th replicate of a 6×2^8 Design, change the treatment combinations for either of the 8 $\times 2^8$ Designs as follows. For Factor A: let levels 1 through 6 remain as shown in the array and let levels 7 and 8 be assigned to any two specific levels of the six level factor. For Factor H through Factor O there will be no changes. The Confounding Patterns given with the Combined 16-Run Designs will remain the unchanged, although the comparisons made by the contrasts for Factor A will be slightly different.

A (1/80)th REPLICATE OF A 5×2^8 DESIGN:

For a (1/80)th replicate of a 5×2^8 Design, change the treatment combinations for either of the 8 $\times 2^8$ Designs as follows. For Factor A: let levels 1 through 5 remain as shown in the array and let levels 6, 7, ans 8 be assigned to any three specific levels of the five level factor. You will collect twice as much data at these three duplicated levels than you will at the other two levels of the five level factor. For Factor H through Factor O there will be no changes. The Confounding Patterns given with the Combined 16-Run Designs will remain the unchanged, although the comparisons made by the contrasts for Factor A will be slightly different.

A Basic 16-Run Design With A Four-Level Factor

The following design is based upon the Basic 16-Run Plackett-Burman Design. It can accommodate one factor at four levels and up to 12 factors at two levels each. When used with thirteen factors it is a (1/1024)th replicate of the fully crossed design.

A BASIC 4×2^{12} DESIGN

TREATMENT COMBINATIONS

Run	A	D	E	F	G	H	I	J	K	L	M	N	O			
1	1	-	-	-	-	-	-	-	-	-	-	-	-	-	-	-
2	1	-	-	-	-	+	+	+	+	+	+	+	+	-	-	-
3	1	+	+	+	+	+	+	+	+	-	-	-	-	-	-	-
4	1	+	+	+	+	-	-	-	-	+	+	+	+	-	-	-
5	2	+	+	-	-	-	-	+	+	+	+	-	-	-	+	+
6	2	+	+	-	-	+	+	-	-	-	-	+	+	-	+	+
7	2	-	-	+	+	+	+	-	-	+	+	-	-	-	+	+
8	2	-	-	+	+	-	-	+	+	-	-	+	+	-	+	+
9	3	-	+	+	-	-	+	+	-	-	+	+	-	+	+	-
10	3	-	+	+	-	+	-	-	+	+	-	-	+	+	+	-
11	3	+	-	-	+	+	-	-	+	-	+	+	-	+	+	-
12	3	+	-	-	+	-	+	+	-	+	-	-	+	+	+	-
13	4	+	-	+	-	-	+	-	+	+	-	+	-	+	-	+
14	4	+	-	+	-	+	-	+	-	-	+	-	+	+	-	+
15	4	-	+	-	+	+	-	+	-	+	-	+	-	+	-	+
16	4	-	+	-	+	-	+	-	+	-	+	-	+	+	-	+
	D	E	F	G	H	I	J	K	L	M	N	O	A	B	C

CONTRAST LABELS

Treatment combinations are defined by the first 13 elements of each row above.

Contrast coefficients are defined by the last 15 columns of the array above.

CONFOUNDING PATTERN FOR THE
BASIC 16-RUN DESIGN WITH A FOUR-LEVEL FACTOR

When the contrast coefficients for the Basic 16-Run Plackett-Burman design (p.40, 41) are used to analyze the data from this experiment the following confounding pattern may be used to interpret the results.

Contrasts A, B, and C will represent the three degrees of freedom for the four-level Factor A. The Main Effects represented by these three contrasts will be denoted by A, A' and A".

Contrast Labels

A	B	C	D	E	F	G	H	I	J	K	L	M	N	O

Main Effects

A	A'	A"	D	E	F	G	H	I	J	K	L	M	N	O

Interactions

-DE	-DF	-DG	-A E	-A D	-A G	-A F	-A I	-A H	-A K	-A J	-A M	-A L	-A O	-A N
-FG	-EG	-EF	-A 'F	-A 'G	-A 'D	-A 'E	-A 'J	-A 'K	-A 'H	-A 'I	-A 'N	-A 'O	-A 'L	-A 'M
-HI	-HJ	-HK	-A"G	-A"F	-A"E	-A"D	-A"K	-A"J	-A"I	-A"H	-A"O	-A"N	-A"M	-A"L
-JK	-IK	-IJ	-HL	-HM	-HN	-HO	-DL	-DM	-DN	-DO	-DH	-DI	-DJ	-DK
-LM	-LN	-LO	-IM	-IL	-IO	-IN	-EM	-EL	-EO	-EN	-EI	-EH	-EK	-EJ
-NO	-MO	-MN	-JN	-JO	-JL	-JM	-FN	-FO	-FL	-FM	-FJ	-FK	-FH	-FI
			-KO	-KN	-KM	-KL	-GO	-GN	-GM	-GL	-GK	-GJ	-GI	-GH

A (1/768)th replicate of a 3 x 2^{12} Design may be obtained by changing Factor A into a three-level factor. This is accomplished by performing Runs 13, 14, 15 and 16 with Factor A set at either level 1 or level 2 or level 3 instead of level 4. (This will result in eight runs involving one of the three levels of Factor A.) The confounding pattern will remain unchanged, but two of the Main Effects for Factor A will represent independent evaluations of the same comparison.

A REFLECTED 16-RUN DESIGN WITH A FOUR-LEVEL FACTOR

The following design is based upon the Reflected 16-Run Plackett-Burman Design. It can accommodate one factor at four levels and up to 12 factors at two levels each. When used with thirteen factors it is a (1/1024)th replicate of the fully crossed design.

A REFLECTED 4×2^{12} DESIGN

TREATMENT COMBINATIONS

Run	A	D	E	F	G	H	I	J	K	L	M	N	O			
1	4	+	+	+	+	+	+	+	+	+	+	+	+	+	+	+
2	4	+	+	+	+	-	-	-	-	-	-	-	-	+	+	+
3	4	-	-	-	-	-	-	-	-	+	+	+	+	+	+	+
4	4	-	-	-	-	+	+	+	+	-	-	-	-	+	+	+
5	3	-	-	+	+	+	+	-	-	-	-	+	+	+	-	-
6	3	-	-	+	+	-	-	+	+	+	+	-	-	+	-	-
7	3	+	+	-	-	-	-	+	+	-	-	+	+	+	-	-
8	3	+	+	-	-	+	+	-	-	+	+	-	-	+	-	-
9	2	+	-	-	+	+	-	-	+	+	-	-	+	-	-	+
10	2	+	-	-	+	-	+	+	-	-	+	+	-	-	-	+
11	2	-	+	+	-	-	+	+	-	+	-	-	+	-	-	+
12	2	-	+	+	-	+	-	-	+	-	+	+	-	-	-	+
13	1	-	+	-	+	+	-	+	-	-	+	-	+	-	+	-
14	1	-	+	-	+	-	+	-	+	+	-	+	-	-	+	-
15	1	+	-	+	-	-	+	-	+	-	+	-	+	-	+	-
16	1	+	-	+	-	+	-	+	-	+	-	+	-	-	+	-
	D	E	F	G	H	I	J	K	L	M	N	O	A	B	C

CONTRAST LABELS

Treatment combinations are defined by the first 13 elements of each row above.

Contrast coefficients are defined by the last 15 columns of the array above.

CONFOUNDING PATTERN FOR THE
REFLECTED 16-RUN DESIGN WITH A FOUR-LEVEL FACTOR

When the contrast coefficients for the Reflected 16-Run Plackett-Burman design (p.52, 53) are used to analyze the data from this experiment the following confounding pattern may be used to interpret the results.

Contrasts A, B, and C will represent the three degrees of freedom for the four-level Factor A. The Main Effects represented by these three contrasts will be denoted by A, -A' and A". The sign change for Contrast B is unavoidable if A' is taken to represent the same comparison between the levels of Factor A in both the Basic Design and the Reflected Design.

Contrast Labels

A	B	C	D	E	F	G	H	I	J	K	L	M	N	O

Main Effects

A	-A'	A"	D	E	F	G	H	I	J	K	L	M	N	O

Interactions

-DE	-DF	-DG	AE	AD	AG	AF	AI	AH	AK	AJ	AM	AL	AO	AN
-FG	-EG	-EF	-A'F	-A'G	-A'D	-A'E	-A'J	-A'K	-A'H	-A'I	-A'N	-A'O	-A'L	-A'M
-HI	-HJ	-HK	A"G	A"F	A"E	A"D	A"K	A"J	A"I	A"H	A"O	A"N	A"M	A"L
JK	IK	IJ	HL	HM	HN	HO	DL	DM	DN	DO	DH	DI	DJ	DK
LM	LN	LO	IM	IL	IO	IN	EM	EL	EO	EN	EI	EH	EK	EJ
NO	MO	MN	JN	JO	JL	JM	FN	FO	FL	FM	FJ	FK	FH	FI
			KO	KN	KM	KL	GO	GN	GM	GL	GK	GJ	GI	GH

Note that interactions involving A' will not be isolated from the main effects by performing both the basic and reflected 16-run studies.

A (1/768)th replicate of a 3×2^{12} Design may be obtained by changing Factor A into a three-level factor. This is accomplished by performing Runs 1, 2, 3, and 4 with Factor A set at either level 1 or level 2 or level 3 instead of level 4. The confounding pattern will remain unchanged, but two of the both Main Effects for Factor A will represent independent evaluations of the same comparison.

A Basic 16-Run Design With Two Four-Level Factors

The following design is based upon the Basic 16-Run Plackett-Burman Design. It can accommodate two factors at four levels and up to 9 factors at two levels each. When used with eleven factors it is a (1/512)th replicate of the fully crossed design.

A BASIC $4^2 \times 2^9$ DESIGN

TREATMENT COMBINATIONS

Run	A	D	E	F	G	I	J	K	M	N	O						
1	1	1	-	-	-	-	-	-	-	-	-	-	-	-	-	-	-
2	1	2	-	-	-	+	+	+	+	+	+	-	-	-	-	+	+
3	1	3	+	+	+	+	+	+	-	-	-	-	-	-	+	+	-
4	1	4	+	+	+	-	-	-	+	+	+	-	-	-	+	-	+
5	2	4	+	-	-	-	+	+	+	-	-	-	+	+	+	-	+
6	2	3	+	-	-	+	-	-	-	+	+	-	+	+	+	+	-
7	2	2	-	+	+	+	-	-	+	-	-	-	+	+	-	+	+
8	2	1	-	+	+	-	+	+	-	+	+	-	+	+	-	-	-
9	3	1	+	+	-	+	+	-	+	+	-	+	+	-	-	-	-
10	3	2	+	+	-	-	-	+	-	-	+	+	+	-	-	+	+
11	3	3	-	-	+	-	-	+	+	+	-	+	+	-	+	+	-
12	3	4	-	-	+	+	+	-	-	-	+	+	+	-	+	-	+
13	4	4	-	+	-	+	-	+	-	+	-	+	-	+	+	-	+
14	4	3	-	+	-	-	+	-	+	-	+	+	-	+	+	+	-
15	4	2	+	-	+	-	+	-	-	+	-	+	-	+	-	+	+
16	4	1	+	-	+	+	-	+	+	-	+	+	-	+	-	-	-

| | | | E | F | G | I | J | K | M | N | O | A | B | C | D | H | L |

CONTRAST LABELS

Treatment combinations are defined by the first 11 elements of each row above.

Contrast coefficients are defined by the last 15 columns of the array above.

CONFOUNDING PATTERN FOR THE
BASIC 16-RUN DESIGN WITH TWO FOUR-LEVEL FACTORS

When the data obtained using the treatment combinations on the previous page are analyzed using the contrast coefficients for the Basic 16-Run Plackett-Burman design (p.40, 41) one may use the following confounding pattern to interpret the results. Contrasts A, B, and C will represent the three degrees of freedom for the four-level Factor A. The Main Effects represented by these three contrasts will be denoted by A, A' and A". Contrasts D, H, and L will represent the three degrees of freedom for the four-level Factor D. The Main Effects represented by these three contrasts will be denoted by D, D' and D".

Contrast Labels

A	B	C	D	E	F	G	H	I	J	K	L	M	N	O

Main Effects

A	A'	A"	D	E	F	G	D'	I	J	K	D"	M	N	O

Interactions

-DE	-DF	-DG	-AE	-AD	-AG	-AF	-AI	-AD'	-AK	-AJ	-AM	-AD"	-AO	-AN
-FG	-EG	-EF	-A'F	-A'G	-A'D	-A'E	-A'J	-A'K	-A'D'	-A'I	-A'N	-A'O	-A'D"	-A'M
-D'I	-D'J	-D'K	-A"G	-A"F	-A"E	-A"D	-A"K	-A"J	-A"I	-A"D'	-A"O	-A"N	-A"M	-A"D"
-JK	-IK	-IJ	-IM	-D'M	-D'N	-D'O	-EM	-DM	-DN	-DO	-EI	-DI	-DJ	-DK
-D"M	-D"N	-D"O	-JN	-D'I	-IO	-IN	-FN	-D"E	-EO	-EN	-FJ	-D'E	-EK	-EJ
-NO	-MO	-MN	-KO	-JO	-D"J	-JM	-GO	-FO	-D"F	-FM	-GK	-FK	-D'F	-FI
			-KN	-KM	-D"K		-GN	-GM	-D"G		-GJ	-GI	-D'G	

A (1/288)th replicate of a $3^2 \times 2^9$ Design may be obtained by changing Factors A and D into three-level factors. A (1/384)th replicate of a $3 \times 4 \times 2^9$ Design may be obtained by changing either Factor A or Factor D into a three-level factor. The change from a four-level factor into a three-level factor is accomplished by replacing the fourth level of the (apparent) four-level factor with some other level of the three level factor. (e.g. all level 4's become level 2.)

Four Level Factor		Three Level Factor
Level 1	remains	Level 1
Level 2	remains	Level 2
Level 3	remains	Level 3
Level 4	**is changed into one of:**	**Level 1 or Level 2 or Level 3**

If Factor A represents a three level factor, two of the Main Effect contrasts for Factor A will represent independent evaluations of the same comparison. If Factor D represents a three level factor, two of the Main Effect contrasts for Factor D will represent independent evaluations of the same comparison.

A REFLECTED 16-RUN DESIGN WITH TWO FOUR-LEVEL FACTORS

The following design is based upon the Reflected 16-Run Plackett-Burman Design. It can accommodate two factors at four levels and up to 9 factors at two levels each. When used with eleven factors it is a (1/512)th replicate of the fully crossed design.

A REFLECTED $4^2 \times 2^9$ DESIGN

TREATMENT COMBINATIONS

Run	A	D	E	F	G	I	J	K	M	N	O						
1	4	4	+	+	+	+	+	+	+	+	+	+	+	+	+	+	+
2	4	3	+	+	+	−	−	−	−	−	−	+	+	+	+	−	−
3	4	2	−	−	−	−	−	−	+	+	+	+	+	+	−	−	+
4	4	1	−	−	−	+	+	+	−	−	−	+	+	+	−	+	−
5	3	1	−	+	+	+	−	−	−	+	+	+	−	−	−	+	−
6	3	2	−	+	+	−	+	+	+	−	−	+	−	−	−	−	+
7	3	3	+	−	−	−	+	+	−	+	+	+	−	−	+	−	−
8	3	4	+	−	−	+	−	−	+	−	−	+	−	−	+	+	+
9	2	4	−	−	+	−	−	+	−	−	+	−	−	+	+	+	+
10	2	3	−	−	+	+	+	−	+	+	−	−	−	+	+	−	−
11	2	2	+	+	−	+	+	−	−	−	+	−	−	+	−	−	+
12	2	1	+	+	−	−	−	+	+	+	−	−	−	+	−	+	−
13	1	1	+	−	+	−	+	−	+	−	+	−	+	−	−	+	−
14	1	2	+	−	+	+	−	+	−	+	−	−	+	−	−	−	+
15	1	3	−	+	−	+	−	+	+	−	+	−	+	−	+	−	−
16	1	4	−	+	−	−	+	−	−	+	−	−	+	−	+	+	+
			E	F	G	I	J	K	M	N	O	A	B	C	D	H	L

CONTRAST LABELS

Treatment combinations are defined by the first 11 elements of each row above.

Contrast coefficients are defined by the last 15 columns of the array above.

CONFOUNDING PATTERN FOR THE
REFLECTED 16-RUN DESIGN WITH TWO FOUR-LEVEL FACTORS

When the data obtained using the treatment combinations on the previous page are analyzed using the contrast coefficients for the Reflected 16-Run Plackett-Burman design (p.52, 53) one may use the following confounding pattern to interpret the results. Contrasts A, B, and C will represent the three degrees of freedom for the four-level Factor A. The Main Effects represented by these three contrasts will be denoted by A, -A' and A". Contrasts D, H, and L will represent the three degrees of freedom for the four-level Factor D. The Main Effects represented by these three contrasts will be denoted by D, -D' and D".   The sign change for Contrasts B and H is unavoidable if A' and D' are taken to represent the same comparisons in both the Basic Design and the Reflected Design.

Contrast Labels

A	B	C	D	E	F	G	H	I	J	K	L	M	N	O

Main Effects

A	-A'	A"	D	E	F	G	-D'	I	J	K	D"	M	N	O

Interactions

DE	DF	DG	AE	AD	AG	AF	AI	AD'	AK	AJ	AM	AD"	AO	AN
FG	EG	EF	-A'F	-A'G	-A'D	-A'E	-A'J	-A'K	A'D'	-A'I	-A'N	-A'O	-A'D"	-A'M
-D'I	-D'J	-D'K	A"G	A"F	A"E	A"D	A"K	A"J	A"I	-A"D'	A"O	A"N	A"M	A"D"
JK	IK	IJ	IM	-D'M	-D'N	-D'O	EM	DM	DN	DO	EI	DI	DJ	DK
D"M	D"N	D"O	JN	D"I	IO	IN	FN	D"E	EO	EN	FJ	-D'E	EK	EJ
NO	MO	MN	KO	JO	D"J	JM	GO	FO	D"F	FM	GK	FK	-D'F	FI
			KN	KM	D"K		GN	GM	D"G		GJ	GI	-D'G	

Note that some two-factor interactions do not display a sign change between the basic design and the reflected design. Thus, there are some interactions that cannot be isolated from the main effects with these designs. Note also that two main effects (A' and D') show a sign change between the basic design and the reflected design.

A (1/288)th replicate of a $3^2 \times 2^9$ Design may be obtained by changing Factors A and D into three-level factors. A (1/384)th replicate of a $3 \times 4 \times 2^9$ Design may be obtained by changing either Factor A or Factor D into a three-level factor. The change from a four-level factor into a three-level factor is described on p. 211.

A Basic 16-Run Design With Three Four-Level Factors

The following design is based upon the Basic 16-Run Plackett-Burman Design. It can accommodate three factors at four levels and up to 6 factors at two levels each. When used with nine factors it is a (1/256)th replicate of the fully crossed design.

A BASIC $4^3 \times 2^6$ DESIGN

TREATMENT COMBINATIONS

Run	A	D	E	F	G	I	K	M	N									
1	1	1	1	−	−	−	−	−	−	−	−	−	−	−	−	−	−	−
2	1	2	2	−	−	+	+	+	+	−	−	−	−	−	+	+	+	+
3	1	3	3	+	+	+	+	−	−	−	−	−	+	+	+	+	−	−
4	1	4	4	+	+	−	−	+	+	−	−	−	+	+	−	−	+	+
5	2	4	3	−	−	−	+	+	−	−	+	+	+	+	−	+	+	−
6	2	3	4	−	−	+	−	−	+	−	+	+	+	+	+	−	−	+
7	2	2	1	+	+	+	−	+	−	−	+	+	−	−	+	−	+	−
8	2	1	2	+	+	−	+	−	+	−	+	+	−	−	−	+	−	+
9	3	1	3	+	−	+	−	+	+	+	+	−	−	+	−	+	−	−
10	3	2	4	+	−	−	+	−	−	+	+	−	−	+	+	−	+	+
11	3	3	1	−	+	−	+	+	+	+	+	−	+	−	+	−	−	−
12	3	4	2	−	+	+	−	−	−	+	+	−	+	−	−	+	+	+
13	4	4	1	+	−	+	+	−	+	+	−	+	+	−	−	−	−	+
14	4	3	2	+	−	−	−	+	−	+	−	+	+	−	+	+	−	+
15	4	2	3	−	+	−	−	−	+	+	−	+	−	+	+	+	+	−
16	4	1	4	−	+	+	+	+	−	+	−	+	−	+	−	−	−	+
				F	G	I	K	M	N	A	B	C	D	E	H	J	L	O

CONTRAST LABELS

Treatment combinations are defined by the first 9 elements of each row above.

Contrast coefficients are defined by the last 15 columns of the array above.

Confounding Pattern for the
Basic 16-Run Design With Three Four-Level Factors

When the data obtained using the treatment combinations on the previous page are analyzed using the contrast coefficients for the Basic 16-Run Plackett-Burman design (p.40, 41) one may use the following confounding pattern to interpret the results. Contrasts A, B, and C will represent the three degrees of freedom for the four-level Factor A. Contrasts D, H, and L will represent the three degrees of freedom for the four-level Factor D. Contrasts E, J, and O will represent the three degrees of freedom for the four-level Factor E.

Contrast Labels

A	B	C	D	E	F	G	H	I	J	K	L	M	N	O

Main Effects

A	A'	A"	D	E	F	G	D'	I	E'	K	D"	M	N	E"

Interactions

A	B	C	D	E	F	G	H	I	J	K	L	M	N	O
-DE	-DF	-DG	-AE	-AD	-AG	-AF	-AI	-AD'	-AK	-AE'	-AM	-AD"	-AE"	-AN
-FG	-EG	-EF	-A'F	-A'G	-A'D	-A'E	-A'E'	-A'K	-A'D'	-A'I	-A'N	-A'E"	-A'D"	-A'M
-D'I	-D'E'	-D'K	-A"G	-A"F	-A"E	-A"D	-A"K	-A"E'	-A"I	-A"D'	-A"E"	-A"N	-A"M	-A"D"
-E'K	-IK	-E'I	-IM	-D'M	-D'N	-D'E"	-EM	-DM	-DN	-DE"	-EI	-DI	-DE'	-DK
-D"M	-D"N	-D"E'	-E'N	-D"I	-E"I	-IN	-FN	-D"E	-D"F	-EN	-E'F	-D'E	-EK	-FI
-E"N	-E"M	-MN	-E"K	-KN	-D"E'	-E'M	-E"G	-E"F	-GM	-FM	-GK	-FK	-D'F	-D'G
					-KM	-D"K		-GN			-D"G		-E'G	-GI

A (1/108)th replicate of a $3^3 \times 2^6$ Design may be obtained by changing Factors A, D, and E into three-level factors.

A (1/144)th replicate of a $3^2 \times 4 \times 2^6$ Design may be obtained by changing any two of the four-level factors into three-level factors.

A (1/192)nd replicate of a $3 \times 4^2 \times 2^6$ Design may be obtained by changing any one of the four-level factors into a three-level factor.

For details of these changes see p. 211.

A Reflected 16-Run Design With Three Four-Level Factors

The following design is based upon the Reflected 16-Run Plackett-Burman Design. It can accommodate three factors at four levels and up to 6 factors at two levels each. When used with nine factors it is a (1/256)th replicate of the fully crossed design.

A BASIC $4^3 \times 2^6$ DESIGN

TREATMENT COMBINATIONS

Run	A	D	E	F	G	I	K	M	N									
1	4	4	4	+	+	+	+	+	+	+	+	+	+	+	+	+	+	+
2	4	3	3	+	+	−	−	−	−	+	+	+	+	+	−	−	−	−
3	4	2	2	−	−	−	−	+	+	+	+	+	−	−	−	−	+	+
4	4	1	1	−	−	+	+	−	−	+	+	+	−	−	+	+	−	−
5	3	1	2	+	+	+	−	−	+	+	−	−	−	−	+	−	−	+
6	3	2	1	+	+	−	+	+	−	+	−	−	−	−	−	+	+	−
7	3	3	4	−	−	−	+	−	+	+	−	−	+	+	−	+	−	+
8	3	4	3	−	−	+	−	+	−	+	−	−	+	+	+	−	+	−
9	2	4	2	−	+	−	+	−	−	−	−	+	+	−	+	−	+	+
10	2	3	1	−	+	+	−	+	+	−	−	+	+	−	−	+	−	−
11	2	2	4	+	−	+	−	−	−	−	−	+	−	+	−	+	+	+
12	2	1	3	+	−	−	+	+	+	−	−	+	−	+	+	−	−	−
13	1	1	4	−	+	−	−	+	−	−	+	−	−	+	+	+	−	+
14	1	2	3	−	+	+	+	−	+	−	+	−	−	+	−	−	+	−
15	1	3	2	+	−	+	+	+	−	−	+	−	+	−	−	−	−	+
16	1	4	1	+	−	−	−	−	+	−	+	−	+	−	+	+	+	−
				F	G	I	K	M	N	A	B	C	D	E	H	J	L	O

CONTRAST LABELS

Treatment combinations are defined by the first 9 elements of each row above.

Contrast coefficients are defined by the last 15 columns of the array above.

CONFOUNDING PATTERN FOR THE
REFLECTED 16-RUN DESIGN WITH THREE FOUR-LEVEL FACTORS

When the data obtained using the treatment combinations on the previous page are analyzed using the contrast coefficients for the Reflected 16-Run Plackett-Burman design (p.52, 53) one may use the following confounding pattern to interpret the results. Contrasts A, B, and C will represent the three degrees of freedom for the four-level Factor A. Contrasts D, H, and L will represent the three degrees of freedom for the four-level Factor D. Contrasts E, J, and O will represent the three degrees of freedom for the four-level Factor E. The sign change for Contrasts B, H, and J is required if A', D', and E' are taken to represent the same comparisons in both the Basic Design and the Reflected Design.

Contrast Labels

A	B	C	D	E	F	G	H	I	J	K	L	M	N	O

Main Effects

A	-A'	A"	D	E	F	G	-D'	I	-E'	K	D"	M	N	E"

Interactions

DE	DF	DG	AE	AD	AG	AF	AI	-AD'	AK	-AE'	AM	AD"	AE"	AN
FG	EG	EF	-A'F	-A'G	-A'D	-A'E	A'E'	-A'K	A'D'	-A'I	-A'N	-A'E"	-A'D"	-A'M
-D'I	D'E'	-D'K	A"G	A"F	A"E	A"D	A"K	-A"E'	A"I	-A"D'	A"E"	A"N	A"M	A"D"
-E'K	IK	-E'I	IM	-D'M	-D'N	-D'E"	EM	DM	DN	DE"	EI	DI	-DE'	DK
D"M	D"N	D"E"	-E'N	D"I	E"I	IN	FN	D"E	D"F	EN	-E'F	-D'E	EK	FI
E"N	E"M	MN	E"K	KN	-D"E'	-E'M	E"G	E"F	GM	FM	GK	FK	-D'F	-D'G
					KM	D"K		GN		D"G		-E'G	GI	

Note that some two-factor interactions do not display a sign change between the basic design and the reflected design. Thus, there are some interactions that cannot be isolated from the main effects with these designs. Note also that three main effects (A', D', and E') show a sign change between the basic design and the reflected design.

A (1/108)th replicate of a $3^3 \times 2^6$ Design may be obtained by changing Factors A, D, and E into three-level factors.

A (1/144)th replicate of a $3^2 \times 4 \times 2^6$ Design may be obtained by changing any two of the four-level factors into three-level factors.

A (1/192)nd replicate of a $3 \times 4^2 \times 2^6$ Design may be obtained by changing any one of the four-level factors into a three-level factor.

For details of these changes see p. 211.

A Basic 16-Run Design With 4 Four-Level Factors

The following design is based upon the Basic 16-Run Plackett-Burman Design. It can accommodate four factors at four levels and up to 3 factors at two levels each. When used with seven factors it is a (1/128)th replicate of the fully crossed design.

A BASIC $4^4 \times 2^3$ DESIGN

TREATMENT COMBINATIONS

Run	A	D	E	F	G	I	N	A	B	C	D	E	F	H	J	K	L	M	O
1	1	1	1	1	-	-	-	-	-	-	-	-	-	-	-	-	-	-	-
2	1	2	2	2	-	+	+	-	-	-	-	-	-	+	+	+	+	+	+
3	1	3	3	3	+	+	-	-	-	-	+	+	+	+	+	+	-	-	-
4	1	4	4	4	+	-	+	-	-	-	+	+	+	-	-	-	+	+	+
5	2	4	3	2	-	-	-	-	+	+	+	+	-	-	+	+	+	+	-
6	2	3	4	1	-	+	+	-	+	+	+	+	-	+	-	-	-	-	+
7	2	2	1	4	+	+	-	-	+	+	-	-	+	+	-	-	+	+	-
8	2	1	2	3	+	-	+	-	+	+	-	-	+	-	+	+	-	-	+
9	3	1	3	4	-	+	+	+	+	-	-	+	+	-	+	-	-	+	-
10	3	2	4	3	-	-	-	+	+	-	-	+	+	+	-	+	+	-	+
11	3	3	1	2	+	-	+	+	+	-	+	-	-	+	-	+	-	+	-
12	3	4	2	1	+	+	-	+	+	-	+	-	-	-	+	-	+	-	+
13	4	4	1	3	-	+	+	+	-	+	+	-	+	-	-	+	+	-	-
14	4	3	2	4	-	-	-	+	-	+	+	-	+	+	+	-	-	+	+
15	4	2	3	1	+	-	+	+	-	+	-	+	-	+	+	-	+	-	-
16	4	1	4	2	+	+	-	+	-	+	-	+	-	-	-	+	-	+	+
				G	I	N	A	B	C	D	E	F	H	J	K	L	M	O

CONTRAST LABELS

Treatment combinations are defined by the first 7 elements of each row above.

Contrast coefficients are defined by the last 15 columns of the array above.

Confounding Pattern for the
Basic 16-Run Design With 4 Four-Level Factors

When the data obtained using the treatment combinations on the previous page are analyzed using the contrast coefficients for the Basic 16-Run Plackett-Burman design (p.40, 41) one may use the following confounding pattern to interpret the results. Contrasts A, B, and C will represent the three degrees of freedom for the four-level Factor A. Contrasts D, H, and L will represent the three degrees of freedom for the four-level Factor D. Contrasts E, J, and O will represent the three degrees of freedom for the four-level Factor E. Contrasts F, K, and M will represent the three degrees of freedom for the four-level Factor F.

Contrast Labels

A	B	C	D	E	F	G	H	I	J	K	L	M	N	O

Main Effects

A	A'	A"	D	E	F	G	D'	I	E'	F'	D"	F"	N	E"

Interactions

A	B	C	D	E	F	G	H	I	J	K	L	M	N	O
-DE	-DF	-DG	-AE	-AD	-AG	-AF	-AI	-AD'	-AF'	-AE'	-AF"	-AD"	-AE"	-AN
-FG	-EG	-EF	-A'F	-A'G	-A'D	-A'E	-A'E	-A'F	-A'D	-A'I	-A'N	-A'E	-A'D	-A'F"
-D'I	-D'E'	-D'F'	-A"G	-A"F	-A"E	-A"D	-A"F	-A"E	-A"I	-A"D'	-A"E'	-A"N	-A"F"	-A"D"
-E'F'	-F'I	-E'I	-F"I	-D'F"	-D'N	-D'E"	-EF"	-DF"	-DN	-DE"	-EI	-DI	-DE'	-DF'
-D"F"	-D"N	-D"E"	-E'N	-D"I	-E"I	-IN	-FN	-D"E	-D"F	-EN	-E'F	-D'E	-EF'	-FI
-E"N	-E"F"	-F"N	-E"F'	-F'N	-D"E'	-E'F"	-E"G	-E"F	-F'G	-D"G	-F'G	-E'G	-D'F	-D'G
						-D"F'		-GN						-GI

A (2/81)st replicate of a $3^4 \times 2^3$ Design may be obtained by changing Factors A, D, E, and F into three-level factors.

A (1/54)th replicate of a $3^3 \times 4 \times 2^3$ Design may be obtained by changing any three of the four-level factors into three-level factors.

A (1/72)nd replicate of a $3^2 \times 4^2 \times 2^3$ Design may be obtained by changing any two of the four-level factors into three-level factors.

A (1/96)th replicate of a $3 \times 4^3 \times 2^3$ Design may be obtained by changing any one of the four-level factors into a three-level factor.

For details of these changes see p. 211.

A Reflected 16-Run Design With 4 Four-Level Factors

The following design is based upon the Reflected 16-Run Plackett-Burman Design. It can accommodate four factors at four levels and up to 3 factors at two levels each. When used with seven factors it is a $(1/128)$th replicate of the fully crossed design.

A REFLECTED $4^4 \times 2^3$ DESIGN

TREATMENT COMBINATIONS

Run	A	D	E	F	G	I	N	A	B	C	D	E	F	H	J	K	L	M	O
1	4	4	4	4	+	+	+	+	+	+	+	+	+	+	+	+	+	+	+
2	4	3	3	3	+	−	−	+	+	+	+	+	+	−	−	−	−	−	−
3	4	2	2	2	−	−	+	+	+	+	−	−	−	−	−	−	+	+	+
4	4	1	1	1	−	+	−	+	+	+	−	−	−	+	+	+	−	−	−
5	3	1	2	3	+	+	+	+	−	−	−	−	+	+	−	−	−	−	+
6	3	2	1	4	+	−	−	+	−	−	−	−	+	−	+	+	+	+	−
7	3	3	4	1	−	−	+	+	−	−	+	+	−	−	+	+	−	−	+
8	3	4	3	2	−	+	−	+	−	−	+	+	−	+	−	−	+	+	−
9	2	4	2	1	+	−	−	−	−	+	+	−	−	+	−	+	+	−	+
10	2	3	1	2	+	+	+	−	−	+	+	−	−	−	+	−	−	+	−
11	2	2	4	3	−	+	−	−	−	+	−	+	+	−	+	−	+	−	+
12	2	1	3	4	−	−	+	−	−	+	−	+	+	+	−	+	−	+	−
13	1	1	4	2	+	−	−	−	+	−	−	+	−	+	+	−	−	+	+
14	1	2	3	1	+	+	+	−	+	−	−	+	−	−	−	+	+	−	−
15	1	3	2	4	−	+	−	−	+	−	+	−	+	−	−	+	−	+	+
16	1	4	1	3	−	−	+	−	+	−	+	−	+	+	+	−	+	−	−
					G	I	N	A	B	C	D	E	F	H	J	K	L	M	O

CONTRAST LABELS

Treatment combinations are defined by the first 7 elements of each row above.

Contrast coefficients are defined by the last 15 columns of the array above.

Confounding Pattern for the Reflected 16-Run Design With 4 Four-Level Factors

When the data obtained using the treatment combinations on the previous page are analyzed using the contrast coefficients for the Reflected 16-Run Plackett-Burman design (p.52, 53) one may use the following confounding pattern to interpret the results. Contrasts A, B, and C will represent the three degrees of freedom for the four-level Factor A. Contrasts D, H, and L will represent the three degrees of freedom for the four-level Factor D. Contrasts E, J, and O will represent the three degrees of freedom for the four-level Factor E. Contrasts F, K, and M will represent the three degrees of freedom for the four-level Factor F. The sign change for Contrasts B, H, J, and K is required if A', D', E', and F are taken to represent the same comparisons in both the Basic Design and the Reflected Design.

Contrast Labels

A	B	C	D	E	F	G	H	I	J	K	L	M	N	O

Main Effects

A	-A'	A"	D	E	F	G	-D'	I	-E'	-F'	D"	F"	N	E"

Interactions

A	B	C	D	E	F	G	H	I	J	K	L	M	N	O
DE	DF	DG	AE	AD	AG	AF	AI	-AD'	-AF'	-AE'	AF"	AD"	AE"	AN
FG	EG	EF	-A'F	-A'G	-A'D	-A'E	A'E	A'F	A'D	-A'I	-A'N	-A'E"	-A'D"	-A'F"
-D'I	D'E'	D'F'	A"G	A"F	A"E	A"D	-A"F'	-A"E'	A"I	-A"D'	A"E'	A"N	A"F"	A"D"
E'F'	-F'I	-E'I	F'I	-D'F"	-D'N	-D'E"	EF"	DF"	DN	DE"	EI	DI	-DE'	-DF'
D"F"	D"N	D"E"	-E'N	D"I	E"I	IN	FN	D"E	D"F	EN	-E'F	-D'E	-EF'	FI
E"N	E"F"	F"N	-E"F'	-F'N	-D"E'	-E'F'	E"G	E"F	F'G	D"G	-F'G	-E'G	-D'F	-D'G
					-D"F'		GN						GI	

Note that some two-factor interactions do not display a sign change between the basic design and the reflected design. Thus, there are some interactions that cannot be isolated from the main effects with these designs. Note also that four main effects (A', D', E', and F') show a sign change between the basic design and the reflected design.

A (2/81)st replicate of a $3^4 \times 2^3$ Design may be obtained by changing Factors A, D, E, and F into three-level factors. For details of these changes see p. 211.

A (1/54)th replicate of a $3^3 \times 4 \times 2^3$ Design may be obtained by changing any three of the four-level factors into three-level factors. For details see p. 211.

A (1/72)nd replicate of a $3^2 \times 4^2 \times 2^3$ Design may be obtained by changing any two of the four-level factors into three-level factors. For details see p. 211.

A (1/96)th replicate of a $3 \times 4^3 \times 2^3$ Design may be obtained by changing any one of the four-level factors into a three-level factor. For details see p. 211.

A BASIC 16-RUN DESIGN WITH FIVE FOUR-LEVEL FACTORS

The following design is based upon the Basic 16-Run Plackett-Burman Design. It can accommodate five factors at four levels. When used with five factors it is a (1/64)th replicate of the fully crossed design.

A BASIC 4^5 DESIGN

Run	A	D	E	F	G	A	B	C	D	E	F	G	H	I	J	K	L	M	N	O
1	1	1	1	1	1	-	-	-	-	-	-	-	-	-	-	-	-	-	-	-
2	1	2	2	2	2	-	-	-	-	-	-	+	+	+	+	+	+	+	+
3	1	3	3	3	3	-	-	-	+	+	+	+	+	+	+	+	-	-	-	-
4	1	4	4	4	4	-	-	-	+	+	+	+	-	-	-	-	+	+	+	+
5	2	4	3	2	1	-	+	+	+	+	-	-	-	-	+	+	+	+	-	-
6	2	3	4	1	2	-	+	+	+	+	-	-	+	+	-	-	-	-	+	+
7	2	2	1	4	3	-	+	+	-	-	+	+	+	+	-	-	+	+	-	-
8	2	1	2	3	4	-	+	+	-	-	+	+	-	-	+	+	-	-	+	+
9	3	1	3	4	2	+	+	-	-	+	+	-	-	+	+	-	-	+	+	-
10	3	2	4	3	1	+	+	-	-	+	+	-	+	-	-	+	+	-	-	+
11	3	3	1	2	4	+	+	-	+	-	-	+	+	-	-	+	-	+	+	-
12	3	4	2	1	3	+	+	-	+	-	-	+	-	+	+	-	+	-	-	+
13	4	4	1	3	2	+	-	+	+	-	+	-	-	+	-	+	+	-	+	-
14	4	3	2	4	1	+	-	+	+	-	+	-	+	-	+	-	-	+	-	+
15	4	2	3	1	4	+	-	+	-	+	-	+	+	-	+	-	+	-	+	-
16	4	1	4	2	3	+	-	+	-	+	-	+	-	+	-	+	-	+	-	+

CONTRAST LABELS

Treatment combinations are defined by the first 5 elements of each row above.

Contrast coefficients are defined by the last 15 columns of the array above.

CONFOUNDING PATTERN FOR THE
BASIC 16-RUN DESIGN WITH FIVE FOUR-LEVEL FACTORS

When the data obtained using the treatment combinations on the previous page are analyzed using the contrast coefficients for the Basic 16-Run Plackett-Burman design (p.40, 41) one may use the following confounding pattern to interpret the results. Contrasts A, B, and C will represent the three degrees of freedom for the four-level Factor A. Contrasts D, H, and L will represent the three degrees of freedom for the four-level Factor D. Contrasts E, J, and O will represent the three degrees of freedom for the four-level Factor E. Contrasts F, K, and M will represent the three degrees of freedom for the four-level Factor F. Contrasts G, I and N will represent the three degrees of freedom for the four level Factor G.

Contrast Labels

A	B	C	D	E	F	G	H	I	J	K	L	M	N	O

Main Effects

A	A'	A"	D	E	F	G	D'	G'	E'	F'	D"	F"	G"	E"

Interactions

-DE	-DF	-DG	-AE	-AD	-AG	-AF	-AG'	-AD'	-AF'	-AE'	-AF"	-AD"	-AE"	-AG"
-FG	-EG	-EF	-A'F	-A'G	-A'D	-A'E	-A'E'	-A'F'	-A'D'	-A'G'	-A'G"	-A'E"	-A'D"	-A'F"
-D'G'	-D'E'	-D'F'	-A"G	-A"F	-A"E	-A"D	-A"F'	-A"E'	-A"G'	-A"D'	-A"E"	-A"G"	-A"F"	-A"D"
-E'F'	-F'G'	-E'G'	-F"G'	-D'F"	-D'G"	-D'E"	-EF"	-DF"	-DG"	-DE"	-EG'	-DG'	-DE'	-DF'
-D"F"	-D"G"	-D"E"	-E'G"	-D'G'	-E'G'	-E'F'	-FG"	-D"E	-D"F	-EG'	-E'F	-D'E	-EF'	-FG'
-E'G"	-E"F"	-F"G"	-E"F'	-F'G"	-D"E'	-D"F'	-E"G	-E"F	-F"G	-D"G	-F'G	-E'G	-D'F	-D'G

A (16/243)rd replicate of a 3^5 Design may be obtained by changing Factors A, D, E, F, and G into three-level factors. For details of these changes see p. 211.

A (4/81)st replicate of a $3^4 \times 4$ Design may be obtained by changing any four of the four-level factors into three-level factors.

A (1/27)th replicate of a $3^3 \times 4^2$ Design may be obtained by changing any three of the four-level factors into three-level factors.

A (1/36)th replicate of a $3^2 \times 4^3$ Design may be obtained by changing any two of the four-level factors into three-level factors.

A (1/48)th replicate of a 3×4^4 Design may be obtained by changing any one of the four-level factors into a three-level factor.

A REFLECTED 16-RUN DESIGN WITH FIVE FOUR-LEVEL FACTORS

The following design is based upon the Reflected 16-Run Plackett-Burman Design. It can accommodate five factors at four levels. When used with seven factors it is a (1/64)th replicate of the fully crossed design.

A REFLECTED 4^5 DESIGN

TREATMENT COMBINATIONS

Run	A	D	E	F	G	A	B	C	D	E	F	G	H	I	J	K	L	M	N	O
1	4	4	4	4	4	+	+	+	+	+	+	+	+	+	+	+	+	+	+	+
2	4	3	3	3	3	+	+	+	+	+	+	+	-	-	-	-	-	-	-	-
3	4	2	2	2	2	+	+	+	-	-	-	-	-	-	-	+	+	+	+	+
4	4	1	1	1	1	+	+	+	-	-	-	-	+	+	+	+	-	-	-	-
5	3	1	2	3	4	+	-	-	-	-	+	+	+	+	-	-	-	-	+	+
6	3	2	1	4	3	+	-	-	-	-	+	+	-	-	+	+	+	+	-	-
7	3	3	4	1	2	+	-	-	+	+	-	-	-	-	+	+	-	-	+	+
8	3	4	3	2	1	+	-	-	+	+	-	-	+	+	-	-	+	+	-	-
9	2	4	2	1	3	-	-	+	+	-	-	+	+	-	-	+	+	-	-	+
10	2	3	1	2	4	-	-	+	+	-	-	+	-	+	+	-	-	+	+	-
11	2	2	4	3	1	-	-	+	-	+	+	-	-	+	+	-	+	-	-	+
12	2	1	3	4	2	-	-	+	-	+	+	-	+	-	-	+	-	+	+	-
13	1	1	4	2	3	-	+	-	-	+	-	+	+	-	+	-	-	+	-	+
14	1	2	3	1	4	-	+	-	-	+	-	+	-	+	-	+	+	-	+	-
15	1	3	2	4	1	-	+	-	+	-	+	-	-	+	-	+	-	+	-	+
16	1	4	1	3	2	-	+	-	+	-	+	-	+	-	+	-	+	-	+	-
						A	B	C	D	E	F	G	H	I	J	K	L	M	N	O

CONTRAST LABELS

Treatment combinations are defined by the first 5 elements of each row above.

Contrast coefficients are defined by the last 15 columns of the array above.

CONFOUNDING PATTERN FOR THE
REFLECTED 16-RUN DESIGN WITH FIVE FOUR-LEVEL FACTORS

When the data obtained using the treatment combinations on the previous page are analyzed using the contrast coefficients for the Reflected 16-Run Plackett-Burman design (p.52, 53) one may use the following confounding pattern to interpret the results. Contrasts A, B, and C will represent the three degrees of freedom for the four-level Factor A. Contrasts D, H, and L will represent the three degrees of freedom for the four-level Factor D. Contrasts E, J, and O will represent the three degrees of freedom for the four-level Factor E. Contrasts F, K, and M will represent the three degrees of freedom for the four-level Factor F. The sign change for Contrasts B, H, J, K, and I is unavoidable if A', D', E', F', and G' are taken to represent the same comparisons in both the Basic Design and the Reflected Design.

Contrast Labels

A	B	C	D	E	F	G	H	I	J	K	L	M	N	O

Main Effects

A	-A'	A"	D	E	F	G	-D'	-G'	-E'	-F'	D"	F"	G"	E"

Interactions

A	B	C	D	E	F	G	H	I	J	K	L	M	N	O
DE	DF	DG	AE	AD	AG	AF	-AG'	-AD'	-AF'	-AE'	AF"	AD"	AE"	AG"
FG	EG	EF	-A'F	-A'G	-A'D	-A'E	A'E	A'F'	A'D	A'G	-A'G"	-A'E"	-A'D"	-A'F"
D'G'	D'E'	D'F'	A"G	A"F	A"E	A"D	-A"F'	-A"E'	-A"G'	-A"D'	A"E"	A"G"	A"F"	A"D"
E'F'	F'G'	E'G'	-F"G'	-D'F"	-D'G"	-D'E"	EF"	DF"	DG"	DE"	-EG'	-DG'	-DE'	-DF'
D"F"	D"G"	D"E"	-E'G"	-D'G"	-E'G"	-E'F"	FG"	D"E	D"F	EG"	-E'F	-D'E	-EF'	-FG'
E"G"	E"F"	F"G"	-E"F'	-F'G"	-D"E'	-D"F'	E"G	E"F	F"G	D"G	-F'G	-E'G	-D'F	-D'G

Note that some two-factor interactions do not display a sign change between the basic design and the reflected design. Thus, there are some interactions that cannot be isolated from the main effects with these designs. Note also that four main effects (A', D', E', F', and G') show a sign change between the basic design and the reflected design.

A (16/243)rd replicate of a 3^5 Design may be obtained by changing Factors A, D, E, F, and G into three-level factors. For details of these changes see p. 211.

A (4/81)st replicate of a $3^4 \times 4$ Design may be obtained by changing any four of the four-level factors into three-level factors.

A (1/27)th replicate of a $3^3 \times 4^2$ Design may be obtained by changing any three of the four-level factors into three-level factors.

A (1/36)th replicate of a $3^2 \times 4^3$ Design may be obtained by changing any two of the four-level factors into three-level factors.

A (1/48)th replicate of a 3×4^4 Design may be obtained by changing any one of the four-level factors into a three-level factor.

A BASIC 32-RUN DESIGN WITH A SIXTEEN-LEVEL FACTOR

One factor at 16 levels and sixteen factors at 2 levels each. A (1/32,768)th Replicate.

Treatment Combinations

Run	A	P	Q	R	S	T	U	V	W	X	Y	Z	1	2	3	4	5
1	1	-	-	-	-	-	-	-	-	-	-	-	-	-	-	-	-
2	1	+	+	+	+	+	+	+	+	+	+	+	+	+	+	+	+
3	2	+	+	+	+	+	+	+	+	-	-	-	-	-	-	-	-
4	2	-	-	-	-	-	-	-	-	+	+	+	+	+	+	+	+
5	3	-	-	-	-	+	+	+	+	+	+	+	+	-	-	-	-
6	3	+	+	+	+	-	-	-	-	-	-	-	-	+	+	+	+
7	4	+	+	+	+	-	-	-	-	+	+	+	+	-	-	-	-
8	4	-	-	-	-	+	+	+	+	-	-	-	-	+	+	+	+
9	5	-	-	+	+	+	+	-	-	-	-	+	+	+	+	-	-
10	5	+	+	-	-	-	-	+	+	+	+	-	-	-	-	+	+
11	6	+	+	-	-	-	-	+	+	-	-	+	+	+	+	-	-
12	6	-	-	+	+	+	+	-	-	+	+	-	-	-	-	+	+
13	7	-	-	+	+	-	-	+	+	+	+	-	-	+	+	-	-
14	7	+	+	-	-	+	+	-	-	-	-	+	+	-	-	+	+
15	8	+	+	-	-	+	+	-	-	+	+	-	-	+	+	-	-
16	8	-	-	+	+	-	-	+	+	-	-	+	+	-	-	+	+
17	9	-	+	+	-	-	+	+	-	-	+	+	-	-	+	+	-
18	9	+	-	-	+	+	-	-	+	+	-	-	+	+	-	-	+
19	10	+	-	-	+	+	-	-	+	-	+	+	-	-	+	+	-
20	10	-	+	+	-	-	+	+	-	+	-	-	+	+	-	-	+
21	11	-	+	+	-	+	-	-	+	+	-	-	+	-	+	+	-
22	11	+	-	-	+	-	+	+	-	-	+	+	-	+	-	-	+
23	12	+	-	-	+	-	+	+	-	+	-	-	+	-	+	+	-
24	12	-	+	+	-	+	-	-	+	-	+	+	-	+	-	-	+
25	13	-	+	-	+	+	-	+	-	-	+	-	+	+	-	+	-
26	13	+	-	+	-	-	+	-	+	+	-	+	-	-	+	-	+
27	14	+	-	+	-	-	+	-	+	-	+	-	+	+	-	+	-
28	14	-	+	-	+	+	-	+	-	+	-	+	-	-	+	-	+
29	15	-	+	-	+	-	+	-	+	+	-	+	-	+	-	+	-
30	15	+	-	+	-	+	-	+	-	-	+	-	+	-	+	-	+
31	16	+	-	+	-	+	-	+	-	+	-	+	-	+	-	+	-
32	16	-	+	-	+	-	+	-	+	-	+	-	+	-	+	-	+
	A	P	Q	R	S	T	U	V	W	X	Y	Z	1	2	3	4	5

CONFOUNDING PATTERNS FOR THE
BASIC 32-RUN DESIGN WITH A SIXTEEN-LEVEL FACTOR

Use contrast coefficients from Basic 32-Run Plackett-Burman design for analysis.

Contrast Labels

A	B	C	D	E	F	G	H	I	J	K	L	M	N	O

Corresponding Main Effects and Two-Factor Interactions

A_1	A_2	A_3	A_4	A_5	A_6	A_7	A_8	A_9	A_{10}	A_{11}	A_{12}	A_{13}	A_{14}	A_{15}
-PQ	-PR	-PS	-PT	-PU	-PV	-PW	-PX	-PY	-PZ	-P1	-P2	-P3	-P4	-P5
-RS	-SQ	-QR	-QU	-QT	-QW	-QV	-QY	-QX	-Q1	-QZ	-Q3	-Q2	-Q5	-Q4
-TU	-TV	-TW	-RV	-RW	-RT	-RU	-RZ	-R1	-RX	-RY	-R4	-R5	-R2	-R3
-VW	-UW	-UV	-SW	-SV	-SU	-ST	-S1	-SZ	-SY	-SX	-S5	-S4	-S3	-S2
-XY	-XZ	-X1	-X2	-X3	-X4	-X5	-T2	-T3	-T4	-T5	-TX	-TY	-TZ	-T1
-Z1	-Y1	-YZ	-Y3	-Y2	-Y5	-Y4	-U3	-U2	-U5	-U4	-UY	-UX	-U1	-UZ
-23	-24	-25	-Z4	-Z5	-Z2	-Z3	-V4	-V5	-V2	-V3	-VZ	-V1	-VX	-VY
-45	-35	-34	-15	-14	-13	-12	-W5	-W4	-W3	-W2	-W1	-WZ	-WY	-WX

Contrast Labels

P	Q	R	S	T	U	V	W	X	Y	Z	1	2	3	4	5

Corresponding Main Effects and Two-Factor Interactions

P	Q	R	S	T	U	V	W	X	Y	Z	1	2	3	4	5
-A_1Q	-A_1P	-A_1S	-A_1R	-A_1U	-A_1T	-A_1W	-A_1V	-A_1Y	-A_1X	-$A_1$1	-A_1Z	-$A_1$3	-$A_1$2	-$A_1$5	-$A_1$4
-A_2R	-A_2S	-A_2P	-A_2Q	-A_2V	-A_2W	-A_2T	-A_2U	-A_2Z	-$A_2$1	-A_2X	-A_2Y	-$A_2$4	-$A_2$5	-$A_2$2	-$A_2$3
-A_3S	-A_3R	-A_3Q	-A_3P	-A_3W	-A_3V	-A_3U	-A_3T	-$A_3$1	-A_3Z	-A_3Y	-A_3X	-$A_3$5	-$A_3$4	-$A_3$3	-$A_3$2
-A_4T	-A_4U	-A_4V	-A_4W	-A_4P	-A_4Q	-A_4R	-A_4S	-$A_4$2	-$A_4$3	-$A_4$4	-$A_4$5	-A_4X	-A_4Y	-A_4Z	-$A_4$1
-A_5U	-A_5T	-A_5W	-A_5V	-A_5Q	-A_5P	-A_5S	-A_5R	-$A_5$3	-$A_5$2	-$A_5$5	-$A_5$4	-A_5Y	-A_5X	-$A_5$1	-A_5Z
-A_6V	-A_6W	-A_6T	-A_6U	-A_6R	-A_6S	-A_6P	-A_6Q	-$A_6$4	-$A_6$5	-$A_6$2	-$A_6$3	-A_6Z	-$A_6$1	-A_6X	-A_6Y
-A_7W	-A_7V	-A_7U	-A_7T	-A_7S	-A_7R	-A_7Q	-A_7P	-$A_7$5	-$A_7$4	-$A_7$3	-$A_7$2	-$A_7$1	-A_7Z	-A_7Y	-A_7X
-A_8X	-A_8Y	-A_8Z	-$A_8$1	-$A_8$2	-$A_8$3	-$A_8$4	-$A_8$5	-A_8P	-A_8Q	-A_8R	-A_8S	-A_8T	-A_8U	-A_8V	-A_8W
-A_9Y	-A_9X	-$A_9$1	-A_9Z	-$A_9$3	-$A_9$2	-$A_9$5	-$A_9$4	-A_9Q	-A_9P	-A_9S	-A_9R	-A_9U	-A_9T	-A_9W	-A_9V
-A_{10}Z	-A_{10}1	-A_{10}X	-A_{10}Y	-A_{10}4	-A_{10}5	-A_{10}2	-A_{10}3	-A_{10}R	-A_{10}S	-A_{10}P	-A_{10}Q	-A_{10}V	-A_{10}W	-A_{10}T	-A_{10}U
-A_{11}1	-A_{11}Z	-A_{11}Y	-A_{11}X	-A_{11}5	-A_{11}4	-A_{11}3	-A_{11}2	-A_{11}S	-A_{11}R	-A_{11}Q	-A_{11}P	-A_{11}W	-A_{11}V	-A_{11}U	-A_{11}T
-A_{12}2	-A_{12}3	-A_{12}4	-A_{12}5	-A_{12}X	-A_{12}Y	-A_{12}Z	-A_{12}1	-A_{12}T	-A_{12}U	-A_{12}V	-A_{12}W	-A_{12}P	-A_{12}Q	-A_{12}R	-A_{12}S
-A_{13}3	-A_{13}2	-A_{13}5	-A_{13}4	-A_{13}Y	-A_{13}X	-A_{13}1	-A_{13}Z	-A_{13}U	-A_{13}T	-A_{13}W	-A_{13}V	-A_{13}Q	-A_{13}P	-A_{13}S	-A_{13}R
-A_{14}4	-A_{14}5	-A_{14}2	-A_{14}3	-A_{14}Z	-A_{14}1	-A_{14}X	-A_{14}Y	-A_{14}V	-A_{14}W	-A_{14}T	-A_{14}U	-A_{14}R	-A_{14}S	-A_{14}P	-A_{14}Q
-A_{15}5	-A_{15}4	-A_{15}3	-A_{15}2	-A_{15}1	-A_{15}Z	-A_{15}Y	-A_{15}X	-A_{15}W	-A_{15}V	-A_{15}U	-A_{15}T	-A_{15}S	-A_{15}R	-A_{15}Q	-A_{15}P

A Reflected 32-Run Design With A Sixteen-Level Factor

One factor at 16 levels and sixteen factors at 2 levels each. A (1/32,768)th Replicate.

Treatment Combinations

Run	A	P	Q	R	S	T	U	V	W	X	Y	Z	1	2	3	4	5
1	16	+	+	+	+	+	+	+	+	+	+	+	+	+	+	+	+
2	16	-	-	-	-	-	-	-	-	-	-	-	-	-	-	-	-
3	15	-	-	-	-	-	-	-	-	+	+	+	+	+	+	+	+
4	15	+	+	+	+	+	+	+	+	-	-	-	-	-	-	-	-
5	14	+	+	+	+	-	-	-	-	-	-	-	-	+	+	+	+
6	14	-	-	-	-	+	+	+	+	+	+	+	+	-	-	-	-
7	13	-	-	-	-	+	+	+	+	-	-	-	-	+	+	+	+
8	13	+	+	+	+	-	-	-	-	+	+	+	+	-	-	-	-
9	12	+	+	-	-	-	-	+	+	+	+	-	-	-	-	+	+
10	12	-	-	+	+	+	+	-	-	-	-	+	+	+	+	-	-
11	11	-	-	+	+	+	+	-	-	+	+	-	-	-	-	+	+
12	11	+	+	-	-	-	-	+	+	-	-	+	+	+	+	-	-
13	10	+	+	-	-	+	+	-	-	-	-	+	+	-	-	+	+
14	10	-	-	+	+	-	-	+	+	+	+	-	-	+	+	-	-
15	9	-	-	+	+	-	-	+	+	-	-	+	+	-	-	+	+
16	9	+	+	-	-	+	+	-	-	+	+	-	-	+	+	-	-
17	8	+	-	-	+	+	-	-	+	+	-	-	+	+	-	-	+
18	8	-	+	+	-	-	+	+	-	-	+	+	-	-	+	+	-
19	7	-	+	+	-	-	+	+	-	+	-	-	+	+	-	-	+
20	7	+	-	-	+	+	-	-	+	-	+	+	-	-	+	+	-
21	6	+	-	-	+	-	+	+	-	-	+	+	-	+	-	-	+
22	6	-	+	+	-	+	-	-	+	+	-	-	+	-	+	+	-
23	5	-	+	+	-	+	-	-	+	-	+	+	-	+	-	-	+
24	5	+	-	-	+	-	+	+	-	+	-	-	+	-	+	+	-
25	4	+	-	+	-	-	+	-	+	+	-	+	-	-	+	-	+
26	4	-	+	-	+	+	-	+	-	-	+	-	+	+	-	+	-
27	3	-	+	-	+	+	-	+	-	+	-	+	-	-	+	-	+
28	3	+	-	+	-	-	+	-	+	-	+	-	+	+	-	+	-
29	2	+	-	+	-	+	-	+	-	-	+	-	+	-	+	-	+
30	2	-	+	-	+	-	+	-	+	+	-	+	-	+	-	+	-
31	1	-	+	-	+	-	+	-	+	-	+	-	+	-	+	-	+
32	1	+	-	+	-	+	-	+	-	+	-	+	-	+	-	+	-
	A	P	Q	R	S	T	U	V	W	X	Y	Z	1	2	3	4	5

CONFOUNDING PATTERNS FOR THE
REFLECTED 32-RUN DESIGN WITH A SIXTEEN-LEVEL FACTOR

Use contrast coefficients for Reflected 32-Run Plackett-Burman design for analysis.

Contrast Labels

A	B	C	D	E	F	G	H	I	J	K	L	M	N	O

Corresponding Main Effects and Two-Factor Interactions

A_1	$-A_2$	A_3	$-A_4$	A_5	$-A_6$	A_7	$-A_8$	A_9	$-A_{10}$	A_{11}	$-A_{12}$	A_{13}	$-A_{14}$	A_{15}
PQ	PR	PS	PT	PU	PV	PW	PX	PY	PZ	P1	P2	P3	P4	P5
RS	SQ	QR	QU	QT	QW	QV	QY	QX	Q1	QZ	Q3	Q2	Q5	Q4
TU	TV	TW	RV	RW	RT	RU	RZ	R1	RX	RY	R4	R5	R2	R3
VW	UW	UV	SW	SV	SU	ST	S1	SZ	SY	SX	S5	S4	S3	S2
XY	XZ	X1	X2	X3	X4	X5	T2	T3	T4	T5	TX	TY	TZ	T1
Z1	Y1	YZ	Y3	Y2	Y5	Y4	U3	U2	U5	U4	UY	UX	U1	UZ
23	24	25	Z4	Z5	Z2	Z3	V4	V5	V2	V3	VZ	V1	VX	VY
45	35	34	15	14	13	12	W5	W4	W3	W2	W1	WZ	WY	WX

Contrast Labels

P	Q	R	S	T	U	V	W	X	Y	Z	1	2	3	4	5

Corresponding Main Effects and Two-Factor Interactions

P	Q	R	S	T	U	V	W	X	Y	Z	1	2	3	4	5
A_1Q	A_1P	A_1S	A_1R	A_1U	A_1T	A_1W	A_1V	A_1Y	A_1X	A_11	A_1Z	A_13	A_12	A_15	A_14
$-A_2R$	$-A_2S$	$-A_2P$	$-A_2Q$	$-A_2V$	$-A_2W$	$-A_2T$	$-A_2U$	$-A_2Z$	$-A_21$	$-A_2X$	$-A_2Y$	$-A_24$	$-A_25$	$-A_22$	$-A_23$
A_3S	A_3R	A_3Q	A_3P	A_3W	A_3V	A_3U	A_3T	A_31	A_3Z	A_3Y	A_3X	A_35	A_34	A_33	A_32
$-A_4T$	$-A_4U$	$-A_4V$	$-A_4W$	$-A_4P$	$-A_4Q$	$-A_4R$	$-A_4S$	$-A_42$	$-A_43$	$-A_44$	$-A_45$	$-A_4X$	$-A_4Y$	$-A_4Z$	$-A_41$
A_5U	A_5T	A_5W	A_5V	A_5Q	A_5P	A_5S	A_5R	A_53	A_52	A_55	A_54	A_5Y	A_5X	A_51	A_5Z
$-A_6V$	$-A_6W$	$-A_6T$	$-A_6U$	$-A_6R$	$-A_6S$	$-A_6P$	$-A_6Q$	$-A_64$	$-A_65$	$-A_62$	$-A_63$	$-A_6Z$	$-A_61$	$-A_6X$	$-A_6Y$
A_7W	A_7V	A_7U	A_7T	A_7S	A_7R	A_7Q	A_7P	A_75	A_74	A_73	A_72	A_71	A_7Z	A_7Y	A_7X
$-A_8X$	$-A_8Y$	$-A_8Z$	$-A_81$	$-A_82$	$-A_83$	$-A_84$	$-A_85$	$-A_8P$	$-A_8Q$	$-A_8R$	$-A_8S$	$-A_8T$	$-A_8U$	$-A_8V$	$-A_8W$
A_9Y	A_9X	A_91	A_9Z	A_93	A_92	A_95	A_94	A_9Q	A_9P	A_9S	A_9R	A_9U	A_9T	A_9W	A_9V
$-A_{10}Z$	$-A_{10}1$	$-A_{10}X$	$-A_{10}Y$	$-A_{10}4$	$-A_{10}5$	$-A_{10}2$	$-A_{10}3$	$-A_{10}R$	$-A_{10}S$	$-A_{10}P$	$-A_{10}Q$	$-A_{10}V$	$-A_{10}W$	$-A_{10}T$	$-A_{10}U$
$A_{11}1$	$A_{11}Z$	$A_{11}Y$	$A_{11}X$	$A_{11}5$	$A_{11}4$	$A_{11}3$	$A_{11}2$	$A_{11}S$	$A_{11}R$	$A_{11}Q$	$A_{11}P$	$A_{11}W$	$A_{11}V$	$A_{11}U$	$A_{11}T$
$-A_{12}2$	$-A_{12}3$	$-A_{12}4$	$-A_{12}5$	$-A_{12}X$	$-A_{12}Y$	$-A_{12}Z$	$-A_{12}1$	$-A_{12}T$	$-A_{12}U$	$-A_{12}V$	$-A_{12}W$	$-A_{12}P$	$-A_{12}Q$	$-A_{12}R$	$-A_{12}S$
$A_{13}3$	$A_{13}2$	$A_{13}5$	$A_{13}4$	$A_{13}Y$	$A_{13}X$	$A_{13}1$	$A_{13}Z$	$A_{13}U$	$A_{13}T$	$A_{13}W$	$A_{13}V$	$A_{13}Q$	$A_{13}P$	$A_{13}S$	$A_{13}R$
$-A_{14}4$	$-A_{14}5$	$-A_{14}2$	$-A_{14}3$	$-A_{14}Z$	$-A_{14}1$	$-A_{14}X$	$-A_{14}Y$	$-A_{14}V$	$-A_{14}W$	$-A_{14}T$	$-A_{14}U$	$-A_{14}R$	$-A_{14}S$	$-A_{14}P$	$-A_{14}Q$
$A_{15}5$	$A_{15}4$	$A_{15}3$	$A_{15}2$	$A_{15}1$	$A_{15}Z$	$A_{15}Y$	$A_{15}X$	$A_{15}W$	$A_{15}V$	$A_{15}U$	$A_{15}T$	$A_{15}S$	$A_{15}R$	$A_{15}Q$	$A_{15}P$

Some interactions will fail to show a change of sign between the basic design and the reflected design. This is due to the negative signs attached to the main effects in the reflected design and is unavoidable when using these designs with factors having more than two levels.

32-RUN DESIGNS HAVING ONE FACTOR WITH NINE TO FIFTEEN LEVELS

The 16 level factor in the previous 32-run designs may be changed into a factor having as few as 9 levels or as many as 15 levels by changing the values in the column for Factor A as indicated below. Since these designs will make Factor A appear to have 15 degrees of freedom regardless of the number of levels present, there will be some redundancy in the effects represented by the contrasts. In spite of this redundancy the contrasts will still be orthogonal. Significant contrasts should be interpreted in terms of the contrast coefficients for that contrast and the factor levels being compared by those coefficients. The confounding patterns will remain as shown for the 32-run designs having one factor with 16 levels. Analyze each of these designs by using the contrasts defined for either the basic 32-run Plackett-Burman design or the reflected 32-run Plackett-Burman design.

As noted earlier, when Factor A has 15 levels or fewer one must use one or more levels to replace the missing levels for the sixteen level factor. Any levels may be used for this, but the levels used must be used consistently throughout the Basic and Reflected studies. Some possible choices are below.

	Basic 32-Run Designs								Reflected 32-Run Designs							
Number of levels:	16	15	14	13	12	11	10	9	16	15	14	13	12	11	10	9
Factor Label:	A	A	A	A	A	A	A	A	A	A	A	A	A	A	A	A
Runs																
1 and 2	1	1	1	1	1	1	1	1	16	1	14	13	12	1	10	9
3 and 4	2	2	2	2	2	2	2	2	15	15	1	7	8	8	9	8
5 and 6	3	3	3	3	3	3	3	3	14	14	14	1	4	6	7	7
7 and 8	4	4	4	4	4	4	4	4	13	13	13	13	1	4	4	5
9 and 10	5	5	5	5	5	5	5	5	12	12	12	12	12	1	2	3
11 and 12	6	6	6	6	6	6	6	6	11	11	11	11	11	11	1	2
13 and 14	7	7	7	7	7	7	7	7	10	10	10	10	10	10	10	1
15 and 16	8	8	8	8	8	8	8	8	9	9	9	9	9	9	9	9
17 and 18	9	9	9	9	9	9	9	9	8	8	8	8	8	8	8	8
19 and 20	10	10	10	10	10	10	10	1	7	7	7	7	7	7	7	7
21 and 22	11	11	11	11	11	11	1	2	6	6	6	6	6	6	6	6
23 and 24	12	12	12	12	12	1	2	3	5	5	5	5	5	5	5	5
25 and 26	13	13	13	13	1	4	4	5	4	4	4	4	4	4	4	4
27 and 28	14	14	14	1	4	6	7	7	3	3	3	3	3	3	3	3
29 and 30	15	15	1	7	8	8	9	8	2	2	2	2	2	2	2	2
31 and 32	16	1	14	13	12	11	10	9	1	1	1	1	1	1	1	1

A BASIC 32-RUN DESIGN WITH AN EIGHT-LEVEL FACTOR

One factor with 8 levels and twenty-four factors with 2 levels each. Use contrast coefficients for the Basic 32-Run Plackett-Burman Design for the analysis of data collected under the following conditions.

Treatment Combinations

Run	A	H I J K	L M N O	P Q R S	T U V W	X Y Z 1	2 3 4 5
1	1	− − − −	− − − −	− − − −	− − − −	− − − −	− − − −
2	1	− − − −	− − − −	+ + + +	+ + + +	+ + + +	+ + + +
3	1	+ + + +	+ + + +	+ + + +	+ + + +	− − − −	− − − −
4	1	+ + + +	+ + + +	− − − −	− − − −	+ + + +	+ + + +
5	2	+ + + +	− − − −	− − − −	+ + + +	+ + + +	− − − −
6	2	+ + + +	− − − −	+ + + +	− − − −	− − − −	+ + + +
7	2	− − − −	+ + + +	+ + + +	− − − −	+ + + +	− − − −
8	2	− − − −	+ + + +	− − − −	+ + + +	− − − −	+ + + +
9	3	− − + +	+ + − −	− − + +	+ + − −	− − + +	+ + − −
10	3	− − + +	+ + − −	+ + − −	− − + +	+ + − −	− − + +
11	3	+ + − −	− − + +	+ + − −	− − + +	− − + +	+ + − −
12	3	+ + − −	− − + +	− − + +	+ + − −	+ + − −	− − + +
13	4	+ + − −	+ + − −	− − + +	− − + +	+ + − −	+ + − −
14	4	+ + − −	+ + − −	+ + − −	+ + − −	− − + +	− − + +
15	4	− − + +	− − + +	+ + − −	+ + − −	+ + − −	+ + − −
16	4	− − + +	− − + +	− − + +	− − + +	− − + +	− − + +
17	5	− + + −	− + + −	− + + −	− + + −	− + + −	− + + −
18	5	− + + −	− + + −	+ − − +	+ − − +	+ − − +	+ − − +
19	5	+ − − +	+ − − +	+ − − +	+ − − +	− + + −	− + + −
20	5	+ − − +	+ − − +	− + + −	− + + −	+ − − +	+ − − +
21	6	+ − − +	− + + −	− + + −	+ − − +	+ − − +	− + + −
22	6	+ − − +	− + + −	+ − − +	− + + −	− + + −	+ − − +
23	6	− + + −	+ − − +	+ − − +	− + + −	+ − − +	− + + −
24	6	− + + −	+ − − +	− + + −	+ − − +	− + + −	+ − − +
25	7	− + − +	+ − + −	− + − +	+ − + −	− + − +	+ − + −
26	7	− + − +	+ − + −	+ − + −	− + − +	+ − + −	− + − +
27	7	+ − + −	− + − +	+ − + −	− + − +	− + − +	+ − + −
28	7	+ − + −	− + − +	− + − +	+ − + −	+ − + −	− + − +
29	8	+ − + −	+ − + −	− + − +	− + − +	+ − + −	+ − + −
30	8	+ − + −	+ − + −	+ − + −	+ − + −	− + − +	− + − +
31	8	− + − +	− + − +	+ − + −	+ − + −	+ − + −	+ − + −
32	8	− + − +	− + − +	− + − +	− + − +	− + − +	− + − +
	A	H I J K	L M N O	P Q R S	T U V W	X Y Z 1	2 3 4 5

CONFOUNDING PATTERNS FOR THE BASIC 32-RUN DESIGN WITH AN EIGHT-LEVEL FACTOR

Contrast Labels

A	B	C	D	E	F	G	H	I	J	K	L	M	N	O	P

Corresponding Main Effects and Two-Factor Interactions

A_1	A_2	A_3	A_4	A_5	A_6	A_7	H	I	J	K	L	M	N	O	P
-HI	-HJ	-HK	-HL	-HM	-HN	-HO	$-A_1I$	$-A_1H$	$-A_1K$	$-A_1J$	$-A_1M$	$-A_1L$	$-A_1O$	$-A_1N$	$-A_1Q$
-JK	-IK	-IJ	-IM	-IL	-IO	-IN	$-A_2J$	$-A_2K$	$-A_2H$	$-A_2I$	$-A_2N$	$-A_2O$	$-A_2L$	$-A_2M$	$-A_2R$
-LM	-LN	-LO	-JN	-JO	-JL	-JM	$-A_3K$	$-A_3J$	$-A_3I$	$-A_3H$	$-A_3O$	$-A_3N$	$-A_3M$	$-A_3L$	$-A_3S$
-NO	-MO	-MN	-KO	-KN	-KM	-KL	$-A_4L$	$-A_4M$	$-A_4N$	$-A_4O$	$-A_4H$	$-A_4I$	$-A_4J$	$-A_4K$	$-A_4T$
-PQ	-PR	-PS	-PT	-PU	-PV	-PW	$-A_5M$	$-A_5L$	$-A_5O$	$-A_5N$	$-A_5I$	$-A_5H$	$-A_5K$	$-A_5J$	$-A_5U$
-RS	-SQ	-QR	-QU	-QT	-QW	-QV	$-A_6N$	$-A_6O$	$-A_6L$	$-A_6M$	$-A_6J$	$-A_6K$	$-A_6H$	$-A_6I$	$-A_6V$
-TU	-TV	-TW	-RV	-RW	-RT	-RU	$-A_7O$	$-A_7N$	$-A_7M$	$-A_7L$	$-A_7K$	$-A_7J$	$-A_7I$	$-A_7H$	$-A_7W$
-VW	-UW	-UV	-SW	-SV	-SU	-ST	-PX	-PY	-PZ	-P1	-P2	-P3	-P4	-P5	-HX
-XY	-XZ	-X1	-X2	-X3	-X4	-X5	-QY	-QX	-Q1	-QZ	-Q3	-Q2	-Q5	-Q4	-IY
-Z1	-Y1	-YZ	-Y3	-Y2	-Y5	-Y4	-RZ	-R1	-RX	-RY	-R4	-R5	-R2	-R3	-JZ
-23	-24	-25	-Z4	-Z5	-Z2	-Z3	-S1	-SZ	-SY	-SX	-S5	-S4	-S3	-S2	-K1
-45	-35	-34	-15	-14	-13	-12	-T2	-T3	-T4	-T5	-TX	-TY	-TZ	-T1	-L2
							-U3	-U2	-U5	-U4	-UY	-UX	-U1	-UZ	-M3
							-V4	-V5	-V2	-V3	-VZ	-V1	-VX	-VY	-N4
							-W5	-W4	-W3	-W2	-W1	-WZ	-WY	-WX	-O5

Contrast Labels

Q	R	S	T	U	V	W	X	Y	Z	1	2	3	4	5

Corresponding Main Effects and Two-Factor Interactions

Q	R	S	T	U	V	W	X	Y	Z	1	2	3	4	5
$-A_1P$	$-A_1S$	$-A_1R$	$-A_1U$	$-A_1T$	$-A_1W$	$-A_1V$	$-A_1Y$	$-A_1X$	$-A_11$	$-A_1Z$	$-A_13$	$-A_12$	$-A_15$	$-A_14$
$-A_2S$	$-A_2P$	$-A_2Q$	$-A_2V$	$-A_2W$	$-A_2T$	$-A_2U$	$-A_2Z$	$-A_21$	$-A_2X$	$-A_2Y$	$-A_24$	$-A_25$	$-A_22$	$-A_23$
$-A_3R$	$-A_3Q$	$-A_3P$	$-A_3W$	$-A_3V$	$-A_3U$	$-A_3T$	$-A_31$	$-A_3Z$	$-A_3Y$	$-A_3X$	$-A_35$	$-A_34$	$-A_33$	$-A_32$
$-A_4U$	$-A_4V$	$-A_4W$	$-A_4P$	$-A_4Q$	$-A_4R$	$-A_4S$	$-A_42$	$-A_43$	$-A_44$	$-A_45$	$-A_4X$	$-A_4Y$	$-A_4Z$	$-A_41$
$-A_5T$	$-A_5W$	$-A_5V$	$-A_5Q$	$-A_5P$	$-A_5S$	$-A_5R$	$-A_53$	$-A_52$	$-A_55$	$-A_54$	$-A_5Y$	$-A_5X$	$-A_51$	$-A_5Z$
$-A_6W$	$-A_6T$	$-A_6U$	$-A_6R$	$-A_6S$	$-A_6P$	$-A_6Q$	$-A_64$	$-A_65$	$-A_62$	$-A_63$	$-A_6Z$	$-A_61$	$-A_6X$	$-A_6Y$
$-A_7V$	$-A_7U$	$-A_7T$	$-A_7S$	$-A_7R$	$-A_7Q$	$-A_7P$	$-A_75$	$-A_74$	$-A_73$	$-A_72$	$-A_71$	$-A_7Z$	$-A_7Y$	$-A_7X$
-HY	-HZ	-H1	-H2	-H3	-H4	-H5	-HP	-HQ	-HR	-HS	-HT	-HU	-HV	-HW
-IX	-I1	-IZ	-I3	-I2	-I5	-I4	-IQ	-IP	-IS	-IR	-IU	-IT	-IW	-IV
-J1	-JX	-JY	-J4	-J5	-J2	-J3	-JR	-JS	-JP	-JQ	-JV	-JW	-JT	-JU
-KZ	-KY	-KX	-K5	-K4	-K3	-K2	-KS	-KR	-KQ	-KP	-KW	-KV	-KU	-KT
-L3	-L4	-L5	-LX	-LY	-LZ	-L1	-LT	-LU	-LV	-LW	-LP	-LQ	-LR	-LS
-M2	-M5	-M4	-MY	-MX	-M1	-MZ	-MU	-MT	-MW	-MV	-MQ	-MP	-MS	-MR
-N5	-N2	-N3	-NZ	-N1	-NX	-NY	-NV	-NW	-NT	-NU	-NR	-NS	-NP	-NQ
-O4	-O3	-O2	-O1	-OZ	-OY	-OX	-OW	-OV	-OU	-OT	-OS	-OR	-OQ	-OP

A Reflected 32-Run Design With An Eight-Level Factor

One factor with 8 levels and twenty-four factors with two levels each.

Treatment Combinations

Run	A	H I J K	L M N O	P Q R S	T U V W	X Y Z 1	2 3 4 5
1	8	+ + + +	+ + + +	+ + + +	+ + + +	+ + + +	+ + + +
2	8	+ + + +	+ + + +	− − − −	− − − −	− − − −	− − − −
3	8	− − − −	− − − −	− − − −	− − − −	+ + + +	+ + + +
4	8	− − − −	− − − −	+ + + +	+ + + +	− − − −	− − − −
5	7	− − − −	+ + + +	+ + + +	− − − −	− − − −	+ + + +
6	7	− − − −	+ + + +	− − − −	+ + + +	+ + + +	− − − −
7	7	+ + + +	− − − −	− − − −	+ + + +	− − − −	+ + + +
8	7	+ + + +	− − − −	+ + + +	− − − −	+ + + +	− − − −
9	6	+ + − −	− − + +	+ + − −	− − + +	+ + − −	− − + +
10	6	+ + − −	− − + +	− − + +	+ + − −	− − + +	+ + − −
11	6	− − + +	+ + − −	− − + +	+ + − −	+ + − −	− − + +
12	6	− − + +	+ + − −	+ + − −	− − + +	− − + +	+ + − −
13	5	− − + +	− − + +	+ + − −	+ + − −	− − + +	− − + +
14	5	− − + +	− − + +	− − + +	− − + +	+ + − −	+ + − −
15	5	+ + − −	+ + − −	− − + +	− − + +	− − + +	− − + +
16	5	+ + − −	+ + − −	+ + − −	+ + − −	+ + − −	+ + − −
17	4	+ − − +	+ − − +	+ − − +	+ − − +	+ − − +	+ − − +
18	4	+ − − +	+ − − +	− + + −	− + + −	− + + −	− + + −
19	4	− + + −	− + + −	− + + −	− + + −	+ − − +	+ − − +
20	4	− + + −	− + + −	+ − − +	+ − − +	− + + −	− + + −
21	3	− + + −	+ − − +	+ − − +	− + + −	− + + −	+ − − +
22	3	− + + −	+ − − +	− + + −	+ − − +	+ − − +	− + + −
23	3	+ − − +	− + + −	− + + −	+ − − +	− + + −	+ − − +
24	3	+ − − +	− + + −	+ − − +	− + + −	+ − − +	− + + −
25	2	+ − + −	− + − +	+ − + −	− + − +	+ − + −	− + − +
26	2	+ − + −	− + − +	− + − +	+ − + −	− + − +	+ − + −
27	2	− + − +	+ − + −	− + − +	+ − + −	+ − + −	− + − +
28	2	− + − +	+ − + −	+ − + −	− + − +	− + − +	+ − + −
29	1	− + − +	− + − +	+ − + −	+ − + −	− + − +	− + − +
30	1	− + − +	− + − +	− + − +	− + − +	+ − + −	+ − + −
31	1	+ − + −	+ − + −	− + − +	− + − +	− + − +	− + − +
32	1	+ − + −	+ − + −	+ − + −	+ − + −	+ − + −	+ − + −
	A	H I J K	L M N O	P Q R S	T U V W	X Y Z 1	2 3 4 5

CONFOUNDING PATTERNS FOR THE
REFLECTED 32-RUN DESIGN WITH AN EIGHT-LEVEL FACTOR

Contrast Labels

A	B	C	D	E	F	G	H	I	J	K	L	M	N	O	P

Corresponding Main Effects and Two-Factor Interactions

A_1	$-A_2$	A_3	$-A_4$	A_5	$-A_6$	A_7	H	I	J	K	L	M	N	O	P
HI	HJ	HK	HL	HM	HN	HO	A_1I	A_1H	A_1K	A_1J	A_1M	A_1L	A_1O	A_1N	A_1Q
JK	IK	IJ	IM	IL	IO	IN	$-A_2$J	$-A_2$K	$-A_2$H	$-A_2$I	$-A_2$N	$-A_2$O	$-A_2$L	$-A_2$M	$-A_2$R
LM	LN	LO	JN	JO	JL	JM	A_3K	A_3J	A_3I	A_3H	A_3O	A_3N	A_3M	A_3L	A_3S
NO	MO	MN	KO	KN	KM	KL	$-A_4$L	$-A_4$M	$-A_4$N	$-A_4$O	$-A_4$H	$-A_4$I	$-A_4$J	$-A_4$K	$-A_4$T
PQ	PR	PS	PT	PU	PV	PW	A_5M	A_5L	A_5O	A_5N	A_5I	A_5H	A_5K	A_5J	A_5U
RS	SQ	QR	QU	QT	QW	QV	$-A_6$N	$-A_6$O	$-A_6$L	$-A_6$M	$-A_6$J	$-A_6$K	$-A_6$H	$-A_6$I	$-A_6$V
TU	TV	TW	RV	RW	RT	RU	A_7O	A_7N	A_7M	A_7L	A_7K	A_7J	A_7I	A_7H	A_7W
VW	UW	UV	SW	SV	SU	ST	PX	PY	PZ	P1	P2	P3	P4	P5	HX
XY	XZ	X1	X2	X3	X4	X5	QY	QX	Q1	QZ	Q3	Q2	Q5	Q4	IY
Z1	Y1	YZ	Y3	Y2	Y5	Y4	RZ	R1	RX	RY	R4	R5	R2	R3	JZ
23	24	25	Z4	Z5	Z2	Z3	S1	SZ	SY	SX	S5	S4	S3	S2	K1
45	35	34	15	14	13	12	T2	T3	T4	T5	TX	TY	TZ	T1	L2
							U3	U2	U5	U4	UY	UX	U1	UZ	M3
							V4	V5	V2	V3	VZ	V1	VX	VY	N4
							W5	W4	W3	W2	W1	WZ	WY	WX	O5

Contrast Labels

Q	R	S	T	U	V	W	X	Y	Z	1	2	3	4	5

Corresponding Main Effects and Two-Factor Interactions

Q	R	S	T	U	V	W	X	Y	Z	1	2	3	4	5
A_1P	A_1S	A_1R	A_1U	A_1T	A_1W	A_1V	A_1Y	A_1X	$A_1$1	A_1Z	$A_1$3	$A_1$2	$A_1$5	$A_1$4
$-A_2$S	$-A_2$P	$-A_2$Q	$-A_2$V	$-A_2$W	$-A_2$T	$-A_2$U	$-A_2$Z	$-A_2$1	$-A_2$X	$-A_2$Y	$-A_2$4	$-A_2$5	$-A_2$2	$-A_2$3
A_3R	A_3Q	A_3P	A_3W	A_3V	A_3U	A_3T	$A_3$1	A_3Z	A_3Y	A_3X	$A_3$5	$A_3$4	$A_3$3	$A_3$2
$-A_4$U	$-A_4$V	$-A_4$W	$-A_4$P	$-A_4$Q	$-A_4$R	$-A_4$S	$-A_4$2	$-A_4$3	$-A_4$4	$-A_4$5	$-A_4$X	$-A_4$Y	$-A_4$Z	$-A_4$1
A_5T	A_5W	A_5V	A_5Q	A_5P	A_5S	A_5R	$A_5$3	$A_5$2	$A_5$5	$A_5$4	A_5Y	A_5X	$A_5$1	A_5Z
$-A_6$W	$-A_6$T	$-A_6$U	$-A_6$R	$-A_6$S	$-A_6$P	$-A_6$Q	$-A_6$4	$-A_6$5	$-A_6$2	$-A_6$3	$-A_6$Z	$-A_6$1	$-A_6$X	$-A_6$Y
A_7V	A_7U	A_7T	A_7S	A_7R	A_7Q	A_7P	$A_7$5	$A_7$4	$A_7$3	$A_7$2	$A_7$1	A_7Z	A_7Y	A_7X
HY	HZ	H1	H2	H3	H4	H5	HP	HQ	HR	HS	HT	HU	HV	HW
IX	I1	IZ	I3	I2	I5	I4	IQ	IP	IS	IR	IU	IT	IW	IV
J1	JX	JY	J4	J5	J2	J3	JR	JS	JP	JQ	JV	JW	JT	JU
KZ	KY	KX	K5	K4	K3	K2	KS	KR	KQ	KP	KW	KV	KU	KT
L3	L4	L5	LX	LY	LZ	L1	LT	LU	LV	LW	LP	LQ	LR	LS
M2	M5	M4	MY	MX	M1	MZ	MU	MT	MW	MV	MQ	MP	MS	MR
N5	N2	N3	NZ	N1	NX	NY	NV	NW	NT	NU	NR	NS	NP	NQ
O4	O3	O2	O1	OZ	OY	OX	OW	OV	OU	OT	OS	OR	OQ	OP

Note that three main effects for Factor A show a change of sign between the basic design and the reflected design.

32-Run Designs Having
One Factor With Five to Seven Levels

The 8 level factor in the previous 32-run designs may be changed into a factor having 5, 6, or 7 levels by changing the values in the column for Factor A as indicated below. Since these designs will make Factor A appear to have 7 degrees of freedom regardless of the number of levels present, there will be some redundancy in the effects represented by the contrasts. In spite of this redundancy the contrasts will still be orthogonal. Significant contrasts should be interpreted in terms of the contrast coefficients for that contrast and the factor levels being compared by those coefficients. The confounding patterns will remain as shown for the 32-run designs having one factor with 8 levels. Analyze each of these designs by using the contrasts defined for either the basic 32-run Plackett-Burman design or the reflected 32-run Plackett-Burman design.

	Basic 32-Run Designs				Reflected 32-Run Designs			
Number of levels:	8	7	6	5	8	7	6	5
Factor Label:	A	A	A	A	A	A	A	A
Runs	Levels							
1, 2, 3 and 4	1	1	1	1	8	1	6	5
5, 6, 7 and 8	2	2	2	2	7	7	1	3
9, 10, 11 and 12	3	3	3	3	6	6	6	1
13, 14, 15 and 16	4	4	4	4	5	5	5	5
17, 18, 19 and 20	5	5	5	5	4	4	4	4
21, 22, 23, and 24	6	6	6	1	3	3	3	3
25, 26, 27 and 28	7	7	1	3	2	2	2	2
29, 30, 31 and 32	8	1	6	5	1	1	1	1

A BASIC 32-RUN DESIGN WITH A FOUR-LEVEL FACTOR

One factor at 4 levels and up to twenty-eight factors at 2 levels each. Use contrast coefficients for the Basic 32-Run Plackett-Burman Design for the analysis of data collected under the following conditions.

Treatment Combinations

Run	A	D	E	F	G	H	I	J	K	L	M	N	O	P	Q	R	S	T	U	V	W	X	Y	Z	1	2	3	4	5
1	1	−	−	−	−	−	−	−	−	−	−	−	−	−	−	−	−	−	−	−	−	−	−	−	−	−	−	−	−
2	1	−	−	−	−	−	−	−	−	−	−	−	−	+	+	+	+	+	+	+	+	+	+	+	+	+	+	+	+
3	1	−	−	−	−	+	+	+	+	+	+	+	+	+	+	+	+	+	+	+	+	−	−	−	−	−	−	−	−
4	1	−	−	−	−	+	+	+	+	+	+	+	+	−	−	−	−	−	−	−	−	+	+	+	+	+	+	+	+
5	1	+	+	+	+	+	+	+	+	−	−	−	−	−	−	−	−	+	+	+	+	+	+	+	+	−	−	−	−
6	1	+	+	+	+	+	+	+	+	−	−	−	−	+	+	+	+	−	−	−	−	−	−	−	−	+	+	+	+
7	1	+	+	+	+	−	−	−	−	+	+	+	+	+	+	+	+	−	−	−	−	+	+	+	+	−	−	−	−
8	1	+	+	+	+	−	−	−	−	+	+	+	+	−	−	−	−	+	+	+	+	−	−	−	−	+	+	+	+
9	2	+	+	−	−	−	−	+	+	+	+	−	−	−	−	+	+	+	+	−	−	−	−	+	+	+	+	−	−
10	2	+	+	−	−	−	−	+	+	+	+	−	−	+	+	−	−	−	−	+	+	+	+	−	−	−	−	+	+
11	2	+	+	−	−	+	+	−	−	−	−	+	+	+	+	−	−	−	−	+	+	−	−	+	+	+	+	−	−
12	2	+	+	−	−	+	+	−	−	−	−	+	+	−	−	+	+	+	+	−	−	+	+	−	−	−	−	+	+
13	2	−	−	+	+	+	+	−	−	−	−	+	+	−	−	+	+	+	+	−	−	+	+	−	−	+	+	+	+
14	2	−	−	+	+	+	+	−	−	−	−	+	+	+	+	−	−	−	−	+	+	−	−	+	+	−	−	+	+
15	2	−	−	+	+	−	−	+	+	+	+	−	−	+	+	−	−	−	−	+	+	+	+	−	−	+	+	−	−
16	2	−	−	+	+	−	−	+	+	+	+	−	−	−	−	+	+	+	+	−	−	+	+	−	−	−	−	+	+
17	3	−	+	+	−	−	+	+	−	−	+	+	−	−	+	+	−	−	+	+	−	−	+	+	−	−	+	+	−
18	3	−	+	+	−	−	+	+	−	−	+	+	−	+	−	−	+	+	−	−	+	+	−	−	+	+	−	−	+
19	3	−	+	+	−	+	−	−	+	+	−	−	+	+	−	−	+	+	−	−	+	−	+	+	−	−	+	+	−
20	3	−	+	+	−	+	−	−	+	+	−	−	+	−	+	+	−	−	+	+	−	+	−	−	+	+	−	−	+
21	3	+	−	−	+	+	−	−	+	−	+	+	−	−	+	+	−	+	−	−	+	+	−	−	+	−	+	+	−
22	3	+	−	−	+	+	−	−	+	−	+	+	−	+	−	−	+	−	+	+	−	−	+	+	−	+	−	−	+
23	3	+	−	−	+	−	+	+	−	+	−	−	+	+	−	−	+	−	+	+	−	+	−	−	+	−	+	+	−
24	3	+	−	−	+	−	+	+	−	+	−	−	+	−	+	+	−	+	−	−	+	−	+	+	−	+	−	−	+
25	4	+	−	+	−	−	+	−	+	+	−	+	−	+	−	+	−	−	+	−	+	−	+	+	−	+	−	+	−
26	4	+	−	+	−	−	+	−	+	+	−	+	−	+	−	+	−	−	+	−	+	+	−	+	−	−	+	−	+
27	4	+	−	+	−	+	−	+	−	−	+	−	+	+	−	+	−	−	+	−	+	+	−	+	−	+	−	+	−
28	4	+	−	+	−	+	−	+	−	−	+	−	+	−	+	−	+	+	−	+	−	+	−	+	−	−	+	−	+
29	4	−	+	−	+	+	−	+	−	−	+	−	+	−	+	−	+	+	−	+	−	+	−	+	−	+	−	+	−
30	4	−	+	−	+	+	−	+	−	−	+	−	+	+	−	+	−	−	+	−	+	−	+	−	+	−	+	−	+
31	4	−	+	−	+	−	+	−	+	+	−	+	−	+	−	+	−	−	+	−	+	+	−	+	−	+	−	+	−
32	4	−	+	−	+	−	+	−	+	+	−	+	−	−	+	−	+	+	−	+	−	+	−	+	−	−	+	−	+
	A	D	E	F	G	H	I	J	K	L	M	N	O	P	Q	R	S	T	U	V	W	X	Y	Z	1	2	3	4	5

CONFOUNDING PATTERNS FOR
THE BASIC 32-RUN DESIGN WITH A FOUR-LEVEL FACTOR

Contrast Labels

A	B	C	D	E	F	G	H	I	J	K	L	M	N	O	P

Corresponding Main Effects and Two-Factor Interactions

A	A'	A"	D	E	F	G	H	I	J	K	L	M	N	O	P
-DE	-DF	-DG	-AE	-AD	-AG	-AF	-AI	-AH	-AK	-AJ	-AM	-AL	-AO	-AN	-AQ
-FG	-EG	-EF	-A'F	-A'G	-A'D	-A'E	-A'J	-A'K	-A'H	-A'I	-A'N	-A'O	-A'L	-A'M	-A'R
-HI	-HJ	-HK	-A"G	-A"F	-A"E	-A"D	-A"K	-A"J	-A"I	-A"H	-A"O	-A"N	-A"M	-A"L	-A"S
-JK	-IK	-IJ	-HL	-HM	-HN	-HO	-DL	-DM	-DN	-DO	-DH	-DI	-DJ	-DK	-DT
-LM	-LN	-LO	-IM	-IL	-IO	-IN	-EM	-EL	-EO	-EN	-EI	-EH	-EK	-EJ	-EU
-NO	-MO	-MN	-JN	-JO	-JL	-JM	-FN	-FO	-FL	-FM	-FJ	-FK	-FH	-FI	-FV
-PQ	-PR	-PS	-KO	-KN	-KM	-KL	-GO	-GN	-GM	-GL	-GK	-GJ	-GI	-GH	-GW
-RS	-SQ	-QR	-PT	-PU	-PV	-PW	-PX	-PY	-PZ	-P1	-P2	-P3	-P4	-P5	-HX
-TU	-TV	-TW	-QU	-QT	-QW	-QV	-QY	-QX	-Q1	-QZ	-Q3	-Q2	-Q5	-Q4	-IY
-VW	-UW	-UV	-RV	-RW	-RT	-RU	-RZ	-R1	-RX	-RY	-R4	-R5	-R2	-R3	-JZ
-XY	-XZ	-X1	-SW	-SV	-SU	-ST	-S1	-SZ	-SY	-SX	-S5	-S4	-S3	-S2	-K1
-Z1	-Y1	-YZ	-X2	-X3	-X4	-X5	-T2	-T3	-T4	-T5	-TX	-TY	-TZ	-T1	-L2
-23	-24	-25	-Y3	-Y2	-Y5	-Y4	-U3	-U2	-U5	-U4	-UY	-UX	-U1	-UZ	-M3
-45	-35	-34	-Z4	-Z5	-Z2	-Z3	-V4	-V5	-V2	-V3	-VZ	-V1	-VX	-VY	-N4
			-15	-14	-13	-12	-W5	-W4	-W3	-W2	-W1	-WZ	-WY	-WX	-O5

Contrast Labels

Q	R	S	T	U	V	W	X	Y	Z	1	2	3	4	5

Corresponding Main Effects and Two-Factor Interactions

Q	R	S	T	U	V	W	X	Y	Z	1	2	3	4	5
-AP	-AS	-AR	-AU	-AT	-AW	-AV	-AY	-AX	-A1	-AZ	-A3	-A2	-A5	-A4
-A'S	-A'P	-A'Q	-A'V	-A'W	-A'T	-A'U	-A'Z	-A'1	-A'X	-A'Y	-A'4	-A'5	-A'2	-A'3
-A"R	-A"Q	-A"P	-A"W	-A"V	-A"U	-A"T	-A"1	-A"Z	-A"Y	-A"X	-A"5	-A"4	-A"3	-A"2
-DU	-DV	-DW	-DP	-DQ	-DR	-DS	-D2	-D3	-D4	-D5	-DX	-DY	-DZ	-D1
-ET	-EW	-EV	-EQ	-EP	-ES	-ER	-E3	-E2	-E5	-E4	-EY	-EX	-E1	-EZ
-FW	-FT	-FU	-FR	-FS	-FP	-FQ	-F4	-F5	-F2	-F3	-FZ	-F1	-FX	-FY
-GV	-GU	-GT	-GS	-GR	-GQ	-GP	-G5	-G4	-G3	-G2	-G1	-GZ	-GY	-GX
-HY	-HZ	-H1	-H2	-H3	-H4	-H5	-HP	-HQ	-HR	-HS	-HT	-HU	-HV	-HW
-IX	-I1	-IZ	-I3	-I2	-I5	-I4	-IQ	-IP	-IS	-IR	-IU	-IT	-IW	-IV
-J1	-JX	-JY	-J4	-J5	-J2	-J3	-JR	-JS	-JP	-JQ	-JV	-JW	-JT	-JU
-KZ	-KY	-KX	-K5	-K4	-K3	-K2	-KS	-KR	-KQ	-KP	-KW	-KV	-KU	-KT
-L3	-L4	-L5	-LX	-LY	-LZ	-L1	-LT	-LU	-LV	-LW	-LP	-LQ	-LR	-LS
-M2	-M5	-M4	-MY	-MX	-M1	-MZ	-MU	-MT	-MW	-MV	-MQ	-MP	-MS	-MR
-N5	-N2	-N3	-NZ	-N1	-NX	-NY	-NV	-NW	-NT	-NU	-NR	-NS	-NP	-NQ
-O4	-O3	-O2	-O1	-OZ	-OY	-OX	-OW	-OV	-OU	-OT	-OS	-OR	-OQ	-OP

The four-level factor may be changed into a three-level factor as described on page 195.

A Reflected 32-Run Design With A Four-Level Factor

One factor at 4 levels and up to twenty-eight factors at 2 levels each. Use contrast coefficients from the Reflected 32-Run Plackett-Burman Design for the analysis of data collected under the following design.

Treatment Combinations

Run	A	D	E	F	G	H	I	J	K	L	M	N	O	P	Q	R	S	T	U	V	W	X	Y	Z	1	2	3	4	5
1	4	+	+	+	+	+	+	+	+	+	+	+	+	+	+	+	+	+	+	+	+	+	+	+	+	+	+	+	+
2	4	+	+	+	+	+	+	+	+	+	+	+	+	-	-	-	-	-	-	-	-	-	-	-	-	-	-	-	-
3	4	+	+	+	+	-	-	-	-	-	-	-	-	-	-	-	-	-	-	-	-	+	+	+	+	+	+	+	+
4	4	+	+	+	+	-	-	-	-	-	-	-	-	+	+	+	+	+	+	+	+	-	-	-	-	-	-	-	-
5	4	-	-	-	-	-	-	-	-	+	+	+	+	+	+	+	+	-	-	-	-	-	-	-	-	+	+	+	+
6	4	-	-	-	-	-	-	-	-	+	+	+	+	-	-	-	-	+	+	+	+	+	+	+	+	-	-	-	-
7	4	-	-	-	-	+	+	+	+	-	-	-	-	-	-	-	-	+	+	+	+	-	-	-	-	+	+	+	+
8	4	-	-	-	-	+	+	+	+	-	-	-	-	+	+	+	+	-	-	-	-	+	+	+	+	-	-	-	-
9	3	-	-	+	+	+	+	-	-	-	-	+	+	+	+	-	-	-	-	+	+	+	+	-	-	-	-	+	+
10	3	-	-	+	+	+	+	-	-	-	-	+	+	-	-	+	+	+	+	-	-	-	-	+	+	+	+	-	-
11	3	-	-	+	+	-	-	+	+	+	+	-	-	-	-	+	+	+	+	-	-	+	+	-	-	-	-	+	+
12	3	-	-	+	+	-	-	+	+	+	+	-	-	+	+	-	-	-	-	+	+	-	-	+	+	+	+	-	-
13	3	+	+	-	-	-	-	+	+	-	-	+	+	+	+	-	-	+	+	-	-	-	-	+	+	-	-	+	+
14	3	+	+	-	-	-	-	+	+	-	-	+	+	-	-	+	+	-	-	+	+	+	+	-	-	+	+	-	-
15	3	+	+	-	-	+	+	-	-	+	+	-	-	-	-	+	+	-	-	+	+	-	-	+	+	-	-	+	+
16	3	+	+	-	-	+	+	-	-	+	+	-	-	+	+	-	-	+	+	-	-	+	+	-	-	+	+	-	-
17	2	+	-	-	+	+	-	-	+	+	-	-	+	+	-	-	+	+	-	-	+	+	-	-	+	+	-	-	+
18	2	+	-	-	+	+	-	-	+	+	-	-	+	-	+	+	-	-	+	+	-	-	+	+	-	-	+	+	-
19	2	+	-	-	+	-	+	+	-	-	+	+	-	-	+	+	-	-	+	+	-	+	-	-	+	+	-	-	+
20	2	+	-	-	+	-	+	+	-	-	+	+	-	+	-	-	+	+	-	-	+	-	+	+	-	-	+	+	-
21	2	-	+	+	-	-	+	+	-	+	-	-	+	+	-	-	+	-	+	+	-	-	+	+	-	+	-	-	+
22	2	-	+	+	-	-	+	+	-	+	-	-	+	-	+	+	-	+	-	-	+	+	-	-	+	+	-	-	+
23	2	-	+	+	-	+	-	-	+	-	+	+	-	-	+	+	-	+	-	-	+	-	+	+	-	+	-	-	+
24	2	-	+	+	-	+	-	-	+	-	+	+	-	+	-	-	+	-	+	+	-	+	-	-	+	-	+	+	-
25	1	-	+	-	+	+	-	+	-	-	+	-	+	+	-	+	-	-	+	-	+	+	-	+	-	-	+	-	+
26	1	-	+	-	+	+	-	+	-	-	+	-	+	-	+	-	+	+	-	+	-	-	+	-	+	+	-	+	-
27	1	-	+	-	+	-	+	-	+	+	-	+	-	-	+	-	+	+	-	+	-	+	-	+	-	-	+	-	+
28	1	-	+	-	+	-	+	-	+	+	-	+	-	+	-	+	-	-	+	-	+	-	+	-	+	+	-	+	-
29	1	+	-	+	-	-	+	-	+	-	+	-	+	+	-	+	-	+	-	+	-	-	+	-	+	-	+	-	+
30	1	+	-	+	-	-	+	-	+	-	+	-	+	-	+	-	+	-	+	-	+	+	-	+	-	+	-	+	-
31	1	+	-	+	-	+	-	+	-	+	-	+	-	-	+	-	+	-	+	-	+	-	+	-	+	-	+	-	+
32	1	+	-	+	-	+	-	+	-	+	-	+	-	+	-	+	-	+	-	+	-	+	-	+	-	+	-	+	-
	A	D	E	F	G	H	I	J	K	L	M	N	O	P	Q	R	S	T	U	V	W	X	Y	Z	1	2	3	4	5

CONFOUNDING PATTERNS FOR
THE REFLECTED 32-RUN DESIGN WITH A FOUR-LEVEL FACTOR

Contrast Labels

A	B	C	D	E	F	G	H	I	J	K	L	M	N	O	P

Corresponding Main Effects and Two-Factor Interactions

A	-A'	A"	D	E	F	G	H	I	J	K	L	M	N	O	P
DE	DF	DG	AE	AD	AG	AF	AI	AH	AK	AJ	AM	AL	AO	AN	AQ
FG	EG	EF	-A'F	-A'G	-A'D	-A'E	-A'J	-A'K	-A'H	-A'I	-A'N	-A'O	-A'L	-A'M	-A'R
HI	HJ	HK	A"G	A"F	A"E	A"D	A"K	A"J	A"I	A"H	A"O	A"N	A"M	A"L	A"S
JK	IK	IJ	HL	HM	HN	HO	DL	DM	DN	DO	DH	DI	DJ	DK	DT
LM	LN	LO	IM	IL	IO	IN	EM	EL	EO	EN	EI	EH	EK	EJ	EU
NO	MO	MN	JN	JO	JL	JM	FN	FO	FL	FM	FJ	FK	FH	FI	FV
PQ	PR	PS	KO	KN	KM	KL	GO	GN	GM	GL	GK	GJ	GI	GH	GW
RS	SQ	QR	PT	PU	PV	PW	PX	PY	PZ	P1	P2	P3	P4	P5	HX
TU	TV	TW	QU	QT	QW	QV	QY	QX	Q1	QZ	Q3	Q2	Q5	Q4	IY
VW	UW	UV	RV	RW	RT	RU	RZ	R1	RX	RY	R4	R5	R2	R3	JZ
XY	XZ	X1	SW	SV	SU	ST	S1	SZ	SY	SX	S5	S4	S3	S2	K1
Z1	Y1	YZ	X2	X3	X4	X5	T2	T3	T4	T5	TX	TY	TZ	T1	L2
23	24	25	Y3	Y2	Y5	Y4	U3	U2	U5	U4	UY	UX	U1	UZ	M3
45	35	34	Z4	Z5	Z2	Z3	V4	V5	V2	V3	VZ	V1	VX	VY	N4
			15	14	13	12	W5	W4	W3	W2	W1	WZ	WY	WX	O5

Contrast Labels

Q	R	S	T	U	V	W	X	Y	Z	1	2	3	4	5

Corresponding Main Effects and Two-Factor Interactions

Q	R	S	T	U	V	W	X	Y	Z	1	2	3	4	5
AP	AS	AR	AU	AT	AW	AV	AY	AX	A1	AZ	A3	A2	A5	A4
-A'S	-A'P	-A'Q	-A'V	-A'W	-A'T	-A'U	-A'Z	-A'1	-A'X	-A'Y	-A'4	-A'5	-A'2	-A'3
A"R	A"Q	A"P	A"W	A"V	A"U	A"T	A"1	A"Z	A"Y	A"X	A"5	A"4	A"3	A"2
DU	DV	DW	DP	DQ	DR	DS	D2	D3	D4	D5	DX	DY	DZ	D1
ET	EW	EV	EQ	EP	ES	ER	E3	E2	E5	E4	EY	EX	E1	EZ
FW	FT	FU	FR	FS	FP	FQ	F4	F5	F2	F3	FZ	F1	FX	FY
GV	GU	GT	GS	GR	GQ	GP	G5	G4	G3	G2	G1	GZ	GY	GX
HY	HZ	H1	H2	H3	H4	H5	HP	HQ	HR	HS	HT	HU	HV	HW
IX	I1	IZ	I3	I2	I5	I4	IQ	IP	IS	IR	IU	IT	IW	IV
J1	JX	JY	J4	J5	J2	J3	JR	JS	JP	JQ	JV	JW	JT	JU
KZ	KY	KX	K5	K4	K3	K2	KS	KR	KQ	KP	KW	KV	KU	KT
L3	L4	L5	LX	LY	LZ	L1	LT	LU	LV	LW	LP	LQ	LR	LS
M2	M5	M4	MY	MX	M1	MZ	MU	MT	MW	MV	MQ	MP	MS	MR
N5	N2	N3	NZ	N1	NX	NY	NV	NW	NT	NU	NR	NS	NP	NQ
O4	O3	O2	O1	OZ	OY	OX	OW	OV	OU	OT	OS	OR	OQ	OP

The four-level factor may be changed into a three-level factor as described on page 195.

A BASIC 32-RUN DESIGN WITH TWO FOUR-LEVEL FACTORS

Two factors at 4 levels and up to twenty-five factors at 2 levels each. Use contrast coefficients for the Basic 32-Run Plackett-Burman Design for the analysis of data collected under the following conditions.

Treatment Combinations

Run	A	D	E	F	G	H	I	J	K	L	M	N	O	P	Q	R	S	T	U	V	W	X	Y	Z	2	3	4
1	1	1	-	-	-	-	-	-	-	-	-	-	-	-	-	-	-	-	-	-	-	-	-	-	-	-	-
2	1	2	-	-	-	-	-	-	-	-	-	-	-	+	+	+	+	+	+	+	+	+	+	+	+	+	+
3	1	1	-	-	-	+	+	+	+	+	+	+	+	+	+	+	+	+	+	+	+	-	-	-	-	-	-
4	1	2	-	-	-	+	+	+	+	+	+	+	+	-	-	-	-	-	-	-	-	+	+	+	+	+	+
5	1	3	+	+	+	+	+	+	+	-	-	-	-	-	-	-	-	+	+	+	+	+	+	+	-	-	-
6	1	4	+	+	+	+	+	+	+	-	-	-	-	+	+	+	+	-	-	-	-	-	-	-	+	+	+
7	1	3	+	+	+	-	-	-	-	+	+	+	+	+	+	+	+	-	-	-	-	+	+	+	-	-	-
8	1	4	+	+	+	-	-	-	-	+	+	+	+	-	-	-	-	+	+	+	+	-	-	-	+	+	+
9	2	3	+	-	-	-	-	+	+	+	+	-	-	-	-	+	+	+	+	-	-	-	-	-	+	+	-
10	2	4	+	-	-	-	-	+	+	+	+	-	-	+	+	-	-	-	-	+	+	+	+	-	-	-	+
11	2	3	+	-	-	+	+	-	-	-	-	+	+	+	+	-	-	-	-	+	+	-	-	+	+	+	-
12	2	4	+	-	-	+	+	-	-	-	-	+	+	-	-	+	+	+	+	-	-	+	+	-	-	-	+
13	2	1	-	+	+	+	+	-	-	+	+	-	-	-	-	+	+	-	-	+	+	+	+	-	+	+	-
14	2	2	-	+	+	+	+	-	-	+	+	-	-	+	+	-	-	+	+	-	-	-	-	+	-	-	+
15	2	1	-	+	+	-	-	+	+	-	-	+	+	+	+	-	-	+	+	-	-	+	+	-	+	+	-
16	2	2	-	+	+	-	-	+	+	-	-	+	+	-	-	+	+	-	-	+	+	-	-	+	-	-	+
17	3	1	+	+	-	-	+	+	-	-	+	+	-	-	+	+	-	+	+	-	-	+	+	-	-	+	+
18	3	2	+	+	-	-	+	+	-	-	+	+	-	+	-	-	+	-	-	+	+	-	-	+	+	-	-
19	3	1	+	+	-	+	-	-	+	+	-	-	+	+	-	-	+	+	-	-	+	-	+	+	-	+	+
20	3	2	+	+	-	+	-	-	+	+	-	-	+	-	+	+	-	-	+	+	-	+	-	-	+	-	-
21	3	3	-	-	+	+	-	-	+	-	+	+	-	-	+	+	-	+	-	-	+	+	-	-	-	+	+
22	3	4	-	-	+	+	-	-	+	-	+	+	-	+	-	-	+	-	+	+	-	-	+	+	+	-	-
23	3	3	-	-	+	-	+	+	-	+	-	-	+	+	-	-	+	-	+	+	-	+	-	-	-	+	+
24	3	4	-	-	+	-	+	+	-	+	-	-	+	-	+	+	-	+	-	-	+	-	+	+	+	-	-
25	4	3	-	+	-	-	+	-	+	+	-	+	-	-	+	-	+	+	-	+	-	-	+	-	+	-	+
26	4	4	-	+	-	-	+	-	+	+	-	+	-	+	-	+	-	-	+	-	+	+	-	+	-	+	-
27	4	3	-	+	-	+	-	+	-	-	+	-	+	+	-	+	-	-	+	-	+	-	+	-	+	-	+
28	4	4	-	+	-	+	-	+	-	-	+	-	+	-	+	-	+	+	-	+	-	+	-	+	-	+	-
29	4	1	+	-	+	+	-	+	-	+	-	+	-	-	+	-	+	-	+	-	+	+	-	+	+	-	+
30	4	2	+	-	+	+	-	+	-	+	-	+	-	+	-	+	-	+	-	+	-	-	+	-	-	+	-
31	4	1	+	-	+	-	+	-	+	-	+	-	+	+	-	+	-	+	-	+	-	+	-	+	-	+	+
32	4	2	+	-	+	-	+	-	+	-	+	-	+	-	+	-	+	-	+	-	+	-	+	-	+	-	-
	A	D	E	F	G	H	I	J	K	L	M	N	O	P	Q	R	S	T	U	V	W	X	Y	Z	2	3	4

CONFOUNDING PATTERNS FOR
THE BASIC 32-RUN DESIGN WITH TWO FOUR-LEVEL FACTORS

Contrast Labels

A   B   C   D   E   F   G   H   I   J   K   L   M   N   O   P

Corresponding Main Effects and Two-Factor Interactions

A	A'	A"	D	E	F	G	H	I	J	K	L	M	N	O	P
-DE	-DF	-DG	-AE	-AD	-AG	-AF	-AI	-AH	-AK	-AJ	-AM	-AL	-AO	-AN	-AQ
-FG	-EG	-EF	-A'F	-A'G	-A'D	-A'E	-A'J	-A'K	-A'H	-A'I	-A'N	-A'O	-A'L	-A'M	-A'R
-HI	-HJ	-HK	-A"G	-A"F	-A"E	-A"D	-A"K	-A"J	-A"I	-A"H	-A"O	-A"N	-A"M	-A"L	-A"S
-JK	-IK	-IJ	-HL	-HM	-HN	-HO	-DL	-DM	-DN	-DO	-DH	-DI	-DJ	-DK	-DT
-LM	-LN	-LO	-IM	-IL	-IO	-IN	-EM	-EL	-EO	-EN	-EI	-EH	-EK	-EJ	-EU
NO	-MO	-MN	-JN	-JO	-JL	-JM	-FN	-FO	-FL	-FM	-FJ	-FK	-FH	-FI	-FV
-PQ	-PR	-PS	-KO	-KN	-KM	-KL	-GO	-GN	-GM	-GL	-GK	-GJ	-GI	-GH	-GW
-RS	-SQ	-QR	-PT	-PU	-PV	-PW	-PX	-PY	-PZ	-D'P	-P2	-P3	-P4	-D"P	-HX
-TU	-TV	-TW	-QU	-QT	-QW	-QV	-QY	-QX	-D'Q	-QZ	-Q3	-Q2	-D"Q	-Q4	-IY
VW	-UW	-UV	-RV	-RW	-RT	-RU	-RZ	-D'R	-RX	-RY	-R4	-D"R	-R2	-R3	-JZ
-XY	-XZ	-D'X	-SW	-SV	-SU	-ST	-D'S	-SZ	-SY	-SX	-D"S	-S4	-S3	-S2	-D'K
-D'Z	-D'Y	-YZ	-X2	-X3	-X4	-D"X	-T2	-T3	-T4	-D'T	-TX	-TY	-TZ	-DT	-L2
-23	-24	-D"2	-Y3	-Y2	-D"Y	-Y4	-U3	-U2	-D"U	-U4	-UY	-UX	-D'U	-UZ	-M3
-D"4	-D"3	-34	-Z4	-D"Z	-Z2	-Z3	-V4	-D"V	-V2	-V3	-VZ	-D'V	-VX	-VY	-N4
			-D'4	-D'3	-D'2	-D"W	-W4	-W3	-W2	-D'W	-WZ	-WY	-WX	-D"O	

Contrast Labels

Q   R   S   T   U   V   W   X   Y   Z   1   2   3   4   5

Corresponding Main Effects and Two-Factor Interactions

Q	R	S	T	U	V	W	X	Y	Z	D'	2	3	4	D"
-AP	-AS	-AR	-AU	-AT	-AW	-AV	-AY	-AX	-AD'	-AZ	-A3	-A2	-AD"	-A4
A'S	-A'P	-A'Q	-A'V	-A'W	-A'T	-A'U	-A'Z	-A'D'	-A'X	-A'Y	-A'4	-A'D"	-A'2	-A'3
A"R	-A"Q	-A"P	-A"W	-A"V	-A"U	-A"T	-A"D'	-A"Z	-A"Y	-A"X	-A"D"	-A"4	-A"3	-A"2
-DU	-DV	-DW	-DP	-DQ	-DR	-DS	-D2	-D3	-D4	-E4	-DX	-DY	-DZ	-EZ
-ET	-EW	-EV	-EQ	-EP	-ES	-ER	-E3	-E2	-D"E	-F3	-EY	-EX	-D'E	-FY
-FW	-FT	-FU	-FR	-FS	-FP	-FQ	-F4	-D"F	-F2	-G2	-FZ	-D'F	-FX	-GX
-GV	-GU	-GT	-GS	-GR	-GQ	-GP	-D"G	-G4	-G3	-HS	-D'G	-GZ	-GY	-HW
-HY	-HZ	-D'H	-H2	-H3	-H4	-D"H	-HP	-HQ	-HR	-IR	-HT	-HU	-HV	-IV
-IX	-D'I	-IZ	-I3	-I2	-D"I	-I4	-IQ	-IP	-IS	-JQ	-IU	-IT	-IW	-JU
-D'J	-JX	-JY	-J4	-D"J	-J2	-J3	-JR	-JS	-JP	-KP	-JV	-JW	-JT	-KT
-KZ	-KY	-KX	-D"K	-K4	-K3	-K2	-KS	-KR	-KQ	-LW	-KW	-KV	-KU	-LS
-L3	-L4	-D"L	-LX	-LY	-LZ	-D'L	-LT	-LU	-LV	-MV	-LP	-LQ	-LR	-MR
-M2	-D"M	-M4	-MY	-MX	-D'M	-MZ	-MU	-MT	-MW	-NU	-MQ	-MP	-MS	-NQ
-D"N	-N2	-N3	-NZ	-D'N	-NX	-NY	-NV	-NW	-NT	-OT	-NR	-NS	-NP	-OP
-O4	-O3	-O2	-D'O	-OZ	-OY	-OX	-OW	-OV	-OU		-OS	-OR	-OQ	

A Reflected 32-Run Design With Two Four-Level Factors

Two factors at 4 levels and twenty-five factors at 2 levels each. Use contrast coefficients for the Reflected 32-Run Plackett-Burman Design for the analysis of data collected under the following plan.

Treatment Combinations

Run	A	D	E	F	G	H	I	J	K	L	M	N	O	P	Q	R	S	T	U	V	W	X	Y	Z	2	3	4
1	4	4	+	+	+	+	+	+	+	+	+	+	+	+	+	+	+	+	+	+	+	+	+	+	+	+	+
2	4	3	+	+	+	+	+	+	+	+	+	+	+	−	−	−	−	−	−	−	−	−	−	−	−	−	−
3	4	4	+	+	+	−	−	−	−	−	−	−	−	−	−	−	−	−	−	−	−	+	+	+	+	+	+
4	4	3	+	+	+	−	−	−	−	−	−	−	+	+	+	+	+	+	+	+	−	−	−	−	−	−	−
5	4	2	−	−	−	−	−	−	−	+	+	+	+	+	+	+	+	−	−	−	−	−	−	−	+	+	+
6	4	1	−	−	−	−	−	−	−	+	+	+	+	−	−	−	−	+	+	+	+	+	+	+	−	−	−
7	4	2	−	−	−	+	+	+	+	−	−	−	−	−	−	−	−	+	+	+	+	−	−	−	+	+	+
8	4	1	−	−	−	+	+	+	+	−	−	−	−	+	+	+	+	−	−	−	−	+	+	+	−	−	−
9	3	2	−	+	+	+	+	−	−	−	−	+	+	+	+	−	−	−	−	+	+	+	+	−	−	−	+
10	3	1	−	+	+	+	+	−	−	−	−	+	+	−	−	+	+	+	+	−	−	−	−	+	+	+	−
11	3	2	−	+	+	−	−	+	+	+	+	−	−	−	−	+	+	+	+	−	−	+	+	−	−	−	+
12	3	1	−	+	+	−	−	+	+	+	+	−	−	+	+	−	−	−	−	+	+	−	−	+	+	+	−
13	3	4	+	−	−	−	−	+	+	−	−	+	+	+	+	−	−	+	+	−	−	−	−	+	−	−	+
14	3	3	+	−	−	−	−	+	+	−	−	+	+	−	−	+	+	−	−	+	+	+	+	−	+	+	−
15	3	4	+	−	−	+	+	−	−	+	+	−	−	−	−	+	+	−	−	+	+	−	−	+	−	−	+
16	3	3	+	−	−	+	+	−	−	+	+	−	−	+	+	−	−	+	+	−	−	+	+	−	+	+	−
17	2	4	−	−	+	+	−	−	+	+	−	−	+	+	−	−	+	+	−	−	+	+	−	−	+	−	−
18	2	3	−	−	+	+	−	−	+	+	−	−	+	−	+	+	−	−	+	+	−	−	+	+	−	+	+
19	2	4	−	−	+	−	+	+	−	−	+	+	−	−	+	+	−	−	+	+	−	+	−	−	+	−	−
20	2	3	−	−	+	−	+	+	−	−	+	+	−	+	−	−	+	+	−	−	+	−	+	+	−	+	+
21	2	2	+	+	−	−	+	+	−	+	−	−	+	+	−	−	+	−	+	+	−	−	+	+	+	−	−
22	2	1	+	+	−	−	+	+	−	+	−	−	+	−	+	+	−	+	−	−	+	+	−	−	−	+	+
23	2	2	+	+	−	+	−	−	+	−	+	+	−	−	+	+	−	+	−	−	+	−	+	+	+	−	−
24	2	1	+	+	−	+	−	−	+	−	+	+	−	+	−	−	+	−	+	+	−	+	−	−	−	+	+
25	1	2	+	−	+	+	−	+	−	−	+	−	+	+	−	+	−	−	+	−	+	+	−	+	−	+	−
26	1	1	+	−	+	+	−	+	−	−	+	−	+	−	+	+	−	+	−	−	+	−	+	−	+	−	+
27	1	2	+	−	+	−	+	−	+	+	−	+	−	−	+	−	+	+	−	+	−	+	−	+	−	+	−
28	1	1	+	−	+	−	+	−	+	+	−	+	−	+	−	−	+	−	+	+	−	+	−	+	−	+	+
29	1	4	−	+	−	−	−	+	+	−	+	−	+	+	−	+	−	+	−	+	−	+	−	+	−	+	−
30	1	3	−	+	−	−	+	+	−	+	−	+	+	−	+	−	+	+	−	+	+	−	+	+	−	+	+
31	1	4	−	+	−	+	−	+	−	+	−	+	−	−	+	−	+	+	−	+	−	+	+	−	+	−	−
32	1	3	−	+	−	+	−	+	−	+	−	+	−	+	−	+	−	+	−	+	−	+	+	+	−	+	+
	A	D	E	F	G	H	I	J	K	L	M	N	O	P	Q	R	S	T	U	V	W	X	Y	Z	2	3	4

CONFOUNDING PATTERNS FOR THE REFLECTED 32-RUN DESIGN WITH TWO FOUR-LEVEL FACTORS

Contrast Labels

A	B	C	D	E	F	G	H	I	J	K	L	M	N	O	P

Corresponding Main Effects and Two-Factor Interactions

A	**-A'**	**A"**	**D**	**E**	**F**	**G**	**H**	**I**	**J**	**K**	**L**	**M**	**N**	**O**	**P**
DE	DF	DG	AE	AD	AG	AF	AI	AH	AK	AJ	AM	AL	AO	AN	AQ
FG	EG	EF	-A'F	-A'G	-A'D	-A'E	-A'J	-A'K	-A'H	-A'I	-A'N	-A'O	-A'L	-A'M	-A'R
HI	HJ	HK	A"G	A"F	A"E	A"D	A"K	A"J	A"I	A"H	A"O	A"N	A"M	A"L	A"S
JK	IK	IJ	HL	HM	HN	HO	DL	DM	DN	DO	DH	DI	DJ	DK	DT
LM	LN	LO	IM	IL	IO	IN	EM	EL	EO	EN	EI	EH	EK	EJ	EU
NO	MO	MN	JN	JO	JL	JM	FN	FO	FL	FM	FJ	FK	FH	FI	FV
PQ	PR	PS	KO	KN	KM	KL	GO	GN	GM	GL	GK	GJ	GI	GH	GW
RS	SQ	QR	PT	PU	PV	PW	PX	PY	PZ	-D'P	P2	P3	P4	D"P	HX
TU	TV	TW	QU	QT	QW	QV	QY	QX	-D'Q	QZ	Q3	Q2	D"Q	Q4	IY
VW	UW	UV	RV	RW	RT	RU	RZ	-D'R	RX	RY	R4	D"R	R2	R3	JZ
XY	XZ	-D'X	SW	SV	SU	ST	-D'S	SZ	SY	SX	D"S	S4	S3	S2	-D'K
-D'Z	-D'Y	YZ	X2	X3	X4	D"X	T2	T3	T4	D'T	TX	TY	TZ	-D'T	L2
23	24	D"2	Y3	Y2	D"Y	Y4	U3	U2	D"U	U4	UY	UX	-D'U	UZ	M3
D"4	D"3	34	Z4	D"Z	Z2	Z3	V4	D"V	V2	V3	VZ	-D'V	VX	VY	N4
				-D'4	-D'3	-D'2	D"W	W4	W3	W2	-D'W	WZ	WY	WX	D"O

Contrast Labels

Q	R	S	T	U	V	W	X	Y	Z	1	2	3	4	5

Corresponding Main Effects and Two-Factor Interactions

Q	R	S	T	U	V	W	X	Y	Z	D	2	3	4	D
AP	AS	AR	AU	AT	AW	AV	AY	AX	-AD'	AZ	A3	A2	AD"	A4
-A'S	-A'P	-A'Q	-A'V	-A'W	-A'T	-A'U	-A'Z	A'D'	-A'X	-A'Y	-A'4	-A'D"	-A'2	-A'3
A"R	A"Q	A"P	A"W	A"V	A"U	A"T	-A"D'	A"Z	A"Y	A"X	A"D"	A"4	A"3	A"2
DU	DV	DW	DP	DQ	DR	DS	D2	D3	D4	E4	DX	DY	DZ	EZ
ET	EW	EV	EQ	EP	ES	ER	E3	E2	D"E	F3	EY	EX	-D'E	FY
FW	FT	FU	FR	FS	FP	FQ	F4	D"F	F2	G2	FZ	-D'F	FX	GX
GV	GU	GT	GS	GR	GQ	GP	D"G	G4	G3	HS	-D'G	GZ	GY	HW
HY	HZ	-D'H	H2	H3	H4	D"H	HP	HQ	HR	IR	HT	HU	HV	IV
IX	-D'I	IZ	I3	I2	D"I	I4	IQ	IP	IS	JQ	IU	IT	IW	JU
-D'J	JX	JY	J4	D"J	J2	J3	JR	JS	JP	KP	JV	JW	JT	KT
KZ	KY	KX	D"K	K4	K3	K2	KS	KR	KQ	LW	KW	KV	KU	LS
L3	L4	D"L	LX	LY	LZ	-D'L	LT	LU	LV	MV	LP	LQ	LR	MR
M2	D"M	M4	MY	MX	-D'M	MZ	MU	MT	MW	NU	MQ	MP	MS	NQ
D"N	N2	N3	NZ	-D'N	NX	NY	NV	NW	NT	OT	NR	NS	NP	OP
O4	O3	O2	-D'O	OZ	OY	OX	OW	OV	OU		OS	OR	OQ	

32-Run Designs With Two Three-Level Factors

The $4^2 \times 2^{25}$ designs on pages 242–245 can be modified into $3^2 \times 2^{25}$ designs by changing both Factors A and D into three level factors. As before, the relationship between the levels for a four-level factor and the levels of the corresponding three-level factor are:

Four Level Factor		Three Level Factor
Level 1	stays	Level 1
Level 2	stays	Level 2
Level 3	stays	Level 3
Level 4	**becomes**	**Level 1 or Level 2 or Level 3**

Since the new three level factor will appear to have three degrees of freedom there will be some redundancy in the analysis. In particular, if Factor A is a three level factor, then two contrasts for Main Effects of Factor A will make the same comparison between the levels of Factor A.

If only one of the four-level factors is modified into a three level factor, then the designs on the previous four pages will be $4 \times 3 \times 2^{25}$ designs.

The confounding pattern for these 32-run designs will remain the same as shown on the preceeding pages, regardless of whether one or two factors are modified into three level factors.

Response plots are still the best way of visualizing the results, especially if a three-level or four-level factor is found to be significant.

32-Run Designs With 3 Three-Level Factors

The $4^3 \times 2^{22}$ designs on pages 248–251 can be modified into $3^3 \times 2^{22}$ designs by changing Factors A, D, and E into three level factors. As before, the relationship between the levels for a four-level factor and the levels of the corresponding three-level factor are as shown on the preceeding page.

If two of the four-level factors are modified into a three level factor, then the designs on the following four pages will be $4 \times 3^2 \times 2^{22}$ designs.

If only one of the four-level factors is modified into a three level factor, then the designs on the following four pages will be $4^2 \times 3 \times 2^{22}$ designs.

The confounding pattern for these 32-run designs will remain the same as shown on the following pages, regardless of whether one or two factors are modified into three level factors. When a four-level factor is converted into a three-level factor there will always be some redundancy in the Main Effects represented by some of the contrasts.

Use response plots to visualize the results, especially if a three-level or four-level factor is found to be significant.

A BASIC 32-RUN DESIGN WITH THREE FOUR-LEVEL FACTORS

Three factors at 4 levels and up to twenty-two factors at 2 levels each. Use contrast coefficients for the Basic 32-Run Plackett-Burman Design for the analysis of data collected under the following conditions.

Treatment Combinations

Run	A	D	E	F	G	H	I	J	K	L	M	N	O	P	Q	S	T	U	V	X	Y	Z	2	3	4
1	1	1	1	-	-	-	-	-	-	-	-	-	-	-	-	-	-	-	-	-	-	-	-	-	-
2	1	3	2	-	-	-	-	-	-	-	-	-	-	+	+	+	+	+	+	+	+	+	+	+	+
3	1	1	2	-	-	+	+	+	+	+	+	+	+	+	+	+	+	+	+	-	-	-	-	-	-
4	1	3	1	-	-	+	+	+	+	+	+	+	+	-	-	-	-	-	-	+	+	+	+	+	+
5	1	4	4	+	+	+	+	+	+	-	-	-	-	-	-	-	+	+	+	+	+	+	-	-	-
6	1	2	3	+	+	+	+	+	+	-	-	-	-	+	+	+	-	-	-	-	-	-	+	+	+
7	1	4	3	+	+	-	-	-	-	+	+	+	+	+	+	+	-	-	-	+	+	+	-	-	-
8	1	2	4	+	+	-	-	-	-	+	+	+	+	-	-	-	+	+	+	-	-	-	+	+	+
9	2	4	3	-	-	-	-	+	+	+	+	-	-	-	-	+	+	+	-	-	-	+	+	+	-
10	2	2	4	-	-	-	-	+	+	+	+	-	-	+	+	-	-	-	+	+	+	-	-	-	+
11	2	4	4	-	-	+	+	-	-	-	-	+	+	+	+	-	-	-	+	-	-	+	+	+	-
12	2	2	3	-	-	+	+	-	-	-	-	+	+	-	-	+	+	+	-	+	+	-	-	-	+
13	2	1	2	+	+	+	+	-	-	+	+	-	-	-	-	+	-	-	+	+	+	-	+	+	-
14	2	3	1	+	+	+	+	-	-	+	+	-	-	+	+	-	+	+	-	-	-	+	-	-	+
15	2	1	1	+	+	-	-	+	+	-	-	+	+	+	+	-	+	+	-	+	+	-	+	+	-
16	2	3	2	+	+	-	-	+	+	-	-	+	+	-	-	+	-	-	+	-	-	+	-	-	+
17	3	1	3	+	-	-	+	+	-	-	+	+	-	-	+	-	-	+	+	-	+	+	-	+	+
18	3	3	4	+	-	-	+	+	-	-	+	+	-	+	-	+	+	-	-	+	-	-	+	-	-
19	3	1	4	+	-	+	-	-	+	+	-	-	+	+	-	+	+	-	-	-	+	+	-	+	+
20	3	3	3	+	-	+	-	-	+	+	-	-	+	-	+	-	-	+	+	+	-	-	+	-	-
21	3	4	2	-	+	+	-	-	+	-	+	+	-	-	+	-	+	-	-	+	-	-	-	+	+
22	3	2	1	-	+	+	-	-	+	-	+	+	-	+	-	+	-	+	+	-	+	+	+	-	-
23	3	4	1	-	+	-	+	+	-	+	-	-	+	+	-	+	-	+	+	+	-	-	-	+	+
24	3	2	2	-	+	-	+	+	-	+	-	-	+	-	+	-	+	-	-	-	+	+	+	-	-
25	4	4	1	+	-	-	+	-	+	+	-	+	-	-	+	+	+	-	+	-	+	-	+	-	+
26	4	2	2	+	-	-	+	-	+	+	-	+	-	+	-	-	-	+	-	+	-	+	-	+	-
27	4	4	2	+	-	+	-	+	-	-	+	-	+	+	-	-	-	+	-	-	+	-	+	-	+
28	4	2	1	+	-	+	-	+	-	-	+	-	+	-	+	+	+	-	+	+	-	+	-	+	-
29	4	1	4	-	+	+	-	+	-	+	-	+	-	-	+	+	-	+	-	+	-	+	+	-	+
30	4	3	3	-	+	+	-	+	-	+	-	+	-	+	-	-	+	-	+	-	+	-	-	+	-
31	4	1	3	-	+	-	+	-	+	-	+	-	+	+	-	-	+	-	+	+	-	+	+	-	+
32	4	3	4	-	+	-	+	-	+	-	+	-	+	-	+	+	-	+	-	-	+	-	-	+	-
	A	D	E	F	G	H	I	J	K	L	M	N	O	P	Q	S	T	U	V	X	Y	Z	2	3	4

CONFOUNDING PATTERNS FOR THE BASIC 32-RUN DESIGN WITH THREE FOUR-LEVEL FACTORS

Contrast Labels

A	B	C	D	E	F	G	H	I	J	K	L	M	N	O	P

Corresponding Main Effects and Two-Factor Interactions

A	A'	A"	D	E	F	G	H	I	J	K	L	M	N	O	P
-DE	-DF	-DG	-AE	-AD	-AG	-AF	-AI	-AH	-AK	-AJ	-AM	-AL	-AO	-AN	-AQ
-FG	-EG	-EF	-A'F	-A'G	-A'D	-A'E	-A'J	-A'K	-A'H	-A'I	-A'N	-A'O	-A'L	-A'M	-A'E'
-HI	-HJ	-HK	-A"G	-A"F	-A"E	-A"D	-A"K	-A"J	-A"I	-A"H	-A"O	-A"N	-A"M	-A"L	-A"S
-JK	-IK	-IJ	-HL	-HM	-HN	-HO	-DL	-DM	-DN	-DO	-DH	-DI	-DJ	-DK	-DT
-LM	-LN	-LO	-IM	-IL	-IO	-IN	-EM	-EL	-EO	-EN	-EI	-EH	-EK	-EJ	-EU
-NO	-MO	-MN	-JN	-JO	-JL	-JM	-FN	-FO	-FL	-FM	-FJ	-FK	-FH	-FI	-FV
-PQ	-E'P	-PS	-KO	-KN	-KM	-KL	-GO	-GN	-GM	-GL	-GK	-GJ	-GI	-GH	-E"G
-E'S	-SQ	-E'Q	-PT	-PU	-PV	-E"P	-PX	-PY	-PZ	-D'P	-P2	-P3	-P4	-D"P	-HX
-TU	-TV	-E'T	-QU	-QT	-E"Q	-QV	-QY	-QX	-D'Q	-QZ	-Q3	-Q2	-D"Q	-Q4	-IY
-E"V	-E"U	-UV	-E'V	-SV	-ET	-E'U	-EZ	-D'E'	-E'X	-E'Y	-E'4	-D"E'	-E'2	-E'3	-JZ
-XY	-XZ	-D'X	-E'S	-X3	-SU	-ST	-D'S	-SZ	-SY	-SX	-D"S	-S4	-S3	-S2	-D'K
-D'Z	-D'Y	-YZ	-X2	-Y2	-X4	-D"X	-T2	-T3	-T4	-D'T	-TX	-TY	-TZ	-DT	-L2
-23	-24	-D"2	-Y3	-D"Z	-D"Y	-Y4	-U3	-U2	-D"U	-U4	-UY	-UX	-D'U	-UZ	-M3
-D"4	-D"3	-34	-Z4	-D'4	-Z2	-Z3	-V4	-D"V	-V2	-V3	-VZ	-D'V	-VX	-VY	-N4
					-D'3	-D'2	-D"E"	-E'4	-E"3	-E"2	-D'E"	-E"Z	-E"Y	-E"X	-D"O

Contrast Labels

Q	R	S	T	U	V	W	X	Y	Z	1	2	3	4	5

Corresponding Main Effects and Two-Factor Interactions

Q	E'	S	T	U	V	E"	X	Y	Z	D'	2	3	4	D"
-AP	-AS	-AE'	-AU	-AT	-AE"	-AV	-AY	-AX	-AD'	-AZ	-A3	-A2	-AD"	-A4
-A'S	-A'P	-A'Q	-A'V	-A'E"	-AT	-A'U	-A'Z	-A'D'	-A'X	-A'Y	-A'4	-A'D"	-A'2	-A'3
-A"E'	-A"Q	-A"P	-A"E"	-A"V	-A"U	-A"T	-A"D'	-A"Z	-A"Y	-A"X	-A"D"	-A"4	-A"3	-A"2
-DU	-DV	-DE"	-DP	-DQ	-DE'	-DS	-D2	-D3	-D4	-E4	-DX	-DY	-DZ	-EZ
-ET	-FT	-EV	-EQ	-EP	-ES	-FQ	-E3	-E2	-D"E	-F3	-EY	-EX	-D'E	-FY
-E"F	-GU	-FU	-E'F	-FS	-FP	-GP	-F4	-D"F	-F2	-G2	-FZ	-D'F	-FX	-GX
-GV	-HZ	-GT	-GS	-E'G	-GQ	-D"H	-D"G	-G4	-G3	-HS	-D'G	-GZ	-GY	-E"H
-HY	-D'I	-D'H	-H2	-H3	-H4	-I4	-HP	-HQ	-E'H	-E'I	-HT	-HU	-HV	-IV
-IX	-JX	-IZ	-I3	-I2	-D'I	-J3	-IQ	-IP	-IS	-JQ	-IU	-IT	-E'I	-JU
-D'J	-KY	-JY	-J4	-D"J	-J2	-K2	-E'J	-JS	-JP	-KP	-JV	-E"J	-JT	-KT
-KZ	-L4	-KX	-D"K	-K4	-K3	-D'L	-KS	-E'K	-KQ	-E'L	-E"K	-KV	-KU	-LS
-L3	-D"M	-D"L	-LX	-LY	-LZ	-MZ	-LT	-LU	-LV	-MV	-LP	-LQ	-E'L	-E'M
-M2	-N2	-M4	-MY	-MX	-D'M	-NY	-MU	-MT	-E"M	-NU	-MQ	-MP	-MS	-NQ
-D'N	-O3	-N3	-NZ	-D'N	-NX	-OX	-NV	-E"N	-NT	-OT	-E'N	-NS	-NP	-OP
-O4		-O2	-D'O	-OZ	-OY		-E"O	-OV	-OU		-OS	-E'O	-OQ	

A Reflected 32-Run Design With Three Four-Level Factors

Three factors at 4 levels and twenty-two factors at 2 levels each. Use contrast coefficients for the Reflected 32-Run Plackett-Burman Design for the analysis of data collected under the following plan.

Treatment Combinations

Run	A	D	E	F	G	H	I	J	K	L	M	N	O	P	Q	S	T	U	V	X	Y	Z	2	3	4
1	4	4	4	+	+	+	+	+	+	+	+	+	+	+	+	+	+	+	+	+	+	+	+	+	+
2	4	2	3	+	+	+	+	+	+	+	+	+	+	−	−	−	−	−	−	−	−	−	−	−	−
3	4	4	3	+	+	−	−	−	−	−	−	−	−	−	−	−	−	−	−	+	+	+	+	+	+
4	4	2	4	+	+	−	−	−	−	−	−	−	−	+	+	+	+	+	+	−	−	−	−	−	−
5	4	1	1	−	−	−	−	−	−	+	+	+	+	+	+	+	−	−	−	−	−	−	+	+	+
6	4	3	2	−	−	−	−	−	−	+	+	+	+	−	−	−	+	+	+	+	+	+	−	−	−
7	4	1	2	−	−	+	+	+	+	−	−	−	−	−	−	−	+	+	+	−	−	−	+	+	+
8	4	3	1	−	−	+	+	+	+	−	−	−	−	+	+	+	−	−	−	+	+	+	−	−	−
9	3	1	2	+	+	+	+	−	−	−	−	+	+	+	+	−	−	−	+	+	+	−	−	−	+
10	3	3	1	+	+	+	+	−	−	−	−	+	+	−	−	+	+	+	−	−	−	+	+	+	−
11	3	1	1	+	+	−	−	+	+	+	+	−	−	−	−	+	+	+	−	+	+	−	−	−	+
12	3	3	2	+	+	−	−	+	+	+	+	−	−	+	+	−	−	−	+	−	−	+	+	+	−
13	3	4	3	−	−	−	−	+	+	−	−	+	+	+	+	−	+	+	−	−	−	+	−	−	+
14	3	2	4	−	−	−	−	+	+	−	−	+	+	−	−	+	−	−	+	+	+	−	+	+	−
15	3	4	4	−	−	+	+	−	−	+	+	−	−	−	−	+	−	−	+	−	−	+	−	−	+
16	3	2	3	−	−	+	+	−	−	+	+	−	−	+	+	−	+	+	−	+	+	−	+	+	−
17	2	4	2	−	+	+	−	−	+	+	−	−	+	+	−	+	+	−	−	+	−	−	+	−	−
18	2	2	1	−	+	+	−	−	+	+	−	−	+	−	+	−	−	+	+	−	+	+	−	+	+
19	2	4	1	−	+	−	+	+	−	−	+	+	−	−	+	−	−	+	+	+	−	−	+	−	−
20	2	2	2	−	+	−	+	+	−	−	+	+	−	+	−	+	+	−	−	−	+	+	−	+	+
21	2	1	3	+	−	−	+	+	−	+	−	−	+	+	−	+	−	+	+	−	+	+	+	−	−
22	2	3	4	+	−	−	+	+	−	+	−	−	+	−	+	+	−	+	−	+	−	−	−	+	+
23	2	1	4	+	−	+	−	−	+	−	+	+	−	−	+	−	+	−	−	−	+	+	+	−	−
24	2	3	3	+	−	+	−	−	+	−	+	+	−	+	−	+	−	+	+	+	−	−	−	+	+
25	1	1	4	−	+	+	−	+	−	−	+	−	+	+	−	−	−	+	−	+	−	+	−	+	−
26	1	3	3	−	+	+	−	+	−	−	+	−	+	−	+	+	+	−	+	−	+	−	+	−	+
27	1	1	3	−	+	−	+	−	+	+	−	+	−	−	+	+	+	−	+	+	−	+	−	+	−
28	1	3	4	−	+	−	+	−	+	+	−	+	−	+	−	−	−	+	−	−	+	−	+	−	+
29	1	4	1	+	−	−	+	−	+	−	+	−	+	+	−	−	+	−	+	−	+	−	−	+	−
30	1	2	2	+	−	−	+	−	+	−	+	−	+	−	+	+	−	+	−	+	−	+	+	−	+
31	1	4	2	+	−	+	−	+	−	+	−	+	−	−	+	+	−	+	−	−	+	−	−	+	−
32	1	2	1	+	−	+	−	+	−	+	−	+	−	+	−	−	+	−	+	+	−	+	+	−	+
	A	D	E	F	G	H	I	J	K	L	M	N	O	P	Q	S	T	U	V	X	Y	Z	2	3	4

CONFOUNDING PATTERNS FOR THE REFLECTED 32-RUN DESIGN WITH THREE FOUR-LEVEL FACTORS

Contrast Labels

A	B	C	D	E	F	G	H	I	J	K	L	M	N	O	P

Corresponding Main Effects and Two-Factor Interactions

A	-A'	A"	D	E	F	G	H	I	J	K	L	M	N	O	P
DE	DF	DG	AE	AD	AG	AF	AI	AH	AK	AJ	AM	AL	AO	AN	AQ
FG	EG	EF	-A'F	-A'G	-A'D	-A'E	-A'J	-A'K	-A'H	-A'I	-A'N	-A'O	-A'L	-A'M	A'E'
HI	HJ	HK	A"G	A"F	A"E	A"D	A"K	A"J	A"I	A"H	A"O	A"N	A"M	A"L	A"S
JK	IK	IJ	HL	HM	HN	HO	DL	DM	DN	DO	DH	DI	DJ	DK	DT
LM	LN	LO	IM	IL	IO	IN	EM	EL	EO	EN	EI	EH	EK	EJ	EU
NO	MO	MN	JN	JO	JL	JM	FN	FO	FL	FM	FJ	FK	FH	FI	FV
PQ	-E'P	PS	KO	KN	KM	KL	GO	GN	GM	GL	GK	GJ	GI	GH	GE"
-E'S	SQ	-E'Q	PT	PU	PV	E"P	PX	PY	PZ	-D'P	P2	P3	P4	D"P	HX
TU	TV	E"T	QU	QT	E"Q	QV	QY	QX	-D'Q	QZ	Q3	Q2	D"Q	Q4	IY
E"V	E"U	UV	-E'V	SV	-ET	-E'U	-E'Z	D'E'	-E'X	-E'Y	-E'4	-D'E'	-E'2	-E'3	JZ
XY	XZ	-D'X	E"S	X3	SU	ST	-D'S	SZ	SY	SX	D"S	S4	S3	S2	-D'K
-D'Z	-D'Y	YZ	X2	Y2	X4	D"X	T2	T3	T4	D"T	TX	TY	TZ	-DT	L2
23	24	D"2	Y3	-D'Z	D"Y	Y4	U3	U2	D"U	U4	UY	UX	-D'U	UZ	M3
D"4	D"3	34	Z4	-D4	Z2	Z3	V4	D"V	V2	V3	VZ	-D'V	VX	VY	N4
					-D'3	-D'2	D"E"	E"4	E"3	E"2	-D'E"	E"Z	E"Y	E"X	D"O

Contrast Labels

Q	R	S	T	U	V	W	X	Y	Z	1	2	3	4	5

Corresponding Main Effects and Two-Factor Interactions

Q	-E'	S	T	U	V	E"	X	Y	Z	D	2	3	4	D
AP	AS	-AE'	AU	AT	AE"	AV	AY	AX	-AD'	AZ	A3	A2	AD"	A4
-A'S	-A'P	-A'Q	-A'V	-A'E"	-AT	-A'U	-A'Z	A'D'	-A'X	-A'Y	-A'4	-A'D"	-A'2	-A'3
-A"E'	A"Q	A"P	A"E"	A"V	A"U	A"T	-A"D'	A"Z	A"Y	A"X	A"D"	A"4	A"3	A"2
DU	DV	DE"	DP	DQ	-DE'	DS	D2	D3	D4	E4	DX	DY	DZ	EZ
ET	FT	EV	EQ	EP	ES	FQ	E3	E2	D"E	F3	EY	EX	-D'E	FY
E"F	GU	FU	-E'F	FS	FP	GP	F4	D"F	F2	G2	FZ	-D'F	FX	GX
GV	HZ	GT	GS	-E'G	GQ	D"H	D'G	G4	G3	HS	-D'G	GZ	GY	E"H
HY	-D'I	-D'H	H2	H3	H4	I4	HP	HQ	-E'H	-E'I	HT	HU	HV	IV
IX	JX	IZ	I3	I2	D'I	J3	IQ	IP	IS	JQ	IU	IT	E'I	JU
-D'J	KY	JY	J4	D"J	J2	K2	-E'J	JS	JP	KP	JV	E"J	JT	KT
KZ	L4	KX	D"K	K4	K3	-D'L	KS	-E'K	KQ	E"L	E"K	KV	KU	LS
L3	D"M	D"L	LX	LY	LZ	MZ	LT	LU	LV	MV	LP	LQ	-E'L	-E'M
M2	N2	M4	MY	MX	-D'M	NY	MU	MT	E"M	NU	MQ	MP	MS	NQ
D"N	O3	N3	NZ	-D'N	NX	OX	NV	E"N	NT	OT	-E'N	NS	NP	OP
O4		O2	-D'O	OZ	OY		E"O	OV	OU		OS	-E'O	OQ	

A BASIC 32-RUN DESIGN WITH 4 FOUR-LEVEL FACTORS

Four factors at 4 levels and up to nineteen factors at 2 levels each. Use contrast coefficients for the Basic 32-Run Plackett-Burman Design for the analysis of data collected under the following conditions.

Treatment Combinations

Run	A	D	E	F	G	H	I	J	K	L	M	N	O	P	Q	T	V	X	Y	Z	2	3	4
1	1	1	1	1	−	−	−	−	−	−	−	−	−	−	−	−	−	−	−	−	−	−	−
2	1	3	2	2	−	−	−	−	−	−	−	−	−	+	+	+	+	+	+	+	+	+	+
3	1	1	2	2	−	+	+	+	+	+	+	+	+	+	+	+	+	−	−	−	−	−	−
4	1	3	1	1	−	+	+	+	+	+	+	+	+	−	−	−	−	+	+	+	+	+	+
5	1	4	4	4	+	+	+	+	+	−	−	−	−	−	−	+	+	+	+	+	−	−	−
6	1	2	3	3	+	+	+	+	+	−	−	−	−	+	+	−	−	−	−	−	+	+	+
7	1	4	3	3	+	−	−	−	−	+	+	+	+	+	+	−	−	+	+	+	−	−	−
8	1	2	4	4	+	−	−	−	−	+	+	+	+	−	−	+	+	−	−	−	+	+	+
9	2	4	3	2	−	−	−	+	+	+	+	−	−	−	−	+	−	−	−	+	+	+	−
10	2	2	4	1	−	−	−	+	+	+	+	−	−	+	+	−	+	+	+	−	−	−	+
11	2	4	4	1	−	+	+	−	−	−	−	+	+	+	+	−	+	−	−	+	+	+	−
12	2	2	3	2	−	+	+	−	−	−	−	+	+	−	−	+	−	+	+	−	−	−	+
13	2	1	2	3	+	+	+	−	−	+	+	−	−	−	−	−	+	+	+	−	+	+	−
14	2	3	1	4	+	+	+	−	−	+	+	−	−	+	+	+	−	−	−	+	−	−	+
15	2	1	1	4	+	−	−	+	+	−	−	+	+	+	+	+	−	+	+	−	+	+	−
16	2	3	2	3	+	−	−	+	+	−	−	+	+	−	−	−	+	−	−	+	−	−	+
17	3	1	3	4	−	−	+	+	−	−	+	+	−	−	+	−	+	−	+	+	−	+	+
18	3	3	4	3	−	−	+	+	−	−	+	+	−	+	−	+	−	+	−	−	+	−	−
19	3	1	4	3	−	+	−	−	+	+	−	−	+	+	−	+	−	−	+	+	−	+	+
20	3	3	3	4	−	+	−	−	+	+	−	−	+	−	+	−	+	+	−	−	+	−	−
21	3	4	2	1	+	+	−	−	+	−	+	+	−	−	+	+	−	+	−	−	−	+	+
22	3	2	1	2	+	+	−	−	+	−	+	+	−	+	−	−	+	−	+	+	+	−	−
23	3	4	1	2	+	−	+	+	−	+	−	−	+	+	−	−	+	+	−	−	−	+	+
24	3	2	2	1	+	−	+	+	−	+	−	−	+	−	+	+	−	−	+	+	+	−	−
25	4	4	1	3	−	−	+	−	+	+	−	+	−	−	+	+	+	−	+	−	+	−	+
26	4	2	2	4	−	−	+	−	+	+	−	+	−	+	−	−	−	+	−	+	−	+	−
27	4	4	2	4	−	+	−	+	−	−	+	−	+	+	−	−	−	−	+	−	+	−	+
28	4	2	1	3	−	+	−	+	−	−	+	−	+	−	+	+	+	+	−	+	−	+	−
29	4	1	4	2	+	+	−	+	−	+	−	+	−	−	+	−	−	+	−	+	+	−	+
30	4	3	3	1	+	+	−	+	−	+	−	+	−	+	−	+	+	−	+	−	−	+	−
31	4	1	3	1	+	−	+	−	+	−	+	−	+	+	−	+	+	+	−	+	+	−	+
32	4	3	4	2	+	−	+	−	+	−	+	−	+	−	+	−	−	−	+	−	−	+	−
	A	D	E	F	G	H	I	J	K	L	M	N	O	P	Q	T	V	X	Y	Z	2	3	4

CONFOUNDING PATTERNS FOR
THE BASIC 32-RUN DESIGN WITH 4 FOUR-LEVEL FACTORS

Contrast Labels

A	B	C	D	E	F	G	H	I	J	K	L	M	N	O	P

Corresponding Main Effects and Two-Factor Interactions

A	A'	A"	D	E	F	G	H	I	J	K	L	M	N	O	P
-DE	-DF	-DG	-AE	-AD	-AG	-AF	-AI	-AH	-AK	-AJ	-AM	-AL	-AO	-AN	-AQ
-FG	-EG	-EF	-A'F	-A'G	-A'D	-A'E	-A'J	-A'K	-A'H	-A'I	-A'N	-A'O	-A'L	-A'M	-A'E'
-HI	-HJ	-HK	-A"G	-A"F	-A"E	-A"D	-A"K	-A"J	-A"I	-A"H	-A"O	-A"N	-A"M	-A"L	-A"F'
-JK	-IK	-IJ	-HL	-HM	-HN	-HO	-DL	-DM	-DN	-DO	-DH	-DI	-DJ	-DK	-DT
-LM	-LN	-LO	-IM	-IL	-IO	-IN	-EM	-EL	-EO	-EN	-EI	-EH	-EK	-EJ	-EF"
-NO	-MO	-MN	-JN	-JO	-JL	-JM	-FN	-FO	-FL	-FM	-FJ	-FK	-FH	-FI	-FV
-PQ	-E'P	-F'P	-KO	-KN	-KM	-KL	-GO	-GN	-GM	-GL	-GK	-GJ	-GI	-GH	-E"G
-E'F'	-F'Q	-E'Q	-PT	-F"P	-PV	-E"P	-PX	-PY	-PZ	-D'P	-P2	-P3	-P4	-D"P	-HX
-F'T	-TV	-E'T	-F"Q	-QT	-E"Q	-QV	-QY	-QX	-D'Q	-QZ	-Q3	-Q2	-D"Q	-Q4	-IY
-E"V	-E"F"	-F'V	-E'V	-F'V	-ET	-E'F"	-EZ	-D'E'	-EX	-E'Y	-E4	-D"E'	-E'2	-E3	-JZ
-XY	-XZ	-D'X	-E"F'	-X3	-X4	-F'T	-D'F'	-F'Z	-F'Y	-F'X	-D"F'	-F'4	-F'3	-F'2	-D'K
-D'Z	-D'Y	-YZ	-X2	-Y2	-D"Y	-D"X	-T2	-T3	-T4	-D'T	-TX	-TY	-TZ	-DT	-L2
-23	-24	-D"2	-Y3	-D"Z	-Z2	-Y4	-F"3	-F"2	-D"F"	-F"4	-F"Y	-F"X	-D'F"	-F"Z	-M3
-D"4	-D"3	-34	-Z4	-D'4	-D'3	-Z3	-V4	-D"V	-V2	-V3	-VZ	-D'V	-VX	-VY	-N4
						-D'2	-D"E"	-E"4	-E'3	-E'2	-D'E'	-E"Z	-E"Y	-E"X	-D"O

Contrast Labels

Q	R	S	T	U	V	W	X	Y	Z	1	2	3	4	5

Corresponding Main Effects and Two-Factor Interactions

Q	E'	F'	T	F"	V	E"	X	Y	Z	D'	2	3	4	D"
-AP	-AF'	-AE'	-AF"	-AT	-AE"	-AV	-AY	-AX	-AD'	-AZ	-A3	-A2	-AD"	-A4
-A'F'	-A'P	-A'Q	-A'V	-A'E"	-AT	-A'F"	-A'Z	-A'D'	-A'X	-A'Y	-A'4	-A'D"	-A'2	-A'3
-A"E'	-A"Q	-A"P	-A"E'	-A"V	-A"F"	-A"T	-A"D'	-A"Z	-A"Y	-A"X	-A"D"	-A"4	-A"3	-A"2
-DF"	-DV	-DE"	-DP	-DQ	-DE'	-DF'	-D2	-D3	-D4	-E4	-DX	-DY	-DZ	-EZ
-ET	-FT	-EV	-EQ	-EP	-EF'	-FQ	-E3	-E2	-D"E	-F3	-EY	-EX	-D'E	-FY
-E"F	-F'G	-GT	-E'F	-E'G	-FP	-GP	-F4	-D"F	-F2	-G2	-FZ	-D'F	-FX	-GX
-GV	-HZ	-D'H	-F'G	-H3	-GQ	-D"H	-D"G	-G4	-G3	-F"H	-D'G	-GZ	-GY	-E"H
-HY	-D'I	-IZ	-H2	-I2	-H4	-I4	-HP	-HQ	-E'H	-E'I	-HT	-F"H	-HV	-IV
-IX	-JX	-JY	-I3	-D"J	-D"I	-J3	-IQ	-IP	-F'I	-JQ	-F'I	-IT	-E'I	-F'J
-D'J	-KY	-KX	-J4	-K4	-J2	-K2	-E'J	-F'J	-JP	-KP	-JV	-E"J	-JT	-KT
-KZ	-L4	-D'L	-D"K	-LY	-K3	-D'L	-F'K	-E'K	-KQ	-E"L	-E'K	-KV	-F"K	-F'L
-L3	-D"M	-M4	-LX	-MX	-LZ	-MZ	-LT	-F"L	-LV	-MV	-LP	-LQ	-E'L	-E"M
-M2	-N2	-N3	-MY	-D'N	-D'M	-NY	-F"M	-MT	-E"M	-F"N	-MQ	-MP	-F'M	-NQ
-D"N	-O3	-O2	-NZ	-OZ	-NX	-OX	-NV	-E"N	-NT	-OT	-E'N	-F'N	-NP	-OP
-O4			-D'O		-OY		-E"O	-OV	-F"O		-F'O	-E'O	-OQ	

A Reflected 32-Run Design With 4 Four-Level Factors

Four factors at 4 levels and nineteen factors at 2 levels each. Use contrast coefficients for the Reflected 32-Run Plackett-Burman Design for the analysis of data collected under the following plan.

Treatment Combinations

Run	A	D	E	F	G	H	I	J	K	L	M	N	O	P	Q	T	V	X	Y	Z	2	3	4
1	4	4	4	4	+	+	+	+	+	+	+	+	+	+	+	+	+	+	+	+	+	+	+
2	4	2	3	3	+	+	+	+	+	+	+	+	+	-	-	-	-	-	-	-	-	-	-
3	4	4	3	3	+	-	-	-	-	-	-	-	-	-	-	-	-	+	+	+	+	+	+
4	4	2	4	4	+	-	-	-	-	-	-	-	-	+	+	+	+	-	-	-	-	-	-
5	4	1	1	1	-	-	-	-	-	+	+	+	+	+	+	-	-	-	-	-	+	+	+
6	4	3	2	2	-	-	-	-	-	+	+	+	+	-	-	+	+	+	+	+	-	-	-
7	4	1	2	2	-	+	+	+	+	-	-	-	-	-	-	+	+	-	-	-	+	+	+
8	4	3	1	1	-	+	+	+	+	-	-	-	-	+	+	-	-	+	+	+	-	-	-
9	3	1	2	3	+	+	+	-	-	-	-	+	+	+	+	-	+	+	+	-	-	-	+
10	3	3	1	4	+	+	+	-	-	-	-	+	+	-	-	+	-	-	-	+	+	+	-
11	3	1	1	4	+	-	-	+	+	+	+	-	-	-	-	+	-	+	+	-	-	-	+
12	3	3	2	3	+	-	-	+	+	+	+	-	-	+	+	-	+	-	-	+	+	+	-
13	3	4	3	2	-	-	-	+	+	-	-	+	+	+	+	+	-	-	-	+	-	-	+
14	3	2	4	1	-	-	-	+	+	-	-	+	+	-	-	-	+	+	+	-	+	+	-
15	3	4	4	1	-	+	+	-	-	+	+	-	-	-	-	-	+	-	-	+	-	-	+
16	3	2	3	2	-	+	+	-	-	+	+	-	-	+	+	+	-	+	+	-	+	+	-
17	2	4	2	1	+	+	-	-	+	+	-	-	+	+	-	+	-	+	-	-	+	-	-
18	2	2	1	2	+	+	-	-	+	+	-	-	+	-	+	-	+	-	+	+	-	+	+
19	2	4	1	2	+	-	+	+	-	-	+	+	-	-	+	-	+	+	-	-	+	-	-
20	2	2	2	1	+	-	+	+	-	-	+	+	-	+	-	+	-	-	+	+	-	+	+
21	2	1	3	4	-	-	+	+	-	+	-	-	+	+	-	-	+	-	+	+	+	-	-
22	2	3	4	3	-	-	+	+	-	+	-	-	+	-	+	+	-	+	-	-	-	+	+
23	2	1	4	3	-	+	-	-	+	-	+	+	-	-	+	+	-	-	+	+	+	-	-
24	2	3	3	4	-	+	-	-	+	-	+	+	-	+	-	-	+	+	-	-	-	+	+
25	1	1	4	2	+	+	-	+	-	-	+	-	+	+	-	-	-	+	-	+	-	+	-
26	1	3	3	1	+	+	-	+	-	-	+	-	+	-	+	+	+	-	+	-	+	-	+
27	1	1	3	1	+	-	+	-	+	+	-	+	-	-	+	+	+	+	-	+	-	+	-
28	1	3	4	2	+	-	+	-	+	+	-	+	-	+	-	-	-	-	+	-	+	-	+
29	1	4	1	3	-	-	+	-	+	-	+	-	+	+	-	+	+	-	+	-	-	+	-
30	1	2	2	4	-	-	+	-	+	-	+	-	+	-	+	-	-	+	-	+	+	-	+
31	1	4	2	4	-	+	-	+	-	+	-	+	-	-	+	-	-	-	+	-	-	+	-
32	1	2	1	3	-	+	-	+	-	+	-	+	-	+	-	+	+	+	-	+	+	-	+
	A	D	E	F	G	H	I	J	K	L	M	N	O	P	Q	T	V	X	Y	Z	2	3	4

Confounding Patterns For
The Reflected 32-Run Design With 4 Four-Level Factors

Contrast Labels

A	B	C	D	E	F	G	H	I	J	K	L	M	N	O	P

Corresponding Main Effects and Two-Factor Interactions

A	-A'	A"	D	E	F	G	H	I	J	K	L	M	N	O	P
DE	DF	DG	AE	AD	AG	AF	AI	AH	AK	AJ	AM	AL	AO	AN	AQ
FG	EG	EF	-A'F	-A'G	-A'D	-A'E	-A'J	-A'K	-A'H	-A'I	-A'N	-A'O	-A'L	-A'M	A'E'
HI	HJ	HK	A"G	A"F	A"E	A"D	A"K	A"J	A"I	A"H	A"O	A"N	A"M	A"L	-A"F
JK	IK	IJ	HL	HM	HN	HO	DL	DM	DN	DO	DH	DI	DJ	DK	DT
LM	LN	LO	IM	IL	IO	IN	EM	EL	EO	EN	EI	EH	EK	EJ	EF"
NO	MO	MN	JN	JO	JL	JM	FN	FO	FL	FM	FJ	FK	FH	FI	FV
PQ	-E'P	-F'P	KO	KN	KM	KL	GO	GN	GM	GL	GK	GJ	GI	GH	GE"
E'F'	-F'Q	-E'Q	PT	F"P	PV	E"P	PX	PY	PZ	-D'P	P2	P3	P4	D"P	HX
F"T	TV	E'T	F"Q	QT	E'Q	QV	QY	QX	-D'Q	QZ	Q3	Q2	D"Q	Q4	IY
E"V	E"F"	F"V	-E'V	-F'V	-ET	-E'F'	-EZ	D'E'	-E'X	-E'Y	-E'4	-D"E'	-E'2	-E'3	JZ
XY	XZ	-D'X	-E"F'	X3	X4	-FT	D'F'	-F'Z	-F'Y	-F'X	-D"F'	-F'4	-F'3	-F'2	-D'K
-D'Z	-D'Y	YZ	X2	Y2	D"Y	D'X	T2	T3	T4	D'T	TX	TY	TZ	-DT	L2
23	24	D"2	Y3	D"Z	Z2	Y4	F"3	F"2	D"F"	F"4	F"Y	F"X	-D'F"	F"Z	M3
D"4	D"3	34	Z4	-D'4	-D'3	Z3	V4	D"V	V2	V3	VZ	-D'V	VX	VY	N4
						-D'2	D"E"	E"4	E"3	E"2	-D'E"	E"Z	E"Y	E"X	D"O

Contrast Labels

Q	R	S	T	U	V	W	X	Y	Z	1	2	3	4	5

Corresponding Main Effects and Two-Factor Interactions

Q	-E'	-F'	T	F"	V	E"	X	Y	Z	D	2	3	4	D
AP	-AF'	-AE'	AF"	AT	AE"	AV	AY	AX	-AD'	AZ	A3	A2	AD"	A4
A'F'	-A'P	-A'Q	-A'V	-A'E"	-AT	-A'F"	-A'Z	A'D'	-A'X	-A'Y	-A'4	-A'D"	-A'2	-A'3
-A"E'	A"Q	A"P	A"E"	A"V	A"F"	A"T	-A"D'	A"Z	A"Y	A"X	A"D"	A"4	A"3	A"2
DF"	DV	DE"	DP	DQ	-DE'	-DF'	D2	D3	D4	E4	DX	DY	DZ	EZ
ET	FT	EV	EQ	EP	-EF'	FQ	E3	E2	D"E	F3	EY	EX	-D'E	FY
E"F	F"G	GT	-E'F	-E'G	FP	GP	F4	D"F	F2	G2	FZ	-D'F	FX	GX
GV	HZ	-D'H	-F'G	H3	GQ	D"H	D"G	G4	G3	-F'H	-D'G	GZ	GY	E"H
HY	-D'I	IZ	H2	I2	H4	I4	HP	HQ	-E'H	-EI	HT	F"H	HV	IV
IX	JX	JY	I3	D"J	D"I	J3	IQ	IP	-F'I	JQ	F"I	IT	E'I	F"J
-D'J	KY	KX	J4	K4	J2	K2	-E'J	-F'J	JP	KP	JV	E"J	JT	KT
KZ	L4	D"L	D"K	LY	K3	-D'L	-F'K	-E'K	KQ	E"L	E"K	KV	F"K	-F'L
L3	D"M	M4	LX	MX	LZ	MZ	LT	F"L	LV	MV	LP	LQ	-E'L	-E'M
M2	N2	N3	MY	-D'N	-D'M	NY	F"M	MT	E"M	F"N	MQ	MP	-F'M	NQ
D"N	O3	O2	NZ	OZ	NX	OX	NV	E"N	NT	OT	-E'N	-F'N	NP	OP
O4			-D'O		OY		E"O	OV	F"O		-F'O	-E'O	OQ	

32-Run Designs With Four Factors
Having Three or Four Levels

The $4^4 \times 2^{19}$ designs on pages 252–255 can be modified into $3^4 \times 2^{19}$ designs by changing Factors A, D, E, and F into three level factors. As before, the relationship between the levels for a four-level factor and the levels of the corresponding three-level factor are:

Four Level Factor		Three Level Factor
Level 1	stays	Level 1
Level 2	stays	Level 2
Level 3	stays	Level 3
Level 4	**becomes**	**Level 1 or Level 2 or Level 3**

Since the new three level factor will appear to have three degrees of freedom there will be some redundancy in the analysis. See p.195 for details.

If three of the four-level factors are modified into three-level factors, then the designs on the previous four pages will be $4 \times 3^3 \times 2^{19}$ designs.

If two of the four-level factors are modified into three-level factors, then the designs on the previous four pages will be $4^2 \times 3^2 \times 2^{19}$ designs.

If only one of the four-level factors is modified into a three level factor, then the designs on the previous four pages will be $4^3 \times 3 \times 2^{19}$ designs.

The confounding pattern for these 32-run designs will remain the same as shown on the preceeding pages, regardless of the number of factors that are modified into three level factors.

Use response plots visualize the results, especially if a three-level or four-level factor is found to be significant.

32-Run Designs With Five Factors
Having Three or Four Levels

The $4^5 \times 2^{16}$ designs on pages 258–261 can be modified into $3^5 \times 2^{16}$ designs by changing Factors A, D, E, F and G into three level factors. As before, the relationship between the levels for a four-level factor and the levels of the corresponding three-level factor are as shown on the preceeding page.

If four of the four-level factors are modified into three level factors, then the designs on the following four pages will be $4 \times 3^4 \times 2^{16}$ designs.

If three of the four-level factors are modified into three level factors, then the designs on the following four pages will be $4^2 \times 3^3 \times 2^{16}$ designs.

If two of the four-level factors are modified into three level factors, then the designs on the following four pages will be $4^3 \times 3^2 \times 2^{16}$ designs.

If only one of the four-level factors is modified into a three level factor, then the designs on the following four pages will be $4^4 \times 3 \times 2^{16}$ designs.

The confounding pattern for these 32-run designs will remain the same as shown on the following pages, regardless of the number of factors which are modified into three level factors.

Use response plots to visualize the results, especially if a three-level or four-level factor is found to be significant.

A BASIC 32-RUN DESIGN WITH FIVE FOUR-LEVEL FACTORS

Five factors at 4 levels and up to sixteen factors at 2 levels each. Use contrast coefficients for the Basic 32-Run Plackett-Burman Design for the analysis of data collected under the following conditions.

Treatment Combinations

Run	A	D	E	F	G	H	I	J	M	N	O	P	Q	T	V	X	Y	Z	2	3	4
1	1	1	1	1	1	-	-	-	-	-	-	-	-	-	-	-	-	-	-	-	-
2	1	3	2	2	1	-	-	-	-	-	-	+	+	+	+	+	+	+	+	+	+
3	1	1	2	2	2	+	+	+	+	+	+	+	+	+	+	-	-	-	-	-	-
4	1	3	1	1	2	+	+	+	+	+	+	-	-	-	-	+	+	+	+	+	+
5	1	4	4	4	3	+	+	+	-	-	-	-	-	+	+	+	+	+	-	-	-
6	1	2	3	3	3	+	+	+	-	-	-	+	+	-	-	-	-	-	+	+	+
7	1	4	3	3	4	-	-	-	+	+	+	+	+	-	-	+	+	+	-	-	-
8	1	2	4	4	4	-	-	-	+	+	+	-	-	+	+	-	-	-	+	+	+
9	2	4	3	2	2	-	-	+	+	-	-	-	-	+	-	-	-	+	+	+	-
10	2	2	4	1	2	-	-	+	+	-	-	+	+	-	+	+	+	-	-	-	+
11	2	4	4	1	1	+	+	-	-	+	+	+	+	-	+	-	-	+	+	+	-
12	2	2	3	2	1	+	+	-	-	+	+	-	-	+	-	+	+	-	-	-	+
13	2	1	2	3	4	+	+	-	+	-	-	-	-	-	+	+	+	-	+	+	-
14	2	3	1	4	4	+	+	-	+	-	-	+	+	+	-	-	-	+	-	-	+
15	2	1	1	4	3	-	-	+	-	+	+	+	+	+	-	+	+	-	+	+	-
16	2	3	2	3	3	-	-	+	-	+	+	-	-	-	+	-	-	+	-	-	+
17	3	1	3	4	1	-	+	+	+	+	-	-	+	-	+	-	+	+	-	+	+
18	3	3	4	3	1	-	+	+	+	+	-	+	-	+	-	+	-	-	+	-	-
19	3	1	4	3	2	+	-	-	-	-	+	+	-	+	-	-	+	+	-	+	+
20	3	3	3	4	2	+	-	-	-	-	+	-	+	-	+	+	-	-	+	-	-
21	3	4	2	1	3	+	-	-	+	+	-	-	+	+	-	+	-	-	-	+	+
22	3	2	1	2	3	+	-	-	+	+	-	+	-	-	+	-	+	+	+	-	-
23	3	4	1	2	4	-	+	+	-	-	+	+	-	-	+	+	-	-	-	+	+
24	3	2	2	1	4	-	+	+	-	-	+	-	+	+	-	-	+	+	+	-	-
25	4	4	1	3	2	-	+	-	-	+	-	-	+	+	+	-	+	-	+	-	+
26	4	2	2	4	2	-	+	-	-	+	-	+	-	-	-	+	-	+	-	+	-
27	4	4	2	4	1	+	-	+	+	-	+	+	-	-	-	-	+	-	+	-	+
28	4	2	1	3	1	+	-	+	+	-	+	-	+	+	+	+	-	+	-	+	-
29	4	1	4	2	4	+	-	+	-	+	-	-	+	-	-	+	-	+	+	-	+
30	4	3	3	1	4	+	-	+	-	+	-	+	-	+	+	-	+	-	-	+	-
31	4	1	3	1	3	-	+	-	+	-	+	+	-	+	+	+	-	+	+	-	+
32	4	3	4	2	3	-	+	-	+	-	+	-	+	-	-	-	+	-	-	+	-
	A	D	E	F	G	H	I	J	M	N	O	P	Q	T	V	X	Y	Z	2	3	4

Confounding Patterns For The Basic 32-Run Design With Five Four-Level Factors

Contrast Labels

A	B	C	D	E	F	G	H	I	J	K	L	M	N	O	P

Corresponding Main Effects and Two-Factor Interactions

A	A'	A"	D	E	F	G	H	I	J	G'	G"	M	N	O	P
-DE	-DF	-DG	-AE	-AD	-AG	-AF	-AI	-AH	-AG'	-AJ	-AM	-AG"	-AO	-AN	-AQ
-FG	-EG	-EF	-A'F	-A'G	-A'D	-A'E	-A'J	-A'G'	-A'H	-A'I	-A'N	-A'O	-A'G"	-A'M	-A'E'
-HI	-HJ	-G'H	-A"G	-A"F	-A"E	-A"D	-A"G'	-A"J	-A"I	-A"H	-A"O	-A"N	-A"M	-A"G"	-A"F'
-G'J	-G'I	-IJ	-G"H	-HM	-HN	-HO	-DG'	-DM	-DN	-DO	-DH	-DI	-DJ	-DG'	-DT
-G"M	-G"N	-G"O	-IM	-G'I	-IO	-IN	-EM	-EG"	-EO	-EN	-EI	-EH	-EG'	-EJ	-EF"
-NO	-MO	-MN	-JN	-JO	-G'J	-JM	-FN	-FO	-FG"	-FM	-FJ	-FG'	-FH	-FI	-FV
-PQ	-E'P	-F'P	-G'O	-G'N	-G'M	-E"P	-GO	-GN	-GM	-D'P	-P2	-GJ	-GI	-GH	-E'G
-E'F'	-F'Q	-E'Q	-PT	-F"P	-PV	-QV	-PX	-PY	-PZ	-QZ	-Q3	-P3	-P4	-D"P	-HX
-F"T	-TV	-E'T	-F"Q	-QT	-E'Q	-E'F"	-QY	-QX	-D'Q	-E'Y	-E'4	-Q2	-D"Q	-Q4	-IY
-E"V	-E"F"	-F"V	-E'V	-F'V	-ET	-F'T	-EZ	-D'E'	-E'X	-F'X	-D"F'	-D"E'	-E'2	-E'3	-JZ
-XY	-XZ	-D'X	-E"F'	-X3	-X4	-D"X	-D'F'	-F'Z	-F'Y	-D'T	-TX	-F'4	-F'3	-F'2	-D'G'
-DZ	-D'Y	-YZ	-X2	-Y2	-D"Y	-Y4	-T2	-T3	-T4	-F"4	-F"Y	-TY	-TZ	-DT	-G"2
-23	-24	-D"2	-Y3	-D"Z	-Z2	-Z3	-F"3	-F"2	-D"F"	-V3	-VZ	-F"X	-D'F"	-F"Z	-M3
-D"4	-D"3	-34	-Z4	-D'4	-D'3	-D'2	-V4	-D"V	-V2	-E"2	-D'E	-D'V	-VX	-VY	-N4
							-D"E"	-E"4	-E"3			-E"Z	-E"Y	-E"X	-D"O

Contrast Labels

Q	R	S	T	U	V	W	X	Y	Z	1	2	3	4	5

Corresponding Main Effects and Two-Factor Interactions

Q	E'	F'	T	F"	V	E"	X	Y	Z	D'	2	3	4	D"
-AP	-AF'	-AE'	-AF"	-AT	-AE"	-AV	-AY	-AX	-AD'	-AZ	-A3	-A2	-AD"	-A4
-A'F'	-A'P	-A'Q	-A'V	-A'E"	-A'T	-A'F'	-A'Z	-A'D'	-A'X	-A'Y	-A'4	-A'D"	-A'2	-A'3
-A"E'	-A"Q	-A"P	-A"E"	-A"V	-A"F"	-A"T	-A"D'	-A"Z	-A"Y	-A"X	-A"D"	-A"4	-A"3	-A"2
-DF"	-DV	-DE"	-DP	-DQ	-DE'	-DF	-D2	-D3	-D4	-E4	-DX	-DY	-DZ	-EZ
-ET	-FT	-EV	-EQ	-EP	-EF'	-FQ	-E3	-E2	-D"E	-F3	-EY	-EX	-D'E	-FY
-E"F	-F"G	-GT	-E'F	-E'G	-FP	-GP	-F4	-D"F	-F2	-G2	-FZ	-D'F	-FX	-GX
-GV	-HZ	-D'H	-F'G	-H3	-GQ	-D"H	-D"G	-G4	-G3	-F'H	-D'G	-GZ	-GY	-E"H
-HY	-D'I	-IZ	-H2	-I2	-H4	-I4	-HP	-HQ	-E'H	-E'I	-HT	-F"H	-HV	-IV
-IX	-JX	-JY	-I3	-D"J	-D'I	-J3	-IQ	-IP	-F'I	-JQ	-F'I	-IT	-E'I	-F"J
-D'J	-G'Y	-G'X	-J4	-G'4	-J2	-G'2	-E'J	-F'J	-JP	-G'P	-JV	-E"J	-JT	-GT
-GZ	-G'4	-D"G"	-D"G'	-G'Y	-G'3	-D'G'	-F'G'	-E'G'	-G'Q	-E"G"	-E"G'	-G'V	-F'G'	-F'G"
-G"3	-D"M	-M4	-G"X	-MX	-G"Z	-MZ	-G"T	-F"G'	-G"V	-MV	-G"P	-G"Q	-E'G'	-E"M
-M2	-N2	-N3	-MY	-D'N	-D'M	-NY	-F"M	-MT	-E"M	-F"N	-MQ	-MP	-F'M	-NQ
-D"N	-O3	-O2	-NZ	-OZ	-NX	-OX	-NV	-E"N	-NT	-OT	-E'N	-F'N	-NP	-OP
-O4			-D'O			-OY	-E"O	-OV	-F"O			-F'O	-E'O	-OQ

A Reflected 32-Run Design With Five Four-Level Factors

Five factors at 4 levels and sixteen factors at 2 levels each. Use contrast coefficients for the Reflected 32-Run Plackett-Burman Design for the analysis of data collected under the following plan.

Treatment Combinations

Run	A	D	E	F	G	H	I	J	M	N	O	P	Q	T	V	X	Y	Z	2	3	4
1	4	4	4	4	4	+	+	+	+	+	+	+	+	+	+	+	+	+	+	+	+
2	4	2	3	3	4	+	+	+	+	+	+	-	-	-	-	-	-	-	-	-	-
3	4	4	3	3	3	-	-	-	-	-	-	-	-	-	-	+	+	+	+	+	+
4	4	2	4	4	3	-	-	-	-	-	-	+	+	+	+	-	-	-	-	-	-
5	4	1	1	1	2	-	-	-	+	+	+	+	+	-	-	-	-	-	+	+	+
6	4	3	2	2	2	-	-	-	+	+	+	-	-	+	+	+	+	+	-	-	-
7	4	1	2	2	1	+	+	+	-	-	-	-	-	+	+	-	-	-	+	+	+
8	4	3	1	1	1	+	+	+	-	-	-	+	+	-	-	+	+	+	-	-	-
9	3	1	2	3	3	+	+	-	-	+	+	+	+	-	+	+	+	-	-	-	+
10	3	3	1	4	3	+	+	-	-	+	+	-	-	+	-	-	-	+	+	+	-
11	3	1	1	4	4	-	-	+	+	-	-	-	-	+	-	+	+	-	-	-	+
12	3	3	2	3	4	-	-	+	+	-	-	+	+	-	+	-	-	+	+	+	-
13	3	4	3	2	1	-	-	+	-	+	+	+	+	+	-	-	-	+	-	-	+
14	3	2	4	1	1	-	-	+	-	+	+	-	-	-	+	+	+	-	+	+	-
15	3	4	4	1	2	+	+	-	+	-	-	-	-	-	+	-	-	+	-	-	+
16	3	2	3	2	2	+	+	-	+	-	-	+	+	+	-	+	+	-	+	+	-
17	2	4	2	1	4	+	-	-	-	-	+	+	-	+	-	+	-	-	+	-	-
18	2	2	1	2	4	+	-	-	-	-	+	-	+	-	+	-	+	+	-	+	+
19	2	4	1	2	3	-	+	+	+	+	-	-	+	-	+	+	-	-	+	-	-
20	2	2	2	1	3	-	+	+	+	+	-	+	-	+	-	-	+	+	-	+	+
21	2	1	3	4	2	-	+	+	-	-	+	+	-	-	+	-	+	+	+	-	-
22	2	3	4	3	2	-	+	+	-	-	+	-	+	+	+	-	-	-	-	+	+
23	2	1	4	3	1	+	-	-	+	+	-	-	+	+	-	-	+	+	+	-	-
24	2	3	3	4	1	+	-	-	+	+	-	+	-	-	+	+	-	-	-	+	+
25	1	1	4	2	3	+	-	+	+	-	+	+	-	-	-	+	-	+	-	+	-
26	1	3	3	1	3	+	-	+	+	-	+	-	+	+	+	-	+	-	+	-	+
27	1	1	3	1	4	-	+	-	-	+	-	-	+	+	+	+	-	+	-	+	-
28	1	3	4	2	4	-	+	-	-	+	-	+	-	-	-	-	+	-	+	-	+
29	1	4	1	3	1	-	+	-	+	-	+	+	-	+	+	-	+	-	-	+	-
30	1	2	2	4	1	-	+	-	+	-	+	-	+	-	-	+	-	+	+	-	+
31	1	4	2	4	2	+	-	+	-	+	-	-	+	-	-	-	+	-	-	+	-
32	1	2	1	3	2	+	-	+	-	+	-	+	-	+	+	+	-	+	+	-	+
	A	D	E	F	G	H	I	J	M	N	O	P	Q	T	V	X	Y	Z	2	3	4

CONFOUNDING PATTERNS FOR THE REFLECTED 32-RUN DESIGN WITH FIVE FOUR-LEVEL FACTORS

Contrast Labels

A	B	C	D	E	F	G	H	I	J	K	L	M	N	O	P

Corresponding Main Effects and Two-Factor Interactions

A	-A'	A"	D	E	F	G	H	I	J	-G'	G"	M	N	O	P
DE	DF	DG	AE	AD	AG	AF	AI	AH	-AG'	AJ	AM	AG"	AO	AN	AQ
FG	EG	EF	-A'F	-A'G	-A'D	-A'E	-A'J	A'G'	-A'H	-A'I	-A'N	-A'O	-A'G"	-A'M	A'E'
HI	HJ	-G'H	A"G	A"F	A"E	A"D	-A"G'	A"J	A'I	A"H	A"O	A"N	A"M	A"G'	-A"F
-G'J	-G'I	IJ	G"H	HM	HN	HO	DG"	DM	DN	DO	DH	DI	DJ	-DG'	DT
G"M	G"N	G"O	IM	G'I	IO	IN	EM	EG"	EO	EN	EI	EH	-EG'	EJ	EF"
NO	MO	MN	JN	JO	G"J	JM	FN	FO	FG"	FM	FJ	-FG'	FH	FI	FV
PQ	-E'P	-F'P	-G'O	-G'N	-G'M	E"P	GO	GN	GM	-D'P	P2	GJ	GI	GH	GE"
E'F'	-F'Q	-E'Q	PT	F"P	PV	QV	PX	PY	PZ	QZ	Q3	P3	P4	D"P	HX
F"T	TV	E'T	F"Q	QT	E'Q	-E'F'	QY	QX	-D'Q	-E'Y	-E'4	Q2	D"Q	Q4	IY
E"V	E"F"	F"V	-E'V	-F'V	-ET	-F'T	-EZ	D'E'	-E'X	-F'X	-D"F'	-D"E'	-E'2	-E'3	JZ
XY	XZ	-D'X	-E"F'	X3	X4	D"X	D'F	-F'Z	-F'Y	D'T	TX	-F'4	-F'3	-F'2	D'G'
-D'Z	-D'Y	YZ	X2	Y2	D"Y	Y4	T2	T3	T4	F"4	F"Y	TY	TZ	-D'T	G"2
23	24	D"2	Y3	D"Z	Z2	Z3	F"3	F"2	D"F"	V3	VZ	F"X	-D'F"	F"Z	M3
D"4	D"3	34	Z4	-D'4	-D'3	-D'2	V4	D"V	V2	E"2	-D'E"	-D'V	VX	VY	N4
							D"E	E"4	E"3			E"Z	E"Y	E"X	

Contrast Labels

Q	R	S	T	U	V	W	X	Y	Z	1	2	3	4	5

Corresponding Main Effects and Two-Factor Interactions

Q	-E'	-F'	T	F"	V	E"	X	Y	Z	D	2	3	4	D
AP	-AF'	-AE'	AF"	AT	AE"	AV	AY	AX	-AD'	AZ	A3	A2	AD"	A4
A'F'	-A'P	-A'Q	-A'V	-A'E"	-AT	-A'F'	-A'Z	A'D'	-A'X	-A'Y	-A'4	-A'D"	-A'2	-A'3
-A"E'	A"Q	A"P	A"E"	A"V	A"F"	A"T	-A"D'	A"Z	A"Y	A"X	A"D	A"4	A"3	A"2
DF"	DV	DE"	DP	DQ	-DE'	-DF'	D2	D3	D4	E4	DX	DY	DZ	EZ
ET	FT	EV	EQ	EP	-EF'	FQ	E3	E2	D"E	F3	EY	EX	-D'E	FY
E"F	F"G	GT	-E'F	-E'G	FP	GP	F4	D"F	F2	G2	FZ	-D'F	FX	GX
GV	HZ	-D'H	-F'G	H3	GQ	D"H	D'G	G4	G3	-F'H	-D'G	GZ	GY	E"H
HY	-D'I	IZ	H2	I2	H4	I4	HP	HQ	-E'H	-E'I	HT	F"H	HV	IV
IX	JX	JY	I3	D"J	D'I	J3	IQ	IP	-F'I	JQ	F"I	IT	E'I	F"J
-D'J	-G'Y	-G'X	J4	-G'4	J2	-G'2	-E'J	-F'J	JP	-G'P	JV	E"J	JT	-GT
-G'Z	G"4	D"G"	-D'G"	G"Y	-G'3	-D'G"	F'G'	E'G'	-G'Q	E"G"	-E'G'	-G'V	-F"G'	-F'G"
G"3	D"M	M4	G"X	MX	G"Z	MZ	G"T	F"G"	G"V	MV	G"P	G"Q	-E'G"	-E'M
M2	N2	N3	MY	-D'N	-D'M	NY	F"M	MT	E"M	F"N	MQ	MP	-F'M	NQ
D"N	O3	O2	NZ	OZ	NX	OX	NV	E"N	NT	OT	-E'N	-F'N	NP	OP
O4			-D'O	OY		E"O	OV	F"O				-F'O	-E'O	OQ

A BASIC 32-RUN DESIGN WITH SIX FOUR-LEVEL FACTORS

Six factors at 4 levels and up to thirteen factors at 2 levels each. Use contrast coefficients for the Basic 32-Run Plackett-Burman Design for the analysis of data collected under the following conditions.

Treatment Combinations

Run	A	D	E	F	G	H	I	J	M	N	O	P	Q	T	X	Y	Z	2	3
1	1	1	1	1	1	1	-	-	-	-	-	-	-	-	-	-	-	-	-
2	1	3	2	2	1	2	-	-	-	-	-	+	+	+	+	+	+	+	+
3	1	1	2	2	2	3	+	+	+	+	+	+	+	+	-	-	-	-	-
4	1	3	1	1	2	4	+	+	+	+	+	-	-	-	+	+	+	+	+
5	1	4	4	4	3	3	+	+	-	-	-	-	-	+	+	+	+	-	-
6	1	2	3	3	3	4	+	+	-	-	-	+	+	-	-	-	-	+	+
7	1	4	3	3	4	1	-	-	+	+	+	+	+	-	+	+	+	-	-
8	1	2	4	4	4	2	-	-	+	+	+	-	-	+	-	-	-	+	+
9	2	4	3	2	2	1	-	+	+	-	-	-	-	+	-	-	+	+	+
10	2	2	4	1	2	2	-	+	+	-	-	+	+	-	+	+	-	-	-
11	2	4	4	1	1	3	+	-	-	+	+	+	+	-	-	-	+	+	+
12	2	2	3	2	1	4	+	-	-	+	+	-	-	+	+	+	-	-	-
13	2	1	2	3	4	3	+	-	+	-	-	-	-	-	+	+	-	+	+
14	2	3	1	4	4	4	+	-	+	-	-	+	+	+	-	-	+	-	-
15	2	1	1	4	3	1	-	+	-	+	+	+	+	+	+	+	-	+	+
16	2	3	2	3	3	2	-	+	-	+	+	-	-	-	-	-	+	-	-
17	3	1	3	4	1	2	+	+	+	+	-	-	+	-	-	+	+	-	+
18	3	3	4	3	1	1	+	+	+	+	-	+	-	+	+	-	-	+	-
19	3	1	4	3	2	4	-	-	-	-	+	+	-	+	-	+	+	-	+
20	3	3	3	4	2	3	-	-	-	-	+	-	+	-	+	-	-	+	-
21	3	4	2	1	3	4	-	-	+	+	-	-	+	+	+	-	-	-	+
22	3	2	1	2	3	3	-	-	+	+	-	+	-	-	-	+	+	+	-
23	3	4	1	2	4	2	+	+	-	-	+	+	-	-	+	-	-	-	+
24	3	2	2	1	4	1	+	+	-	-	+	-	+	+	-	+	+	+	-
25	4	4	1	3	2	2	+	-	-	+	-	-	+	+	-	+	-	+	-
26	4	2	2	4	2	1	+	-	-	+	-	+	-	-	+	-	+	-	+
27	4	4	2	4	1	4	-	+	+	-	+	+	-	-	-	+	-	+	-
28	4	2	1	3	1	3	-	+	+	-	+	-	+	+	+	-	+	-	+
29	4	1	4	2	4	4	-	+	-	+	-	-	+	-	+	-	+	+	-
30	4	3	3	1	4	3	-	+	-	+	-	+	-	+	-	+	-	-	+
31	4	1	3	1	3	2	+	-	+	-	+	+	-	+	+	-	+	+	-
32	4	3	4	2	3	1	+	-	+	-	+	-	+	-	-	+	-	-	+
	A	D	E	F	G	H	I	J	M	N	O	P	Q	T	X	Y	Z	2	3

Confounding Patterns For
The Basic 32-Run Design With Six Four-Level Factors

Contrast Labels

A	B	C	D	E	F	G	H	I	J	K	L	M	N	O	P

Corresponding Main Effects and Two-Factor Interactions

A	A'	A"	D	E	F	G	H	I	J	G'	G"	M	N	O	P
-DE	-DF	-DG	-AE	-AD	-AG	-AF	-AI	-AH	-AG'	-AJ	-AM	-AG"	-AO	-AN	-AQ
-FG	-EG	-EF	-A'F	-A'G	-A'D	-A'E	-A'J	-A'G'	-A'H	-A'I	-A'N	-A'O	-A'G"	-A'M	-A'E'
-HI	-HJ	-G'H	-A"G	-A"F	-A"E	-A"D	-A"G'	-A"J	-A"I	-A"H	-A"O	-A"N	-A"M	-A"G"	-A"F'
-G'J	-G'I	-IJ	-G"H	-HM	-HN	-HO	-DG"	-DM	-DN	-DO	-DH	-DI	-DJ	-DG'	-DT
-G"M	-G"N	-G"O	-IM	-G'I	-IO	-IN	-EM	-EG"	-EO	-EN	-EI	-EH	-EG'	-EJ	-EF"
-NO	-MO	-MN	-JN	-JO	-G"J	-JM	-FN	-FO	-FG"	-FM	-FJ	-FG'	-FH	-FI	-FH'
-PQ	-E'P	-F'P	-G'O	-G'N	-G'M	-E"P	-GO	-GN	-GM	-D'P	-P2	-GJ	-GI	-GH	-E'G
-E'F'	-F'Q	-E'Q	-PT	-F"P	-H'P	-H'Q	-PX	-PY	-PZ	-QZ	-Q3	-P3	-H"P	-D"P	-HX
-F'T	-TH'	-E'T	-F"Q	-QT	-E"Q	-E'F"	-QY	-QX	-D'Q	-E'Y	-E"H"	-Q2	-D"Q	-H'Q	-IY
-E"H'	-E'F"	-F'H'	-E'H'	-F'H'	-ET	-FT	-EZ	-D'E'	-EX	-F'X	-D'F	-D"E'	-E'2	-E'3	-JZ
-XY	-XZ	-D'X	-E'F"	-X3	-H"X	-D'X	-D'F'	-F'Z	-F'Y	-D'T	-TX	-F'H"	-F'3	-F'2	-D'G'
-D'Z	-D'Y	-YZ	-X2	-Y2	-D"Y	-H'Y	-T2	-T3	-H'T	-F"H"	-F'Y	-TY	-TZ	-DT	-G"2
-23	-H"2	-D"2	-Y3	-D"Z	-Z2	-Z3	-F"3	-F"2	-D"F"	-H3	-H'Z	-F"X	-D'F"	-F"Z	-M3
-D"H"	-D"3	-H"3	-H'Z	-D'H"	-D3	-D2	-D"E"	-D"H"	-H2	-E"2	-D'E"	-D'H'	-H'X	-H'Y	-H"N
							-E"H"	-E'3			-E"Z	-E"Y	-E"X	-D'O	

Contrast Labels

Q	R	S	T	U	V	W	X	Y	Z	1	2	3	4	5

Corresponding Main Effects and Two-Factor Interactions

Q	E'	F'	T	F"	H'	E"	X	Y	Z	D'	2	3	H"	D"
-AP	-AF'	-AE'	-AF"	-AT	-AE"	-AH'	-AY	-AX	-AD'	-AZ	-A3	-A2	-AD"	-AH"
-A'F'	-A'P	-A'Q	-A'H'	-A'E'	-AT	-A'F"	-A'Z	-A'D'	-A'X	-A'Y	-A'H"	-A'D"	-A'2	-A'3
-A"E'	-A"Q	-A"P	-A"E'	-A"H'	-A"F'	-A"T	-A"D'	-A"Z	-A"Y	-A"X	-A"D"	-A"H"	-A"3	-A"2
-DF"	-DH'	-DE"	-DP	-DQ	-DE'	-DF'	-D2	-D3	-DH"	-EH"	-DX	-DY	-DZ	-EZ
-ET	-FT	-EH'	-EQ	-EP	-EF'	-FQ	-E3	-E2	-D"E	-F3	-EY	-EX	-D'E	-FY
-E"F	-F"G	-GT	-E'F	-E'G	-FP	-GP	-FH"	-D"F	-F2	-G2	-FZ	-D'F	-FX	-GX
-GH'	-HZ	-D'H	-F'G	-H3	-GQ	-D"H	-D"G	-GH"	-G3	-F'H	-D'G	-GZ	-GY	-E"H
-HY	-DI	-IZ	-H2	-I2	-D'I	-H'I	-HP	-HQ	-E'H	-EI	-HT	-F"H	-E'I	-H'I
-IX	-JX	-JY	-I3	-D"J	-J2	-J3	-IQ	-IP	-F'I	-JQ	-F"I	-IT	-JT	-F"J
-D'J	-G'Y	-G'X	-H"J	-G'H"	-G3	-G'2	-E'J	-F'J	-JP	-G'P	-H'J	-E"J	-F"G'	-GT
-G'Z	-G"H"	-D"G"	-D'G'	-G'Y	-G"Z	-D'G"	-F'G'	-E'G'	-G'Q	-E"G"	-E"G'	-G'H'	-E'G"	-F'G"
-G"3	-D"M	-H"M	-G'X	-MX	-D'M	-MZ	-G'T	-F"G'	-G"H'	-H'M	-G"P	-G'Q	-F'M	-E'M
-M2	-N2	-N3	-MY	-D'N	-NX	-NY	-F"M	-MT	-E'M	-F'N	-MQ	-MP	-NP	-NQ
-D"N	-O3	-O2	-NZ	-OZ	-OY	-OX	-H'N	-E'N	-NT	-OT	-E'N	-F'N	-OQ	-OP
-H"O			-D'O				-E"O	-H'O	-F'O		-F'O	-E'O		

A Reflected 32-Run Design With Six Four-Level Factors

Six factors at 4 levels and thirteen factors at 2 levels each. Use contrast coefficients for the Reflected 32-Run Plackett-Burman Design for the analysis of data collected under the following plan.

Treatment Combinations

Run	A	D	E	F	G	H	I	J	M	N	O	P	Q	T	X	Y	Z	2	3
1	4	4	4	4	4	4	+	+	+	+	+	+	+	+	+	+	+	+	+
2	4	2	3	3	4	3	+	+	+	+	+	-	-	-	-	-	-	-	-
3	4	4	3	3	3	2	-	-	-	-	-	-	-	-	+	+	+	+	+
4	4	2	4	4	3	1	-	-	-	-	-	+	+	+	-	-	-	-	-
5	4	1	1	1	2	2	-	-	+	+	+	+	+	-	-	-	-	+	+
6	4	3	2	2	2	1	-	-	+	+	+	-	-	+	+	+	+	-	-
7	4	1	2	2	1	4	+	+	-	-	-	-	-	+	-	-	-	+	+
8	4	3	1	1	1	3	+	+	-	-	-	+	+	-	+	+	+	-	-
9	3	1	2	3	3	4	+	-	-	+	+	+	+	-	+	+	-	-	-
10	3	3	1	4	3	3	+	-	-	+	+	-	-	+	-	-	+	+	+
11	3	1	1	4	4	2	-	+	+	-	-	-	-	+	+	+	-	-	-
12	3	3	2	3	4	1	-	+	+	-	-	+	+	-	-	-	+	+	+
13	3	4	3	2	1	2	-	+	-	+	+	+	+	+	-	-	+	-	-
14	3	2	4	1	1	1	-	+	-	+	+	-	-	-	+	+	-	+	+
15	3	4	4	1	2	4	+	-	+	-	-	-	-	-	-	-	+	-	-
16	3	2	3	2	2	3	+	-	+	-	-	+	+	+	+	+	-	+	+
17	2	4	2	1	4	3	-	-	-	-	+	+	-	+	+	-	-	+	-
18	2	2	1	2	4	4	-	-	-	-	+	-	+	-	-	+	+	-	+
19	2	4	1	2	3	1	+	+	+	+	-	-	+	-	+	-	-	+	-
20	2	2	2	1	3	2	+	+	+	+	-	+	-	+	-	+	+	-	+
21	2	1	3	4	2	1	+	+	-	-	+	+	-	-	-	+	+	+	-
22	2	3	4	3	2	2	+	+	-	-	+	-	+	+	+	-	-	-	+
23	2	1	4	3	1	3	-	-	+	+	-	-	+	+	-	+	+	+	-
24	2	3	3	4	1	4	-	-	+	+	-	+	-	-	+	-	-	-	+
25	1	1	4	2	3	3	-	+	+	-	+	+	-	-	+	-	+	-	+
26	1	3	3	1	3	4	-	+	+	-	+	-	+	+	-	+	-	+	-
27	1	1	3	1	4	1	+	-	-	+	-	-	+	+	+	-	+	-	+
28	1	3	4	2	4	2	+	-	-	+	-	+	-	-	-	+	-	+	-
29	1	4	1	3	1	1	+	-	+	-	+	+	-	+	-	+	-	-	+
30	1	2	2	4	1	2	+	-	+	-	+	-	+	-	+	-	+	+	-
31	1	4	2	4	2	3	-	+	-	+	-	-	+	-	-	+	-	-	+
32	1	2	1	3	2	4	-	+	-	+	-	+	-	+	+	-	+	+	-
	A	D	E	F	G	H	I	J	M	N	O	P	Q	T	X	Y	Z	2	3

CONFOUNDING PATTERNS FOR THE REFLECTED 32-RUN DESIGN WITH SIX FOUR-LEVEL FACTORS

Contrast Labels

A	B	C	D	E	F	G	H	I	J	K	L	M	N	O	P

Corresponding Main Effects and Two-Factor Interactions

A	-A'	A"	D	E	F	G	H	I	J	-G'	G"	M	N	O	P
DE	DF	DG	AE	AD	AG	AF	AI	AH	AG'	AJ	AM	AG"	AO	AN	AQ
FG	EG	EF	-A'F	-A'G	-A'D	-A'E	-A'J	A'G'	-A'H	-A'I	-A'N	-A'O	-A'G"	-A'M	A'E'
HI	HJ	-G'H	A'G	A"F	A"E	A"D	A"G'	A"J	A'I	A"H	A"O	A"N	A"M	A"G"	-A"F'
-G'J	-G'I	IJ	G"H	HM	HN	HO	DG"	DM	DN	DO	DH	DI	DJ	DG'	DT
G"M	G"N	G"O	IM	G"I	IO	IN	EM	EG"	EO	EN	EI	EH	-EG'	EJ	EF"
NO	MO	MN	JN	JO	G"J	JM	FN	FO	FG"	FM	FJ	FG'	FH	FI	-FH'
PQ	-E'P	-F'P	-G'O	-G'N	-G'M	E"P	GO	GN	GM	-D'P	P2	GJ	GI	GH	E'G
E'F'	-F'Q	-E'Q	PT	F"P	-H'P	-H'Q	PX	PY	PZ	QZ	Q3	P3	H"P	D"P	HX
F"T	TH'	E'T	F"Q	QT	E"Q	-E'F"	QY	QX	-D'Q	-E'Y	-E'H"	Q2	D"Q	H"Q	IY
E"H'	E"F'	F"H'	E'H'	F'H'	-ET	-FT	-EZ	-D'E'	-E'X	-F'X	-D"F	-D"E'	-E'2	-E'3	JZ
XY	XZ	-D'X	-E"F'	X3	H'X	D'X	D'F	-FZ	-F'Y	D'T	TX	-F'H"	-F'3	-F'2	D'G'
-DZ	-D'Y	YZ	X2	Y2	D'Y	H'Y	T2	T3	H'T	F"H'	F"Y	TY	TZ	-DT	G"2
23	H"2	D"2	Y3	D"Z	Z2	Z3	F"3	F"2	D"F"	-H3	-H'Z	F"X	-D'F"	F"Z	M3
D"H"	D"3	H"3	H"Z	-D'H"	-D3	-D2	D"E"	-D"H'	-H2	E'2	-D'E"	D'H'	-H'X	-H'Y	D"O
							E"H"	E"3			E'Z	E'Y	E'X	D"O

Contrast Labels

Q	R	S	T	U	V	W	X	Y	Z	1	2	3	4	5

Corresponding Main Effects and Two-Factor Interactions

Q	-E'	-F'	T	F"	-H'	E"	X	Y	Z	-D'	2	3	H"	D"
AP	-AF'	-AE'	AF"	AT	AE"	-AH'	AY	AX	-AD'	AZ	A3	A2	AD"	AH"
A'F'	-A'P	-A'Q	A'H'	-A'E"	-AT	-A'F"	-A'Z	A'D'	-A'X	-A'Y	-A'H"	-A'D"	-A'2	-A'3
-A"E'	A"Q	A"P	A"E'	-A"H'	A"F"	A"T	-A"D'	A"Z	A"Y	A"X	A"D"	A"H'	A"3	A"2
DF"	-DH'	DE"	DP	DQ	-DE'	-DF'	D2	D3	DH"	EH'	DX	DY	DZ	EZ
ET	FT	-EH'	EQ	EP	-EF'	FQ	E3	E2	D"E	F3	EY	EX	-D'E	FY
E"F	F"G	GT	-E'F	-E'G	FP	GP	FH"	D"F	F2	G2	FZ	-D'F	FX	GX
-GH'	HZ	-D'H	-F'G	H3	GQ	D"H	D"G	GH"	G3	-F'H	-D'G	GZ	GY	E"H
HY	-D'I	IZ	H2	I2	D'I	H'I	HP	HQ	-E'H	-E'I	HT	F"H	E'I	-H'I
IX	JX	JY	I3	D"J	J2	J3	IQ	IP	-F'I	JQ	F'I	IT	JT	F"J
-D'J	-G'Y	-G'X	H"J	-G'H"	-G'3	-G'2	-E'J	-F'J	JP	-G'P	-H'J	E"J	-F"G'	-GT
-G'Z	G"H"	D"G"	D"G'	G"Y	G"Z	-D'G"	F'G'	-E'G'	G'Q	E"G"	E"G'	G'H'	-E'G"	-F'G"
G"3	D"M	H"M	G"X	MX	D"M	MZ	G"T	F"G"	-G"H'	-H'M	G"P	G"Q	-F'M	-E'M
M2	N2	N3	MY	-D'N	NX	NY	F"M	MT	E"M	F"N	MQ	MP	NP	NQ
D"N	O3	O2	NZ	OZ	OY	OX	-H'N	E"N	NT	OT	-E'N	-F'N	OQ	OP
H"O			-D'O				E'O	-H'O	F'O		-F'O	-E'O		

32-Run Designs With Six Factors
Having Three or Four Levels

The $4^6 \times 2^{13}$ designs on pages 262–265 can be modified into $3^6 \times 2^{13}$ designs by changing Factors A, D, E, F, G and H into three level factors. As before, the relationship between the levels for a four-level factor and the levels of the corresponding three-level factor are:

Four Level Factor		Three Level Factor
Level 1	stays	Level 1
Level 2	stays	Level 2
Level 3	stays	Level 3
Level 4	**becomes**	**Level 1 or Level 2 or Level 3**

Since the new three level factor will appear to have three degrees of freedom there will be some redundancy in the analysis. See p. 195 for more details.

If five of the four-level factors are modified into three-level factors, then the designs on the previous four pages will be $4 \times 3^5 \times 2^{13}$ designs.

If four of the four-level factors are modified into three-level factors, then the designs on the previous four pages will be $4^2 \times 3^4 \times 2^{13}$ designs.

If three of the four-level factors are modified into three-level factors, then the designs on the previous four pages will be $4^3 \times 3^3 \times 2^{13}$ designs.

If two of the four-level factors are modified into three-level factors, then the designs on the previous four pages will be $4^4 \times 3^2 \times 2^{13}$ designs.

If only one of the four-level factors is modified into a three level factor, then the designs on the previous four pages will be $4^5 \times 3 \times 2^{13}$ designs.

The confounding pattern for these 32-run designs will remain the same as shown on the preceeding pages, regardless of the number of factors that are modified into three level factors.

Use response plots visualize the results, especially if a three-level or four-level factor is found to be significant.

32-RUN DESIGNS WITH SEVEN FACTORS HAVING THREE OR FOUR LEVELS

The $4^7 \times 2^{10}$ designs on pages 268–271 can be modified into $3^7 \times 2^{10}$ designs by changing Factors A, D, E, F, G, H and I into three level factors. As before, the relationship between the levels for a four-level factor and the levels of the corresponding three-level factor are as shown on the preceeding page.

If six of the four-level factors are modified into three level factors, then the designs on the following four pages will be $4 \times 3^6 \times 2^{10}$ designs.

If five of the four-level factors are modified into three level factors, then the designs on the following four pages will be $4^2 \times 3^5 \times 2^{10}$ designs.

If four of the four-level factors are modified into three level factors, then the designs on the following four pages will be $4^3 \times 3^4 \times 2^{10}$ designs.

If three of the four-level factors are modified into three level factors, then the designs on the following four pages will be $4^4 \times 3^3 \times 2^{10}$ designs.

If two of the four-level factors are modified into three level factors, then the designs on the following four pages will be $4^5 \times 3^2 \times 2^{10}$ designs.

If only one of the four-level factors is modified into a three level factor, then the designs on the following four pages will be $4^6 \times 3 \times 2^{10}$ designs.

The confounding pattern for these 32-run designs will remain the same as shown on the following pages, regardless of the number of factors which are modified into three level factors.

Use response plots to visualize the results, especially if a three-level or four-level factor is found to be significant.

A Basic 32-Run Design With Seven Four-Level Factors

Seven factors at 4 levels and up to ten factors at 2 levels each. Use contrast coefficients for the Basic 32-Run Plackett-Burman Design for the analysis of data collected under the following conditions.

Treatment Combinations

Run	A	D	E	F	G	H	I	J	M	N	O	P	Q	X	Y	Z	2
1	1	1	1	1	1	1	1	-	-	-	-	-	-	-	-	-	-
2	1	3	2	2	1	2	2	-	-	-	-	+	+	+	+	+	+
3	1	1	2	2	2	3	3	+	+	+	+	+	+	-	-	-	-
4	1	3	1	1	2	4	4	+	+	+	+	-	-	+	+	+	+
5	1	4	4	4	3	3	3	+	-	-	-	-	-	+	+	+	-
6	1	2	3	3	3	4	4	+	-	-	-	+	+	-	-	-	+
7	1	4	3	3	4	1	1	-	+	+	+	+	+	+	+	+	-
8	1	2	4	4	4	2	2	-	+	+	+	-	-	-	-	-	+
9	2	4	3	2	2	1	2	+	+	-	-	-	-	-	-	+	+
10	2	2	4	1	2	2	1	+	+	-	-	+	+	+	+	-	-
11	2	4	4	1	1	3	4	-	-	+	+	+	+	-	-	+	+
12	2	2	3	2	1	4	3	-	-	+	+	-	-	+	+	-	-
13	2	1	2	3	4	3	4	-	+	-	-	-	-	+	+	-	+
14	2	3	1	4	4	4	3	-	+	-	-	+	+	-	-	+	-
15	2	1	1	4	3	1	2	+	-	+	+	+	+	+	+	-	+
16	2	3	2	3	3	2	1	+	-	+	+	-	-	-	-	+	-
17	3	1	3	4	1	2	4	+	+	+	-	-	+	-	+	+	-
18	3	3	4	3	1	1	3	+	+	+	-	+	-	+	-	-	+
19	3	1	4	3	2	4	2	-	-	-	+	+	-	-	+	+	-
20	3	3	3	4	2	3	1	-	-	-	+	-	+	+	-	-	+
21	3	4	2	1	3	4	2	-	+	+	-	-	+	+	-	-	-
22	3	2	1	2	3	3	1	-	+	+	-	+	-	-	+	+	+
23	3	4	1	2	4	2	4	+	-	-	+	+	-	+	-	-	-
24	3	2	2	1	4	1	3	+	-	-	+	-	+	-	+	+	+
25	4	4	1	3	2	2	3	-	-	+	-	-	+	-	+	-	+
26	4	2	2	4	2	1	4	-	-	+	-	+	-	+	-	+	-
27	4	4	2	4	1	4	1	+	+	-	+	+	-	-	+	-	+
28	4	2	1	3	1	3	2	+	+	-	+	-	+	+	-	+	-
29	4	1	4	2	4	4	1	+	-	+	-	-	+	+	-	+	+
30	4	3	3	1	4	3	2	+	-	+	-	+	-	-	+	-	-
31	4	1	3	1	3	2	3	-	+	-	+	+	-	+	-	+	+
32	4	3	4	2	3	1	4	-	+	-	+	-	+	-	+	-	-
	A	D	E	F	G	H	I	J	M	N	O	P	Q	X	Y	Z	2

CONFOUNDING PATTERNS FOR THE BASIC 32-RUN DESIGN WITH SEVEN FOUR-LEVEL FACTORS

Contrast Labels

A	B	C	D	E	F	G	H	I	J	K	L	M	N	O	P

Corresponding Main Effects and Two-Factor Interactions

A	A'	A"	D	E	F	G	H	I	J	G'	G"	M	N	O	P
-DE	-DF	-DG	-AE	-AD	-AG	-AF	-AI	-AH	-AG'	-AJ	-AM	-AG"	-AO	-AN	-AQ
-FG	-EG	-EF	-A'F	-A'G	-A'D	-A'E	-A'J	-A'G'	-A'H	-A'I	-A'N	-A'O	-A'G"	-A'M	-A'E'
-HI	-HJ	-G'H	-A"G	-A"F	-A"E	-A"D	-A"G'	-A"J	-A"I	-A"H	-A"O	-A"N	-A"M	-A"G"	-A"F'
-G'J	-G'I	-IJ	-G"H	-HM	-HN	-HO	-DG"	-DM	-DN	-DO	-DH	-DI	-DJ	-DG'	-DI'
-G"M	-G"N	-G"O	-IM	-G'I	-IO	-IN	-EM	-EG'	-EO	-EN	-EI	-EH	-EG'	-EJ	-EF"
-NO	-MO	-MN	-JN	-JO	-G"J	-JM	-FN	-FO	-FG"	-FM	-FJ	-FG'	-FH	-FI	-FH'
-PQ	-E'P	-F'P	-G'O	-G'N	-G'M	-E"P	-GO	-GN	-GM	-D'P	-P2	-GJ	-GI	-GH	-E"G
-E'F'	-F'Q	-E'Q	-I'P	-F"P	-H'P	-H'Q	-PX	-PY	-PZ	-QZ	-I'Q	-I'P	-H"P	-D"P	-HX
-F'T	-H'T	-E'T	-F"Q	-I'Q	-E"Q	-E'F"	-QY	-QX	-D'Q	-E'Y	-E'H"	-Q2	-D"Q	-H'Q	-IY
-E"H'	-E"F"	-F"H'	-E'H'	-ET'	-FI'	-EZ	-D'E	-E'X	-F'X	-D"F'	-D"E'	-E'2	-EI'	-JZ	
-XY	-XZ	-D'X	-E'F"	-I'X	-H"X	-D"X	-D'F	-F'Z	-F'Y	-D'T	-I'X	-F'H"	-FT'	-F'2	-D'G'
-DZ	-D'Y	-YZ	-X2	-Y2	-D"Y	-H"Y	-I'2	-F"2	-H'T	-F"H"	-F'Y	-I'Y	-IZ	-DT'	-G"2
-I'2	-H"2	-D'2	-I'Y	-D'Z	-Z2	-I'Z	-F"I'	-D"H'	-D"F'	-HT"	-H'Z	-F"X	-D'F'	-F"Z	-I'M
-D"H'	-D'T'	-H'T'	-H"Z	-D'H"	-DT"	-D'2	-D"E'	-E"H"	-H2	-E"2	-D'E'	-D'H'	-H'X	-H'Y	-H"N
									-E'T'				-E'Z	-E"Y	-E"X	-D"O

Contrast Labels

Q	R	S	T	U	V	W	X	Y	Z	1	2	3	4	5

Corresponding Main Effects and Two-Factor Interactions

Q	E'	F'	I'	F"	H'	E"	X	Y	Z	D'	2	I"	H"	D"
-AP	-AF'	-AE'	-AF"	-AI'	-AE"	-AH'	-AY	-AX	-AD'	-AZ	-AI"	-A2	-AD"	-AH"
-A'F'	-A'P	-A'Q	-A'H'	-A'E'	-A'T	-A'F"	-A'Z	-A'D'	-A'X	-A'Y	-A'H"	-A'D"	-A'2	-A'T'
-A"E'	-A"Q	-A"P	-A"E'	-A"H'	-A"F"	-A"T	-A"D'	-A"Z	-A"Y	-A"X	-A"D"	-A"H"	-A"T'	-A"2
-DF"	-DH'	-DE"	-DP	-DQ	-DE'	-DF'	-D2	-DI"	-DH'	-EH"	-DX	-DY	-DZ	-EZ
-EI'	-FI'	-EH'	-EQ	-EP	-EF'	-FQ	-EI"	-E2	-D"E	-FI"	-EY	-EX	-D'E	-FY
-E'F'	-F"G	-GI'	-E'F	-E'G	-FP	-GP	-FH"	-D"F	-F2	-G2	-FZ	-D'F	-FX	-GX
-GH'	-HZ	-D'H	-F'G	-HI'	-GQ	-D"H	-D'G	-GH"	-GI"	-F'H	-D'G	-GZ	-GY	-E"H
-HY	-DI'	-IZ	-H2	-I2	-D'I	-H'I	-HP	-HQ	-E'H	-EI	-HI'	-F"H	-E'I	-H'I
-IX	-JX	-JY	-H'J	-D'J	-J2	-I'J	-IQ	-IP	-F'I	-JQ	-F'I	-E'J	-I'J	-F"J
-D'J	-G'Y	-G'X	-D'G'	-G'H"	-GT'	-G'2	-E'J	-F'J	-JP	-G'P	-H'J	-G'H'	-F"G'	-G'T'
-G'Z	-G"H"	-D"G"	-G'X	-G'Y	-G'Z	-D"G"	-F'G'	-E'G'	-G'Q	-E"G"	-E'G'	-G'Q	-E'G"	-F'G"
-G"T'	-D"M	-H"M	-MY	-MX	-D"M	-MZ	-G'T	-F"G"	-G"H'	-H'M	-G"P	-MP	-F'M	-E'M
-M2	-N2	-I'N	-NZ	-D'N	-NX	-NY	-F"M	-I'M	-E"M	-F'N	-MQ	-F'N	-NP	-NQ
-D"N	-I'O	-O2	-D'O	-OZ	-OY	-OX	-H'N	-E"N	-I'N	-I'O	-E'N	-E'O	-OQ	-OP
-H"O							-E"O	-H'O	-F"O		-F'O			

269

A Reflected 32-Run Design With Seven Four-Level Factors

Seven factors at 4 levels and ten factors at 2 levels each. Use contrast coefficients for the Reflected 32-Run Plackett-Burman Design for the analysis of data collected under the following plan.

Treatment Combinations

Run	A	D	E	F	G	H	I	J	M	N	O	P	Q	X	Y	Z	2
1	4	4	4	4	4	4	4	+	+	+	+	+	+	+	+	+	+
2	4	2	3	3	4	3	3	+	+	+	+	-	-	-	-	-	-
3	4	4	3	3	3	2	2	-	-	-	-	-	-	+	+	+	+
4	4	2	4	4	3	1	1	-	-	-	-	+	+	-	-	-	-
5	4	1	1	1	2	2	2	-	+	+	+	+	+	-	-	-	+
6	4	3	2	2	2	1	1	-	+	+	+	-	-	+	+	+	-
7	4	1	2	2	1	4	4	+	-	-	-	-	-	-	-	-	+
8	4	3	1	1	1	3	3	+	-	-	-	+	+	+	+	+	-
9	3	1	2	3	3	4	3	-	-	+	+	+	+	+	+	-	-
10	3	3	1	4	3	3	4	-	-	+	+	-	-	-	-	+	+
11	3	1	1	4	4	2	1	+	+	-	-	-	-	+	+	-	-
12	3	3	2	3	4	1	2	+	+	-	-	+	+	-	-	+	+
13	3	4	3	2	1	2	1	+	-	+	+	+	+	-	-	+	-
14	3	2	4	1	1	1	2	+	-	+	+	-	-	+	+	-	+
15	3	4	4	1	2	4	3	-	+	-	-	-	-	-	-	+	-
16	3	2	3	2	2	3	4	-	+	-	-	+	+	+	+	-	+
17	2	4	2	1	4	3	1	-	-	-	+	+	-	+	-	-	+
18	2	2	1	2	4	4	2	-	-	-	+	-	+	-	+	+	-
19	2	4	1	2	3	1	3	+	+	+	-	-	+	+	-	-	+
20	2	2	2	1	3	2	4	+	+	+	-	+	-	-	+	+	-
21	2	1	3	4	2	1	3	+	-	-	+	+	-	-	+	+	+
22	2	3	4	3	2	2	4	+	-	-	+	-	+	+	-	-	-
23	2	1	4	3	1	3	1	-	+	+	-	-	+	-	+	+	+
24	2	3	3	4	1	4	2	-	+	+	-	+	-	+	-	-	-
25	1	1	4	2	3	3	2	+	+	-	+	+	-	+	-	+	-
26	1	3	3	1	3	4	1	+	+	-	+	-	+	-	+	-	+
27	1	1	3	1	4	1	4	-	-	+	-	-	+	+	-	+	-
28	1	3	4	2	4	2	3	-	-	+	-	+	-	-	+	-	+
29	1	4	1	3	1	1	4	-	+	-	+	+	-	-	+	-	-
30	1	2	2	4	1	2	3	-	+	-	+	-	+	+	-	+	+
31	1	4	2	4	2	3	2	+	-	+	-	-	+	-	+	-	-
32	1	2	1	3	2	4	1	+	-	+	-	+	-	+	-	+	+
	A	D	E	F	G	H	I	J	M	N	O	P	Q	X	Y	Z	2

Confounding Patterns For
The Reflected 32-Run Design With Seven Four-Level Factors

Contrast Labels

| A | B | C | D | E | F | G | H | I | J | K | L | M | N | O | P |

Corresponding Main Effects and Two-Factor Interactions

A	-A'	A"	D	E	F	G	H	I	J	-G'	G"	M	N	O	P
DE	DF	DG	AE	AD	AG	AF	AI	AH	-AG'	AJ	AM	AG"	AO	AN	AQ
FG	EG	EF	-A'F	-A'G	-A'D	-A'E	-A'J	A'G'	-A'H	-A'I	-A'N	-A'O	-A'G"	-A'M	A'E'
HI	HJ	-G'H	A"G	A"F	A"E	A"D	-A"G'	A"J	A"I	A"H	A"O	A"N	A"M	A"G"	-A"F'
-G'J	-G'I	IJ	G"H	HM	HN	HO	DG"	DM	DN	DO	DH	DI	DJ	-DG'	-DI'
G"M	G"N	G"O	IM	G'I	IO	IN	EM	EG"	EO	EN	EI	EH	-EG'	EJ	EF"
NO	MO	MN	JN	JO	G"J	JM	FN	FO	FG"	FM	FJ	-FG'	FH	FI	-FH'
PQ	-E'P	-F'P	-G'O	-G'N	-G'M	E"P	GO	GN	GM	-D'P	P2	GJ	GI	GH	E"G
E'F'	-F'Q	-E'Q	-I'P	F"P	-H'P	-H'Q	PX	PY	PZ	QZ	I'Q	I'P	H"P	D"P	HX
-F'T	HT	-E'T	F"Q	-I'Q	E"Q	-E'F'	QY	QX	-D'Q	-E'Y	-E'H"	Q2	D"Q	H"Q	IY
-E"H'	E"F"	-F"H'	E'H'	F'H'	ET	FI'	-EZ	D'E'	-EX	-F'X	-D"F'	-D"E'	-E'2	-ET"	JZ
XY	XZ	-D'X	-E"F'	I'X	H'X	D'X	D'F'	-F'Z	-F'Y	-D'T'	-I'X	-F'H'	-F'I'	-F'2	D'G'
-D'Z	-D'Y	YZ	X2	Y2	D"Y	H"Y	-I'2	F"2	-H'T'	F"H'	F"Y	-I'Y	-I'Z	DT	G"2
I"2	H"2	D"2	I'Y	D'Z	Z2	I'Z	F'I'	-D"H'	D"F"	-H'T	-H'Z	F"X	-D'F'	F"Z	I"M
D"H"	D"T"	H'T'	H"Z	-D'H"	-DT"	-D'2	D"E'	E"H"	-H'2	E"2	-D'E"	D'H'	-H'X	-H'Y	H"N
									E'T"			E"Z	E"Y	E"X	D"O

Contrast Labels

| Q | R | S | T | U | V | W | X | Y | Z | 1 | 2 | 3 | 4 | 5 |

Corresponding Main Effects and Two-Factor Interactions

Q	-E'	-F'	-I'	F"	-H'	E"	X	Y	Z	-D'	2	I"	H"	D"
AP	-AF'	-AE'	AF"	-AI'	AE"	-AH'	AY	AX	-AD'	AZ	AI"	A2	AD"	AH"
A'F'	-A'P	-A'Q	A'H'	-A'E'	A'T'	-A'F'	-A'Z	A'D'	-A'X	-A'Y	-A'H"	-A'D"	-A'2	-A'T'
-A"E'	A"Q	A"P	A"E"	-A"H'	A"F"	-A"T'	-A"D'	A"Z	A"Y	A"X	A"D"	A"H"	A"T'	A"2
DF"	-DH'	DE"	DP	DQ	-DE'	-DF'	D2	DI'	DH"	DX	DY	DZ		EZ
-EI'	-FI'	-EH'	EQ	EP	-EF'	FQ	EI"	E2	D"E	FI"	EY	EX	-D'E	FY
E"F'	F"G	-GI'	-E'F	-E'G	FP	GP	FH"	D"F	F2	G2	FZ	-D'F	FX	GX
-GH'	HZ	-D'H	-F'G	HI"	GQ	D"H	D'G	GH"	GI'	-F'H	-D'G	GZ	GY	E"H
HY	-D'I	IZ	H2	I2	D'I	H'I	HP	HQ	-E'H	-E'I	-HI'	F"H	E'I	-H'I
IX	JX	JY	H"J	D"J	J2	I"J	IQ	IP	-F'I	JQ	F"I	E"J	-I'J	F"J
-D'J	-G'Y	-G'X	-D"G'	-G'H"	-GT'	-G'2	-E'J	-F'J	JP	-G'P	-H'J	G'H'	-F"G'	G'T
-GZ	G"H'	D"G'	G'X	G"Y	G'Z	-D'G'	F'G'	E'G'	-G'Q	E'G"	-E'G	G'Q	-E'G"	-F'G"
G'T'	D"M	H"M	MY	MX	D"M	MZ	-G'T	F"G"	-G"H'	-H'M	G"P	MP	-F'M	-E'M
M2	N2	I'N	NZ	-D'N	NX	NY	F"M	-I'M	E"M	F"N	MQ	-F'N	NP	NQ
D"N	I'O	O2	-D'O	OZ	OY	OX	-H'N	E"N	-I'N	-I'O	-E'N	-E'O	OQ	OP
H"O							E"O	-H'O	F"O	-F'O				

271

A BASIC 32-RUN DESIGN WITH EIGHT FOUR-LEVEL FACTORS

Eight factors at 4 levels and up to seven factors at 2 levels each. Use contrast coefficients for the Basic 32-Run Plackett-Burman Design for the analysis of data collected under the following conditions.

Treatment Combinations

Run	A	D	E	F	G	H	I	J	M	N	O	Q	X	Y	2
1	1	1	1	1	1	1	1	1	-	-	-	-	-	-	-
2	1	3	2	2	1	2	2	2	-	-	-	+	+	+	+
3	1	1	2	2	2	3	3	3	+	+	+	+	-	-	-
4	1	3	1	1	2	4	4	4	+	+	+	-	+	+	+
5	1	4	4	4	3	3	3	4	-	-	-	-	+	+	-
6	1	2	3	3	3	4	4	3	-	-	-	+	-	-	+
7	1	4	3	3	4	1	1	2	+	+	+	+	+	+	-
8	1	2	4	4	4	2	2	1	+	+	+	-	-	-	+
9	2	4	3	2	2	1	2	4	+	-	-	-	-	-	+
10	2	2	4	1	2	2	1	3	+	-	-	+	+	+	-
11	2	4	4	1	1	3	4	2	-	+	+	+	-	-	+
12	2	2	3	2	1	4	3	1	-	+	+	-	+	+	-
13	2	1	2	3	4	3	4	1	+	-	-	-	+	+	+
14	2	3	1	4	4	4	3	2	+	-	-	+	-	-	-
15	2	1	1	4	3	1	2	3	-	+	+	+	+	+	+
16	2	3	2	3	3	2	1	4	-	+	+	-	-	-	-
17	3	1	3	4	1	2	4	4	+	+	-	+	-	+	-
18	3	3	4	3	1	1	3	3	+	+	-	-	+	-	+
19	3	1	4	3	2	4	2	2	-	-	+	-	-	+	-
20	3	3	3	4	2	3	1	1	-	-	+	+	+	-	+
21	3	4	2	1	3	4	2	1	+	+	-	+	+	-	-
22	3	2	1	2	3	3	1	2	+	+	-	-	-	+	+
23	3	4	1	2	4	2	4	3	-	-	+	-	+	-	-
24	3	2	2	1	4	1	3	4	-	-	+	+	-	+	+
25	4	4	1	3	2	2	3	1	-	+	-	+	-	+	+
26	4	2	2	4	2	1	4	2	-	+	-	-	+	-	-
27	4	4	2	4	1	4	1	3	+	-	+	-	-	+	+
28	4	2	1	3	1	3	2	4	+	-	+	+	+	-	-
29	4	1	4	2	4	4	1	4	-	+	-	+	+	-	+
30	4	3	3	1	4	3	2	3	-	+	-	-	-	+	-
31	4	1	3	1	3	2	3	2	+	-	+	-	+	-	+
32	4	3	4	2	3	1	4	1	+	-	+	+	-	+	-
	A	D	E	F	G	H	I	J	M	N	O	Q	X	Y	2

CONFOUNDING PATTERNS FOR
THE BASIC 32-RUN DESIGN WITH EIGHT FOUR-LEVEL FACTORS

Contrast Labels

A	B	C	D	E	F	G	H	I	J	K	L	M	N	O	P

Corresponding Main Effects and Two-Factor Interactions

A	A'	A"	D	E	F	G	H	I	J	G'	G"	M	N	O	J'
-DE	-DF	-DG	-AE	-AD	-AG	-AF	-AI	-AH	-AG'	-AJ	-AM	-AG"	-AO	-AN	-AQ
-FG	-EG	-EF	-A'F	-A'G	-A'D	-A'E	-A'J	-A'G'	-A'H	-A'I	-A'N	-A'O	-A'G"	-A'M	-A'E'
-HI	-HJ	-G'H	-A"G	-A"F	-A"E	-A"D	-A"G'	-A"J	-A"I	-A"H	-A"O	-A"N	-A"M	-A"G"	-A"F
-G'J	-G'I	-IJ	-G"H	-HM	-HN	-HO	-DG"	-DM	-DN	-DO	-DH	-DI	-DJ	-DG'	-DI'
-G"M	-G"N	-G"O	-IM	-G"I	-IO	-IN	-EM	-EG"	-EO	-EN	-EI	-EH	-EG'	-EJ	-EF"
-NO	-MO	-MN	-JN	-JO	-G"J	-JM	-FN	-FO	-FG"	-FM	-FJ	-FG'	-FH	-FI	-FH'
-J'Q	-E'J	-F'J	-G'O	-G'N	-G'M	-E"J	-GO	-GN	-GM	-D'J	-J'2	-GJ	-GI	-GH	-E'G
-E'F'	-F'Q	-E'Q	-I'J	-F"J	-H'J	-H'Q	-J'X	-J'Y	-D'Q	-QJ'	-I'Q	-I'J	-H"J	-D"J	-HX
-F"T	-HT	-E'T	-F"Q	-I'Q	-E"Q	-E'F"	-QY	-QX	-E'X	-E'Y	-E'H"	-Q2	-D"Q	-H"Q	-IY
-E"H'	-E"F"	-F"H'	-E'H'	-F'H'	-E'T	-F'T	-EJ"	-D'E	-F'Y	-F'X	-D"F	-D"E	-E'2	-ET"	-D'G'
-XY	-J'X	-D'X	-E'F'	-I'X	-H"X	-D'X	-D'F	-F'J"	-H'T	-D'T	-I'X	-F'H'	-FI'	-F'2	-G"2
-D'J"	-D'Y	-J"Y	-X2	-Y2	-D"Y	-H"Y	-I'2	-F"2	-D"F"	-F'H"	-F"Y	-I'Y	-I'J"	-D'T	-I"M
-I"2	-H"2	-D"2	-I'Y	-D"J'	-J'2	-I"J'	-F"T	-D"H'	-H'2	-HT'	-HJ'	-F'X	-D'F'	-F"J'	-H'N
-D"H'	-D'T	-H'T'	-H'J"	-D'H"	-DT'	-D'2	-D"E'	-E"H"	-E'T'	-E'2	-D'E'	-D"H'	-H'X	-H'Y	-D"O
													-E'J"	-E"Y	-E"X

Contrast Labels

Q	R	S	T	U	V	W	X	Y	Z	1	2	3	4	5

Corresponding Main Effects and Two-Factor Interactions

Q	E'	F'	I'	F"	H'	E"	X	Y	J"	D'	2	I"	H"	D"
-AJ'	-AF	-AE'	-AF"	-AI'	-AE"	-AH'	-AY	-AX	-AD'	-AJ"	-AI"	-A2	-AD"	-AH"
-A'F	-A'J	-A'Q	-A'H'	-A'E"	-A'T	-A'F"	-A'J"	-A'D'	-A'X	-A'Y	-A'H"	-A'D"	-A'2	-A'T"
-A"E'	-A"Q	-A"J'	-A"E"	-A"H'	-A"F"	-A"T	-A"D'	-A"J"	-A"Y	-A"X	-A"D"	-A"H"	-A"T'	-A"2
-DF"	-DH	-DE"	-DJ	-DQ	-DE'	-DF'	-D2	-DI'	-DH"	-EH'	-DX	-DY	-DJ'	-EJ"
-EI'	-FI'	-EH'	-EQ	-EJ'	-EF'	-FQ	-EI"	-E2	-D"E	-FI'	-EY	-EX	-D'E	-FY
-E'F	-F'G	-GI'	-E'F	-E'G	-FJ'	-GJ'	-FH'	-D"F	-F2	-G2	-FJ'	-D'F	-FX	-GX
-GH'	-HJ"	-D'H	-F'G	-HI"	-GQ	-D"H	-D'G	-GH"	-GI'	-FH	-D'G	-GJ"	-GY	-E"H
-HY	-D'I	-IJ"	-H2	-I2	-D'I	-H"I	-HJ	-HQ	-E'H	-EI	-HI'	-F"H	-E'I	-HI'
-IX	-JX	-JY	-H"J	-D"J	-J2	-I"J	-IQ	-IJ'	-F'I	-JQ	-F'I	-E'J	-I'J	-F"J
-D'J	-G'Y	-G'X	-D"G'	-G'H"	-GT'	-G'2	-E'J	-F'J	-G'Q	-G'J'	-H'J	-G'H'	-F"G'	-GT'
-G'J'	-G"H"	-D"G"	-G"X	-G"Y	-G"J'	-D'G"	-F'G'	-E'G'	-G"H'	-E"G'	-E'G'	-G"Q	-E'G"	-F'G'
-G'T	-D"M	-H"M	-MY	-MX	-D'M	-J"M	-G'T	-F"G'	-E"M	-H'M	-G"J'	-J'M	-F'M	-E'M
-M2	-N2	-I'N	-J'N	-D'N	-NX	-NY	-F"M	-I'M	-I'N	-F"N	-MQ	-F'N	-J'N	-NQ
-D'N	-I'O	-O2	-D'O	-J'O	-OY	-OX	-H'N	-E'N	-F"O	-I'O	-E'N	-E'O	-OQ	-J'O
-H"O							-E"O	-H'O			-F'O			

A Reflected 32-Run Design With Eight Four-Level Factors

Eight factors at 4 levels and seven factors at 2 levels each. Use contrast coefficients for the Reflected 32-Run Plackett-Burman Design for the analysis of data collected under the following plan.

Treatment Combinations

Run	A	D	E	F	G	H	I	J	M	N	O	Q	X	Y	2
1	4	4	4	4	4	4	4	4	+	+	+	+	+	+	+
2	4	2	3	3	4	3	3	3	+	+	+	-	-	-	-
3	4	4	3	3	3	2	2	2	-	-	-	-	+	+	+
4	4	2	4	4	3	1	1	1	-	-	-	+	-	-	-
5	4	1	1	1	2	2	2	1	+	+	+	+	-	-	+
6	4	3	2	2	2	1	1	2	+	+	+	-	+	+	-
7	4	1	2	2	1	4	4	3	-	-	-	-	-	-	+
8	4	3	1	1	1	3	3	4	-	-	-	+	+	+	-
9	3	1	2	3	3	4	3	1	-	+	+	+	+	+	-
10	3	3	1	4	3	3	4	2	-	+	+	-	-	-	+
11	3	1	1	4	4	2	1	3	+	-	-	-	+	+	-
12	3	3	2	3	4	1	2	4	+	-	-	+	-	-	+
13	3	4	3	2	1	2	1	4	-	+	+	+	-	-	-
14	3	2	4	1	1	1	2	3	-	+	+	-	+	+	+
15	3	4	4	1	2	4	3	2	+	-	-	-	-	-	-
16	3	2	3	2	2	3	4	1	+	-	-	+	+	+	+
17	2	4	2	1	4	3	1	1	-	-	+	-	+	-	+
18	2	2	1	2	4	4	2	2	-	-	+	+	-	+	-
19	2	4	1	2	3	1	3	3	+	+	-	+	+	-	+
20	2	2	2	1	3	2	4	4	+	+	-	-	-	+	-
21	2	1	3	4	2	1	3	4	-	-	+	-	-	+	+
22	2	3	4	3	2	2	4	3	-	-	+	+	+	-	-
23	2	1	4	3	1	3	1	2	+	+	-	+	-	+	+
24	2	3	3	4	1	4	2	1	+	+	-	-	+	-	-
25	1	1	4	2	3	3	2	4	+	-	+	-	+	-	-
26	1	3	3	1	3	4	1	3	+	-	+	+	-	+	+
27	1	1	3	1	4	1	4	2	-	+	-	+	+	-	-
28	1	3	4	2	4	2	3	1	-	+	-	-	-	+	+
29	1	4	1	3	1	1	4	1	+	-	+	-	-	+	-
30	1	2	2	4	1	2	3	2	+	-	+	+	+	-	+
31	1	4	2	4	2	3	2	3	-	+	-	+	-	+	-
32	1	2	1	3	2	4	1	4	-	+	-	-	+	-	+
	A	D	E	F	G	H	I	J	M	N	O	Q	X	Y	2

CONFOUNDING PATTERNS FOR
THE REFLECTED 32-RUN DESIGN WITH EIGHT FOUR-LEVEL FACTORS

Contrast Labels

A	B	C	D	E	F	G	H	I	J	K	L	M	N	O	P

Corresponding Main Effects and Two-Factor Interactions

A	-A'	A"	D	E	F	G	H	I	J	-G'	G"	M	N	O	-J'
DE	DF	DG	AE	AD	AG	AF	AI	AH	-AG'	AJ	AM	AG"	AO	AN	AQ
FG	EG	EF	-A'F	-A'G	-A'D	-A'E	-A'J	A'G	-A'H	-A'I	-A'N	-A'O	-A'G"	-A'M	A'E'
HI	HJ	-G'H	A"G	A"F	A"E	A"D	-A"G'	A"J	A"I	A"H	A"O	A"N	A"M	A"G"	-A"F'
-G'J	-G'I	IJ	G"H	HM	HN	HO	DG"	DM	DN	DO	DH	DI	DJ	-DG'	-DI'
G"M	G"N	G"O	IM	G"I	IO	IN	EM	EG"	EO	EN	EI	EH	-EG'	EJ	EF"
NO	MO	MN	JN	JO	G"J	JM	FN	FO	FG"	FM	FJ	-FG'	FH	FI	-FH'
-J'Q	E'J	F'J	-G'O	-G'N	-G'M	-E'J	GO	GN	GM	D'J	-J'2	GJ	GI	GH	E'G
E'F	-F'Q	-E'Q	I'J	-F'J	H'J	-H'Q	-J'X	-J'Y	-D'Q	J'Q	I'Q	-I'J	-H'J	-D"J	HX
-F'T	HT	-E'T	F"Q	-I'Q	E'Q	-E'F"	QY	QX	-EX	-E'Y	-E'H"	Q2	D"Q	H'Q	IY
-E'H'	E'F"	-F"H'	E'H'	F'H'	ET	FT	-EJ'	D'E'	-F'Y	-F'X	-D"F'	-D'E'	-E'2	-ET'	D'G'
XY	J'X	-D'X	-E"F'	I'X	H'X	D'X	D'F'	-F'J'	-H'T	-D'T	-I'X	-F'H'	-FI'	-F'2	G"2
-D'J'	-D'Y	J'Y	X2	Y2	D'Y	H'Y	-I'2	F"2	D"F'	F"H'	F'Y	-I'Y	-I'J'	DI'	I"M
I'2	H"2	D"2	I'Y	D'J"	J'2	I'J'	F"I'	-D"H'	-H'2	-HI'	-H'J'	F'X	-D'F'	F"J'	H'N
D"H"	D'T'	H'T'	H"J'	-D'H"	-DI'	-D'2	D"E'	E'H"	E'T'	E'2	-D'E"	D'H'	-H'X	-H'Y	D"O
												E"J'	E"Y	E"X	

Contrast Labels

Q	R	S	T	U	V	W	X	Y	Z	1	2	3	4	5

Corresponding Main Effects and Two-Factor Interactions

Q	-E'	-F'	-I'	F"	-H'	E"	X	Y	J"	-D'	2	I"	H"	D"
-AJ'	-AF'	-AE'	AF"	-AI'	AE"	-AH'	AY	AX	-AD'	AJ"	AI"	A2	AD"	AH"
A'F'	A'J'	-A'Q	A'H'	-A'E'	AT'	-A'F"	-A'J'	A'D'	-A'X	-A'Y	-A'H"	-A'D"	-A'2	-A'T"
-A"E'	A"Q	-A"J'	A"E'	-A"H'	A"F'	-A"T'	-A"D'	A"J"	A"Y	A"X	A"D"	A"H"	A"T'	A"2
DF"	-DH'	DE"	-DJ'	DQ	-DE'	-DF'	D2	DI"	DH"	EH'	DX	DY	DJ"	EJ"
-EI'	-FI'	-EH'	EQ	-EJ'	-EF'	FQ	EI"	E2	D"E	FI"	EY	EX	-D'E	FY
E"F	F"G	-GI'	-E'F	-E'G	-FJ'	-GJ'	FH"	D"F	F2	G2	FJ"	-D'F	FX	GX
-GH'	HJ'	-D'H	-F'G	HI"	GQ	D"H	D"G	GH"	GI"	-F'H	-D'G	GJ"	GY	E"H
HY	-DI'	IJ"	H2	I2	D'I	H'I	-HJ	HQ	-E'H	-EI	-HI'	F"H	E'I	-H'I
IX	JX	JY	H'J	D'J	J2	I'J	IQ	-IJ	-F'I	JQ	F'I	E'J	-I'J	F"J
-D'J	-G'Y	-G'X	-D'G'	-G'H"	-GT'	-G'2	-E'J	-F'J	-G'Q	G'J'	-H'J	G'H'	-F"G'	G'T'
-G'J'	G"H'	D"G'	G'X	G'Y	G"J'	-D'G'	FG'	E'G'	-G"H'	E'G"	G'Q	-E'G'	-E'G"	-F'G"
G'T'	D"M	H"M	MY	MX	D'M	J'M	-G'T	F"G'	E"M	-H'M	-G"J'	-J'M	-F'M	-E'M
M2	N2	I'N	J'N	-D'N	NX	NY	F"M	-I'M	-I'N	F'N	MQ	-F'N	-J'N	NQ
D'N	I'O	O2	-D'O	J'O	OY	OX	-H'N	E'N	F'O	-I'O	-E'N	-E'O	OQ	-J'O
H"O							E"O	-H'O			-F'O			

275

32-Run Designs With Eight Factors Having Three or Four Levels

The $4^8 \times 2^7$ designs on pages 272–275 can be modified into $3^8 \times 2^7$ designs by changing Factors A, D, E, F, G, H, I and J into three level factors. As before, the relationship between the levels for a four-level factor and the levels of the corresponding three-level factor are:

Four Level Factor		Three Level Factor
Level 1	stays	Level 1
Level 2	stays	Level 2
Level 3	stays	Level 3
Level 4	**becomes**	**Level 1 or Level 2 or Level 3**

Since the new three level factor will appear to have three degrees of freedom there will be some redundancy in the analysis. See page 195 for details.

If seven of the four-level factors are modified into three-level factors, then the designs on the previous four pages will be $4 \times 3^7 \times 2^7$ designs.

If six of the four-level factors are modified into three-level factors, then the designs on the previous four pages will be $4^2 \times 3^6 \times 2^7$ designs.

If five of the four-level factors are modified into three-level factors, then the designs on the previous four pages will be $4^3 \times 3^5 \times 2^7$ designs.

If four of the four-level factors are modified into three-level factors, then the designs on the previous four pages will be $4^4 \times 3^4 \times 2^7$ designs.

If three of the four-level factors are modified into three-level factors, then the designs on the previous four pages will be $4^5 \times 3^3 \times 2^7$ designs.

If two of the four-level factors are modified into three-level factors, then the designs on the previous four pages will be $4^6 \times 3^2 \times 2^7$ designs.

If only one of the four-level factors is modified into a three level factor, then the designs on the previous four pages will be $4^7 \times 3 \times 2^7$ designs.

The confounding pattern for these 32-run designs will remain the same as shown on the preceeding pages, regardless of the number of factors that are modified into three level factors.

Use response plots visualize the results, especially if a three-level or four-level factor is found to be significant.

32-Run Designs With Nine Factors
Having Three or Four Levels

The $4^9 \times 2^4$ designs on the following four pages (pp.278–281) can be modified into $3^9 \times 2^4$ designs by changing Factors A, D, E, F, G, H, I, J and M into three level factors. As before, the relationship between the levels for a four-level factor and the levels of the corresponding three-level factor are as shown on the preceeding page.

If eight of the four-level factors are modified into three level factors, then the designs on the following four pages will be $3^8 \times 2^4$ designs.

If seven of the four-level factors are modified into three level factors, then the designs on the following four pages will be $4 \times 3^7 \times 4^2 \times 2^4$ designs.

If six of the four-level factors are modified into three level factors, then the designs on the following four pages will be $4^3 \times 3^6 \times 2^4$ designs.

If five of the four-level factors are modified into three level factors, then the designs on the following four pages will be $4^4 \times 3^5 \times 2^4$ designs.

If four of the four-level factors are modified into three level factors, then the designs on the following four pages will be $4^5 \times 3^4 \times 2^4$ designs.

If three of the four-level factors are modified into three level factors, then the designs on the following four pages will be $4^6 \times 3^3 \times 2^4$ designs.

If two of the four-level factors are modified into three level factors, then the designs on the following four pages will be $4^7 \times 3^2 \times 2^4$ designs.

If only one of the four-level factors is modified into a three level factor, then the designs on the following four pages will be $4^8 \times 3 \times 2^4$ designs.

The confounding pattern for these 32-run designs will remain the same as shown on the following pages, regardless of the number of factors which are modified into three level factors.

Use response plots to visualize the results, especially if a three-level or four-level factor is found to be significant.

A BASIC 32-RUN DESIGN WITH NINE FOUR-LEVEL FACTORS

Nine factors at 4 levels and up to four factors at 2 levels each. Use contrast coefficients for the Basic 32-Run Plackett-Burman Design for the analysis of data collected under the following conditions.

Treatment Combinations

Run	A	D	E	F	G	H	I	J	M	N	O	X	Y
1	1	1	1	1	1	1	1	1	1	-	-	-	-
2	1	3	2	2	1	2	2	2	2	-	-	+	+
3	1	1	2	2	2	3	3	3	3	+	+	-	-
4	1	3	1	1	2	4	4	4	4	+	+	+	+
5	1	4	4	4	3	3	3	4	1	-	-	+	+
6	1	2	3	3	3	4	4	3	2	-	-	-	-
7	1	4	3	3	4	1	1	2	3	+	+	+	+
8	1	2	4	4	4	2	2	1	4	+	+	-	-
9	2	4	3	2	2	1	2	4	4	-	-	-	-
10	2	2	4	1	2	2	1	3	3	-	-	+	+
11	2	4	4	1	1	3	4	2	2	+	+	-	-
12	2	2	3	2	1	4	3	1	1	+	+	+	+
13	2	1	2	3	4	3	4	1	4	-	-	+	+
14	2	3	1	4	4	4	3	2	3	-	-	-	-
15	2	1	1	4	3	1	2	3	2	+	+	+	+
16	2	3	2	3	3	2	1	4	1	+	+	-	-
17	3	1	3	4	1	2	4	4	3	+	-	-	+
18	3	3	4	3	1	1	3	3	4	+	-	+	-
19	3	1	4	3	2	4	2	2	1	-	+	-	+
20	3	3	3	4	2	3	1	1	2	-	+	+	-
21	3	4	2	1	3	4	2	1	3	+	-	+	-
22	3	2	1	2	3	3	1	2	4	+	-	-	+
23	3	4	1	2	4	2	4	3	1	-	+	+	-
24	3	2	2	1	4	1	3	4	2	-	+	-	+
25	4	4	1	3	2	2	3	1	2	+	-	-	+
26	4	2	2	4	2	1	4	2	1	+	-	+	-
27	4	4	2	4	1	4	1	3	4	-	+	-	+
28	4	2	1	3	1	3	2	4	3	-	+	+	-
29	4	1	4	2	4	4	1	4	2	+	-	+	-
30	4	3	3	1	4	3	2	3	1	+	-	-	+
31	4	1	3	1	3	2	3	2	4	-	+	+	-
32	4	3	4	2	3	1	4	1	3	-	+	-	+
	A	D	E	F	G	H	I	J	M	N	O	X	Y

CONFOUNDING PATTERNS FOR
THE BASIC 32-RUN DESIGN WITH NINE FOUR-LEVEL FACTORS

Contrast Labels

A   B   C   D   E   F   G   H   I   J   K   L   M   N   O   P

Corresponding Main Effects and Two-Factor Interactions

A	A'	A"	D	E	F	G	H	I	J	G'	G"	M	N	O	J'
-DE	-DF	-DG	-AE	-AD	-AG	-AF	-AI	-AH	-AG'	-AJ	-AM	-AG"	-AO	-AN	-AM'
-FG	-EG	-EF	-A'F	-A'G	-A'D	-A'E	-A'J	-A'G'	-A'H	-A'I	-A'N	-A'O	-A'G"	-A'M	-A'E'
-HI	-HJ	-G'H	-A"G	-A"F	-A"E	-A"D	-A"G'	-A"J	-A"I	-A"H	-A"O	-A"N	-A"M	-A"G"	-A"F'
-G'J	-GI	-IJ	-G"H	-HM	-HN	-HO	-DG"	-DM	-DN	-DO	-DH	-DI	-DJ	-DG'	-DI'
-G"M	-G"N	-G"O	-IM	-G"I	-IO	-IN	-EM	-EG"	-EO	-EN	-EI	-EH	-EG'	-EJ	-EF"
-NO	-MO	-MN	-JN	-JO	-G"J	-JM	-FN	-FO	-FG"	-FM	-FJ	-FG'	-FH	-FI	-FH'
-J'M'	-E'J	-F'J	-G'O	-G'N	-G'M	-E'J	-GO	-GN	-GM	-D'J	-J'M"	-GJ	-GI	-GH	-E"G
-E'F	-F'M'	-E'M'	-IJ	-F'J	-H'J	-H'M'	-J'X	-J'Y	-D'M'	-J'M'	-I'M'	-I'J	-H'J	-D'J	-HX
-F"I	-HT	-E'T	-F"M'	-I'M'	-E'M'	-E'F'	-M'Y	-M'X	-E'X	-E'Y	-E'H"	-D'E'	-D"M'	-H'M'	-IY
-E"H'	-E'F'	-F"H'	-E'H'	-F'H'	-ET'	-FT'	-EJ"	-D'E	-F'Y	-F'X	-D"F	-F'H"	-E'M'	-ET'	-D'G'
-XY	-J'X	-D'X	-E"F'	-I'X	-H"X	-D'X	-D'F	-F'J"	-H'T	-D'T	-I'X	-I'Y	-FT'	-F"M'	-G"M'
-D'J'	-D'Y	-J'Y	-M"X	-M"Y	-D"Y	-H"Y	-I'M"	-F"M'	-D"F"	-F"H'	-F"Y	-F"X	-I'J'	-D'T'	-I'M'
-I'M"	-H"M'	-D"M'	-I'Y	-D'J'	-J"M'	-I'J'	-F"T	-D"H'	-H'M"	-HT'	-H'J'	-D'H'	-D'F'	-F"J'	-H'N
-D"H'	-D'T'	-HT'	-H'J'	-D'H'	-DT'	-D'M'	-D"E'	-E'H"	-ET'	-E'M'	-D'E'	-E'J'	-H'X	-H'Y	-D'O
													-E"Y	-E'X	

Contrast Labels

Q   R   S   T   U   V   W   X   Y   Z   1   2   3   4   5

Corresponding Main Effects and Two-Factor Interactions

M'	E'	F'	I'	F"	H'	E"	X	Y	J"	D'	M"	I"	H"	D"
-AJ'	-AF'	-AE'	-AF"	-AI'	-AE"	-AH'	-AY	-AX	-AD'	-AJ"	-AI"	-AM"	-AD"	-AH"
-A'F'	-A'J'	-A'M'	-A'H'	-A'E'	-AT'	-A'F"	-A'J"	-A'D'	-A'X	-A'Y	-A'H"	-A'D"	-A'M"	-AT"
-A"E'	-A"M'	-A"J'	-A"E"	-A"H'	-A"F"	-A"T	-A"D'	-A"J"	-A"Y	-A"X	-A"D"	-A"H"	-A"T"	-A"M"
-DF"	-DH'	-DE"	-DJ'	-DM'	-DE'	-DF'	-DM"	-DI'	-DH"	-EH"	-DX	-DY	-DJ"	-EJ"
-EI'	-FI'	-EH'	-EM'	-EJ'	-EF'	-FM'	-EI"	-EM"	-D"E	-FI"	-EY	-EX	-D'E	-FY
-E"F	-F"G	-GI'	-E'F	-E'G	-FJ'	-GJ'	-FH"	-D"F	-FM"	-GM'	-FJ'	-D'F	-FX	-GX
-GH'	-HJ'	-D'H	-F'G	-HI'	-GM'	-D"H	-D'G	-GH'	-GI"	-F'H	-D'G	-GJ"	-GY	-E"H
-HY	-DT	-IJ"	-HM"	-IM'	-DT	-H'T	-HJ'	-HM'	-E'H	-ET	-HT'	-F"H	-E'T	-HT
-IX	-JX	-JY	-H'J	-D'J	-JM"	-I'J	-IM'	-IJ'	-FT	-JM'	-F'T	-E'J	-TJ	-F"J
-D'J	-G'Y	-G'X	-D"G'	-G'H"	-GT	-G'M"	-E'J	-FJ	-G'M'	-G'J'	-H'J	-G'H'	-F"G'	-GT'
-G'J"	-G'H"	-D"G'	-G'X	-G'Y	-G"J"	-D'G"	-F'G'	-E'G'	-G"H'	-E'G"	-E'G'	-G"M'	-E'G"	-F'G'
-G"T	-D"M	-H"M	-MY	-MX	-D"M	-J"M	-G"T	-F"G"	-E'M	-H'M	-G"J'	-J'M	-F'M	-E'M
-D"N	-M"N	-I'N	-J"N	-D'N	-NX	-NY	-F"M	-I'M	-IN	-F"N	-E'N	-F'N	-J'N	-M'N
-H"O	-I'O	-M"O	-D'O	-J'O	-OY	-OX	-H'N	-E'N	-F'O	-I'O	-F'O	-E'O	-M'O	-J'O
							-E"O	-H'O						

A Reflected 32-Run Design With Nine Four-Level Factors

Nine factors at 4 levels and four factors at 2 levels each. Use contrast coefficients for the Reflected 32-Run Plackett-Burman Design for the analysis of data collected under the following plan.

Treatment Combinations

Run	A	D	E	F	G	H	I	J	M	N	O	X	Y
1	4	4	4	4	4	4	4	4	4	+	+	+	+
2	4	2	3	3	4	3	3	3	3	+	+	-	-
3	4	4	3	3	3	2	2	2	2	-	-	+	+
4	4	2	4	4	3	1	1	1	1	-	-	-	-
5	4	1	1	1	2	2	2	1	4	+	+	-	-
6	4	3	2	2	2	1	1	2	3	+	+	+	+
7	4	1	2	2	1	4	4	3	2	-	-	-	-
8	4	3	1	1	1	3	3	4	1	-	-	+	+
9	3	1	2	3	3	4	3	1	1	+	+	+	+
10	3	3	1	4	3	3	4	2	2	+	+	-	-
11	3	1	1	4	4	2	1	3	3	-	-	+	+
12	3	3	2	3	4	1	2	4	4	-	-	-	-
13	3	4	3	2	1	2	1	4	1	+	+	-	-
14	3	2	4	1	1	1	2	3	2	+	+	+	+
15	3	4	4	1	2	4	3	2	3	-	-	-	-
16	3	2	3	2	2	3	4	1	4	-	-	+	+
17	2	4	2	1	4	3	1	1	2	-	+	+	-
18	2	2	1	2	4	4	2	2	1	-	+	-	+
19	2	4	1	2	3	1	3	3	4	+	-	+	-
20	2	2	2	1	3	2	4	4	3	+	-	-	+
21	2	1	3	4	2	1	3	4	2	-	+	-	+
22	2	3	4	3	2	2	4	3	1	-	+	+	-
23	2	1	4	3	1	3	1	2	4	+	-	-	+
24	2	3	3	4	1	4	2	1	3	+	-	+	-
25	1	1	4	2	3	3	2	4	3	-	+	+	-
26	1	3	3	1	3	4	1	3	4	-	+	-	+
27	1	1	3	1	4	1	4	2	1	+	-	+	-
28	1	3	4	2	4	2	3	1	2	+	-	-	+
29	1	4	1	3	1	1	4	1	3	-	+	-	+
30	1	2	2	4	1	2	3	2	4	-	+	+	-
31	1	4	2	4	2	3	2	3	1	+	-	-	+
32	1	2	1	3	2	4	1	4	2	+	-	+	-
	A	D	E	F	G	H	I	J	M	N	O	X	Y

CONFOUNDING PATTERNS FOR
THE REFLECTED 32-RUN DESIGN WITH NINE FOUR-LEVEL FACTORS

Contrast Labels

A	B	C	D	E	F	G	H	I	J	K	L	M	N	O	P

Corresponding Main Effects and Two-Factor Interactions

A	-A'	A"	D	E	F	G	H	I	J	-G'	G"	M	N	O	-J'
DE	DF	DG	AE	AD	AG	AF	AI	AH	-AG'	AJ	AM	AG"	AO	AN	-AM'
FG	EG	EF	-A'F	-A'G	-A'D	-A'E	-A'J	A'G'	-A'H	-A'I	-A'N	-A'O	-A'G"	-A'M	A'E'
HI	HJ	-G'H	A"G	A"F	A"E	A"D	-A"G'	A"J	A"I	A"H	A"O	A"N	A"M	A"G"	-A"F'
-G'J	-G'I	IJ	G"H	HM	HN	HO	DG"	DM	DN	DO	DH	DI	DJ	-DG'	-DI'
G"M	G"N	G'O	IM	G'I	IO	IN	EM	EG"	EO	EN	EI	EH	-EG'	EJ	EF"
NO	MO	MN	JN	JO	G"J	JM	FN	FO	FG"	FM	FJ	-FG'	FH	FI	-FH'
J'M'	E'J	F'J	-G'O	-G'N	-G'M	-E"J	GO	GN	GM	D'J	-J'M"	GJ	GI	GH	E"G
E'F'	F'M'	E'M'	I'J	-F'J	H'J	H'M'	-J'X	-J'Y	D'M'	-J'M'	-I'M'	-I'J	-H'J	-D'J	HX
-F'I'	HT	-E'T	-F"M'	I'M'	-E'M'	-E'F'	-M'Y	-M'X	-E'X	-E'Y	-E'H"	-D"E	-D'M'	-H'M'	IY
-E"H'	E'F'	-F"H'	E'H'	F'H'	ET	FT	-EJ'	D'E'	-F'Y	-F'X	-D'F	-F'H"	-E'M'	-ET'	D'G'
XY	J'X	-D'X	-E"F'	I'X	H'X	D'X	D'F'	-FJ'	-H'T	-D'T	-IX	-TY	-FT'	-F'M'	G"M"
-D'J'	-D'Y	J'Y	M'X	M'Y	D"Y	H'Y	I'M'	-F'M'	D"F'	F"H'	F'Y	F'X	-I'J	D'T	I'M
-I'M'	-H"M'	-D"M'	I'Y	D"J'	J'M'	I'J'	F'I'	-D"H'	-H'M'	-HT	-H'J'	D'H'	-D'F'	F"J'	H'N
D"H'	D'T'	H'T'	H'J'	-D'H"	-DT'	-D'M'	D"E'	E'H"	ET'	-E"M'	-D'E'	E'J'	-H'X	-H'Y	D'O
													E'Y	E'X	

Contrast Labels

Q	R	S	T	U	V	W	X	Y	Z	1	2	3	4	5

Corresponding Main Effects and Two-Factor Interactions

-M'	-E'	-F'	-I'	F"	-H'	E"	X	Y	J"	-D'	M"	I"	H"	D"
-AJ	-AF	-AE	AF"	-AI	AE"	-AH	AY	AX	-AD'	AJ"	AI"	AM"	AD"	AH"
A'F	A'J	A'M	A'H'	-A'E"	AT	-A'F'	-A'J"	A'D	-A'X	-A'Y	-A'H"	-A'D"	-A'M"	-AT'
-A"E'	-A"M'	-A"J	A"E'	-A"H'	A"F"	-A"T	-A"D	A"J'	A"Y	A"X	A"D'	A"H"	A"T'	A"M"
DF"	-DH'	DE"	-DJ'	-DM'	-DE'	-DF'	DM"	DI"	DH"	EH"	DX	DY	DJ'	EJ"
-EI'	-FI'	-EH'	-EM'	-EJ'	-EF'	-FM'	EI"	EM"	D'E	FI"	EY	EX	-D'E	FY
E"F	F"G	-GI'	-E'F	-E'G	-FJ'	-GJ'	FH"	D"F	FM"	GM"	FJ"	-D'F	FX	GX
-GH'	HJ'	-D'H	-F'G	HI"	-GM'	D"H	D'G	GH"	GI"	-F'H	-D'G	GJ"	GY	E"H
HY	-D'I	IJ"	HM"	IM"	D'I	H'I	-HJ	-HM'	-E'H	-E'I	-H'I	F"H	E'I	-HI
IX	JX	JY	H'J	D'J	JM"	I'J	-IM'	-IJ	-FI	-JM'	F"I	E"J	-I'J	F"J
-D'J	-G'Y	-G'X	-D"G'	-G'H"	-GT'	-G'M"	-E'J	-F'J	G'M'	G'J'	-H'J	G'H'	-F"G'	G'T
-G'J"	G"H'	D"G"	G'X	G'Y	G"J'	-D'G"	F'G'	E'G'	-G"H'	E"G'	-E"G'	-G"M'	-E'G"	-F'G"
G'T'	D'M'	H"M	MY	MX	D'M	J'M	-G'T	F"G'	E'M	-H'M	-G'J	-J'M	-F'M	-E'M
D"N	M"N	I'N	J'N	-D'N	NX	NY	F'M	-I'M	-I'N	F"N	-E'N	-F'N	-J'N	-M'N
H"O	I'O	M"O	-D'O	J'O	OY	OX	-H'N	E'N	F'O	-I'O	-F'O	-E'O	-M'O	-J'O
					E"O	-H'O	E"O							

Appendices

Percentiles for the F-Distribution

90th Percentiles
$\alpha = 0.10$

Tabled values are the 90th percentiles of the F-distribution. If the F-ratio follows an F-distribution, then the calculated value of the F-ratio will be less than the tabled value approximately 90 percent of the time, and it will exceed the tabled value approximately 10 percent of the time.

v_1 = Degrees of Freedom for the Numerator of the F-ratio

v_2	1	2	3	4	5	6	7	8	9	10	12	15	20	24	30	40	60	120	inf.
1	39.9	49.5	53.6	55.8	57.2	58.2	58.9	59.4	59.9	60.2	60.7	61.2	61.7	62.0	62.3	62.5	62.8	63.1	63.3
2	8.53	9.00	9.16	9.24	9.29	9.33	9.35	9.37	9.38	9.39	9.41	9.42	9.44	9.45	9.46	9.47	9.47	9.48	9.49
3	5.54	5.46	5.39	5.34	5.31	5.28	5.27	5.25	5.24	5.23	5.22	5.20	5.18	5.18	5.17	5.16	5.15	5.14	5.13
4	4.54	4.32	4.19	4.11	4.05	4.01	3.98	3.95	3.94	3.92	3.90	3.87	3.84	3.83	3.82	3.80	3.79	3.78	3.76
5	4.06	3.78	3.62	3.52	3.45	3.40	3.37	3.34	3.32	3.30	3.27	3.24	3.21	3.19	3.17	3.16	3.14	3.12	3.10
6	3.78	3.46	3.29	3.18	3.11	3.05	3.01	2.98	2.96	2.94	2.90	2.87	2.84	2.82	2.80	2.78	2.76	2.74	2.72
7	3.59	3.26	3.07	2.96	2.88	2.83	2.78	2.75	2.72	2.70	2.67	2.63	2.59	2.58	2.56	2.54	2.51	2.49	2.47
8	3.46	3.11	2.92	2.81	2.73	2.67	2.62	2.59	2.56	2.54	2.50	2.46	2.42	2.40	2.38	2.36	2.34	2.32	2.29
9	3.36	3.01	2.81	2.69	2.61	2.55	2.51	2.47	2.44	2.42	2.38	2.34	2.30	2.28	2.25	2.23	2.21	2.18	2.16
10	3.28	2.92	2.73	2.61	2.52	2.46	2.41	2.38	2.35	2.32	2.28	2.24	2.20	2.18	2.16	2.13	2.11	2.08	2.06
11	3.23	2.86	2.66	2.54	2.45	2.39	2.34	2.30	2.27	2.25	2.21	2.17	2.12	2.10	2.08	2.05	2.03	2.00	1.97
12	3.18	2.81	2.61	2.48	2.39	2.33	2.28	2.24	2.21	2.19	2.15	2.10	2.06	2.04	2.01	1.99	1.96	1.93	1.90
13	3.14	2.76	2.56	2.43	2.35	2.28	2.23	2.20	2.16	2.14	2.10	2.05	2.01	1.98	1.96	1.93	1.90	1.88	1.85
14	3.10	2.73	2.52	2.39	2.31	2.24	2.19	2.15	2.12	2.10	2.05	2.01	1.96	1.94	1.91	1.89	1.86	1.83	1.80
15	3.07	2.70	2.49	2.36	2.27	2.21	2.16	2.12	2.09	2.06	2.02	1.97	1.92	1.90	1.87	1.85	1.82	1.79	1.76
16	3.05	2.67	2.46	2.33	2.24	2.18	2.13	2.09	2.06	2.03	1.99	1.94	1.89	1.87	1.84	1.81	1.78	1.75	1.72
18	3.01	2.62	2.42	2.29	2.20	2.13	2.08	2.04	2.00	1.98	1.93	1.89	1.84	1.81	1.78	1.75	1.72	1.69	1.66
20	2.97	2.59	2.38	2.25	2.16	2.09	2.04	2.00	1.96	1.94	1.89	1.84	1.79	1.77	1.74	1.71	1.68	1.64	1.61
22	2.95	2.56	2.35	2.22	2.13	2.06	2.01	1.97	1.93	1.90	1.86	1.81	1.76	1.73	1.70	1.67	1.64	1.60	1.57
24	2.93	2.54	2.33	2.19	2.10	2.04	1.98	1.94	1.91	1.88	1.83	1.78	1.73	1.70	1.67	1.64	1.61	1.57	1.53
26	2.91	2.52	2.31	2.17	2.08	2.01	1.96	1.92	1.88	1.86	1.81	1.76	1.71	1.68	1.65	1.61	1.58	1.54	1.50
28	2.89	2.50	2.29	2.16	2.06	2.00	1.94	1.90	1.87	1.84	1.79	1.74	1.69	1.66	1.63	1.59	1.56	1.52	1.48
30	2.88	2.49	2.28	2.14	2.05	1.98	1.93	1.88	1.85	1.82	1.77	1.72	1.67	1.64	1.61	1.57	1.54	1.50	1.46
40	2.84	2.44	2.23	2.09	2.00	1.93	1.87	1.83	1.79	1.76	1.71	1.66	1.61	1.57	1.54	1.51	1.47	1.42	1.38
60	2.79	2.39	2.18	2.04	1.95	1.87	1.82	1.77	1.74	1.71	1.66	1.60	1.54	1.51	1.48	1.44	1.40	1.35	1.29
120	2.75	2.35	2.13	1.99	1.90	1.82	1.77	1.72	1.68	1.65	1.60	1.55	1.48	1.45	1.41	1.37	1.32	1.26	1.19
inf.	2.71	2.30	2.08	1.94	1.85	1.77	1.72	1.67	1.63	1.60	1.55	1.49	1.42	1.38	1.34	1.30	1.24	1.17	1.00

v_2 = Degrees of Freedom for the denominator of the F-ratio.

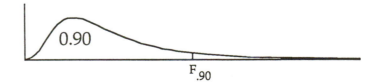

0.90

$F_{.90}$

Percentiles for the F-Distribution

95th Percentiles
$\alpha = 0.05$

Tabled values are the 95th percentiles of the F-distribution.   If the F-ratio follows an F-distribution, then the calculated value of the F-ratio will be less than the tabled value approximately 95 percent of the time, and it will exceed the tabled value approximately 5 percent of the time.

v_1 = Degrees of Freedom for the Numerator of the F-ratio

v_2	1	2	3	4	5	6	7	8	9	10	12	15	20	24	30	40	60	120	inf.
1	161.4	199.5	215.7	224.6	230.2	234.0	236.8	238.9	240.5	241.9	243.9	245.9	248.0	249.1	250.1	251.1	252.2	253.3	254.3
2	18.51	19.00	19.16	19.25	19.30	19.33	19.35	19.37	19.38	19.40	19.41	19.43	19.45	19.45	19.46	19.47	19.48	19.49	19.50
3	10.13	9.55	9.28	9.12	9.01	8.94	8.89	8.85	8.81	8.79	8.74	8.70	8.66	8.64	8.62	8.59	8.57	8.55	8.53
4	7.71	6.94	6.59	6.39	6.26	6.16	6.09	6.04	6.00	5.96	5.91	5.86	5.80	5.77	5.75	5.72	5.69	5.66	5.63
5	6.61	5.79	5.41	5.19	5.05	4.95	4.88	4.82	4.77	4.74	4.68	4.62	4.56	4.53	4.50	4.46	4.43	4.40	4.36
6	5.99	5.14	4.76	4.53	4.39	4.28	4.21	4.15	4.10	4.06	4.00	3.94	3.87	3.84	3.81	3.77	3.74	3.70	3.67
7	5.59	4.74	4.35	4.12	3.97	3.87	3.79	3.73	3.68	3.64	3.57	3.51	3.44	3.41	3.38	3.34	3.30	3.27	3.23
8	5.32	4.46	4.07	3.84	3.69	3.58	3.50	3.44	3.39	3.35	3.28	3.22	3.15	3.12	3.08	3.04	3.01	2.97	2.93
9	5.12	4.26	3.86	3.63	3.48	3.37	3.29	3.23	3.18	3.14	3.07	3.01	2.94	2.90	2.86	2.83	2.79	2.75	2.71
10	4.96	4.10	3.71	3.48	3.33	3.22	3.14	3.07	3.02	2.98	2.91	2.85	2.77	2.74	2.70	2.66	2.62	2.58	2.54
11	4.84	3.98	3.59	3.36	3.20	3.09	3.01	2.95	2.90	2.85	2.79	2.72	2.65	2.61	2.57	2.53	2.49	2.45	2.40
12	4.75	3.89	3.49	3.26	3.11	3.00	2.91	2.85	2.80	2.75	2.69	2.62	2.54	2.51	2.47	2.43	2.38	2.34	2.30
13	4.67	3.81	3.41	3.18	3.03	2.92	2.83	2.77	2.71	2.67	2.60	2.53	2.46	2.42	2.38	2.34	2.30	2.25	2.21
14	4.60	3.74	3.34	3.11	2.96	2.85	2.76	2.70	2.65	2.60	2.53	2.46	2.39	2.35	2.31	2.27	2.22	2.18	2.13
15	4.54	3.68	3.29	3.06	2.90	2.79	2.71	2.64	2.59	2.54	2.48	2.40	2.33	2.29	2.25	2.20	2.16	2.11	2.07
16	4.49	3.63	3.24	3.01	2.85	2.74	2.66	2.59	2.54	2.49	2.42	2.35	2.28	2.24	2.19	2.15	2.11	2.06	2.01
18	4.41	3.55	3.16	2.93	2.77	2.66	2.58	2.51	2.46	2.41	2.34	2.27	2.19	2.15	2.11	2.06	2.02	1.97	1.92
20	4.35	3.49	3.10	2.87	2.71	2.60	2.51	2.45	2.39	2.35	2.28	2.20	2.12	2.08	2.04	1.99	1.95	1.90	1.84
22	4.30	3.44	3.05	2.82	2.66	2.55	2.46	2.40	2.34	2.30	2.23	2.15	2.07	2.03	1.98	1.94	1.89	1.84	1.78
24	4.26	3.40	3.01	2.78	2.62	2.51	2.42	2.36	2.30	2.25	2.18	2.11	2.03	1.98	1.94	1.89	1.84	1.79	1.73
26	4.23	3.37	2.98	2.74	2.59	2.47	2.39	2.32	2.27	2.22	2.15	2.07	1.99	1.95	1.90	1.85	1.80	1.75	1.69
28	4.20	3.34	2.95	2.71	2.56	2.45	2.36	2.29	2.24	2.19	2.12	2.04	1.96	1.91	1.87	1.82	1.77	1.71	1.65
30	4.17	3.32	2.92	2.69	2.53	2.42	2.33	2.27	2.21	2.16	2.09	2.01	1.93	1.89	1.84	1.79	1.74	1.68	1.62
40	4.08	3.23	2.84	2.61	2.45	2.34	2.25	2.18	2.12	2.08	2.00	1.92	1.84	1.79	1.74	1.69	1.64	1.58	1.51
60	4.00	3.15	2.76	2.53	2.37	2.25	2.17	2.10	2.04	1.99	1.92	1.84	1.75	1.70	1.65	1.59	1.53	1.47	1.39
120	3.92	3.07	2.68	2.45	2.29	2.17	2.09	2.02	1.96	1.91	1.83	1.75	1.66	1.61	1.55	1.50	1.43	1.35	1.25
inf.	3.84	3.00	2.60	2.37	2.21	2.10	2.01	1.94	1.88	1.83	1.75	1.67	1.57	1.52	1.46	1.39	1.32	1.22	1.00

v_2 = Degrees of Freedom for the denominator of the F-ratio.

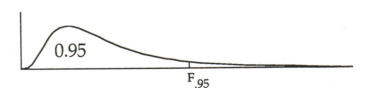

Percentiles for the F-Distribution

99th Percentiles
$\alpha = 0.01$

Tabled values are the 99th percentiles of the F-distribution.   If the F-ratio follows an F-distribution, then the calculated value of the F-ratio will be less than the tabled value approximately 99 percent of the time, and it will exceed the tabled value approximately 1 percent of the time.

v_1 = Degrees of Freedom for the Numerator of the F-ratio

v_2	1	2	3	4	5	6	7	8	9	10	12	15	20	24	30	40	60	120	inf.
1	4052.	5000.	5403.	5625.	5764.	5859.	5928.	5981.	6022.	6056.	6106.	6157.	6209.	6235.	6261.	6287.	6313.	6339.	6366.
2	98.5	99.0	99.2	99.3	99.3	99.3	99.4	99.4	99.4	99.4	99.4	99.4	99.4	99.5	99.5	99.5	99.5	99.5	99.5
3	34.1	30.8	29.5	28.7	28.2	27.9	27.7	27.5	27.4	27.2	27.1	26.9	26.7	26.6	26.5	26.4	26.3	26.2	26.1
4	21.2	18.0	16.7	16.0	15.5	15.2	15.0	14.8	14.7	14.6	14.4	14.2	14.0	13.9	13.8	13.8	13.7	13.6	13.5
5	16.3	13.3	12.1	11.4	11.0	10.7	10.5	10.3	10.2	10.1	9.89	9.72	9.55	9.47	9.38	9.29	9.20	9.11	9.02
6	13.8	10.9	9.78	9.15	8.75	8.47	8.26	8.10	7.98	7.87	7.72	7.56	7.40	7.31	7.23	7.14	7.06	6.97	6.88
7	12.3	9.55	8.45	7.85	7.46	7.19	6.99	6.84	6.72	6.62	6.47	6.31	6.16	6.07	5.99	5.91	5.82	5.74	5.65
8	11.3	8.65	7.59	7.01	6.63	6.37	6.18	6.03	5.91	5.81	5.67	5.52	5.36	5.28	5.20	5.12	5.03	4.95	4.86
9	10.6	8.02	6.99	6.42	6.06	5.80	5.61	5.47	5.35	5.26	5.11	4.96	4.81	4.73	4.65	4.57	4.48	4.40	4.31
10	10.0	7.56	6.55	5.99	5.64	5.39	5.20	5.06	4.94	4.85	4.71	4.56	4.41	4.33	4.25	4.17	4.08	4.00	3.91
11	9.65	7.21	6.22	5.67	5.32	5.07	4.89	4.74	4.63	4.54	4.40	4.25	4.10	4.02	3.94	3.86	3.78	3.69	3.60
12	9.33	6.93	5.95	5.41	5.06	4.82	4.64	4.50	4.39	4.30	4.16	4.01	3.86	3.78	3.70	3.62	3.54	3.45	3.36
13	9.07	6.70	5.74	5.21	4.86	4.62	4.44	4.30	4.19	4.10	3.96	3.82	3.66	3.59	3.51	3.43	3.34	3.25	3.17
14	8.86	6.51	5.56	5.04	4.69	4.46	4.28	4.14	4.03	3.94	3.80	3.66	3.51	3.43	3.35	3.27	3.18	3.09	3.00
15	8.68	6.36	5.42	4.89	4.56	4.32	4.14	4.00	3.89	3.80	3.67	3.52	3.37	3.29	3.21	3.13	3.05	2.96	2.87
16	8.53	6.23	5.29	4.77	4.44	4.20	4.03	3.89	3.78	3.69	3.55	3.41	3.26	3.18	3.10	3.02	2.93	2.84	2.75
18	8.29	6.01	5.09	4.58	4.25	4.01	3.84	3.71	3.60	3.51	3.37	3.23	3.08	3.00	2.92	2.84	2.75	2.66	2.57
20	8.10	5.85	4.94	4.43	4.10	3.87	3.70	3.56	3.46	3.37	3.23	3.09	2.94	2.86	2.78	2.69	2.61	2.52	2.42
22	7.95	5.72	4.82	4.31	3.99	3.76	3.59	3.45	3.35	3.26	3.12	2.98	2.83	2.75	2.67	2.58	2.50	2.40	2.31
24	7.82	5.61	4.72	4.22	3.90	3.67	3.50	3.36	3.26	3.17	3.03	2.89	2.74	2.66	2.58	2.49	2.40	2.31	2.21
26	7.72	5.53	4.64	4.14	3.82	3.59	3.42	3.29	3.18	3.09	2.96	2.81	2.66	2.58	2.50	2.42	2.33	2.23	2.13
28	7.64	5.45	4.57	4.07	3.75	3.53	3.36	3.23	3.12	3.03	2.90	2.75	2.60	2.52	2.44	2.35	2.26	2.17	2.06
30	7.56	5.39	4.51	4.02	3.70	3.47	3.30	3.17	3.07	2.98	2.84	2.70	2.55	2.47	2.39	2.30	2.21	2.11	2.01
40	7.31	5.18	4.31	3.83	3.51	3.29	3.12	2.99	2.89	2.80	2.66	2.52	2.37	2.29	2.20	2.11	2.02	1.92	1.80
60	7.08	4.98	4.13	3.65	3.34	3.12	2.95	2.82	2.72	2.63	2.50	2.35	2.20	2.12	2.03	1.94	1.84	1.73	1.60
120	6.85	4.79	3.95	3.48	3.17	2.96	2.79	2.66	2.56	2.47	2.34	2.19	2.03	1.95	1.86	1.76	1.66	1.53	1.38
inf.	6.63	4.61	3.78	3.32	3.02	2.80	2.64	2.51	2.41	2.32	2.18	2.04	1.88	1.79	1.70	1.59	1.47	1.32	1.00

v_2 = Degrees of Freedom for the denominator of the F-ratio.

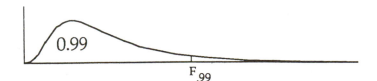

Approximate Percentiles of the Max-F Distribution

Given k-1 independent estimates of V(X), such as k-1 contrast sums of squares for an orthogonal array, the Maximum F Ratio is the ratio of (the largest estimate) to (the average of the p smallest estimates). This ratio will exceed the corresponding tabled values approximately α percent of the time when all contrasts are unbiased estimates of V(X).

p	1-α	k-1 = 7	k-1 = 11	k-1 = 15	k-1 = 19	k-1 = 23	k-1 = 27	k-1 = 31
2	.50	49 ± 3	155 ± 10	321 ± 20	745 ± 48	915 ± 66	1305 ± 71	1916 ± 120
	.75	139 ± 11	472 ± 33	966 ± 70	2300 ± 175	2753 ± 185	3943 ± 296	6130 ± 500
	.90	398 ± 46	1440 ± 150	3308 ± 425	7200 ± 750	8600 ± 800	13630 ± 1600	19400 ± 2100
	.95	847 ± 127	3310 ± 490	7700 ± 1300	15500 ± 2000	18000 ± 2200	30600 ± 6000	43600 ± 8000
3	.50	23 ± 1	75 ± 4	157 ± 7	360 ± 17	423 ± 18	628 ± 30	920 ± 50
	.75	49 ± 3	171 ± 8	377 ± 21	863 ± 44	1012 ± 61	1485 ± 75	2260 ± 140
	.90	111 ± 8	414 ± 36	892 ± 68	2121 ± 152	2391 ± 205	3553 ± 297	5550 ± 470
	.95	193 ± 16	794 ± 76	1623 ± 215	3686 ± 496	4688 ± 510	6083 ± 666	10530 ± 1660
4	.50	13 ± 1	43 ± 2	91 ± 3	201 ± 7	244 ± 10	365 ± 14	527 ± 20
	.75	24 ± 1	88 ± 4	191 ± 10	431 ± 22	519 ± 27	771 ± 39	1131 ± 45
	.90	46 ± 3	182 ± 12	395 ± 29	930 ± 50	1156 ± 80	1588 ± 117	2432 ± 172
	.95	69 ± 4	296 ± 34	609 ± 51	1491 ± 127	1844 ± 180	2673 ± 227	4020 ± 360
5	.50		27 ± 1	59 ± 2	126 ± 4	169 ± 6	245 ± 9	351 ± 12
	.75		52 ± 2	113 ± 4	248 ± 10	329 ± 15	488 ± 20	696 ± 26
	.90		100 ± 6	219 ± 15	482 ± 31	618 ± 32	980 ± 70	1315 ± 78
	.95		146 ± 9	331 ± 24	746 ± 66	923 ± 52	1550 ± 130	1990 ± 167
6	.50		18 ± 1	40 ± 2	94 ± 3	119 ± 4	172 ± 6	252 ± 9
	.75		32 ± 1	71 ± 3	174 ± 7	217 ± 9	316 ± 10	470 ± 21
	.90		55 ± 2	128 ± 7	314 ± 18	384 ± 24	565 ± 28	870 ± 60
	.95		79 ± 6	189 ± 12	468 ± 45	556 ± 44	848 ± 50	1288 ± 80
7	.50			30 ± 1	66 ± 2	87 ± 2	128 ± 4	186 ± 6
	.75			51 ± 2	118 ± 4	151 ± 5	224 ± 8	324 ± 11
	.90			86 ± 4	202 ± 11	262 ± 11	390 ± 20	571 ± 30
	.95			120 ± 6	283 ± 25	369 ± 22	564 ± 37	811 ± 59
8	.50			23 ± 1	51 ± 2	65 ± 2	96 ± 3	144 ± 4
	.75			38 ± 1	87 ± 3	110 ± 4	162 ± 5	243 ± 9
	.90			60 ± 2	143 ± 7	184 ± 8	268 ± 12	414 ± 21
	.95			83 ± 5	198 ± 10	258 ± 15	378 ± 24	590 ± 60
9	.50				41 ± 1	53 ± 1	77 ± 1	114 ± 3
	.75				68 ± 2	85 ± 3	127 ± 3	187 ± 5
	.90				109 ± 5	135 ± 6	203 ± 6	308 ± 14
	.95				151 ± 9	184 ± 11	269 ± 11	416 ± 21
10	.50				33 ± 1	42 ± 1	62 ± 2	91 ± 3
	.75				52 ± 2	67 ± 2	101 ± 4	148 ± 5
	.90				80 ± 4	105 ± 4	159 ± 7	235 ± 9
	.95				109 ± 5	139 ± 6	211 ± 10	322 ± 19

.50   .25   .15

Max-F$_{.50}$ Max-F$_{.75}$ Max-F$_{.90}$ Max-F$_{.95}$

Scree Plot and Normal Probability Plot For 8-Run Design

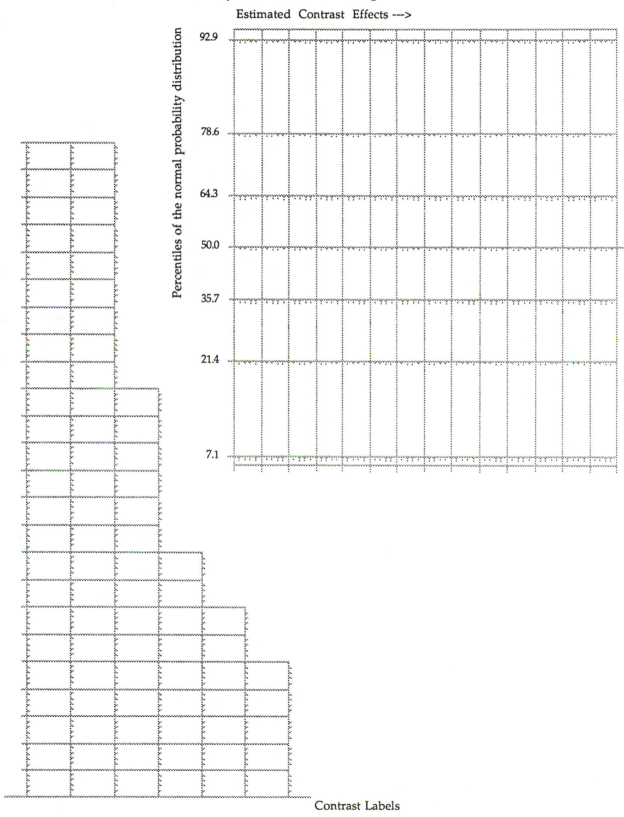

Scree Plot and Normal Probability Plot For 12-Run Design

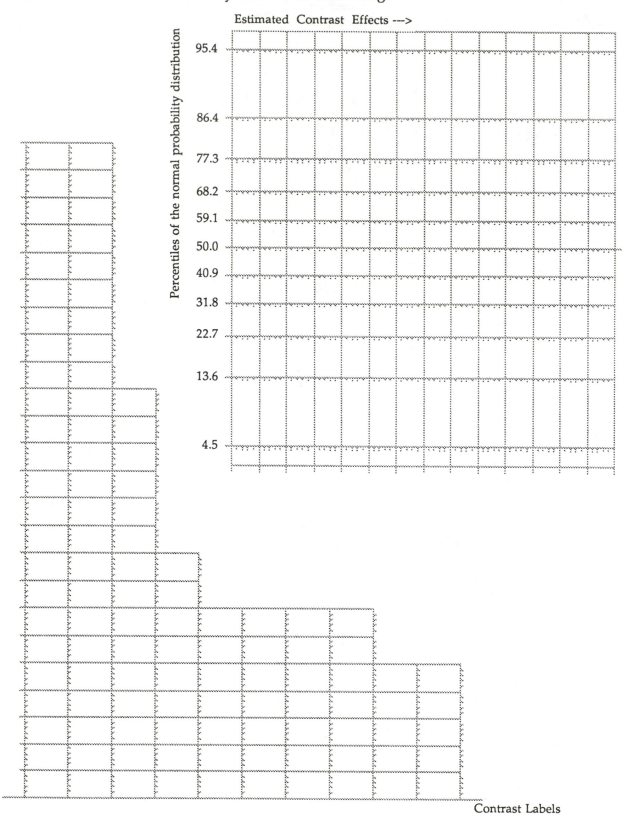

Scree Plot and Normal Probability Plot For 16-Run Design

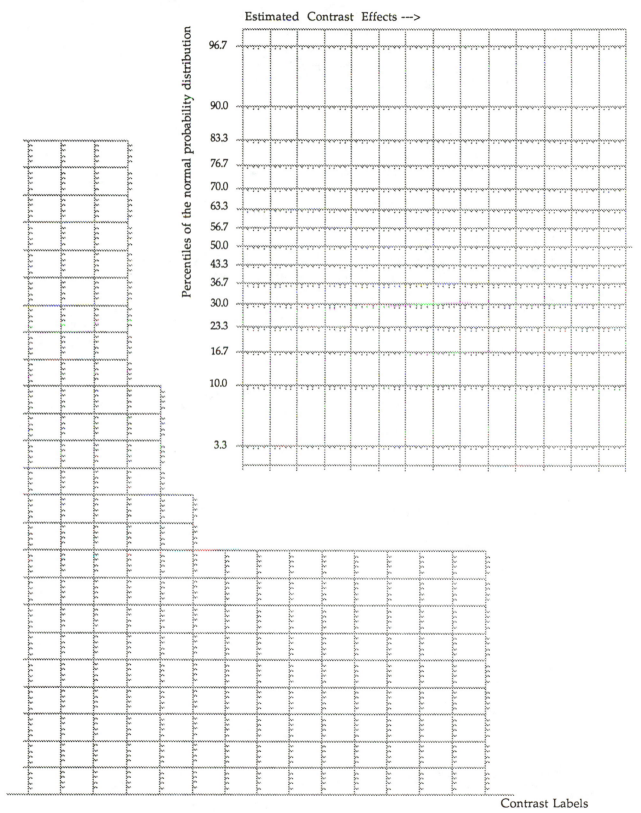

Estimated Contrast Effects --->

Percentiles of the normal probability distribution

Sums of Squares for Contrasts

Contrast Labels

Scree Plot and Normal Probability Plot For 20-Run Design

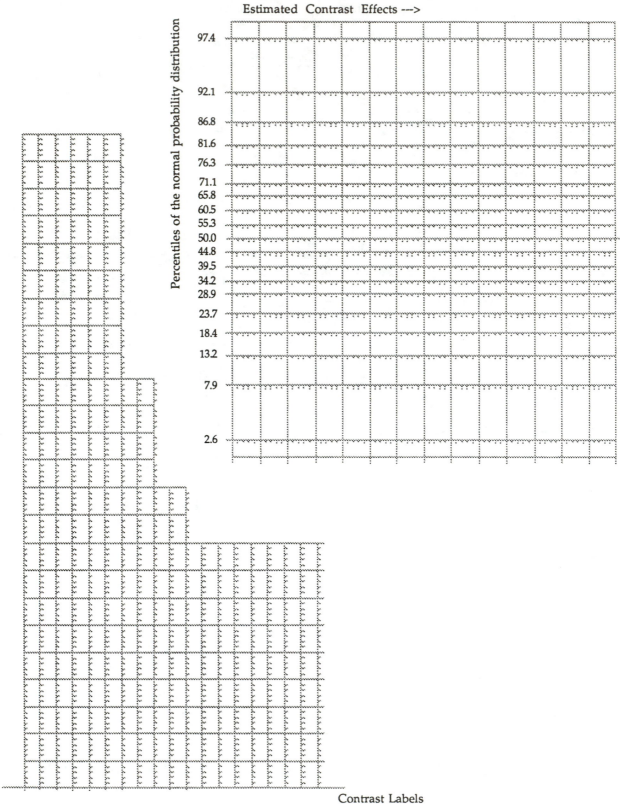

Estimated Contrast Effects --->

Percentiles of the normal probability distribution

Sums of Squares for Contrasts

Contrast Labels

Scree Plot and Normal Probability Plot For 24-Run Design

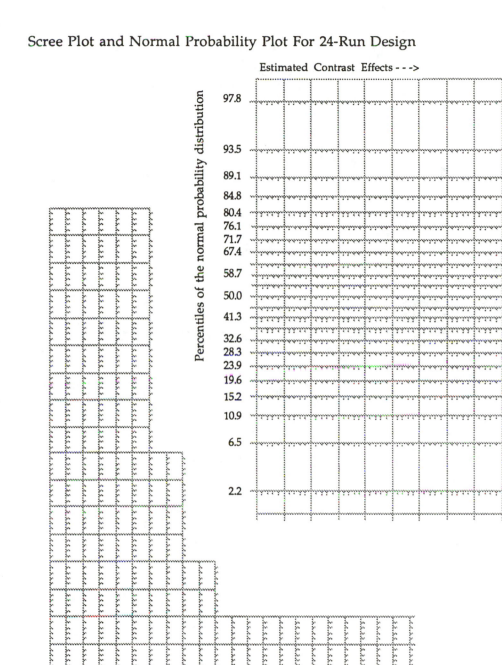

Scree Plot and Normal Probability Plot For 28-Run Design

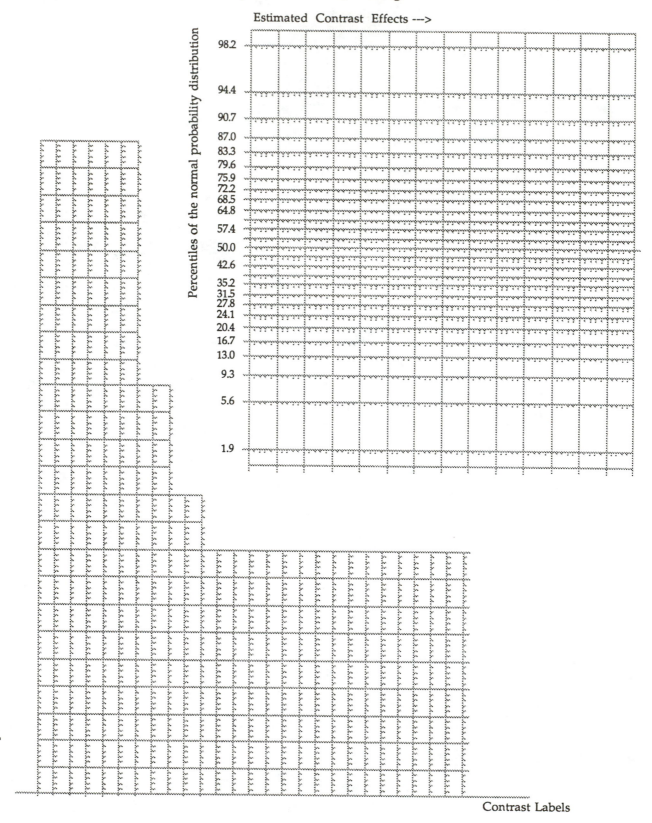

Estimated Contrast Effects --->

Percentiles of the normal probability distribution

Sums of Squares for Contrasts

Contrast Labels

Scree Plot and Normal Probability Plot For 32-Run Design

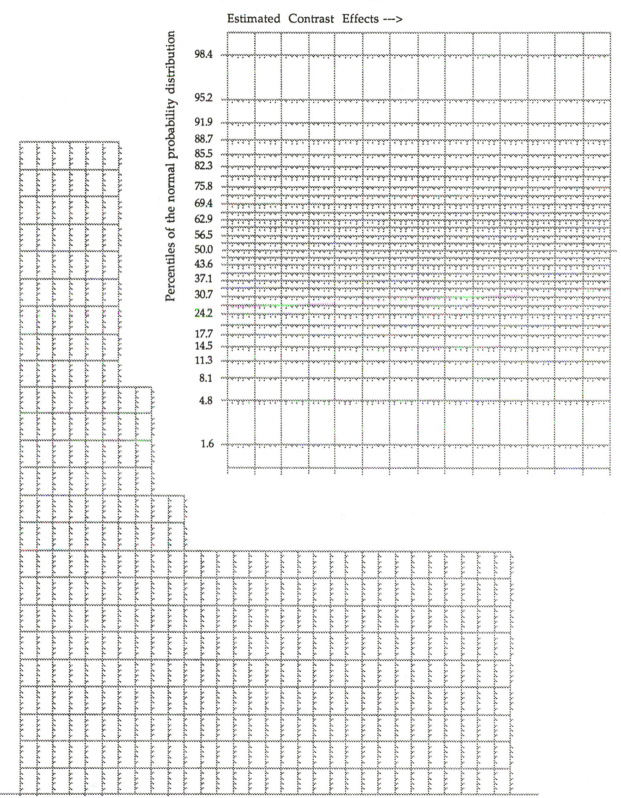

Estimated Contrast Effects --->

Percentiles of the normal probability distribution

Sums of Squares for Contrasts

Contrast Labels

Response Plot

Response Variable Plotted: _____

Factors:

_____

_____

Response Plot

Response Variable Plotted: _____

Factors:

_____

_____

_____

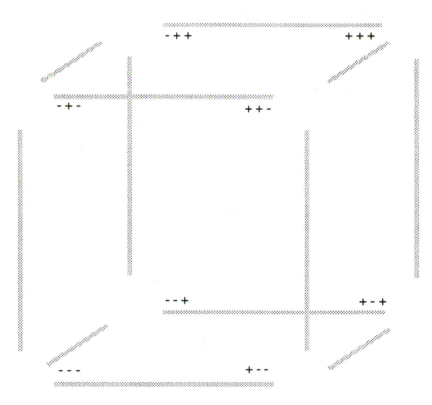

Response Plots

Response Variable(s) Plotted: _____

_____

Factors:

_____

_____

_____

_____

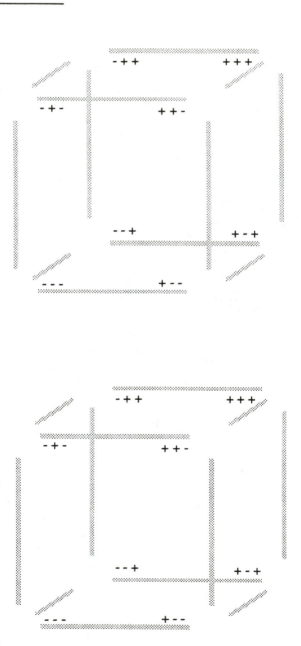

A Basic 32-Run Design With 6 Factors at Two Levels

A One-Half Replicate of a 2^6 design: Resolution VI:

Main effects are A, C, G, O, U, 5
(use these columns in Basic 32-Run Design to define treatment combinations)

Generating Relation: **I = ACGOU5**

Contrast Label	Effects		
A	A		CGOU5
B	–AC		–GOU5
C	C		AGOU5
D	–CG		–AOU5
E		ACG	OU5
F	–AG		–COU5
G	G		ACOU5
H	–GO		–ACU5
I		AGO	CU5
J	–U5		–ACGO
K		AU5	CGO
L	–CO		–AGU5
M		ACO	GU5
N	–AO		–CGU5
O	O		ACGU5
P	–O5		–ACGU
Q		AO5	CGU
R	–GU		–ACO5
S		AGU	CO5
T	–AU		–CGO5
U	U		ACGO5
V	–CU		–AGO5
W		ACU	GO5
X	–G5		–ACOU
Y		AG5	COU
Z	–OU		–ACG5
1		AOU	CG5
2	–C5		–AGOU
3		AC5	GOU
4	–A5		–CGOU
5	5		ACGOU

When using the Reflected 32-Run Plackett-Burman Design change all negative signs above into positive signs.

A Basic 32-Run Design With 7 Factors at Two Levels

A One-Quarter Replicate of a 2^7 design: Resolution IV:

Main effects are A, C, G, K, O, Y, 5

Generating Relation: $I = AGY5 = CGKO = ACKOY5$

Contrast Label	Effects			
A	A	GY5	ACGKO	CKOY5
B	–AC	–CGY5	–AGKO	–KOY5
C	C	GKO	ACGY5	AKOY5
D	–CG	–KO	–ACY5	–AGKOY5
E	ACG	CY5	AKO	GKOY5
F	–AG	–Y5	–ACKO	–CGKOY5
G	G	AY5	CKO	ACGKOY5
H	–GO	–CK	–AOY5	–ACGKY5
I	AGO	OY5	ACK	CGKY5
J	–AK	–ACGO	–COY5	–GKY5
K	K	CGO	ACOY5	AGKY5
L	–CO	–GK	–AKY5	–ACGOY5
M	ACO	AGK	KY5	CGOY5
N	–AO	–GOY5	–ACGK	–CKY5
O	O	CGK	AGOY5	ACKY5
P	–O5	–AGOY	–CGK5	–ACKY
Q	AO5	GOY	CKY	ACGK5
R	–KY	–ACO5	–CGOY	–AGK5
S	CO5	GK5	AKY	ACGOY
T	–K5	–CGO5	–ACOY	–AGKY
U	COY	AK5	GKY	ACGO5
V	–OY	–AGO5	–ACK5	–CGKY
W	GO5	AOY	CK5	ACGKY
X	–G5	–AY	–CKO5	–ACGKOY
Y	Y	AG5	ACKO5	CGKOY
Z	–CY	–ACG5	–AKO5	–GKOY
1	CG5	ACY	KO5	AGKOY
2	–C5	–ACGY	–GKO5	–AKOY
3	AC5	CGY	KOY	AGKO5
4	–A5	–GY	–CKOY	–ACGKO5
5	5	AGY	ACKOY	CGKO5

When using the Reflected 32-Run Plackett-Burman Design change all negative signs above into positive signs.

A Basic 32-Run Design With 8 Factors at Two Levels

A One-Eighth Replicate of a 2^8 design: Resolution IV: Main effects are A, C, G, K, O,W, Y , 5

Generating Relation: I = AGY5 = CGKO = ACKOY5 = GOW5 = AOWY = CKW5 = ACGKWY

Contrast Label	Effects							
A	A	GY5	OWY	ACGKO	CKOY5	AGOW5	ACKW5	CGKWY
B	–AC	–CGY5	–AGKO	–KOY5	–COWY	–AKW5	–GKWY	–ACGOW5
C	C	GKO	KW5	ACGY5	AKOY5	CGOW5	ACOWY	AGKWY
D	–CG	–KO	–ACY5	–COW5	–GKW5	–AKWY	–ACGOWY	–AGKOY5
E	ACG	CY5	AKO	KWY	GKOY5	ACOW5	CGOWY	AGKW5
F	–AG	–Y5	–ACKO	–AOW5	–CKWY	–GOWY	–ACGKW5	–CGKOY5
G	G	AY5	CKO	OW5	AGOWY	CGKW5	ACKWY	ACGKOY5
H	–GO	–W5	–CK	–AOY5	–AGWY	–ACGKY5	–CGKOW5	–ACKOWY
I	AGO	OY5	ACK	AW5	GWY	CGKY5	CKOWY	ACGKOW5
J	–AK	–ACGO	–GKY5	–ACW5	–CGWY	–COY5	–KOWY	–AGKOW5
K	K	CGO	CW5	AGKY5	ACGWY	GKOW5	AKOWY	ACOY5
L	–CO	–GK	–AKY5	–CGW5	–ACWY	–KOW5	–AGKOWY	–ACGOY5
M	ACO	AGK	KY5	CWY	ACGW5	CGOY5	AOKW5	GKOWY
N	–AO	–WY	–GOY5	–ACGK	–CKY5	–AGW5	–ACKOW5	–CGKOWY
O	O	CGK	GW5	AWY	ACKY5	AGOY5	CKOW5	ACGKOWY
P	–O5	–GW	–AGOY	–CGK5	–ACKY	–AWY5	–CKOW	–ACGKOWY5
Q	AO5	GOY	CKY	AGW	WY5	ACGK5	AOCKW	CGKOWY5
R	–KY	–ACO5	–CGOY	–AGK5	–ACGW	–CWY5	–AOKW	–GKOWY5
S	CO5	GK5	AKY	CGW	KOW	ACWY5	ACGOY	AGKOWY5
T	–K5	–CW	–CGO5	–AGKY	–ACOY	–GKOW	–ACGWY5	–AKOWY5
U	COY	AK5	GKY	ACW	ACGO5	CGWY5	AGOKW	KOWY5
V	–AW	–OY	–AGO5	–ACK5	–CGKY	–GWY5	–ACGKOW	–CKOWY5
W	W	AOY	CK5	GO5	ACGKY	AGWY5	CGKOW	ACKOWY5
X	–G5	–AY	–OW	–CKO5	–CGKW	–ACGKOY	–AGOWY5	–ACKWY5
Y	Y	AG5	AOW	ACKO5	CGKOY	GOWY5	ACGKW	CKWY5
Z	–CY	–ACG5	–AKO5	–GKOY	–ACOW	–AGKW	–KWY5	–CGOWY5
1	CG5	ACY	KO5	COW	GKW	AGKOY	AKWY5	ACGOWY5
2	–C5	–KW	–ACGY	–GKO5	–AKOY	–CGOW	–ACOWY5	–AGKWY5
3	AC5	AKW	CGY	KOY	AGKO5	ACGOW	COWY5	GKWY5
4	–A5	–GY	–CKOY	–AGOW	–OWY5	–ACKW	–ACGKO5	–CGKWY5
5	5	AGY	CKW	GOW	CGKO5	ACKOY	AOWY5	ACGKWY5

When using the Reflected 32-Run Plackett-Burman Design change all negative signs above into positive signs.

A Basic 32-Run Design With 9 Factors at Two Levels

A One-Sixteenth Replicate of a 2^9 design: Resolution IV:

Main effects are A, C, E, G, K, O, W, Y , 5

Generating Relation: I = AGY5 = CGKO = ACKOY5 = GOW5 = AOWY = CKW5 = ACGKWY

= ACEG = CEY5 = AEKO = EGKOY5 = ACEOW5 = CEGOWY = AEGKW5 = EKWY

Contrast Label	Effects						
A	A	GY5	CEG	EKO	OWY		
B		–AC	–EG	–AEY5	–AGKO	–AKW5	–CEKO	–CGY5
					–COWY	–EOW5	–GKWY	–KOY5
C	C	GKO	KW5	AEG	EY5		
D		–AE	–CG	–KO	–ACY5	–AKWY	–COW5	
					–GKW5	–EGY5	–EOWY	
E	E	ACG	AKO	CY5	KWY		
F		–AG	–CE	–Y5	–ACKO	–AOW5	–CKWY	
					–EGKO	–EKW5	–GOWY	
G	G	ACE	AY5	CKO	OW5		
H		–CK	–GO	–W5	–ACEO	–AEGK	–AGWY	
					–AOY5	–CEWY	–EKY5	
I		ACK	AGO	AW5	CEO	EGK	GWY	OY5
J		–AK	–EO	–ACGO	–ACW5	–AEWY	–CEGK	–COY5
					–CGWY	–EGW5	–GKY5	–KOWY
K	K	AEO	CGO	CW5	EWY		
L		–CO	–GK	–ACEK	–ACWY	–AEGO	–AEW5	–AKY5
					–CGW5	–EGWY	–EOY5	–KOW5
M		ACO	AGK	CEK	CWY	EGO	EW5	KY5
N		–AO	–EK	–WY	–ACGK	–AGW5	–CEGO	
					–CEW5	–CKY5	–GOY5	
O	O	AEK	AWY	CGK	GW5		

A Basic 32-Run Design With 9 Factors at Two Levels

Contrast Label	Effects						
P		–GW	–O5	–ACEW	–ACKY	–AEK5	–AGOY	–AWY5
					–CEOY	–CGK5	–CKOW	–EGKY
Q		AGW	AO5	CEW	CKY	EK5	GOY	WY5
R		–EW	–KY	–ACO5	–ACGW	–AEOY	–AGK5	–AOKW
					–CEK5	–CGOY	–CWY5	–EGO5
S		AEW	AKY	CGW	GK5	CO5	EOY	KOW
T		–CW	–K5	–ACOY	–AEGW	–AEO5	–AGKY	–CEKY
					–CGO5	–EGOY	–EWY5	–GKOW
U		ACW	AK5	COY	EGW	EO5	GKY	
V		–AW	–OY	–ACK5	–AEKY	–AGO5	–CEGW	–CEO5
					–CGKY	–EGK5	–EKOW	–GWY5
W	W	AOY	CK5	EKY	GO5			
X		–AY	–G5	–OW	–ACE5	–AEKW	–CEGY	
					–CKO5	–CGKW	–EKOY	
Y	Y	AG5	AOW	CE5	EKW			
Z		–CY	–E5	–ACG5	–ACOW	–AEGY	–AGKW	–AKO5
					–CEKW	–EGOW	–GKOY	–KWY5
1		ACY	AE5	CG5	COW	EGY	GKW	KO5
2		–C5	–EY	–KW	–ACGY	–AEG5	–AEOW	
					–AKOY	–CGOW	–GKO5	
3		AC5	AEY	AKW	CGY	EG5	EOW	KOY
4		–A5	–GY	–ACEY	–AGOW	–ACKW	–CEG5	–CEOW
					–CKOY	–EGKW	–EKO5	–OWY5
5	5	AGY	CEY	CKW	GOW			

When using the reflected 32-Run Plackett-Burman Design change all negative signs above into positive signs.

DESIGN INDEX

The following table indexes the designs in this book according to the number of factors at each of the different numbers of factor levels. The purpose of this index is to help the user quickly find all the designs that might fit a particular situation.

Index